Asset Management

Portfolio Construction, Performance and Returns

Edited by

Stephen Satchell

Professor, Sydney University, Australia

palgrave
macmillan

Editor
Stephen Satchell
Sydney University
Australia

ISBN 978-3-319-30793-0 ISBN 978-3-319-30794-7 (eBook)
DOI 10.1007/978-3-319-30794-7

Printed on acid-free paper

This Palgrave Macmillan imprint is published by Springer Nature
The registered company is Springer International Publishing AG Switzerland

Contents

List of Figures and Tables

Figures

Tables

List of Contributors

Arindam Bandopadhyaya is Professor of Finance and Director of Financial Services Forum and Online Programs at the University of Massachusetts at Boston, USA.

Ron Bird is Professor Emeritus at the University of Technology Sydney, Australia.

David Blake is Director of the Pensions Institute and Professor at Cass Business School, City University of London, UK.

David Blitz is Head of Quantitative Equities Research at Robeco, The Netherlands.

Sebastian Ceria is Chief Executive Officer of Axioma. Before founding Axioma, Ceria was Associate Professor of Decision, Risk and Operations at Columbia Business School, USA, from 1993 to 1998. Ceria has worked extensively in the area of optimization and its application to portfolio management. He is the author of many articles in publications including *Management Science, Mathematical Programming,* and *Optima and Operations Research.*

Gordon L. Clark is Professor and Director of the Smith School at Oxford University, is Sir Louis Matheson Distinguished Visiting Professor in the Department of Banking and Finance at Monash University, Australia, and is Visiting Professor at Stanford University, USA. His most recent books are the co-authored *Saving for Retirement: Intention, Context and Behaviour* and *Sovereign Wealth Funds*. He is completing with Ashby Monk *Institutional Investors in Global Markets: An Organizational Perspective* to be published in 2017.

Christian L. Dunis is a founding partner at Acanto Research, Germany, and Emeritus Professor of Banking & Finance, Liverpool John Moores University, UK.

Julius Hemminki holds an MSc in Economics from Aalto University School of Business (former by Helsinki School of Economics), Finland. He works as senior key account manager at Klarna, a Swedish e-commerce company that provides payment services for online storefronts.

Richard Ho previously worked at Barclays Capital Ltd.

Soosung Hwang is Professor of Financial Economics in the Department of Economics, Sungkyunkwan University, Seoul, Korea. He received his PhD from the Cambridge University, UK, and has worked as a fund manager and a consultant in finance. His research interests include finance, financial econometrics, real estate economics and finance, and behavioural finance.

Garud Iyengar is a professor in the Department of Industrial Engineering and Operations Research, Columbia University, USA.

Roy Kouwenberg is Associate Professor and Chair of the PhD Program at Mahidol University, Thailand, and visiting researcher at the Erasmus School of Economics, The Netherlands. His research interests include investments, quantitative finance and behavioural economics. His work has been published in the *Journal of Financial Economics*, the *Review of Economics & Statistics* and *Management Science*, amongst others. Roy received his PhD in Finance from Erasmus University Rotterdam and he is a CFA charterholder. The article (Chapter 5 of this book) was written while Roy was working at AEGON Asset Management, The Hague.

Anne Leah Jones is Assistant Professor of Accounting at Suffolk University, Boston, USA.

Bruce N. Lehmann is a Professor of Economics and Finance at the School of Global Policy and Strategy at the University of California, San Diego, USA.

Alfred Ka Chun Ma is Managing Director, CAC at Algo Financial Services Group.

Vesa Puttonen is Professor of Finance at Aalto University School of Business, Finland. His areas of expertise include topics such as financial institutions, financial services marketing, mutual funds and behavioural finance. He also serves as a board member at Taaleri Private Bank, Finland.

Garrett Quigley is co-founder and co-Chief Investment Officer of Global Systematic Investors LLP. Prior to founding GSI, Garrett was the Investment Director at Dimensional Fund Advisors Ltd, London (DFAL) where he served as Chairman of the London Investment Committee. He has presented widely on investment strategy and research at conferences and seminars and is currently a Director of INQUIRE UK.

He received his BA from Trinity College, Dublin and holds an MSc in Finance from London Business School, UK.

Stephen Satchell is Professor of Finance at Sydney University, Australia. His research covers a number of topics in the broad areas of econometrics, finance, risk measurement and utility theory, and his current research looks at alternative methods of portfolio construction and risk management, as well as work on non-linear dynamic models. Stephen has strong links with Inquire (Institute for Quantitative Investment Research), is on the management committee of LQG (London Quant Group), and is a Fellow of Trinity College Cambridge.

Alan Scowcroft has retired after having served as Managing Director of UBS Ltd.

Gary Shannon was an associate researcher with CIBEF.

Rex A. Sinquefield is co-founder and former co-chairman of Dimensional Fund Advisors. He also is co-founder of the Show-Me Institute. He has contributed numerous articles to books and academic and professional journals. Best known among these are the studies of rates of return in *Stocks Bonds, Bills and Inflation,* which he co-authored with Roger Ibbotson. He was one of the first successfully to apply the academic findings of modern finance to money management. In the early 1970s he and his colleagues at American National Bank of Chicago pioneered many of the first index funds in the US. Rex received his BS from St Louis University and his MBA from the University of Chicago.

Robert A. Stubbs is Vice President, Strategic Innovation at Axioma, Inc. Stubbs joined Axioma in 2000 and is the head of the recently launched Innovation Lab at Axioma. Prior to his most recent position, Stubbs was the head of research at Axioma for more than ten years. In this role, he developed a robust portfolio in optimization technology and made numerous contributions to classical portfolio optimization techniques such as developing an algorithm for solving portfolio rebalancing problems with a limit on the number of assets in the portfolio.

Laurens Swinkels teaches in the Finance Department of the Erasmus School of Economics (ESE) at Erasmus University Rotterdam and Erasmus Research Institute of Management (ERIM), The Netherlands.

Allan Timmermann is Atkinson/Epstein Endowed Chair and Professor of Finance at Rady School of Management at the University of San Diego, USA. He is also Co-Director of the Master of Finance Program at the school.

Roger Urwin is Global Head of Investment Content at Towers Watson, UK.

Jonathan Whitaker worked as a research analyst with GT Capital in Melbourne at the time of writing, having previously been a research associate in the Finance and Economics School at the University of Technology, Sydney (UTS), Australia. He holds an honours degree in Physics from UTS and a Masters in Statistics from the University of New South Wales. He previously held a number of positions in medical physics.

Introduction

Stephen Satchell

This book presents 14 papers that have appeared in the Journal of Asset Management since its inception and have been frequently cited. I have ordered them by date of publication. Many of the papers are highly topical and any aspiring quant would benefit greatly from reading them. Whilst the book has not been compiled on a thematic basis, various themes emerge naturally; there are useful contributions to such areas as pension fund asset management, optimisation, risk management, smart beta, and Exchange Traded Funds (ETFs); to name a subset of possible themes.

I would like to thank all the participants; authors referees, users, and publishing staff, who have contributed to the success of the journal throughout the 21st century.

I list below the chapter titles, the authors, and the abstracts. The abstracts have been amended in places where I have added my own thoughts on the material, which, to reassure authors, have been uniformly positive.

Chapter 1: Performance of UK Equity Unit Trusts

Garrett Quigley and Rex A. Sinquefield, 2000

The authors examine the performance of all UK unit trusts that concentrate their investments on UK equities. This study covers the period from January 1978 to December 1997. They compare the returns of these unit trusts with a three-factor model which takes into account their exposure to market, value, and size risk. Once they control these risk factors, they find that managers, net of expenses, reliably underperform the market. The news is worse for small-company unit trusts. Contrary to the notion that small-company shares offer abundant 'beat the market' opportunities, the authors find that small-company trusts are the worst performers. They also examine performance persistence. Net of expenses, good performance does not reliably persist, but bad performance does.

Chapter 2: A Demystification of the Black–Litterman Model: Managing Quantitative and Traditional Portfolio Construction

Stephen Satchell and Alan Scowcroft, 2000

This chapter discusses the details of Bayesian portfolio construction procedures, which have become popular in the asset management industry as Black–Litterman models. It explains their construction, presents some extensions, and asserts that the models are valuable tools for financial management. The chapter presents examples of Bayesian asset allocation portfolio construction models and illustrates the combination of judgemental and quantitative views. The Black–Litterman model has the potential to integrate diverse approaches, based on a Bayesian methodology that effectively updates currently held opinions with data to form new opinions. It concludes by stating that these models are potentially of considerable importance in the management of the investment process in modern financial institutions where both viewpoints are represented. The discussion includes an exposition of these models for the possibility of application by readers. It presents a theorem of Bayes and related assumptions.

Chapter 3: Tracking Error: *Ex ante* versus *ex post* Measures

Stephen E. Satchell and Soosung Hwang, 2001

In this chapter, the authors show that *ex ante* and *ex post* tracking errors must necessarily differ, since portfolio weights are *ex post* stochastic in nature. In particular, *ex post* tracking error is always larger in expectation than *ex ante* tracking error. Their results imply that fund managers have, on average, a higher *ex post* tracking error than their planned tracking error, and thus unless these results are considered, any performance fee based on *ex post* tracking error is unfavourable to fund managers.

Chapter 4: Performance Clustering and Incentives in the UK Pension Fund Industry

David Blake, Bruce N. Lehmann and Allan Timmermann, 2002

Despite pension fund managers being largely unconstrained in their investment decisions, this chapter reports evidence of clustering in the performance of a large cross-section of UK pension fund managers around the median fund manager. This finding is explained in terms of the predominance of a single investment style (balanced management), the fee structures, and incentives operating in the UK pension fund industry to maximise relative rather than absolute performance, the high concentration in the UK pension fund, industry and the low turnover of fund managers. Fund size appears to be the only variable that can account for an important fraction of the cross-sectional variation in measured performance.

Chapter 5: Do Hedge Funds Add Value to a Passive Portfolio? Correcting for Non-Normal Returns and Disappearing Funds

Roy Kouwenberg, 2003

Hedge funds have greatly increased their assets under management in the last decades, partly driven by investments from institutions such as pension funds and endowments funds. This chapter considers the added value of an investment in hedge funds from the perspective of a passive investor. The Zurich Hedge Fund Universe is used for the empirical investigation, over the period 1995–2000. The database includes a large number of funds that have disappeared over the years, which reduces the impact of survivorship bias. It is found that hedge fund alphas are positive, even after correcting for the non-normality of the hedge fund return distribution. Over longer periods, however, the added value of hedge funds is severely hampered by the large number of funds disappearing from the database, usually after poor performance. Investors can avoid some of the disappearing and bad performing funds by requiring a track record of good performance.

Chapter 6: The Performance of Value and Momentum Investment Portfolios: Recent Experience in the Major European Markets – Parts 1 and 2

Ron Bird and Jonathan Whitaker, 2003

Value and momentum investing are two approaches to investing which have been increasingly utilised either overtly or covertly by fund managers. Consistent with their increasing popularity, a number of academic studies have found such strategies being capable of outperforming traditional benchmarks. The majority of these studies have been focused on the US market and covered the 1980s and

1990s, during which time there was a consistent upward trend in stock prices. In this chapter the authors examine a wide selection of value and momentum strategies applied to the major European markets over the period 1990–2002. This period captures evidence that certain implementations of value and momentum investing performed particularly well over this period across the European markets, with the outperformance from value being confined to the correction period, while that from momentum occurred during the run-up during the 1990s.

Chapter 7: Cointegration Portfolios of European Equities for Index Tracking and Market Neutral Strategies

Christian L. Dunis and Richard Ho, 2005

Traditional quantitative portfolio construction relies on the analysis of correlations between assets. Over the last ten years, following the generalised use of the JP Morgan RiskMetrics approach, quantitative portfolio managers have made increasing use of conditional correlations. If correlations are indeed time-varying, their many changes unfortunately make them a difficult tool to use in practice when managing quantitative portfolios, as the frequent rebalancing they imply may be very costly. In this chapter, the authors use the concept of cointegration, which relies on the long-term relationship between time series, and thus assets, to devise quantitative European equities portfolios in the context of two applications: a classic index tracking strategy and a long/short equity market neutral strategy. Data are used from the Dow Jones EUROStoxx50 index and its constituent stocks from 4 January 1999 to 30 June 2003. The results show that the designed portfolios are strongly cointegrated with the benchmark and indeed demonstrate good tracking performance. In the same vein, the long/short market neutral strategy generates steady returns under adverse market circumstances but, contrary to expectations, does not minimise volatility.

Chapter 8: Emerging Markets of South-East and Central Asia: Do They Still Offer a Diversification Benefit?

Christian L. Dunis and Gary Shannon, 2005

The aim of this chapter is to check whether, despite the growing world economic integration and progressive lifting of capital controls, emerging markets still offer international investors a valuable diversification benefit. The study covers emerging markets from South-East Asia (Indonesia, the Philippines, and Malaysia) and Central Asia (Korea, Taiwan, China, and India) over the period from 31 August 1999 to 29 August 2003 (a period characterised by both bull and bear stock markets), with the US, the UK, and Japan as the reference 'established' markets. It uses several state-of-the-art techniques: multivariate cointegration and vector autoregression models (VARs) with the analysis of variance decomposition (VDC), time-varying correlations with Kalman filter models, and the computation of conditional variances and covariances to devise optimal investment portfolios.

The existence of one cointegrating vector is found between the emerging markets considered and each 'established' market. Furthermore, the results for the time-varying parameter models using Kalman filters show that all emerging markets have become more closely integrated with the Japanese market. In contrast, the results 0for the US and UK time-varying parameter models indicate that several emerging markets have seen their level of integration remain steady or decline over the review period. Finally, the results of the conditional covariance approach indicate that international diversification was still beneficial for a US investor during that period. In addition, it is shown that an optimised portfolio containing emerging market stocks outperformed a portfolio consisting purely of US stocks over the out-of-sample period from 1 September 2003 to 5 July 2005.

Chapter 9: Measuring Investor Sentiment in Equity Markets

Arindam Bandopadhyaya and Anne Leah Jones, 2006

Recently, investor sentiment has become the focus of many studies on asset pricing. Research has demonstrated that changes in investor sentiment may trigger changes in asset prices, and that investor sentiment may be an important component of the market pricing process. Some authors suggest that shifts in investor sentiment may in some instances better explain short-term movement in asset prices than any other set of fundamental factors. This chapter develops an Equity Market Sentiment Index from publicly available data, and then demonstrates how this measure can be used in a stock market setting by studying the price movements of a group of firms which represent a stock market index. News events that affect the underlying market studied are quickly captured by changes in this measure of investor sentiment, and the sentiment measure is capable of explaining a significant proportion of the changes in the stock market index.

Chapter 10: Incorporating Estimation Errors into Portfolio Selection: Robust Portfolio Construction

Sebastián Ceria and Robert A. Stubbs, 2006

The authors explore the negative effect that estimation error has on mean-variance optimal portfolios. It is shown that asset weights in mean-variance optimal portfolios are very sensitive to slight changes in input parameters. This instability is magnified by the presence of constraints that asset managers typically impose on their portfolios. The authors use robust mean variance, a new technique which is based on robust optimisation, a deterministic framework designed to explicitly consider parameter uncertainty in optimisation problems. Alternative uncertainty regions that create a less conservative robust problem are introduced. In fact, the authors' proposed approach does not assume that all estimation errors will negatively affect the portfolios, as is the case in traditional robust optimisation, but rather that there are as many errors with negative consequences as there are errors with positive consequences. The authors demonstrate through extensive computational experiments that portfolios generated with their proposed robust mean variance o scenarios. Additionally, they find that robust mean variance portfolios are usually less sensitive to input parameters. Without endorsing commercial products, it is fair to say that notions of robust mean variance have expanded the number of approaches that portfolio constructors can implement.

Chapter 11: Best-Practice Pension Fund Governance

Gordon L. Clark and Roger Urwin, 2008

The authors argue that good governance by institutional asset owners makes a significant incremental difference to value creation, as measured by their long-term risk-adjusted rate of return. Drawing upon best-practice case studies, it is argued that the principles of good governance can be summarised by organisational *coherence*, including an institution's clarity of mission and its capacities; *people*, including who is involved in the investment process, their skills and responsibilities; and *process*, including how investment decision-making is managed and implemented. Using the case studies to develop the principles and practice of good governance, there are a number of lessons to be learnt from these exemplars whatever the nature, scope, and location of the institution – summarised through a set of 12 findings about global best-practice with implications for large and small institutions. Implications are also drawn for the design and management of sovereign funds, which are increasingly important for national welfare in global financial markets. In conclusion, the authors see the challenge of governance as having two facets: to facilitate adaptation to the functional imperatives of operating in global markets given the heritage of an institution and, over the long-term, to undertake reforms such that institutional form and structure are consistent with the principles developed herein.

Chapter 12: Fundamental Indexation in Europe

Julius Hemminki and Vesa Puttonen, 2008

The authors examine the benefits of fundamental indexation using European data. Our findings suggest that by re-weighting a capitalisation-weighted market index by certain fundamental values, it is possible to produce consistently higher returns and higher risk-adjusted returns. Some of these fundamental portfolios produce consistent and significant benefits compared to the capitalisation-weighted portfolio. Thus, their results are in line with Arnott *et al.* (2005) from the US markets. Readers may compare this chapter with the subsequent one.

Chapter 13: Fundamental Indexation: An Active Value Strategy in Disguise

David Blitz and Laurens Swinkels, 2008

In this chapter, the authors critically examine the novel concept of fundamental indexation. They argue that fundamental indexation is by definition nothing more than an elegant value strategy, because the weights of stocks in a fundamental index and a cap-weighted index only differ as a result of differences in valuation ratios. Moreover, fundamental indices resemble active investment strategies more than classic passive indices because: (i) they appear to be at odds with market equilibrium; (ii) they do not represent a buy-and-hold strategy: and (iii) they require several subjective choices. Last but not least, because fundamental indices are primarily designed for simplicity and appeal, they are unlikely to be the most efficient way of benefiting from the value premium. Compared to more sophisticated, multi-factor quantitative strategies, fundamental indexation is likely to be an even more inferior proposition. This argument is of some importance, not least because of the deluge of smart beta products being touted in the market that justify their existence based on fundamental indexation.

Chapter 14: A Robust Optimization Approach to Pension Fund Management

Garud Iyengar and Alfred Ka Chun Ma, 2010

In this chapter, the authors propose a robust optimisation-based framework for defined benefit pension fund management. They show that this framework allows one to flexibly model many features of the pension fund management problem. Their approach is a computationally tractable alternative to the stochastic programming-based approaches. They illustrate the important features of the robust approach using a specific numerical example.

1
Performance of UK Equity Unit Trusts

Garrett Quigley
is Vice President and Portfolio Manager at Dimensional Fund Advisors Ltd, London. He received his BA from Trinity College, Dublin, and his MSc from Brunel University. Garrett joined Dimensional in 1992 and manages European equity investments in a range of portfolios covering large cap and small cap stocks in both developed and emerging markets.

Rex A. Sinquefield
is Chairman and Chief Investment Officer of Dimensional Fund Advisors Inc., Santa Monica. Rex received his BS from St Louis University and his MBA from the University of Chicago. He has contributed numerous articles to books and academic and professional journals. Best known among these are the studies of rates of return in Stocks Bonds, Bills and Inflation, which he co-authored with Roger Ibbotson. He was one of the first successfully to apply the academic findings of modern finance to money management. In the early 1970s he and his colleagues at American National Bank of Chicago pioneered many of the first index funds in the US.

Introduction

Studies of money manager performance are the bottom line test of market efficiency. They do not claim to uncover specific types of market failure as do the 'anomalies' literature of the 1980s and the behavioural finance literature of today. Rather, money manager studies ask whether there are market failures, regardless of type, that are systematically exploitable. In our opinion, the conclusion of the literature to date is a resounding 'No'.

Nearly all the studies thus far confine themselves to managers' efforts to outperform the US equity markets. Among the more recent are those by Davis (1999), Carhart (1997a), Malkiel (1995) and Elton *et al.* (1993). There are few studies of non-US markets.[1] This paper closes that gap

Reprinted from 'Performance of UK equity unit trusts' by Garrett Quigley and Rex A. Sinquefield in *Journal of Asset Management*, 1, 2000, pp. 72–92, DOI:10.1057/palgrave.jam.2240006. With kind permission from Palgrave Macmillan Ltd.

slightly by examining the performance of all UK equity unit trusts that concentrate their investments in the UK. With respect to the UK market, this paper deals with two popular claims by money managers and consultants: (1) money managers can outperform markets; and (2) this is especially so in the case of small stocks. The evidence we present here contradicts both of these claims.

We organise the paper as follows. First, we give a general description of our data and the classification of unit trusts, followed by the details of the UK treatment of dividends and taxes and the way in which this affects the computation of rates of return for unit trusts. The models that we use for performance measurement and the performance results for portfolios of unit trusts are then presented. We base these portfolios on descriptive classifications and then on the unit trust's exposure to well-known risk factors. The penultimate section examines whether performance persists, and the final section gives the conclusion.

Data

This study examines all UK equity unit trusts (UTs) from the Micropal (now S & P Micropal) database that existed any time between 1978 and 1997 and were authorised for sale to the public. We include only those UTs that invest primarily in UK equities and are classified by the Association of Unit Trusts and Investment Funds (AUTIF) as Growth and Income, Growth, Equity Income or Smaller Companies. In order to qualify as 'UK' a UT must have at least 80 per cent of its investments in the UK. AUTIF defines the four equity-only sectors as follows (*Unit Trust Yearbooks*, 1992–1997):

- *Growth and Income*: to produce a combination of both growth and income with a dividend yield of between 80 and 100 per cent of the yield of the FTA All Share Index;
- *Growth*: to produce capital growth;
- *Equity Income*: to produce a dividend yield in excess of 110 per cent of the yield of the FTA All Share Index;
- *Smaller Companies*: to invest at least 80 per cent of their assets in those companies that form the Extended Hoare Govett Smaller Companies Index. The Hoare Govett Smaller Companies Index (HGSC) contains the smallest tenth by market capitalisation of the main UK equity market. The Extended HGSC also includes stocks quoted on the Unlisted Securities Market, which fall within the HGSC's market capitalisation limit.[2]

We exclude unauthorised UTs because we have insufficient information to determine their investment objectives. We also exclude all international, sector specialist, balanced and fixed income UTs. Authorised UTs are approved – authorised – for sale to the public, while unauthorised UTs are not. Micropal advises us that their dividend data on dead UTs prior to 1978 are incomplete. Because we want to work with total returns, which naturally includes dividends, we commence our sample period in January 1978. Overall, we have data for 473 UTs which were still alive at the end of 1997 and 279 UTs which existed for some period between January 1978 and December 1997 but were not alive in January 1998. At year-end 1997, the aggregate value of the UK equity unit trusts we study was about £163 billion and the entire domestic UK equity market was about £1.3 trillion. By comparison, at year-end 1997 US domestic equity mutual funds had an aggregate value of £973 billion and the entire US equity market was £6.0 trillion.

Because we have data on live and dead UTs, we believe our database is free of survivor bias. This bias afflicts nearly all commercial databases of manager performance, mutual fund or otherwise. Poorly performing funds often do not survive to the end of the sample period and get dropped from the database even though they are investment options while they exist. The opportunity set investors face through time is the combined universe of live and dead funds. This universe has lower returns than the set of surviving funds.

Micropal's time series

Micropal provides us with a monthly time series of returns for all the UTs covered by this study. There are several features of UK law, Micropal convention and data availability that complicate the computation of returns. These features involve the tax treatment of dividends, bid/offer spreads, and the reinvestment of dividends expense information.

Taxation of dividends

In the UK, a corporation paying a dividend of £1 would pay £0.2 in taxes, the Advance Corporation Tax (ACT), and distribute £0.8 to the unit trust with an accompanying tax credit for the ACT paid. The unit trust pays this money as a dividend by declaring a gross dividend of £1 and distributing £0.8 in cash and £0.2 as a tax credit. A taxable investor would report £1 dividend income and £0.2 taxes already paid. Note that the example is for an ACT rate of 20 per cent, the current rate. In 1978, the rate was 33 per cent and gradually fell to 20 per cent. These higher earlier rates explain why the difference between live gross and live net returns are so high, 1.36 per cent per year (Table 1.1). Until July 1997, a UK tax-exempt investor such as a pension fund could reclaim the tax credit as cash. In the budget of July 1997, the ability of such investors to reclaim the tax credit was abolished.

Because we want to evaluate the performance of the unit trusts, and not their investors, we use returns gross of the ACT. For surviving trusts, we have returns gross and net of the ACT. For dead trusts, only net returns are available. We are unable to gross up the dead trusts on an individual basis because individual dividend histories are unavailable. So we pursue a second-best approach of making an aggregate adjustment to the net returns of the dead trusts. Specifically, each month we calculate the difference between the gross and net return of the surviving trusts and add this difference to the net returns of the dead trusts. In the various tests we perform throughout the paper, we form portfolios. The adjustment that grosses up the net returns takes place on a portfolio by portfolio basis. The implied assumption is that there is no average difference between the dividend yields of surviving trusts and dead trusts. More on this later.

Bid/offer spreads

UTs are quoted on a bid/offer basis, where the offer price is the price at which the manager sells units, and the bid price is the price at which the manager buys them back. Among the items accounting for the difference between the bid and offer prices are the initial charge (sales load), typically 5–6 per cent, stamp duty (presently 0.5 per cent for purchases only), dealing charges (commissions) and the bid/offer spreads of the underlying securities. The returns that Micropal provides ignore bid/offer spreads at the point of initial investment, and therefore calculate returns bid price to bid price. This suits our purpose because we want to measure the performance of the unit trust managers rather than that of the clients.

Dividend reinvestment

We have returns for two types of unit trusts, one that distributes dividends on a regular basis, an income unit, and one that accumulates dividends inside the unit trust, an accumulation unit. Generally, when both units are available, they are like two classes of shares for the same underlying portfolio. For income units, Micropal's return series assumes reinvestment of dividends at the offer price. This means that the investor pays the full bid/offer spread when reinvesting dividends.

An investor's total return from a UT that reinvests dividends at the offer price is obviously less than if dividends are reinvested at the bid price. The latter case corresponds more closely to the investment performance of the UT manager. Unfortunately, this series is unavailable from Micropal. Fortunately, the effect on returns is trivial. At the end of February 1998 the average bid/offer spread was 5.0 per cent and the average yield was 2.1 per cent per year. The cost of investing these dividends at this spread is about 0.8 basis points per month. For Small Company UTs, the average monthly cost is 0.6 basis points because of their below-average dividend yields.

Accumulation units do not pay the initial charge on the reinvestment of dividends. Where a UT provides accumulation units along with income units, the returns series of the accumulation units is preferable and is the one we use. Of the 279 non-surviving UTs, 83 are accumulation units and 196 are income units. For the 473 live funds, 93 are accumulation units and 376 are income units.

Expenses

Information on historical investment management fees and total expense ratios (TERs) are not readily available. The only source for TERs is the annual report of each UT, many of which no longer exist. Prior to 1998, there was no industry-wide publication that collected and reported this information. From 1998, Fitzrovia International Limited has published a book that includes TERs. In order to test performance gross of TERs, we choose a second-best approach. We collect a sample of 394 TERs that are closest to year-end 1996 and apply each TER as if it were constant over the life of the UT. The average TER for this sample is 1.35 per cent per year.

Time series tests

In the tests that follow, we form for each month equal weighted portfolios of UTs, using sorting and classification rules appropriate to each test. We avoid survivor bias by including each dead UT through the last month it reports a return. A portfolio that holds a UT that dies, equally weights the remaining UTs. This is similar to the methodology of Carhart (1997a).[3] We cannot purge all survivor bias, however. If a unit trust dies in the month following the last reported return, then the return in the month of death is omitted. That return is probably below the average return of the other unit trusts. This omission causes a small but unmeasurable overstatement of aggregate unit trusts' performance.

Performance measurement

Our primary model of performance measurement is the Fama–French three-factor model, which we compare with the Sharpe–Lintner Capital Asset Pricing Model (CAPM) (Sharpe, 1964; Lintner, 1965). Fama and French (1992, 1993) show that, along with a market factor, size and value (book-to-market) factors help explain both the temporal and cross-sectional variation in stock returns.[4]

We estimate performance relative to the CAPM and Fama–French three-factor models as:

$$R_p(t) - R_f(t) = a + \beta[R_m(t) - R_f(t)] + e(t) \tag{1}$$

$$R_p(t) - R_f(t) = a + b[R_m(t) - R_f(t)] + sSMB(t) + hHML(t) + e(t) \tag{2}$$

where $R_p(t)$ is the return of a unit trust in month *t*, $R_f(t)$ is return of one month UK Treasury bills (henceforth month *t* is understood), and R_m is the total return of the FTA All Share Index (FTA). *SMB* is a size factor which is measured by the monthly return of the HGSC (ex investment trusts) minus the FTA total return (Dimson and Marsh, 1995–98). *HML* is a value (book-to-market) factor which is the return of the top 30 per cent of companies ranked by book-to-market minus the FTA total return. Details on the sources and construction of these series are in the Appendix.

In the above models, *a* is the regression intercept or alpha which estimates a portfolio's average excess return, that is, the return that is in excess of that which is caused by the portfolio's exposure to risk factors. In Equation (1), coefficient β measures the portfolio's exposure to a market factor in the CAPM. In Equation (2), *b* measures the portfolio's sensitivity to the market return, *s* to a size factor and *h* to a value factor. A positive *s* says the portfolio has net exposure to small stocks, while a negative value indicates net exposure to large stocks. A positive *h* indicates net exposure to value stocks, and a negative value indicates net exposure to growth stocks. Each of these coefficients comes with a *t* statistic that indicates how precisely the coefficient is estimated. The R^2 tells what portion of the variance of the dependent variable – the UT – is explained by the regression.

The economic environment and the performance of all UK equity unit trusts

Table 1.1 shows summary statistics for selected equity series, t-bills, the regression independent variables as well as the aggregate returns of all our UK UTs. The returns of all three equity series were high at roughly

18 per cent per year for both the market (FTA) and small stocks, and almost 21 per cent for value stocks (all returns are in sterling). By contrast, the MSCI World ex UK (net) returns 15 per cent per year for the same period. The cross correlations of the independent variables are near zero.

For the UTs, we calculate for each month an equal weighted average for five sets of data:

1. Live Gross – the gross (of tax) returns of all UTs that were still in existence at the end of 1997;
2. Live Net – the net (of tax) returns of all UTs that were still in existence at the end of 1997;
3. Dead Net – the net (of tax) returns of all UTs that were no longer in existence at the end of 1997;
4. Live and Dead Net – the net (of tax) returns of all UTs whether or not in existence at the end of 1997;
5. Live and Dead Gross – the gross (of tax) returns of all UTs whether or not in existence at the end of 1997. The earlier section on 'Taxation of dividends' describes how we estimate the gross returns for dead UTs.

The ACT tax – the difference between the Live Gross and the Live Net – costs investors 1.36 per cent per year compounded and lowers the alpha from both the one-factor and the three-factor model 10 basis points per month.

Our estimate of survivorship bias is 0.7 per cent per year. This is the difference between the compound returns of the live UTs and the combined set of live and dead UTs. It is striking how poorly the non-surviving UTs perform. They underperform the survivors by 2.31 per cent per year and the full sample by 1.61 per cent per year. Other estimates of survivor bias are 1 per cent per year for US equity mutual funds from Carhart (1997b), and 1.4 per cent from Malkiel (1995). (See also Elton *et al.*, 1996; Brown *et al.*, 1992.)

The regression results reveal strong patterns. The three-factor model market betas are all higher than the CAPM betas. The same is true for the R^2 values. The UTs in aggregate have a high *SMB* exposure and a modest yet significant *HML* exposure. The alphas all shift down in the three-factor model results by about 5 basis points per month, indicating that the UTs' performance is lower once we take size and book-to-market exposures into account. After adding back taxes to the overall group – Live and Dead Gross – we get a three-factor alpha of –9 basis

Table 1.1A Summary statistics for UK market, value and small stock indices, t-bills and factor returns in sterling, 1978–97

	UK market	**UK value**	**UK small stocks**	**UK t-bills**	**Market factor**	**Value factor**	**Size factor**
Average return monthly	1.53	1.73	1.50	0.84	0.69	0.20	−0.03
Standard deviation, monthly	4.87	5.29	4.72	0.27	4.87	2.25	2.67
Annual compound return	18.33	20.88	18.01	10.60	7.03	2.13	−0.79

Correlation of regression independent variables (factor returns):

	Market	**Value**	**Size**
Market	1.0		
Value	−0.03	1.0	
Size	−0.32	0.15	1.0

Table 1.1B Summary performance and CAPM and three-factor regressions of all UK equity unit trusts from 1978 to 1997 (regressions are based on monthly returns)

Survival	Tax status	Avg. No. funds	ACR	STD	CAPM					Three-factor model								
					alpha	t(alpha)	b	t(b−1)[a]	Adj. R^2	alpha	t(alpha)	b	t(b−1)	s	t(s)	h	t(h)	Adj. R^2
Live	Gross	262.5	17.60	12.40	0.01	0.16	0.88	−8.14	0.935	−0.04	−1.02	0.95	−6.95	0.37	25.71	0.07	4.25	0.984
Live	Net	262.5	16.24	12.21	−0.09	−1.17	0.88	−8.17	0.934	−0.14	−3.65	0.94	−7.00	0.37	25.34	0.07	4.37	0.983
Dead	Net	105.0	13.93	11.95	−0.25	−2.99	0.86	−8.40	0.917	−0.30	−7.23	0.93	−7.39	0.42	25.76	0.07	3.58	0.979
Live and Dead	Net	367.4	15.54	12.11	−0.13	−1.77	0.87	−8.30	0.930	−0.18	−4.85	0.94	−7.25	0.38	25.54	0.07	4.26	0.983
Live and Dead	Gross	367.4	16.89	12.28	−0.04	−0.48	0.87	−8.26	0.931	−0.09	−2.30	0.94	−7.23	0.38	25.98	0.07	4.14	0.983

Each month, we calculate the total returns of equal weight portfolios of the following categories of all UK equity unit trusts that invest in the UK.

Live Gross: those surviving through to December 1997, gross of UK income tax; Live Net: those surviving through to December 1997, net of UK income tax; Dead Net: those not surviving through to December 1997, net of UK income tax; Live and Dead Net: those surviving and those not surviving through to December 1997, net of UK income tax; Live and Dead Gross: those surviving and those not surviving through to December 1997, net of UK income tax plus the Live Gross return minus the Live Net return.

ACR is the annual compound return of each portfolio. STD is the annual standard deviation of each portfolio. Alpha is expressed as per cent excess return per month. R^2 are adjusted for degrees of freedom.

[a]We test the *t*-statistic of $b - 1$ to measure how reliably b differs from 1.

points per month with a *t*-statistic of −2.3. Our overall conclusion is that before bid/offer spreads but after expenses, these UTs, as a group, generate 20-year performance that is reliably negative relative to a three-factor model.

The average TER of 1.35 per cent per year, or 11 basis points per month, suggests that, gross of all expenses, the excess return of the average manager is around 2 basis points, which is not significantly different from zero (the standard error of the overall alpha is 3.74 basis points). Net of expenses, however, the average investor experiences a risk-adjusted loss of 9 basis points per month on a bid-to-bid basis, which excludes the initial costs of investing. No one invests costlessly. Even an index investor incurs custody and administration expenses of 2–3 basis points per month. The TERs include such costs.

Performance of UK equity unit trusts by sector

Table 1.2 shows the results when the UTs are arranged by AUTIF category. As in Table 1.1, the market betas and the R^2 in the three-factor model are systematically higher than in the one-factor model, and the alphas are correspondingly lower. For the group Live and Dead Gross, the Equity Income and Smaller Companies sectors exhibit the largest differences between the two models. In the case of Equity Income, it is the relatively high *HML* coefficient that causes the difference. For the Smaller Companies sector, the cause is the huge *SMB* exposure of 1.0 in the three-factor regression. Once we control for the size exposure, the beta increases to 0.96 from 0.8 and the R^2 goes up from 0.68 to 0.965. UK Smaller Company UTs live up to their name and do indeed concentrate on small-company stocks.

Overall, the three-factor model explains almost all of the variance in the returns of these UTs and is an improvement on the CAPM. Further, the three-factor model alphas say that in no AUTIF sector did UTs in aggregate beat the market.

Performance of UK equity unit trusts ranked by SMB and HML exposure

It is a common claim that markets for small stocks are less efficient than those for large stocks.[5] We test that proposition directly by comparing the performance of small-company UTs to that of large-company UTs. We then make the same comparison for value and growth UTs.

We investigate the small-stock argument by forming portfolios based on prior *SMB* exposure. Each year we rank all UTs based on their *SMB* exposure over the prior three-year period. If a UT starts within the three-year period, we include it if it has at least 30 months of returns. Based

Table 1.2 Summary performance, CAPM and three-factor regressions of UK equity unit trusts from 1978 to 1997 by AUTIF sector (regressions are based on monthly returns)

AUTIF sector	Survival	Tax status	Avg. No. Funds	ACR	STD	CAPM					Three-factor model								
						alpha	t(alpha)	b	$t(b-1)$	Adj. R^2	alpha	t(alpha)	b	$t(b-1)$	s	$t(s)$	h	$t(h)$	Adj. R^2
Growth and income	Live	Gross	87.2	17.64	12.00	0.00	0.04	0.90	−9.71	0.971	−0.03	−0.74	0.93	−8.08	0.17	11.15	0.07	4.17	0.983
	Live	Net	87.2	16.26	11.81	−0.10	−1.95	0.90	−9.65	0.971	−0.13	−3.30	0.93	−8.01	0.17	11.06	0.07	4.28	0.982
	Dead	Net	29.3	14.77	11.78	−0.19	−3.05	0.86	−10.97	0.951	−0.23	−4.45	0.90	−9.57	0.18	8.94	0.10	4.56	0.967
	Live and Dead	Net	116.6	15.80	11.75	−0.13	−2.41	0.89	−10.49	0.967	−0.16	−3.86	0.92	−9.07	0.17	10.53	0.08	4.60	0.980
	Live and Dead	Gross	116.6	17.18	11.91	−0.03	−0.49	0.89	−10.57	0.968	−0.06	−1.42	0.92	−9.14	0.17	10.60	0.08	4.50	0.980
Growth	Live	Gross	82.7	17.33	12.37	−0.02	−0.28	0.90	−5.98	0.930	−0.06	−1.24	0.97	−2.84	0.37	18.51	0.03	1.33	0.972
	Live	Net	82.7	16.33	12.23	−0.09	−1.18	0.90	−6.04	0.930	−0.13	−2.66	0.97	−2.96	0.36	18.39	0.03	1.47	0.972
	Dead	Net	32.8	14.02	11.96	−0.27	−3.10	0.92	−4.45	0.921	−0.30	−5.60	0.99	−0.45	0.41	19.39	−0.02	−0.78	0.970
	Live and Dead	Net	115.5	15.51	12.10	−0.16	−2.00	0.91	−5.39	0.933	−0.19	−4.10	0.98	−1.84	0.38	20.23	0.01	0.60	0.976
	Live and Dead	Gross	115.5	16.49	12.22	−0.08	−1.09	0.92	−5.32	0.933	−0.12	−2.60	0.98	−1.71	0.38	20.47	0.01	0.45	0.976
Equity Income	Live	Gross	56.8	18.23	13.51	0.07	0.78	0.85	−8.53	0.912	−0.01	−0.12	0.91	−7.40	0.30	13.60	0.21	8.47	0.961
	Live	Net	56.8	16.22	13.27	−0.08	−0.93	0.85	−8.59	0.911	−0.15	−2.67	0.91	−7.49	0.30	13.50	0.21	8.50	0.960
	Dead[a]	Net	25.9	13.88	14.65	−0.22	−2.50	0.82	−9.76	0.897	−0.30	−4.55	0.87	−8.97	0.27	10.24	0.24	8.02	0.944
	Live and Dead	Net	82.5	15.44	13.10	−0.13	−1.50	0.84	−9.28	0.908	−0.20	−3.50	0.89	−8.51	0.30	12.95	0.22	8.74	0.958
	Live and Dead	Gross	82.5	17.44	13.32	0.02	0.20	0.84	−9.24	0.909	−0.06	−0.99	0.90	−8.44	0.30	13.09	0.22	8.73	0.959
Smaller Companies	Live	Gross	35.8	17.44	14.98	0.07	0.42	0.79	−5.95	0.669	0.00	0.00	0.96	−2.67	1.00	41.03	−0.09	−3.33	0.959
	Live	Net	35.8	16.52	14.83	0.01	0.04	0.79	−5.99	0.669	−0.07	−1.07	0.96	−2.77	1.00	40.92	−0.09	−3.18	0.959
	Dead	Net	17.1	12.81	16.12	−0.27	−1.52	0.81	−5.26	0.669	−0.35	−4.95	0.99	−0.93	1.01	36.18	−0.08	−2.42	0.949
	Live and Dead	Net	52.9	15.60	14.89	−0.07	−0.39	0.80	−5.73	0.682	−0.14	−2.47	0.97	−2.08	1.00	43.62	−0.07	−2.88	0.965
	Live and Dead	Gross	52.9	16.52	15.05	0.00	0.00	0.80	−5.69	0.682	−0.08	−1.31	0.98	−1.98	1.00	43.82	−0.08	−3.04	0.965

Each month, we calculated total returns of equal weight portfolios of the following categories of UK equity unit trusts grouped by AUTIF sectors. See Table 1.1 for abbreviations and explanations.

[a]Series ends 10/97.

on these rankings, we form ten equal weight portfolios, each containing the same number of UTs. We gross up the net-of-tax returns of the dead UTs in each portfolio by the difference between Live Gross and Live Net returns for that portfolio. ANOVA tests confirm that UTs that are most alike in a sorting variable, in this case *SMB*, have the least cross-sectional disparity in pre-tax dividend yield. We follow this procedure for all tests in this paper. We hold the ten portfolios for one year and then reform them at the start of the next year. This produces a time series of portfolios of UTs. The top *SMB* portfolio will always contain the UTs with the highest *SMB* exposure over the preceding three-year period and the lowest SMB portfolio will always contain the UTs with the lowest *SMB* exposure over the preceding three-year period. If a UT in a portfolio drops out of the database over the following year, we include its return through the last month it reports. The return of the portfolio in the next month is the equally weighted average of the remaining UTs. We use data from the 1975–77 period, even though the dividend information is unreliable, because the dividends do not appear to affect three-factor risk estimates (for example, these are almost identical for the Live Gross and Live Net series in Tables 1.1 and 1.2). Since we need three years to generate the first rank, our series will start in January 1978 so that, when we test the portfolios, the UT returns have correct dividend data.

We use the three-factor model to compare and evaluate the performance of these ten *SMB* portfolios. The results are in Table 1.3. The degree of *SMB* exposure of these portfolios is in exactly the same order as the pre-formation ordering. The portfolio of UTs with the highest prior three-year *SMB* exposure produces the highest post-formation *SMB* exposure (0.97), and the portfolio of UTs with the lowest prior three-year *SMB* exposure produces the lowest post-formation *SMB* exposure (0.03). The relative exposure to *SMB* over a three-year period is a strong predictor of relative exposure in the following year, and there is a wide spread of *SMB* exposure among UTs. The three-factor alphas of these portfolios tell us how well they perform relative to the size and book-to-market (value) risks they assume. The four small-company portfolios have excess returns (alphas) that are reliably negative. The claim that small-company stocks, at least those in the UK, are inefficiently priced in exploitable ways is a myth. If the small-company UTs were horses, they would be glue.

While the risk-adjusted and absolute returns of the top five *SMB* exposure portfolios become worse as *SMB* exposure increases, there is no pattern to either the risk-adjusted or absolute returns of the bottom five *SMB* portfolios. However, all of the three-factor alphas are negative.

Table 1.3 Portfolios of unit trusts from 1978 to 1997 based on prior three-year three-factor model SMB loadings (regressions are based on monthly returns)

SMB decile	Avg. No. funds	ACR	STD	CAPM					Three-factor model								
				alpha	*t*(alpha)	*b*	*t*(*b*−1)	Adj. R^2	alpha	*t*(alpha)	*b*	*t*(*b*−1)	*s*	*t*(*s*)	*h*	*t*(*h*)	Adj. R^2
High	31.0	15.39	15.57	−0.08	−0.48	0.80	−5.52	0.681	−0.17	−2.48	0.98	−1.59	0.97	34.89	0.00	0.07	0.949
2	30.8	15.57	14.41	−0.09	−0.58	0.81	−6.29	0.755	−0.16	−3.10	0.96	−3.59	0.83	40.23	0.00	−0.02	0.969
3	31.3	16.43	13.13	−0.05	−0.47	0.85	−6.76	0.856	−0.12	−2.19	0.95	−4.28	0.56	25.34	0.09	3.71	0.963
4	31.2	16.49	12.17	−0.06	−0.69	0.86	−7.98	0.910	−0.12	−2.47	0.93	−6.38	0.40	21.02	0.11	5.30	0.972
5	31.0	17.71	12.14	0.02	0.22	0.88	−7.69	0.933	−0.04	−0.68	0.94	−5.64	0.30	14.82	0.11	4.95	0.969
6	30.9	16.98	12.12	−0.05	−0.65	0.90	−6.79	0.942	−0.09	−1.71	0.95	−4.39	0.26	12.75	0.09	4.05	0.969
7	31.1	17.11	12.33	−0.04	−0.76	0.92	−7.05	0.961	−0.08	−1.84	0.95	−4.97	0.19	10.56	0.10	5.12	0.976
8	31.2	17.25	12.46	−0.04	−0.80	0.92	−7.56	0.972	−0.07	−1.73	0.95	−5.77	0.13	8.18	0.09	5.04	0.981
9	30.9	16.18	12.14	−0.12	−2.67	0.94	−6.29	0.976	−0.14	−3.15	0.96	−4.66	0.08	4.73	0.04	1.78	0.979
Low	31.3	17.03	11.94	−0.06	−1.33	0.93	−7.29	0.977	−0.07	−1.44	0.94	−6.38	0.03	1.59	0.01	0.56	0.977

Each year we rank all unit trusts based on their three-factor *SMB* exposure over the prior three-year period. If a unit trust starts within the three-year period, it is included if it has at least 30 months of returns. Based on these rankings, we form ten portfolios with the same number of unit trusts in each portfolio. The ten portfolios are held for one year and then reformed each year. If a unit trust ends during a year, it is included until the last month it reports a return. A monthly total return series is estimated for each portfolio by calculating each month the average post-tax return of the live and dead unit trusts and adding the difference between the average pre-tax return and the average post-tax return of the live unit trusts.

See Table 1.1 for abbreviations.

We perform a similar analysis to see how well 'value' managers perform. Each year we rank all UTs based on their *HML* exposure over the prior three-year period, and we form ten portfolios in exactly the same way as we did for *SMB* ranking above. So our top *HML* portfolio will always contain the UTs with the highest *HML* exposure over the preceding three-year period, and the lowest *HML* portfolio will always contain the UTs with the lowest *HML* exposure over the preceding three-year period. The results are in Table 1.4. The three-factor model results show that there is some persistence in relative exposure to *HML* in these portfolios, but it is weak with a spread of only 0.2 between the highest and lowest *HML* portfolios. This suggests that there are few, if any, UK UTs that have a consistently high exposure to value stocks or a consistently high exposure to growth stocks.

There is some inadvertent connection between the unconditional sorts on *SMB* and *HML*. The highest and lowest *SMB* portfolios have the lowest *HML*s and the highest and lowest *HML* portfolios have the highest *SMB*s. To control for interaction effects, we perform a joint sort. At the start of each year, we sort UTs on prior three-year *SMB* exposure into three equal groups. Within each *SMB* group, we sort on *HML* exposure into three sub-groups, creating nine *SMB/HML* portfolios. We calculate the returns for these portfolios in the same way as before, reforming portfolios each year. The results of this analysis are in Table 1.5.

As expected, the portfolios in each *SMB* group in Table 1.5 have roughly the same *SMB* exposure. Within each *SMB* group, the spread in *HML* exposure is roughly the same, but about 65 per cent of what it was in the unconditional *HML* sort. There is a bit of a performance pattern in that the smaller-company UTs have significantly negative alphas in all three *HML* subgroups. If there are inefficiencies in the small-company UK stocks, the unit trust managers studied here do not exploit them. In the two remaining *SMB* groups, three of six alphas are reliably negative. Davis (1999) performs a similar analysis of US mutual funds and finds that there is no evidence of outperformance in any style group.

Persistence of performance

Our analysis of performance persistence first looks at raw return. Each year, we form ten portfolios of UTs based on the rank of their total return over the previous year. The results, in Table 1.6, show a marked persistence in return over a one-year period. The spread in annual performance between best and worst one-year return portfolios is 3.54 per cent. These results might suggest a market failure and thus an easy

Table 1.4 Portfolios of unit trusts from 1978 to 1997 based on prior three-year three-factor model HML loadings (regressions are based on monthly returns)

HML decile	Avg. No. funds	ACR	STD	CAPM					Three-factor model								
				alpha	*t*(alpha)	*b*	*t*(*b*−1)	Adj. R^2	alpha	*t*(alpha)	*b*	*t*(*b*−1)	*s*	*t*(*s*)	*h*	*t*(*h*)	Adj. R^2
High	30.9	17.19	12.84	0.00	0.02	0.85	−7.41	0.873	−0.08	−1.25	0.93	−5.54	0.43	17.54	0.20	7.02	0.953
2	31.2	17.19	12.96	−0.02	−0.26	0.88	−7.19	0.926	−0.08	−1.39	0.94	−5.07	0.30	13.63	0.14	5.62	0.964
3	31.2	16.75	12.46	−0.06	−0.78	0.89	−7.13	0.936	−0.11	−2.43	0.95	−5.00	0.31	17.09	0.13	6.16	0.975
4	30.9	17.00	12.36	−0.04	−0.63	0.90	−7.38	0.947	−0.09	−1.91	0.95	−5.13	0.28	15.74	0.09	4.32	0.976
5	31.1	16.72	12.76	−0.06	−0.92	0.89	−8.19	0.949	−0.10	−2.13	0.94	−6.14	0.26	14.34	0.07	3.43	0.974
6	31.1	17.05	12.05	−0.03	−0.45	0.88	−7.92	0.938	−0.07	−1.74	0.95	−5.99	0.35	21.87	0.03	1.65	0.980
7	31.3	16.34	11.76	−0.09	−1.34	0.90	−6.95	0.946	−0.13	−2.97	0.96	−4.36	0.31	18.11	0.04	2.22	0.978
8	31.3	16.09	12.06	−0.11	−1.44	0.90	−6.22	0.934	−0.14	−2.99	0.97	−3.15	0.36	19.26	0.00	−0.17	0.975
9	30.8	15.94	12.45	−0.11	−1.08	0.88	−6.17	0.892	−0.14	−2.70	0.97	−2.99	0.49	23.33	−0.03	−1.12	0.967
Low	31.0	16.48	12.57	−0.04	−0.34	0.84	−6.58	0.832	−0.10	−1.73	0.95	−3.82	0.64	27.99	0.00	−0.07	0.962

Each year we rank all unit trusts based on their three-factor *HML* exposure over the prior three-year period.

See Table 1.3 for explanation.

See Table 1.1 for abbreviations.

Table 1.5 Portfolios of unit trusts from 1978 to 1997 based on prior three-year three-factor model SMB and HML loadings (regressions are based on monthly returns)

SMB tritile	*HML* tritile	Avg. No. funds	ACR	STD	CAPM					Three-factor model								
					alpha	t(alpha)	*b*	t(*b*−1)	Adj. R^2	alpha	t(alpha)	*b*	t(*b*−1)	*s*	t(*s*)	*h*	t(*h*)	Adj. R^2
	High	34.4	15.97	14.15	−0.07	−0.50	0.82	−6.42	0.792	−0.15	−2.38	0.95	−3.67	0.69	27.40	0.10	3.65	0.953
High	Med.	34.6	15.38	13.65	−0.11	−0.83	0.82	−6.59	0.796	−0.18	−3.42	0.95	−4.17	0.73	35.03	0.02	0.85	0.968
	Low	34.5	16.00	14.03	−0.06	−0.39	0.82	−5.85	0.754	−0.13	−2.19	0.97	−2.38	0.83	34.75	−0.01	−0.36	0.960
	High	34.6	17.13	12.97	−0.03	−0.35	0.89	−7.16	0.929	−0.09	−1.66	0.94	−5.27	0.28	13.18	0.17	7.27	0.966
Med.	Med.	34.5	18.11	11.90	0.04	0.65	0.88	−8.53	0.946	0.00	−0.02	0.93	−6.73	0.27	14.81	0.09	4.43	0.975
	Low	34.5	16.36	11.97	−0.09	−1.24	0.91	−6.12	0.937	−0.13	−2.42	0.96	−3.25	0.31	14.67	0.04	1.77	0.968
	High	34.7	17.47	12.35	−0.01	−0.24	0.91	−7.86	0.960	−0.05	−1.05	0.93	−6.35	0.13	6.65	0.13	5.61	0.971
Low	Med.	34.5	16.94	11.97	−0.07	−1.63	0.94	−7.32	0.980	−0.09	−2.16	0.95	−5.80	0.07	4.55	0.05	2.82	0.983
	Low	34.6	16.30	12.07	−0.12	−2.72	0.95	−5.82	0.979	−0.12	−2.91	0.96	−4.38	0.07	3.92	0.00	−0.23	0.980

Each year we rank all unit trusts based on their three-factor *SMB* exposure over the prior three-year period. If a unit trust starts within the three-year period, it is included if it has at least 30 months of returns. Based on these rankings, we form three groups with the same number of unit trusts in each group. Within each group we rank all unit trusts according to their *HML* exposure over the same three-year period and then form three *HML*-based portfolios with each containing the same number of unit trusts. This produces nine *SMB/HML* portfolios. We hold them for one year and then repeat the formation process. If a unit trust ends during a year, it is included until the last month it reports a return. A monthly total return series is estimated for each portfolio by calculating each month the average post-tax return of the live and dead unit trusts and adding the difference between the average pre-tax return and the average post-tax return of the live unit trusts.

See Table 1.1 for abbreviations.

Table 1.6 Portfolios of unit trusts from 1981 to 1997 based on prior one-year return (regressions are based on monthly returns)

PR1YR decile	Avg. No. funds	Turn-over	ACR	STD	CAPM					Three-factor model									
					alpha	t(alpha)	b	$t(b-1)$	Adj. R^2	alpha	t(alpha)	b	$t(b-1)$	s	$t(s)$	h	$t(h)$	Adj. R^2
High	35.6	83.0	18.57	12.64	0.08	0.58	0.90	−3.72	0.836	0.07	0.87	0.99	−0.70	0.60	20.06	−0.02	−0.55	0.946
2	35.3	88.0	18.04	12.28	0.04	0.41	0.88	−5.92	0.895	0.02	0.29	0.94	−4.42	0.44	18.56	0.04	1.46	0.962
3	35.7	87.7	17.54	12.41	−0.01	−0.11	0.90	−6.21	0.935	−0.04	−0.78	0.95	−4.95	0.32	16.36	0.07	3.09	0.974
4	35.4	88.7	17.52	12.63	−0.02	−0.25	0.91	−6.04	0.949	−0.05	−0.93	0.95	−4.62	0.28	14.92	0.06	2.86	0.977
5	35.3	92.7	17.65	12.59	−0.01	−0.11	0.91	−5.82	0.946	−0.05	−0.99	0.95	−4.56	0.26	13.17	0.11	4.92	0.974
6	35.3	90.2	17.60	12.63	−0.01	−0.13	0.91	−6.14	0.945	−0.05	−0.98	0.94	−4.98	0.26	12.91	0.11	4.64	0.973
7	34.8	88.0	16.84	12.87	−0.07	−0.91	0.92	−5.28	0.943	−0.11	−2.24	0.96	−3.75	0.29	15.74	0.10	4.71	0.977
8	35.1	89.3	16.45	13.66	−0.08	−0.98	0.89	−6.30	0.927	−0.12	−2.04	0.94	−5.02	0.33	14.86	0.08	3.11	0.967
9	34.8	89.0	15.28	13.45	−0.16	−1.58	0.88	−5.50	0.896	−0.18	−2.70	0.95	−3.67	0.42	16.35	0.03	0.94	0.956
Low	34.3	82.7	15.03	15.48	−0.17	−1.31	0.88	−4.62	0.843	−0.20	−2.56	0.96	−2.38	0.54	17.90	0.06	1.75	0.941

Each year we rank all unit trusts based on their prior one-year total return. If a unit trust starts within the year, we exclude it. Based on these rankings, we form ten portfolios with the same number of unit trusts in each portfolio. We hold the ten portfolios for one year and then reform them at the end of each year. If a unit trust ends during a year, we include it through the last month it reports a return. We calculate a time series for each portfolio by calculating each month the average post-tax return of the live and dead unit trusts and adding the difference between the average pre-tax return and the average post-tax return of the live unit trusts.

See Table 1.1 for abbreviations.

beat-the-market strategy. However, this lusty interpretation seems to fall flat.

First, the turnover from this strategy is over 80 per cent per year. The average bid/offer spread is 5 per cent. Together, these two would wipe out all gains even if the pattern in Table 1.6 repeats itself perfectly.

Secondly, the three-factor alphas of the top two portfolios, while positive, are not statistically significant. The three-factor regressions distinguish between performance due to market, size and value risk factors and that due to the managers' ability to generate returns above those he gets for simple risk bearing. The returns that result from risk bearing are in principle available from structured or index-like portfolios. The three-factor alphas imply that even the best of the UTs did not earn returns above these kinds of strategies. By contrast, the negative alphas of the bottom four portfolios are all significant at the 5 per cent level. This echoes studies of US mutual funds, notably Carhart (1997a) and Malkiel (1995), which show that poor performance persists but good performance does not.

Now we examine persistence in risk-adjusted performance. We sort UTs on three-year three-factor alphas (PR3YA), form ten portfolios as before and compute returns over the next 12 months. We repeat this procedure for the end of each December. The first three-year regression period is 1978–80, so the monthly time series runs from 1981 to 1997. The results, in Table 1.7, are similar to those in Table 1.6, namely, a clear persistence in both absolute and risk-adjusted return over a one-year period. The spread in annual compound returns between the top and bottom PR3YA portfolios is now 2.95 per cent, and the spread in three-factor model alphas for these portfolios is 0.27 per cent per month. Again as in Table 1.6, only the top two PR3YA portfolios have positive three-factor model alphas, neither of which is remotely reliable. Even the largest alpha, for the highest prior-alpha portfolio is only 4 basis points, 0.6 standard errors, above zero. The other eight PR3YA portfolios have negative three-factor model alphas, and the bottom two are significant beyond the 5 per cent level.

To see whether the patterns in Table 1.7, weak though they are, persist through time, we compare the performance of PR3YA sorted portfolios at different periods after formation. For the three-year regression 1978–80, post-formation year 1 is 1981, year 2 is 1982 and year 3 is 1983. The next three-year regression is 1979–81, and the post-formation years are 1982, 1983, and 1984 and so on. We keep the post-formation sample sizes the same so the 'year 1' periods run from 1981 to 1995, 'year 2' periods from 1982 to 1996 and 'year 3' from 1983 to 1997. Table 1.8 gives the results.

Table 1.7 Portfolios of unit trusts from 1981 to 1997 based on prior three-year three-factor model alpha (regressions are based on monthly returns)

PR3YA decile	Avg. No. funds	Turn-over	ACR	STD	CAPM					Three-factor model								
					alpha	*t*(alpha)	*b*	*t*(*b*−1)	Adj. R^2	alpha	*t*(alpha)	*b*	*t*(*b*−1)	*s*	*t*(*s*)	*h*	*t*(*h*)	Adj. R^2
High	31.4	53	17.82	12.78	0.04	0.34	0.85	−5.53	0.836	0.04	0.59	0.95	−4.03	0.62	26.93	−0.03	−0.96	0.965
2	31.4	75	17.82	12.62	0.03	0.31	0.87	−7.10	0.911	0.01	0.20	0.93	−6.57	0.41	20.94	0.02	1.05	0.973
3	31.6	80	17.29	12.49	−0.02	−0.30	0.89	−6.30	0.933	−0.05	−1.04	0.94	−5.08	0.33	16.98	0.06	2.76	0.974
4	31.2	87	17.33	12.94	−0.04	−0.51	0.92	−5.26	0.950	−0.07	−1.43	0.96	−3.57	0.28	15.46	0.07	3.49	0.978
5	31.0	87	17.46	12.87	−0.03	−0.39	0.92	−5.48	0.952	−0.05	−1.13	0.96	−3.78	0.28	15.97	0.05	2.59	0.980
6	31.3	84	17.72	12.94	−0.01	−0.10	0.92	−5.83	0.952	−0.04	−0.83	0.96	−4.41	0.27	15.11	0.08	3.68	0.979
7	30.9	86	17.18	12.90	−0.04	−0.55	0.91	−5.44	0.941	−0.08	−1.50	0.96	−3.88	0.29	14.33	0.09	3.87	0.973
8	31.2	80	16.99	13.09	−0.05	−0.64	0.91	−5.39	0.932	−0.10	−1.96	0.96	−3.99	0.33	16.88	0.12	5.24	0.975
9	30.3	78	16.33	13.25	−0.10	−1.04	0.91	−4.76	0.914	−0.14	−2.26	0.96	−2.80	0.37	16.10	0.09	3.34	0.965
Low	30.4	53	14.87	13.83	−0.18	−1.57	0.88	−5.20	0.867	−0.23	−3.50	0.95	−3.50	0.51	20.47	0.10	3.40	0.960

Each year we rank all unit trusts based on their three-factor alpha over the prior three-year period.

See Table 1.3 for explanation.

See Table 1.1 for abbreviations.

Table 1.8 Three-factor-model alphas for portfolios that are formed based on prior three-year three-factor-model alphas, net and gross of total annual expenses[a]

PR3YA decile	Avg. PR3YA	Ann. exp.	Net of total annual expenses						Gross of total annual expenses					
			Number of years after portfolio formation						Number of years after portfolio formation					
			1		2		3		1		2		3	
Test period			1981–95		1982–96		1983–97		1981–95		1982–96		1983–97	
High	0.52	1.36	0.03	(0.45)	−0.03	(−0.54)	−0.10	(−1.83)	0.14	(2.19)	0.08	(1.37)	0.02	(0.34)
2	0.16	1.27	0.02	(0.29)	−0.05	(−0.95)	−0.10	(−1.73)	0.12	(2.17)	0.05	(1.02)	0.01	(0.12)
3	0.02	1.26	−0.05	(−0.87)	−0.08	(−1.64)	−0.08	(−1.51)	0.06	(0.99)	0.02	(0.40)	0.03	(0.51)
4	−0.08	1.29	−0.07	(−1.40)	−0.03	(−0.59)	−0.07	(−1.40)	0.03	(0.64)	0.08	(1.47)	0.04	(0.75)
5	−0.15	1.28	−0.05	(−1.11)	−0.10	(−2.00)	−0.10	(−2.08)	0.05	(1.04)	0.00	(0.09)	0.01	(0.12)
6	−0.23	1.31	−0.04	(−0.77)	−0.05	(−0.95)	−0.08	(−1.69)	0.07	(1.36)	0.06	(1.26)	0.03	(0.62)
7	−0.31	1.31	−0.08	(−1.41)	−0.10	(−1.85)	−0.04	(−0.65)	0.03	(0.51)	0.01	(0.18)	0.07	(1.19)
8	−0.42	1.33	−0.12	(−2.20)	−0.06	(−1.06)	−0.07	(−1.33)	−0.01	(−0.17)	0.05	(0.93)	0.04	(0.80)
9	−0.56	1.44	−0.16	(−2.39)	−0.13	(−1.85)	−0.06	(−0.93)	−0.04	(−0.58)	−0.01	(−0.09)	0.06	(0.90)
Low	−0.96	1.49	−0.26	(−3.74)	−0.11	(−1.60)	−0.08	(−1.18)	−0.14	(−1.95)	0.02	(0.25)	0.05	(0.73)

Average	−0.20	1.33	−0.08		−0.07		−0.08		0.03		0.04		0.03	
rank r		−0.53	0.94**		0.72*		−0.12		0.92**		0.62		−0.76*	
1–10			0.29	(3.40)	0.08	(0.85)	−0.02	(−0.24)	0.28	(3.27)	0.06	(0.73)	−0.03	(−0.39)
1–All alpha			0.08	(1.53)	0.02	(0.31)	−0.04	(−0.89)	0.08	(1.54)	0.02	(0.32)	−0.04	(−0.87)

[a]The test portfolios correspond respectively to all first years following portfolio formation, all second years following formation and all third years following formation. Regressions use monthly data. *t*-statistics are in parentheses.

Each year we rank all unit trusts based on their three-factor alphas over the prior three-year period. If a unit trust starts with the three-year period, we include it if it has at least 30 months of returns. Based on these rankings, we form ten portfolios with the same number of unit trusts in each portfolio. The ten portfolios are held for one year and then re-formed each year. If a unit trust ends during a year, it is included until the last month it reports a return. A monthly total return series is estimated for each portfolio by calculating each month the average post-tax return of the live and dead unit trusts and adding the difference between the average pre-tax return and the average post-tax return of the live unit trusts. Annual expenses are estimated for each portfolio by calculating the average TER of those unit trusts for which a TER is available. Returns gross of total annual expenses are calculated by adding one-twelfth of the annual expenses to the net-of-expenses returns.

We then examine this time series in three parts. First, we examine the set of years where each year is the first year following portfolio formation. We then examine the set of years where each year is the second year following portfolio formation, and then the set where each year is year three following portfolio formation. For example, for alphas based on 1978–80, year 1 return is 1981, year 2 is 1982, etc.

PR3YA is the average prior three-year three-factor alpha of the UTs in each decile. Rank r is the Spearman rank correlation coefficient between the pre-formation deciles and the post-formation alphas. The 1–10 alpha is the three-factor-model alpha of the series produced by subtracting the monthly return of the top PR3YA decile portfolio from that of the bottom PR3YA decile portfolio. The 1–All alpha is the three-factor-model alpha of the series produced by subtracting the monthly return of the top PR3YA decile portfolio from that of the portfolio of all unit trusts.

*Denotes significance at five per cent level for a two-sided test.

**Denotes significance at one per cent level for a two-sided test.

Year 1 results obviously repeat the pattern in Table 1.7, even though the point estimates differ because of the change in sample sizes. By year 2 the pattern of persistence attenuates somewhat, and by year 3 it disappears entirely. The rank correlation between pre- and post-formation alphas drops from 0.94 in year 1, 0.72 in year 2 to an insignificant −0.12 in year 3. One final test compares the 'high' portfolio with first, the 'low' portfolio, and then with the entire sample. The '1–10 alpha' comes from the three-factor regression of the 'high minus low' portfolio, and the '1–All' alpha from the regression of the 'high' minus the 'Live and Dead Gross' series from Table 1.1. Only in year 1 are these alphas significant, and this is clearly due to the low returns of the poorest performing portfolios.

Table 1.8 also shows the results of this experiment where the returns are grossed up by an estimate of total annual expenses. Recall that expense information is available only for surviving trusts, so we estimate the gross-of-expense returns for each of the ten portfolios by adding back to each portfolio the average expense of just the survivors of each group.

Now finally, there is some evidence that winners repeat. The top two ' high' portfolios have significant alphas in the year after portfolio formation, although we will soon see that this persistence is confined to just one size group of firms. Losers also repeat. Even giving expenses back to the ' low' portfolio does not prevent a nearly significant negative alpha. We will see that this phenomenon is not confined to one size group. The persistence in year one is strong but falls off quickly thereafter.

Because there is a wide range in the size exposure of UTs, we repeat these tests of persistence but condition them on size. First, we form three groups based on prior three-year *SMB* loading and then, within each group, we sort based on PR3YA. Table 1.9 gives the net-of-expense results. The persistence of poor performance does not discriminate by size. In each of the size groups, significant negative alphas persist through year one. For big firms, those with low *SMB* exposure, such alphas make it to year two. In a similar analysis of US mutual funds, Davis (1999) finds no evidence of positive persistence but, in the case of funds with high *SMB* exposure, reliable evidence of persistence of negative alphas. There is some correlation between expenses and performance. In each size group, the worst performing portfolio has the highest expenses (Table 1.9). The correlation may be stronger than it appears because we do not have annual expenses for dead trusts. These trusts may well have higher average expenses than survivors. What happens when we add back expenses?

Table 1.9 also gives the gross-of-expense results. Again, as in Table 1.8, we have some evidence of positive as well as negative persistence, both of which occur in the high *SMB* group. The negative persistence needs no explanation. However, the positive persistence of the high PR3YA small-stock trusts calls for one. Market efficiency would seem to preclude such persistence. In defence of market efficiency, however, the observed persistence, even if it continues, is not exploitable. The bid/offer spreads of these UTs are almost three times as large as the alphas in year one. So from a practical viewpoint, the persistence is useless, even though from a theoretical viewpoint it is intriguing. One possible explanation is that of Carhart (1997a), who shows that the persistence of US mutual funds occurs because of persistence in the underlying stocks they buy. However, he also shows that when managers try to exploit this persistence effect (by buying the previous year's winner stocks), they fail to generate higher absolute returns than managers who do not. It would require further research to determine whether this explanation applied to UK UTs.[6]

Summary and conclusions

This examination of UK equity unit trusts says that UK money managers are unable to outperform markets in any meaningful sense, that is, once we take into account their exposure to market, value and size risk. This result is analogous to most studies of US money managers. Even more dramatic than these overall results are the findings for the small-company UTs. Contrary to the notion that small-company shares offer abundant 'beat-the-market' opportunities, we find that small-company UTs are the worst performers. In fact, their performance failure is persistent and reliable.

In methodology, this study leans heavily on the same kind of three-factor model that Fama and French find well describes the behaviour of US equity markets. For the UK market, the three-factor model has better explanatory power than a one-factor model, especially for UTs that invest heavily in small companies.

Does performance persist? Yes, but only poor performance. As others find for US mutual funds, so we find in the UK. Losers repeat, winners do not. Only after adding back estimated expenses can we find evidence that the most successful UTs repeat their winning performance. (Ironically, so do the losers.) The winners' repeat performance, gross of expenses, is intriguing but not exploitable because of high turnover costs.

Overall, this study, like all mutual fund studies, does not enlighten us about what kinds of market failures occur. It does say that if there are any, UK equity managers do not exploit them.

Table 1.9 Three-factor-model alphas, net and gross of total expenses, for portfolios that are formed first on the prior three-year SMB, and then on the prior three-year three-factor-model alphas[a]

SMB tritile	PR3YA tritile	Avg. PR3YA	Ann. exp.	Net of total annual expenses						Gross of total annual expenses					
				Number of years after portfolio formation						Number of years after portfolio formation					
				1		2		3		1		2		3	
Test period				1981–95		1982–96		1983–97		1981–95		1982–96		1983–97	
	High	0.27	1.32	0.03	(0.44)	−0.07	(−1.22)	−0.11	(−1.98)	0.14	(2.23)	0.04	(0.60)	0.00	(0.00)
	Med.	−0.27	1.28	−0.03	(−0.58)	−0.10	(−1.49)	−0.11	(−1.74)	0.07	(1.26)	0.00	(0.07)	0.00	(−0.02)
High	Low	−0.81	1.48	−0.26	(−3.72)	−0.09	(−1.43)	−0.07	(−1.11)	−0.14	(−1.98)	0.03	(0.45)	0.05	(0.84)
	High–Low	1.08	−0.16	0.29	(4.01)	0.02	(0.27)	−0.04	(−0.62)	0.28	(3.83)	0.01	(0.10)	−0.05	(−0.83)
	High–Med.	0.54	0.04	0.06	(1.11)	0.03	(0.49)	0.00	(−0.04)	0.06	(1.17)	0.03	(0.54)	0.00	(0.02)
	High	0.16	1.29	−0.01	(−0.09)	−0.02	(−0.31)	−0.06	(−1.08)	0.10	(1.63)	0.09	(1.48)	0.05	(0.78)
	Med.	−0.21	1.26	−0.04	(−0.76)	−0.05	(−0.85)	−0.05	(−1.00)	0.06	(1.06)	0.06	(1.08)	0.05	(0.92)
Med.	Low	−0.60	1.40	−0.12	(−2.15)	−0.07	(−1.30)	−0.04	(−0.79)	−0.01	(−0.11)	0.05	(0.85)	0.07	(1.37)
	High–Low	0.76	−0.10	0.12	(2.25)	0.05	(0.92)	−0.02	(−0.42)	0.11	(2.08)	0.04	(0.77)	−0.03	(−0.60)
	High–Med.	0.37	0.04	0.04	(0.81)	0.03	(0.62)	−0.01	(−0.19)	0.04	(0.87)	0.03	(0.69)	−0.01	(−0.13)

	High	0.10	1.29	−0.05	(−0.86)	−0.07	(−1.29)	−0.06	(−1.25)	0.06	(1.04)	0.04	(0.66)	0.04	(0.82)
	Med.	−0.18	1.33	−0.07	(−1.56)	−0.07	(−1.53)	−0.09	(−1.94)	0.04	(0.75)	0.04	(0.78)	0.02	(0.50)
Low	Low	−0.47	1.36	−0.15	(−3.09)	−0.12	(−2.53)	−0.10	(−1.88)	−0.04	(−0.79)	−0.01	(−0.21)	0.01	(0.25)
	High–Low	0.57	−0.07	0.10	(2.17)	0.05	(1.12)	0.04	(0.79)	0.10	(2.05)	0.05	(1.00)	0.03	(0.66)
	High–Med.	0.28	−0.05	0.03	(0.71)	0.00	(0.07)	0.02	(0.71)	0.02	(0.61)	0.00	(−0.03)	0.02	(0.60)

[a]See Table 1.8.

Each year we rank all unit trusts based on their three-factor *SMB* exposure over the prior three-year period. If a unit trust starts within the three-year period, we include it if it has at least 30 months of returns. Based on these rankings, we form three groups with the same number of unit trusts in each group. Within each of these groups we rank on the basis of the three-factor alphas from the prior three-year period and form three equal weight portfolios. This produces nine *SMB*/PR3YA portfolios. We estimate a monthly total return series for each portfolio by calculating each month the average post-tax return of the live and dead unit trusts and adding the difference between the average pre-tax return and the average post-tax return of the live unit trusts. Annual expenses are estimated for each portfolio by calculating the average TER of those unit trusts for which a TER is available. Returns gross of total annual expenses are calculated by adding one-twelfth of the annual expenses to the net-of-expenses returns.

We then examine each time series as described in Table 1.8.

PR3YA is the average prior three-year three-factor alpha of the UTs in each tritile. High-Low alphas are the three-factor-model alphas of the series produced by subtracting the monthly return of the High PR3YA tritile portfolio from the Low PR3YA tritile portfolio within each *SMB* group. High-Med. alphas are the three-factor-model alphas of the series produced by subtracting the monthly return of the High PR3YA tritile portfolio from the Med. PR3YA tritile portfolio within each *SMB* group.

Acknowledgments

We benefited from the comments of many individuals. Special thanks to Mark Carhart and Ken French who both provided extensive comments and considerable discussion. We also thank participants at the finance workshops at the University of Missouri (Columbia) and DePaul University (Chicago). Other individuals who were most helpful are David Booth, Truman Clark, George Constantinides, Jim Davis, Gene Fama, Gene Fama Jr, Donald Keim and Jeanne Sinquefield. Thanks also to John Richardson at Micropal and the staff of AUTIF.

Notes

1. In the course of writing this paper, we were made aware of another paper that examines the performance of a broad array of unit trusts, including those covered here. There are differences in time period of coverage and methodology. That paper is by David Blake and Alan Timmerman (1998) 'Mutual Fund Performance: Evidence from the UK', *European Finance Review*, 2, 57–77.
2. The Unlisted Securities Market was closed in December 1996 and most of the companies in this market moved to either a full listing or to the Alternative Investment Market.
3. We equal-weight the monthly returns, since this gives the average return of the UTs in a portfolio each month. This is the standard approach in studies of this kind. An alternative is to weight each UT return by the value of assets in the UT. However, we do not have a database with the history of the value of assets for each UT.
4. For an application of the Fama–French cross-sectional methodology to UK stock returns, see Strong and Xu (1997).
5. See, for example, '25 Years of Indexing: An Analysis of the Costs and Benefits', PricewaterhouseCoopers and Barclays Global Investors, pp. 18–20, where an analysis is made of the returns of small-company funds compared with small-company benchmarks, suggesting that the funds outperform the benchmarks by more than 2 per cent p.a.
6. We have looked at non-overlapping three-year sub-period analyses of the above sorting procedures, which we do not show in the interests of brevity (details are available on request). For the nine *SMB*/PR3YA portfolios, there is no three-year sub-period where the alpha of the net returns is significantly positive. Interestingly, however, the average non-overlapping three-year alpha is three basis points less than the average full-period alpha across all nine portfolios.

References

Brown, S. J., Goetzmann, W., Ibbotson, R. G. and Ross, S. A. (1992) 'Survivorship Bias in Performance Studies', *Review of Financial Studies*, 5, 553–80.

Carhart, M. M. (1997a) 'On Persistence in Mutual Fund Performance', *Journal of Finance*, 52(1), 57–82.

Carhart, M. M. (1997b) 'Mutual Fund Survivorship', Working Paper, Goldman Sachs Asset Management, New York.

Davis, J. L. (1999) 'Mutual Fund Performance and Manager Style', Working Paper, Dimensional Fund Advisors, Santa Monica.

Dimson, E. and Marsh, P. (1995–98) *Hoare Govett Smaller Companies Index, ABN* AMRO Hoare Govett, London.

Elton, E. J., Gruber, M. J., Das, S. and Hlavka, M. (1993) 'Efficiency with Costly Information: A Reinterpretation of Evidence from Managed Portfolios', *Review of Financial Studies,* 6(1), 1–21.

Elton, E. J., Gruber, M. J. and Blake, C. R. (1996) 'Survivorship Bias and Mutual Fund Performance', *Review of Financial Studies,* 9(4), 1097–120.

Fama, E. F. and French, K. R. (1992) 'The Cross-Section of Expected Stock Returns', *Journal of Finance,* 47, 427–65.

Fama, E. F. and French, K. R. (1993) 'Common Risk Factors in the Returns on Stocks and Bonds', *Journal of Financial Economics,* 33, 3–56.

Lintner, J. (1965) 'The Valuation of Risky Assets and the Selection of Risky Investments in Stock Portfolios and Capital Budgets', *Review of Economics and Statistics,* 47, 13–37.

Malkiel, B. G. (1995) 'Returns from Investing in Equity Mutual Funds 1971 to 1991', *Journal of Finance,* 50(2), 549–72.

Sharpe, W. F. (1964) 'Capital Asset Prices: A Theory of Market Equilibrium under Conditions of Risk', *Journal of Finance,* 19, 425–42.

Strong, N. and Xinzhong G. Xu (1997) 'Explaining the Cross-Section of UK Expected Stock Returns', *British Accounting Review,* 1, 1–23.

Unit Trust Yearbooks (1992–1997) FT Business Publications, London.

Appendix: Sources and descriptions of data

- Risk free rate is the return of one month UK Treasury bills and was supplied by BZW (now Barclays Capital).
- The market return is the total return of the Financial Times Actuaries All Share Index (FTA) and was supplied by BZW.
- The UK Value Index from 1978 to 1995 was supplied by Fama and French and was calculated by ranking UK companies in the MSCI Index based on their book-to-market ratios at the start of July each year and forming a market capitalisation weighted portfolio from the top 30 per cent of companies ranked by book to market, holding for one year and reforming the portfolio each year. From January 1996, it is the monthly return of the UK section of the DFA International Value Series. The DFA International Value Series buys the top 30 per cent of companies ranked by book to market in each market it invests in and weights each company in proportion to its market capitalisation. It will continue to hold a company until it moves below the 50th percentile of companies ranked by book to market.
- The *SMB* (small minus big) series for the three-factor model tests is the return of the Hoare Govett Smaller Companies Index (total return, ex investment trusts) minus the FTA total return.
- The *HML* (high minus low book-to-market) series from 1978 to 1995 for the three-factor model tests is the monthly return of the UK Value index minus the FTA total return.

2

A Demystification of the Black–Litterman Model: Managing Quantitative and Traditional Portfolio Construction

*Stephen Satchell**

is a fellow of Trinity College, Cambridge, a lecturer in Economics at Cambridge University and a Visiting Professor at City University Business School, London. His specialities are finance and econometrics, on which he has written at least 80 papers. An academic advisor and consultant to a wide range of financial institutions covering areas such as actuarial valuation, asset management, risk management and strategy design, Dr Satchell has links with research organisations such as the Department of Applied Economics (Cambridge) and INQUIRE, and has doctorates from the Universities of Cambridge and London.

Alan Scowcroft

was educated at Ruskin College, Oxford and Wolfson College, Cambridge where he was awarded the Jennings prize for academic achievement. He taught econometrics at Clare College, Cambridge before joining Phillips and Drew as an econometrician in 1984. There he worked with the leading macro research group of the time building macro-econometric forecasting models and developing innovative software for solving large scale dynamic input-output models. In 1991 he established the equities quantitative research group at UBS with Alun Jones and since that time has worked on every aspect of quantitative modelling from stock valuation to TAA. He has been closely associated with the pioneering work on equity style and portfolio analysis developed by UBS Warburg. Mr Scowcroft's research interests include practical applications of Bayesian econometrics and portfolio optimisation. He is currently the head of equities quantitative research at UBS Warburg.

**Trinity College, Cambridge University, Trinity Lane, Cambridge CB2 1TQ, UK*
Tel: 44(0) 1223 338409; Fax: 44(0) 1223 335475; e-mail: ses11@econ.cam.ac.uk

Reprinted from 'A demystification of the Black–Litterman model: Managing quantitative and traditional portfolio construction' by Stephen Satchell and Alan Scowcroft in *Journal of Asset Management*, 1, 2000, pp. 138–150, DOI:10.1057/palgrave.jam.2240011. With kind permission from Palgrave Macmillan Ltd.

Introduction

One of the major difficulties in financial management is trying to integrate quantitative and traditional management into a joint framework. Typically, traditional fund managers are resistant to quantitative management, as they feel that techniques of mean-variance analysis and related procedures do not capture effectively their value added. Quantitative managers often regard their judgmental colleagues as idiot savants. Senior management is rarely prepared to intervene when managers are successful and profitable, however they made their decisions. These disharmonies can make company-wide risk-management and portfolio analysis non-operational and can have deleterious effects on company profitability and staff morale.

One model which has the potential to be used to integrate these diverse approaches is the Black-Litterman (BL) model (Black and Litterman, 1991, 1992). This is based on a Bayesian methodology which effectively updates currently held opinions with data to form new opinions. This framework allows the judgmental managers to give their views/forecasts, these views are added to the quantitative model and the final forecasts reflect a blend of both viewpoints. A lucid discussion of the model appears in Lee (1999).

Given the importance of this model, however, there appears to be no readable description of the mathematics underlying it. The purpose of this paper is to present such a description. In the second and third sections we describe the workings of the model and present some examples. In the fourth section we present an alternative formulation which takes into account prior beliefs on volatility. In the second and third sections, particular attention is paid to the interesting issue of how to connect the subjective views of our managers into information usable in the model. This is not a trivial matter and lies at the heart of Bayesian analysis. Indeed Rev. Bayes had such misgivings about applying Bayes theorem to real-world phenomena that he did not publish his paper (Bayes, 1763): it was presented to the Royal Society by his literary executor (Bernstein, 1996: 129–34).

Workings of the model

Before we present Bayes' theorem and its application by BL to asset management problems, we shall present our notation and basic concepts. We assume that there is an $(n \times 1)$ vector of asset returns $\mathbf{r}$; these are, typically, excess returns measured in the domestic currency and subtracting the domestic cash return which is not included in the vectors. With this convention the asset returns have a well-defined n-dimensional covariance matrix Σ; in particular, their covariance matrix is non-singular. If the returns for period t are denoted by $\mathbf{r}_t$, we shall write $E(\mathbf{r})$ to mean expected forecasted returns. This is shorthand for $E(\mathbf{r}_{t+1}|\Im_t)$, where $\Im_t$ refers to all information up to and including period t. A second related concept is the $(n \times 1)$ vector π representing equilibrium excess returns, either in terms of a theory such as the capital asset pricing model (CAPM) or in the sense of the prevailing supply of value-weighted assets. The latter interpretation corresponds to a global market portfolio demonetised in domestic currency.

Algebraically, assuming the validity of the CAPM,

$$\pi = \beta(\mu_{\mathrm{m}} - r_{\mathrm{f}})$$

where μ_{m} is the return on the global market in domestic currency, r_{f} is the riskless (cash) domestic rate of return, β is an $(n \times 1)$ vector of asset betas, where

$$\beta = \mathrm{Cov}(\mathbf{r}, \mathbf{r}' \, \mathbf{w}_{\mathrm{m}})/\sigma_{\mathrm{m}}^2$$

where $\mathbf{r}' \, \mathbf{w}_{\mathrm{m}}$ is the return on the global market, $\mathbf{w}_{\mathrm{m}}$ are the weights on the global market, determined by market values, and σ_{m}^2 is the variance of the rate of return on the world market.

If we let $\Sigma = \mathrm{Cov}(\mathbf{r}, \mathbf{r}')$ be the covariance matrix of the n asset classes, then

$$\pi = \delta \Sigma \mathbf{w}_{\mathrm{m}}$$

where $\delta = (\mu_{\mathrm{m}} - r_{\mathrm{f}})/\sigma_{\mathrm{m}}^2$ is a positive constant. If returns were arithmetic with no reinvestment, δ would be invariant to time, since both numerator and denominator would be linear in time. However, if compounding is present, there may be some time effect.

In this paper, we shall only consider (global) equity in our n assets. Extending the model to domestic and foreign equities and bonds presents few difficulties.

Considering Foreign Exchange (*FX*) as an additional asset class does present difficulties as we need to 'convert' currencies into a domestic value, which requires making assumptions about hedge ratios. Black (1990) proves that, in an international CAPM (ICAPM)[1] under very stringent assumptions, all investors hedge the same proportion of overseas investment, and uses this result to justify a global or universal hedging factor which is the same for all investors facing all currencies. Adler and Prasad (1992) discuss Black's result and show how restrictive the result actually is.

It is natural to think of π as being the implied returns from the equilibrium model and, as the above discussion shows, these would depend upon our data and represent the input of the quantitative manager. How can we represent the views of the fund managers? To answer this question, consider Bayes' theorem. In the notation we have defined above, Bayes' theorem states that

$$\mathrm{pdf}(E(\mathbf{r}) \mid \pi) = \frac{\mathrm{pdf}(\pi \mid E(\mathbf{r}))\mathrm{pdf}(E(\mathbf{r}))}{\mathrm{pdf}(\pi)}$$

where pdf(.) means probability density function. The above terms have the following interpretations:

- pdf($E(\mathbf{r})$) is the prior pdf that expresses the (prior) views of the fund manager/investor
- pdf(π) represents the marginal pdf of equilibrium returns. In the treatment that follows, it is not modelled. As we will demonstrate, it disappears in the constant of integration.
- pdf($\pi | E(\mathbf{r})$) is the conditional pdf of the data equilibrium return, given the forecasts held by the investor.

The result of the theorem pdf($E(\mathbf{r}) \mid \pi$) is the 'combined' return or posterior forecast given the equilibrium information. It represents the forecasts of the manager/investor after updating for the information from the quantitative model.

The contribution of BL was to place this problem into a tractable form with a prior distribution that was both sensible and communicable to investors. Bayesian analysis has, historically, been weakened by difficulties in matching tractable mathematical distributions to individual's views.

We now review and extend BL's results. We make the following assumptions:

A1 pdf($E(\mathbf{r})$) is represented in the following way. The investor has a set of k beliefs represented as linear relationships. More formally, we know the $(k \times n)$ matrix $\mathbf{P}$ and a known $(k \times 1)$ vector $\mathbf{q}$. Let $y = \mathbf{P}E(\mathbf{r})$ be a $(k \times 1)$ vector. It is assumed that $\mathbf{y} \sim N(\mathbf{q},\Omega)$, where Ω is a $(k \times k)$ diagonal matrix with diagonal elements ω_{ii}. A larger ω_{ii} represents a larger degree of disbelief in the relationship represented by y_i, $\omega_{ii} = 0$ represents absolute certainty, and, as a practical matter, we bound ω_{ii} above zero. The parameters $\mathbf{q}$ and Ω are called by Bayesians *hyperparameters*; they parameterise the prior pdf and are known to the investor.

A2 pdf($\pi | E(\mathbf{r})$) is assumed to be $N(E(\mathbf{r}), \tau\Sigma)$ where Σ is the covariance matrix of excess returns and τ is a (known) scaling factor often set to 1. This assumption means that the equilibrium excess returns conditional upon the individual's forecasts equals the individual's forecast on average. This may not hold in practice as the authors have met many practitioners who have exhibited the most alarming biases relative to the market view. The conditioning needs to be understood in the sense that, if all individuals hold this view and invest in a CAPM-type world, then π represents the equilibrium returns conditional upon the individuals' common beliefs.[2]

Given A1 and A2, it is a straightforward result to show the following theorem.

Theorem 1. The pdf of $E(\mathbf{r})$ given π is given by

$$\begin{aligned} \text{pdf}(E(\mathbf{r}) \mid \pi) \sim N([&(\tau \Sigma)^{-1} + \mathbf{P}'\Omega^{-1}\mathbf{P}]^{-1} \\ &[(\tau \Sigma)^{-1}\pi + \mathbf{P}'\Omega^{-1}\mathbf{q}], \\ &[(\tau \Sigma)^{-1} + \mathbf{P}'\Omega^{-1}\mathbf{P}]^{-1}] \end{aligned}$$

Proof: See Appendix.

We emphasise that Theorem 1 is a result known to Bayesian econometricians and to BL, although they did not report the variance formula in the papers. Also, our interpretation of what is prior and what is sample information may differ from BL.

It should be clear from the previous analysis that neither A1 nor A2 are essential for the model to be used. Most priors used in finance, however, tend to convey little information about the investors' beliefs. Various alternatives such as a diffuse prior (see Harvey and Zhou (HZ), 1990: Equation 6; or Klein and Bawa (KB) 1976: Equation 3) or the more detailed priors presented in Hamilton (1994: Chap. 12) cannot be easily understood in behavioural terms. In Bayesian terms, the prior chosen by BL is called the natural conjugate prior.

Extensions could be considered for volatilities as well. The natural *equilibrium* value for volatility is the Black–Scholes (BS) model, so that if option data were available, the prior on volatility could be updated by the *observed* implied volatility. Unfortunately, the *pdf* of implied volatility would depend on the nature of the stochastic volatility ignored by the BS formula, and there appears to be no simple way forward. An alternative would be to formulate a prior on τ. Although we have no obvious data to update our beliefs, a solution similar to Proposition 12.3 in Hamilton (1994) could be attempted. We present details in the fourth section.

Examples

In this section, we consider various examples which illustrate the methodology.

Example 1

In this example, we consider the case where a sterling-based investor believes that the Swiss equity market will outperform the German by 0.5 per cent per annum. All returns are measured in sterling and are unhedged. This is a modest target and is intended to emphasise that the forecast represents a new *equilibrium* and not short-term outperformance. In the notation of the second section, we have one belief, $k = 1$ in A1. Using the universe of 11 European equity markets listed in Table 2.2, **P** is a (1×11) vector of the form

$$\mathbf{P} = [1, -1, 0, 0, 0, 0, 0, 0, 0, 0, 0]$$

and $\mathbf{q} = 0.5$ per cent. Table 2.1 lists the parameters used to compute the conditional forecast.

The computed values $E(\mathbf{r} \mid \pi)$ are shown in Table 2.2. In addition to the prior view of the relative performance of Swiss and German markets, larger changes from the implied view for other markets are associated with low covariance with the Swiss market. In Table 2.3, we report certain key parameters associated with our portfolio construction.

Table 2.1 Bayesian parameters

Parameter	Value	Symbol
Delta	5.00	δ
Tau	1.00	τ
View	0.05	q
Confidence	0.05	ω

Table 2.2 Forecast results

Market	Bench weight	Swiss Cov × 100	π	$E(r\|\pi)$	Difference
Switzerland	0.0982	0.1884	5.34	5.53	+0.19
Germany	0.1511	0.0724	6.46	6.31	−0.15
Denmark	0.0136	0.0766	5.31	5.29	−0.02
Spain	0.0409	0.0666	8.07	7.99	−0.08
Finland	0.0125	0.0666	10.69	10.55	−0.14
France	0.1234	0.1016	7.93	7.89	−0.03
Italy	0.0568	0.0061	8.06	7.88	−0.18
Netherlands	0.0870	0.0826	5.64	5.62	−0.03
Norway	0.0103	0.0979	8.43	8.40	−0.03
Sweden	0.0474	0.0776	7.71	7.67	−0.04
UK	0.3588	0.0784	6.33	6.33	−0.00

Table 2.3 Optimisation parameters

Parameter	Value
Risk aversion λ	2.5
Tracking error limit	2.5
Portfolio beta	1.0

We now consider the impact of the conditional forecast in an optimisation problem, where the objective is a simple mean-variance utility function. The risk-aversion parameter has been set with reference to delta. The beta of the portfolio and the sum of the weights are constrained to unity. The results presented in Table 2.4, show, as expected, a switch from the German to the Swiss market. Some large differences in forecasts, Italy for example, are translated into small changes in the portfolio weights as the optimiser takes into account the benchmark weight, the asset beta and the impact of covariances.

In both this and the following example, currency holdings were free to vary between zero and minus the market weight (ie from unhedged to fully hedged). The assumed benchmark holding of currency is zero for all markets. The solution weights for currencies, which are not shown in the table, are all negligible.

The Sharpe ratio for the solution is 0.16 with a tracking error[3] of 0.39, the portfolio is beta constrained to 1.0.

Table 2.4 Optimisation results

Market	Beta	Benchmark weight (%)	Solution weight (%)	Difference
Switzerland	0.80	9.82	12.19	+2.37
Germany	0.97	15.11	12.81	−2.30
Denmark	0.80	1.36	1.22	−0.14
Spain	1.20	4.09	4.27	+0.18
Finland	1.57	1.25	1.37	+0.11
France	1.18	12.34	12.61	+0.27
Italy	1.20	5.68	5.63	−0.05
Netherlands	0.85	8.70	8.04	−0.66
Norway	1.25	1.03	1.10	+0.07
Sweden	1.15	4.74	4.77	+0.02
UK	0.95	35.88	36.00	+0.12

Table 2.5 Bayesian parameters

Parameter	Value	Symbol
Delta	3.000	δ
Tau	1.000	τ
View	0.015	q
Confidence	0.025	ω

Example 2

In this second example, we consider the case where a US dollar-based investor believes that six *hard currency* markets will outperform nine other European markets, on average, by 1.5 per cent per annum. This could be interpreted as a possible EMU scenario. As in Example 1, this still represents one view and **P** is now a (1 × 15) vector equal to

$$[1/6 \ldots 1/6 \; - \; 1/9 \ldots - 1/9]$$

The values for the other parameters are as shown in Table 2.5. Note that Delta (δ) has now been set at 3 to ensure that the level of the conditional forecast accords with historical experience.

The conditional forecast is shown in Table 2.6. The difference between the implied and conditional forecasts is broadly in line with the imposed view, with the exception that the forecast for Ireland actually goes down while Switzerland increases slightly.

Table 2.6 Forecast results

	Bench weight	π	$E(r\mid\pi)$	Difference
'Hard' markets				
Austria	0.0060	14.84	15.05	+0.21
Belgium	0.0244	13.75	13.83	+0.08
France	0.1181	14.86	14.98	+0.12
Germany	0.1446	13.57	13.60	+0.04
Netherlands	0.0832	12.33	12.38	+0.06
Ireland	0.0076	11.18	11.03	−0.15
'Soft' markets				
Denmark	0.0130	12.24	11.92	−0.32
Finland	0.0120	18.83	17.58	−1.24
Italy	0.0543	16.62	15.42	−1.20
Norway	0.0098	15.55	15.04	−0.51
Portugal	0.0049	11.84	11.67	−0.17
Spain	0.0392	13.63	13.03	−0.60
Sweden	0.0454	13.04	12.28	−0.76
Switzerland	0.0940	13.27	13.29	+0.02
UK	0.3433	12.74	12.68	−0.06

Table 2.7 Optimisation parameters

Parameter	Value
Risk aversion λ	1.5
Tracking error limit	2.5
Portfolio beta	1.0

To consider the impact of the conditional forecast, we solve a simple optimisation problem, where, as in Example 1, the asset weights are constrained to be positive and sum to unity. The asset beta is constrained to unity and currency weights are free to vary between unhedged and fully hedged for each market. The tracking error is bounded at 2.5 (see Table 2.7).

The optimisation results are shown in Table 2.8 and not surprisingly show a positive tilt in favour of the *strong currency* markets. Interestingly, even though the optimiser was free to hold currency up to a fully hedged position, all the solution weights for currencies are zero. The Sharpe ratio for the solution is 0.18 with a tracking error of 1.8. The portfolio beta is constrained to unity.

Table 2.8 Optimisation results

Market	Beta	Benchmark weight (%)	Solution weight (%)	Difference
Austria	1.09	0.60	3.27	+2.67
Belgium	1.02	2.44	4.82	+2.38
France	1.10	11.81	15.90	+4.09
Germany	1.00	14.46	18.63	+4.17
Netherlands	0.92	8.32	9.28	+0.96
Ireland	0.84	0.76	3.39	+2.63
Denmark	0.91	1.30	0.00	−1.30
Finland	1.37	1.20	0.00	−1.20
Italy	1.22	5.43	2.66	−2.77
Norway	1.14	0.98	0.00	−0.98
Portugal	0.88	0.49	0.00	−0.49
Spain	1.01	3.92	0.98	−2.94
Sweden	0.97	4.54	1.82	−2.72
Switzerland	0.98	9.40	6.79	−2.61
UK	0.95	34.33	32.46	−1.88

Overall, we feel that the examples justify our confidence in the approach. Care needs to be taken interpreting the conditional forecast, however, since it is the product of the prior view *and* the data model. In these examples, the data model has been taken to be the implied excess returns generated by a mean-variance optimisation problem. Even though such excess returns can be counter-intuitive, as in the case of Ireland in Example 2, they may be understood as the extent to which the neutral forecast has to change to reflect properly the views held by the investor. When these excess returns are subsequently fed back into the optimisation process, the investor's optimal weights will reflect the prior view.

It is this usage of implied excess returns in the data model which also helps to address one of the principal reservations many practitioners have with respect to the use of optimisers in portfolio construction, namely their extreme sensitivity to changes in forecasts. Raw forecast alphas are inevitably volatile and, if used as optimiser inputs, give rise to completely unacceptable revisions to portfolio weights. By combining neutral model forecasts with the investor's views, the Bayesian formulation produces robust inputs for the optimiser.

Alternative formulations

In this section, we present two alternative formulations of the BL model, the first of which takes into account prior beliefs about overall volatility.

To do this, we make the following adjustment. We shall assume that τ is now unknown and stochastic so that

A3

$\text{pdf}(\pi \mid E(\mathbf{r}),\tau) \sim N(E(\mathbf{r}), \tau\Sigma)$.

Furthermore,

$\text{pdf}(E(\mathbf{r}) \mid \tau) \sim N(\mathbf{q}, \tau\Omega)$,

A4 The marginal (prior) pdf of $\omega = 1/\tau$ is given by the following,[4]

$$\text{pdf}(\omega) = \frac{(\lambda/2)^{m/2}\omega^{(m/2)^{-1}}\exp\left(-\frac{\lambda\omega}{2}\right)}{\Gamma(m/2)},$$

$$0 < \omega < \infty$$

This pdf has two hyperparameters m and λ, and we assume it is independent of pdf(π).

Remark 1. Here we treat τ as a fundamental parameter that measures the overall dispersion of π about $E(\mathbf{r})$. Considering pdf$(E(\mathbf{r}) \mid \tau)$, we define the elements of Ω relative to τ so that $\omega_{ii} = 1$ reflects a degree of disbelief equal in scale to the dispersion measure of π about $E(\mathbf{r})$, a value $\omega_{ii} > 1$ implies greater disbelief than before and an increase in τ not only moves the dispersion of equilibrium expected returns about the forecasts but also increases the overall degree of disbelief in the forecasts.

Remark 2. The prior pdf of $\omega = 1/\tau$ is a scale gamma, where ω is often called the precision. It follows that $E(\omega) = m\lambda$ and Var$(\omega) = 2m\lambda^2$. This means that for fixed $E(\omega)$ as $m \to \infty$, Var$(\omega) \to 0$ and hence is a more reliable prior.

We are now in a position to state our new result which is, again, a standard result in the Bayesian literature. For a similar result, see Hamilton (1994, Proposition 12.3).

Theorem 2. If we assume A3 and A4, then

$$\text{pdf}(E(\mathbf{r}) \mid \pi) \propto [m + (E(\mathbf{r}) - \theta)' \, \lambda\star \, V\,(E(\mathbf{r}) - \theta)]^{-(m+n)/2}$$

which is a multivariate t distribution. The vector θ is the term $E(\mathbf{r} \mid \pi)$ given in Theorem 1, the matrix $\boldsymbol{V}$ is the Var$(\mathbf{r} \mid \pi)$ given in Theorem 1 while

$$\lambda^\star = \frac{m}{\lambda + \mathbf{A} - \mathbf{C}'\mathbf{H}^{-1}\mathbf{C}}$$

where **A**, **C**, **H** are defined in the proof of Theorem 1.

Proof: See Appendix.
An immediate corollary of Theorem 2 is the following.

Corollary 2.1: pdf($\omega | E(\mathbf{r}), \pi$) is a scale gamma with 'degrees of freedom' $m + n$ and scale factor $\mathbf{G} + \boldsymbol{\lambda}$, where $\mathbf{G} = (\pi - E(\mathbf{r}))' \Sigma^{-1} (\pi - E(\mathbf{r})) + (\mathbf{P}E(\mathbf{r}) - \mathbf{q})' \Omega^{-1} (\mathbf{P}E(\mathbf{r}) - \mathbf{q})$.

Proof: See Appendix.
The consequence of Corollary 2.1 is that we can now compute

$$E(\omega | E(\mathbf{r}), \pi) = (m + n)(\mathbf{G} + \boldsymbol{\lambda})$$

and

$$\mathrm{Var}(\omega | E(\mathbf{r}), \pi) = 2(m + n)(\mathbf{G} + \boldsymbol{\lambda})^2$$

The increase in precision can be computed as

$$\begin{aligned} &E(\omega \mid E(r), \pi) - E(w) \\ &\quad = (m+n)(\mathbf{G}+\lambda) - m\lambda \\ &\quad = m\mathbf{G} + n(\mathbf{G}+\lambda) \end{aligned}$$

It is interesting to note that, although our expected returns now have a multivariate *t* distribution, such a returns distribution is consistent with mean-variance analysis and the CAPM. [This is proved in Klein and Bawa (1976)]. Thus, our extended analysis leaves us with a mean vector and a covariance matrix which, up to a scale factor, are the same as before. What we gain is that probability computations will now involve the use of the *t* distribution. This will give the same probabilities as the normal for large *m*, but for small *m* will put more weights in the tails of our forecast distribution. Thus, we can manipulate this feature to give extra diagnostics to capture uncertainties about our forecasts.

We do not present numerical calculations for this model, as the nature of the prior is too complex to capture the beliefs of a typically non-mathematical fund manager. However, in our experience, fund managers are able to provide a range of scenarios for expected returns and associate probabilities with these scenarios. We shall explore such a model next, this being the second 'extension' of the BL model referred to earlier.

A5 The prior pdf for $E(\mathbf{r})$ is of the form $\mathbf{P}E(\mathbf{r}) = q_i$, $i = 1,\ldots,m$. Each (vector value q_i has prior probability p_i, where $\sum_{i=1}^{m} p_i = 1$ $\boldsymbol{P}$ and $E(\mathbf{r})$ have the same definition as before.

If we combine A5 with A3, it is straightforward to compute

$$p_i^\star = \text{prob}(\boldsymbol{P}E(\mathbf{r}) = q_i \mid \pi); \sum_{i=1}^{m} p_i^\star = 1$$

$$p_i^\star = \frac{\text{pdf}(\pi \mid \boldsymbol{P}E(\mathbf{r}) = q_i)\,\text{prob}(E(\mathbf{r}) = q_i)}{\text{pdf}(\pi)}$$

and

$$\text{pdf}(\pi) = \sum_{i=1}^{m} \text{pdf}(\pi \mid \boldsymbol{P}E(\mathbf{r}) = q_i)\ \text{prob}(E(\mathbf{r}) = q_i)$$

$$\text{pdf}(\pi \mid \boldsymbol{P}E(\mathbf{r}) = q_i) = \varphi_i = \left(\frac{1}{2\pi}\right)^{k/2} \frac{1}{\det(\boldsymbol{P}\sum \boldsymbol{P}')} \exp\left(\frac{-(\boldsymbol{P}\pi - q_i)'(\boldsymbol{P}\sum \boldsymbol{P}')^{-1}(\boldsymbol{P}\pi - q_i)}{2\tau}\right) \tag{1}$$

Combining the above, we deduce that $p_i^\star$ the posterior probability of scenario *i* becomes

$$p_i^\star = \frac{p_i\varphi_i}{\sum_{i=1}^{m} p_i\varphi_i} \tag{2}$$

Equation (2) gives us an updating rule on the prior probabilities which allows us to rescale our p_i by value of the likelihood function with expected returns evaluated at q_i normalised so that the sum of the weights is one. Thus, if the equilibrium return $\mathbf{p}$ satisfied the π condition $\mathbf{P}\boldsymbol{\pi} = q_i$, φ_i would reach its maximum value. We note that since the term in front of the exponential in (1) is common for all φ_i, we can simplify $p_i^\star$ to be

$$\frac{p_i \exp\left(\frac{-(\boldsymbol{P}\pi - q_i)'(\boldsymbol{P}\sum \boldsymbol{P}')^{-1}(\boldsymbol{P}\pi - q_i)}{2\tau}\right)}{\sum_{i=1}^{m} p_i \exp\left(\frac{-(\boldsymbol{P}\pi - q_i)'(\boldsymbol{P}\sum \boldsymbol{P}')^{-1}(\boldsymbol{P}\pi - q_i)}{2\tau}\right)} \tag{3}$$

Table 2.9 Posterior probabilities

Scenario outperformance (%)	Prior probability (%)	Posterior probability (%)
0.5	10.00	10.07
1.0	10.00	10.06
1.5	10.00	10.05
2.0	10.00	10.04
2.5	10.00	10.02
3.0	10.00	10.00
3.5	10.00	9.98
4.0	10.00	9.96
4.5	10.00	9.93
5.0	10.00	9.90

Our new weights take a maximum value of 1 and a minimum value of 0. Table 2.9 provides an illustration of the calculations based on ten scenarios for the EMU example given in the third section. Column one shows the assumed outperformance of the strong currency markets for each scenario. For simplicity, we have assumed that the manager believes each scenario to be equally likely; $p_i = 0.1$. The calculated posterior probabilities p_i^* show clearly that substantial outperformance is much less likely given the historic covariances between these markets. In this example, each scenario is associated with only one view. If the scenario contained many views, the posterior probability would still relate to the entire scenario and not an individual view.

In practical terms, the judgmental fund manager can use the posterior probability p_i^* as a consistency check of the prior belief associated with scenario i expressed as probability p_i. If the scenario seems unlikely when tested against the data using (3) the confidence numbers ω_{ii} defined in A1 can be revised upwards accordingly. Equation (3) can therefore be regarded as a useful adjunct to Theorem 1 by helping the rational manager formulate the inputs required in a Bayesian manner. As observed by no less an authority than Harry Markowitz, 'the rational investor is a *Bayesian*' (Markowitz, 1987: 57, italics in original).

Conclusion

We have presented several examples of Bayesian asset allocation portfolio construction models and showed how they combine judgmental and quantitative views. It is our belief that these models are potentially of considerable importance in the management of the investment process in modern financial institutions where both viewpoints are represented. We present an exposition of these models so that readers should be able to apply these methods themselves. We also present several extensions.

Notes

1. Here we use the acronym ICAPM to mean international CAPM. The standard usage for ICAPM is for intertemporal CAPM. Since the international CAPM is a particular application of Merton's intertemporal CAPM, this should cause no confusion.
2. This rather loose interpretation can be tightened; see Hiemstra (1997) for a construction of a CAPM model based on heterogeneous expectations by investors.
3. The tracking error or active risk of a portfolio is conventionally defined as the annualised standard deviation of portfolio active return (ie the excess return attributable to holding portfolio weights different from the benchmark weights).
4. $\Gamma(.)$ is the gamma function, $\Gamma(n) = \int_0^\infty x^{n-1} \exp(-x)\,dx$.

References

Adler, M. and Prasad, B. (1992) 'On Universal Currency Hedges', *Journal of Financial and Quantitative Analysis,* 27(1), 19–39.

Bayes, T. (1763) 'An Essay Toward Solving a Problem in the Doctrine of Chances', *Philosophical Transactions,* Essay LII, 370–418.

Bernstein, P. L. (1996) *Against the Gods,* John Wiley, Chichester.

Black, F. (1989) 'Universal Hedging: Optimal Currency Risk and Reward in International Equity Portfolios', *Financial Analysts Journal,* July–Aug., 16–22, reprinted in *Financial Analysts Journal,* Jan–Feb., 161–7.

Black, F. (1990) 'Equilibrium Exchange Rate Hedging', *Journal of Finance,* July, 45(3), 899–907

Black, F. and Litterman, R. (1991) 'Global Asset Allocation with Equities, Bonds and Currencies', Goldman Sachs and Co., October.

Black, F. and Litterman, R. (1992) 'Global Portfolio Optimization', *Financial Analysts Journal,* Sept–Oct, 28–43.

Hamilton, J. (1994) *Time Series Analysis,* Breedon University Press, Princeton, NJ.

Harvey, C. R. and Zhou, G. (1990) 'Bayesian Inference in Asset Pricing Tests', *Journal of Financial Economics,* 26, 221–54.

Hiemstra, C. (1997) *Addressing Nonlinear Dynamics in Asset Prices with a Behavioural Capital Asset Pricing Model,* Accounting and Finance Department, University of Strathclyde.

Klein, R. W. and Bawa, V. S. (1976) 'The Effect of Estimation Risk on Optimal Portfolio Choice', *Journal of Financial Economics,* 3, 215–31.

Lee, W. (1999) 'Advanced Theory and Methodology of Tactical Asset Allocation', unpublished manuscript, available at http://faculty.fuqua.duke.edu/~charvey/Teaching/BA453_2000/lee.pdf
Markowitz, H. (1987) 'Mean-Variance Analysis in Portfolio Choice and Capital Markets, Basil Blackwell, Oxford.
Zellner, A. (1971) *An Introduction to Bayesian Inference in Econometrics*, John Wiley, New York.

Appendix

Proof of Theorem 1

Using Bayes' theorem and Assumptions A1 and A2, we see that

$$\text{pdf}(E(\mathbf{r})\,|\,\pi) = \frac{k\exp(-\frac{1}{2\tau}(\pi - E(\mathbf{r}))'\Sigma^{-1}(\pi - E(\mathbf{r})) - \frac{1}{2}(\mathbf{P}E(\mathbf{r}) - \mathbf{q})'\Omega^{-1}(\mathbf{P}E(\mathbf{r}) - \mathbf{q}))}{\text{pdf}(\pi)}$$

where k is an appropriate constant.

We next simplify the quadratic term in the exponent.

$$\begin{aligned}
&E(\mathbf{r})'(\tau\Sigma)^{-1}E(\mathbf{r}) - 2\pi(\tau\Sigma)^{-1}E(\mathbf{r}) + \pi'(\tau\Sigma)^{-1}\pi + E(\mathbf{r})'\mathbf{P}'\Omega^{-1}\mathbf{P}E(\mathbf{r}) - 2\mathbf{q}'\Omega^{-1}\mathbf{P}E(\mathbf{r}) \\
&\quad + \mathbf{q}'\Omega^{-1}\mathbf{q} \\
&= E(\mathbf{r})'((\tau\Sigma)^{-1} + \mathbf{P}'\Omega\mathbf{P})((\tau\Sigma)^{-1} + \mathbf{P}'\Omega^{-1}\mathbf{P})^{-1}((\tau\Sigma)^{-1} + \mathbf{P}'\Omega^{-1}\mathbf{P})E(\mathbf{r}) - 2(\pi'(\tau\Sigma)^{-1} \\
&\quad + \mathrm{q}'\Omega^{-1}\mathbf{P})((\tau\Sigma)^{-1} + \mathbf{P}'\Omega^{-1}\mathbf{P})^{-1}((\tau\Sigma)^{-1} + \mathbf{P}'\Omega^{-1}E(\mathbf{r})) + \mathrm{q}'\Omega^{-1}\mathbf{q} + \pi'(\tau\Sigma)^{-1}\pi
\end{aligned}$$

Let

$$\begin{aligned}
&\mathrm{C} = (\tau\Sigma)^{-1}\pi + \mathbf{P}'\Omega^{-1}\mathbf{q} \\
&\mathrm{H} = (\tau\Sigma)^{-1} + \mathbf{P}'\Omega^{-1}\mathbf{P}, \text{ we note that H is symmetrical so } \mathrm{H} = \mathrm{H}' \\
&\mathrm{A} = \mathbf{q}'\Omega^{-1}\mathbf{q} + \pi'(\tau\Sigma)^{-1}\pi
\end{aligned}$$

We can rewrite the exponent as equal to

$$\begin{aligned}
&E(\mathbf{r})'\mathrm{H}'\mathrm{H}^{-1}\mathrm{H}E(\mathbf{r}) - 2\mathrm{C}'\mathrm{H}^{-1}\mathrm{H}E(\mathbf{r}) + \mathrm{A} \\
&= (\mathrm{H}E(\mathbf{r}) - \mathrm{C})'\mathrm{H}^{-1}(\mathrm{H}E(\mathbf{r}) - \mathrm{C}) + \mathrm{A} - \mathrm{C}'\mathrm{H}^{-1}\mathrm{C} \\
&= (E(\mathbf{r}) - \mathrm{H}^{-1}\mathrm{C})'\mathrm{H}(E(\mathbf{r}) - \mathrm{H}^{-1}\mathrm{C}) + \mathrm{A} - \mathrm{C}'\mathrm{H}^{-1}\mathrm{C}
\end{aligned}$$

In terms of $E(\mathbf{r})$, terms such as $\mathrm{A} - \mathrm{C}'\mathrm{HC}$ disappear into the constant of integration. Thus,

$$\text{pdf}(E(\mathbf{r})\,|\,\pi) \propto \exp(-\tfrac{1}{2}E(\mathbf{r}) - \mathrm{H}^{-1}\mathrm{C})'\mathrm{H}(E(\mathbf{r}) - \mathrm{H}^{-1}\mathrm{C})) \tag{A1}$$

so that $E(\mathbf{r})\,|\,\pi$ has mean $= \mathrm{H}^{-1}\,\mathrm{C}$ (A2)

$$= [(\tau\Sigma)^{-1} + \mathbf{P}'\Omega^{-1}\mathbf{P}]^{-1}\,[(\tau\Sigma)^{-1}\pi + \mathbf{P}'\Omega^{-1}\mathbf{q}] \tag{A3}$$

and $$\text{Var}(\mathbf{r}|\pi) = [(\tau\Sigma)^{-1} + \mathbf{P}'\Omega^{-1}\mathbf{P}]^{-1} \tag{A4}$$

Proof of Theorem 2

First

$$\text{pdf}(E(\mathbf{r}), w \mid \pi) = \frac{\text{pdf}(\pi \mid E(\mathbf{r}), w)\,\text{pdf}(E(\mathbf{r}) \mid w)\,\text{pdf}(w)}{\text{pdf}(\pi)} \tag{A5}$$

From Assumption A3, we can write

$$\text{pdf}(\pi \mid E(\mathbf{r}), w)\text{pdf}(E(\mathbf{r}) \mid w) = kw^{n/2} \exp-\left(\frac{w\mathbf{G}}{2}\right) \tag{A6}$$

where $\mathbf{G} = (\pi - \text{E}(\mathbf{r}))'\boldsymbol{\Sigma}^{-1}(\pi - E(\mathbf{r})) + (\mathbf{P}E(\mathbf{r}) - \mathbf{q})'\boldsymbol{\Omega}^{-1}(PE(\mathbf{r}) - \mathbf{q})$

If we now use Assumption 4 and Equation (A6), we see that

$$\text{pdf}(E(\mathbf{r}), w \mid \pi) = \frac{k\exp\left(-\frac{w}{2}(\mathbf{G}+\lambda)\right)\left(\left(\frac{\lambda}{2}\right)^{m/2} w^{(m+n)/2-1}\right)}{\Gamma\left(\frac{m}{2}\right)\text{pdf}(\pi)} \tag{A7}$$

To compute pdf($E(r)$ $|\pi$), we integrate out w.

Let

$$v = \frac{w}{2}(\mathbf{G}+\lambda),\ w = \frac{2v}{(\mathbf{G}+\lambda)},\ dw = \frac{2}{(\mathbf{G}+\lambda)}dv$$

$$\text{pdf}(E(\mathbf{r})|\pi) = k'\left(\frac{\lambda}{2}\right)^{m/2}\int_0^{\infty}\exp(-v)\left(\frac{2v}{\mathbf{G}+\lambda}\right)^{(m+n)/2-1}\left(\frac{2}{\mathbf{G}+\lambda}\right)dv \tag{A8}$$

then

$$= \frac{k'\left(\frac{\lambda}{2}\right)^{m/2} 2^{(m+n)/2}\Gamma\left(\frac{m+n}{2}\right)}{\Gamma\left(\frac{m}{2}\right)(\mathbf{G}+\lambda)^{(m+n)/2}} \tag{A9}$$

The multivariate t is defined (see Zellner, 1971: 383, B20) for matrices $\theta(l \times 1)$ and $\mathbf{V}(l \times l)$ and positive constant v as

$$\text{pdf}(\mathbf{x} \mid \boldsymbol{\theta}, \mathbf{V}, v, l) = \frac{v^{v/2}\Gamma((v+l)/2|\mathbf{V}|^{1/2}[v + (\mathbf{x}-\boldsymbol{\theta})'\,\mathbf{V}(\mathbf{x}-\boldsymbol{\theta})]^{(l+v)/2}}{\pi^{1/2}\Gamma(v/2)}$$

If we re-write $\mathbf{G} + \lambda$ in terms of **A**, **C** and **H** as defined in the proof of Theorem 1, we see that

$$\mathbf{G} + \lambda = (E(\mathbf{r}) - \mathbf{H}^{-1}\mathbf{C})'\mathbf{H}(E(\mathbf{r}) - \mathbf{H}^{-1}\mathbf{C}) + \mathbf{A} - \mathbf{C}'\mathbf{H}^{-1}\mathbf{C} + \lambda$$

$$\propto (E(\mathbf{r}) - \mathbf{H}^{-1}\mathbf{C})'\frac{m\mathbf{H}}{\lambda + \mathbf{A} - \mathbf{C}'\mathbf{H}^{-1}\mathbf{C}}(E(\mathbf{r}) - \mathbf{H}^{-1}\mathbf{C}) + m \tag{A10}$$

This shows that pdf($E(\mathbf{r})\,|\,\pi$) is multivariate t,

$$\theta = \mathbf{H}^{-1}\mathbf{C} \text{ (as before)}$$

$$\mathbf{V} = \frac{m}{\lambda + \mathbf{A} - \mathbf{C}'\mathbf{H}^{-1}\mathbf{C}}\mathbf{H},\, l = n \text{ and } v = m.$$

Proof of Corollary 2.1

Factorising pdf($E(\mathbf{r}), w\,|\,\pi$) = pdf($w\,|\,E(\mathbf{r}),\ \pi$)pdf($E(\mathbf{r})\ |\ \pi$) gives us

$$\mathrm{pdf}(w \mid E(\mathbf{r}), \pi) = \frac{\mathrm{pdf}(E(\mathbf{r}), w \mid \pi)}{\mathrm{pdf}(E(\mathbf{r}) \mid \pi)}$$

thus

$$\mathrm{pdf}(w \mid E(\mathbf{r}), \pi) = \frac{\dfrac{k \exp\left(-\dfrac{w}{2}(\mathbf{G}+\lambda)\right)\left(\dfrac{\lambda}{2}\right)^{m/2} w^{(m+n)/2-1}}{\Gamma\left(\dfrac{m}{2}\right)\mathrm{pdf}(\pi)}}{\dfrac{k'\left(\dfrac{\lambda}{2}\right)^{m/2} 2^{(m+n)/2}\,\Gamma\left(\dfrac{m+n}{2}\right)}{(\mathbf{G}+\lambda)^{(m+n)/2}\,\Gamma\left(\dfrac{m}{2}\right)\mathrm{pdf}(\pi)}} \tag{A11}$$

using Equations (A6) and (A7).

Simplifying,

$$\mathrm{pdf}(w \mid E(\mathbf{r}), \pi) = \frac{k'' \exp\left(-\dfrac{w}{2}(\mathbf{G}+\lambda)\right) w^{(m+n)/2-1}\mathbf{G}^{(m+n)/2}}{\Gamma\left(\dfrac{m+n}{2}\right)} \tag{A12}$$

3
Tracking Error: *Ex Ante* Versus *Ex Post* Measures

*Stephen E. Satchell**
is a Fellow in Trinity College and a Reader in Financial Econometrics in the Faculty of Economics and Politics, Cambridge University, UK. He has PhDs from the London School of Economics and Politics and Cambridge University. His interests include finance, econometrics, decision theory and forecasting.

Soosung Hwang
is a Lecturer in Finance in the Faculty of Finance, City University Business School, London, and an Honorary Research Associate of the Department of Applied Economics, Cambridge University. He received his PhD from the Cambridge University. His research interests include finance, financial econometrics and behavioural finance.

**Faculty of Economics and Politics, Austin Robinson Building, Sidgwick Avenue, Cambridge CB3 9DD, UK. Tel: +44 (0)1223 335213; Fax: +44 (0)1223 335475*

Introduction

Portfolio performance is usually evaluated against a prespecified benchmark portfolio. One most frequently used measure is tracking error (TE), sometimes defined as differences between portfolio returns and the benchmark portfolio returns. TE is simple and easy to calculate as well as a powerful tool in structuring and managing index funds. Two common sources of tracking errors come from the attempts to outperform the benchmark and the passive portfolio replication of the benchmark by a sampled portfolio.

In the analysis of TE, outperforming the benchmark is equivalent to having a positive expected TE; we call the mean TE 'expected relative return' in this study. The risk related to TE is measured by the volatility of the difference between managed portfolio returns and benchmark returns. The volatility is called TE throughout our study.[1] Thus,

Reprinted from 'Tracking error: *Ex ante* versus *ex post* measures' by Stephen E. Satchell and Soosung Hwang in *Journal of Asset Management*, 2, 2001, pp. 241–246, DOI:10.1057/palgrave.jam.2240049. With kind permission from Palgrave Macmillan Ltd.

minimising TE as well as maximising expected relative return is a sensible goal for investors.

Most studies on TE have concentrated on how to minimise TE, or how to maximise expected relative return for a given TE; see Larsen and Resnick (1998) and Baierl and Chen (2000). Roll (1992) derived an efficient portfolio in 'TE – expected relative return' space and showed that a Markowitz efficient frontier dominates the efficient frontier derived with TE.

Pope and Yadav (1994), on the other hand, showed that serial correlation of the returns differences between an index fund portfolio and the underlying benchmark portfolio results in a biased estimate of TE. For example, the annual TE calculated with the daily TE will not be a good estimate of the true annual TE in the presence of serial correlation.

In this paper, we suggest a different source of bias in the TE, which arises from the stochastic nature of portfolio weights. We compare two measures of TE, *ex ante* and *ex post,* and show that the bias comes from the unconditionally stochastic nature of portfolio weights. That is, since portfolio weights are themselves random variables, there is additional variation *ex post* not accounted for *ex ante*. Therefore, the bias can only be found in active portfolios. We show, however, that it will be also found in passive portfolios whose portfolio weights are not stochastic due to rebalancings.

We use two different measures for TE: one is the variance (standard deviation) of the returns difference between the portfolio and the benchmark portfolio, and the other is the mean absolute deviations (MAD) of them. TE measured with standard deviation (variance) will be denoted as TE_{SD} (for variance, TE^2_{SD}), while TE measured with the MAD will be represented as TE_{MAD}. We show that when the difference between portfolio weights and the benchmark portfolio weights is stochastic, *ex ante* TE_{SD} (TE^2_{SD}) is on average downward biased. The results in this study imply that the realised TE_{SD} is typically larger than the planned TE_{SD}. On the other hand, we cannot conclude whether *ex ante* TE_{MAD} is downward or upward biased in the presence of stochastic difference between portfolio weights and the benchmark portfolio weights.

For asset management firms who try to maximise expected relative return and minimise TE_{SD}, our study can provide solace for these firms whose *ex post* TE_{SD} becomes larger than the *ex ante* TE_{SD} the firms explained to their clients. Our results also suggest that if an investment technology firm presents models which claim to use *ex ante* TE_{SD} to forecast *ex post* TE_{SD} accurately, one of the following two explanations may be true; the firm has included either a fudge factor or some rather sophisticated analysis based on the nature of the strategy that the fund will follow over the holding period. The latter method includes very difficult problems, however, and we feel that the former is more likely. Of course there is nothing wrong with 'fudge' factors if they deliver the right answer, but typically clients would like to be told how the fudge operates.

This paper is organised as follows. In the next section, we first present definitions of TE, and then in the third section we show that when portfolio weights are stochastic, *ex ante* TE_{SD} is downward biased. The Conclusion follows.

Definitions of TE

We introduce two different measures of TE to investigate *ex ante* and *ex post* differences in these measures. The first measure for TE is simply the standard deviation (or variance) of difference between portfolio returns and the benchmark portfolio returns, ie TE_{SD}. Roll (1992) analysed the relationship between the expected relative return and TE_{SD}, and showed that the locus of minimum TE_{SD} portfolios for given expected relative return is located on the right of the global efficient frontier, unless the benchmark happens to be MV efficient. Thus, if the benchmark is global inefficient, the minimum TE_{SD} portfolios will be inefficient.

Formally, let $\mathbf{r}_t$ be a vector of rates of return at time t with mean vector θ and covariance matrix $\boldsymbol{\Omega}$. Let the active portfolio weights at time t be the vector $\mathbf{a}_t$ and the benchmark weights be the vector $\mathbf{b}_t$. Then

$$\begin{aligned} TE_{SD,t} &= \sqrt{\mathrm{var}(\mathbf{a}_t'\mathbf{r}_t - \mathbf{b}_t'\mathbf{r}_t)} \\ &= \sqrt{(\mathbf{a}_t - \mathbf{b}_t)'\,\mathrm{var}(\mathbf{r}_t)(\mathbf{a}_t - \mathbf{b}_t)} \\ &= \sqrt{(\mathbf{a}_t - \mathbf{b}_t)'\boldsymbol{\Omega}(\mathbf{a}_t - \mathbf{b}_t)} \end{aligned} \tag{1}$$

It is well understood that the portfolio weights, $\mathbf{w}_t$, which is assumed to be non-stochastic *ex ante*, will be stochastic *ex post*. *Since ex post* TE is computing TE from the actual portfolio returns, r_{pt}, where $r_{pt} = \mathbf{w}_{t-1}'\mathbf{r}_t$, then a time series calculation of TE would involve, over a period from $t = 1, \ldots, T$, the terms, $r_{p1}, r_{p2}, \ldots, r_{pT}$, or $\mathbf{w}_0'\mathbf{r}_1, \mathbf{w}_1'\mathbf{r}_2, \ldots, \mathbf{w}_{T-1}'\mathbf{r}_T$. Conclusions about forecast failure arise from comparisons of *ex ante* TE given by (1) versus the *ex post* $\hat{TE}_{SD}$ given by

$$\hat{TE}_{SD} = \sqrt{\frac{1}{T-1}\sum_{t=1}^{T}(r_{pt} - \bar{r}_p)^2} \tag{2}$$

Consider a fixed strategy such that at $t = 0$, we fix the weights $\mathbf{w}_0$. For randomness in $\mathbf{w}_0$ not to enter into the calculation, we would require that $\mathbf{w}_{t-1}$ would be rebased/rebalanced back to $\mathbf{w}_0$ within the time period from $t - 1$ to t, and this would need to happen for all periods from $t = 0$ to $t = T - 1$.

Barring the above case, all common strategies including passive strategies such as buy and hold, or 'semi-active' ones such as quarterly rebalancing, tilting, etc., will involve $\mathbf{w}_t$ being stochastic. The same will apply (obviously) to cap-weighted strategies.

Another definition of TE we use in this study is MAD of difference between portfolio returns and the benchmark portfolio returns, ie TE_{MAD}. Rudolf *et al.* (1999) argued that the quadratic form of TE^2_{SD} is difficult to interpret, and that 'portfolio managers typically think in terms of linear and not quadratic deviation from a benchmark'. TE_{MAD} is defined as

$$\hat{TE}_{\text{MAD}} = \frac{1}{T-1}\sum_{t=1}^{T}\left|r_{\text{pt}} - \bar{r}_p\right| \tag{3}$$

Rudolf *et al.* (1999), after comparing (2), (3), and some of their variants, argued that if performance fees of fund managers are linear, TE_{MAD} describes investors' risk attitudes better than squared deviation. Most commercial packages, however, use TE_{SD} in (2) rather than TE_{MAD}.

In this study, our main concern is to investigate the effects of the stochastic nature of portfolio weights on the relationship between *ex ante* and *ex post* TE_{SD} defined in (2). As in Rudolf *et al.* (1999), however, if the performance fees of fund managers have a linear relationship with TE_{MAD}, it is also interesting to investigate the case.

Active management and bias in tracking error

It is our contention that the underestimation of TE comes from all portfolio construction, not just active management. In the conventional calculation, weights, $\mathbf{w}_t$, are fixed at time t and portfolio return $r_{\text{pt}+1}$ can be written as

$$r_{\text{pt}+1} = \mathbf{w}_t'\mathbf{r}_{t+1}$$

so

$$\begin{aligned} \text{var}(r_{\text{pt}+1}) &= \text{var}(\mathbf{w}_t'\mathbf{r}_{t+1}) \\ &= \mathbf{w}_t'\,\boldsymbol{\Omega}\mathbf{w}_t \end{aligned} \tag{4}$$

where $\boldsymbol{\Omega}$ is the conditional (or unconditional) covariance matrix of $\mathbf{r}_{t+1}$, $\mathbf{w}_t$ being treated as fixed and $E(\mathbf{r}_{t+1}) = \boldsymbol{\mu}$ again being interpreted conditionally or unconditionally.

Let $\mathbf{e}$ be a vector of ones, ie., $\mathbf{e} = (1\ 1\ .\ .\ .\ 1)'$. Then, if we compute variances, we need $\mathbf{e}'\mathbf{w}_t = 1$. If we compute TE, however, then we have

$\mathbf{e}'\mathbf{w}_t = 0$. Note that using the notation in Equation (1), we can write $\mathbf{w}_t = \mathbf{a}_t - \mathbf{b}_t$. Otherwise the problems are the same.

We first propose Theorem 1 for the relationship between *ex post* and *ex ante* TE^2_{SD}.

Theorem 1

If $\mathbf{w}_t$ *that satisfies* $\mathbf{e}'\mathbf{w}_t = 0$ *is stochastic, ie* $\mathbf{w}_t = \boldsymbol{\mu}_w \mathbf{v}_t$, *where* $\mathbf{v}_t \sim (0, \boldsymbol{\Omega}_w)$, *then the* ex post *variance of the difference between portfolio returns and benchmark portfolio returns,* $\hat{TE}^2_{\mathrm{SD}}$, *can be decomposed as follows;*

$$\hat{TE}^2_{SD} = \boldsymbol{\mu}'\boldsymbol{\Omega}_w\boldsymbol{\mu} + tr(\boldsymbol{\Omega}\boldsymbol{\Omega}_w) + \boldsymbol{\mu}'_w\boldsymbol{\Omega}_w \tag{5}$$

Proof. *Since (4) is the population mean of the* ex post $\hat{TE}^2_{\mathrm{SD}}$ *given by (2),*

$$\begin{aligned}
\hat{TE}^2_{\mathrm{SD}} &= \mathrm{var}(r_{\mathrm{pt}+1}) \\
&= \mathrm{var}[E(r_{\mathrm{pt}+1}|\mathbf{w}_t)] + E[\mathrm{var}(r_{\mathrm{pt}+1})|\mathbf{w}_t] \\
&= \mathrm{var}(\mathbf{w}'_t\boldsymbol{\mu}) + E(\mathbf{w}'_t\boldsymbol{\Omega}\mathbf{w}_t) \\
&= \mathrm{var}(\mathbf{w}'_t\boldsymbol{\mu}) + E[(\boldsymbol{\mu}_w + \mathbf{v}_t)'\boldsymbol{\Omega} \\
&\quad (\boldsymbol{\mu}_w + \mathbf{v}_t)] \\
&= \mathrm{var}(\mathbf{w}'_t\boldsymbol{\mu}) + E[\mathbf{v}'_t\boldsymbol{\Omega}\mathbf{v}_t + 2\mathbf{v}'_t\boldsymbol{\Omega}\boldsymbol{\mu}_w \\
&\quad + \boldsymbol{\mu}'_w\boldsymbol{\Omega}\boldsymbol{\mu}_w] \\
&= \boldsymbol{\mu}'\boldsymbol{\Omega}_w\boldsymbol{\mu} + tr(\boldsymbol{\Omega}\boldsymbol{\Omega}_w) \\
&\quad + \boldsymbol{\mu}'_w\boldsymbol{\Omega}\boldsymbol{\mu}_w. \quad QED
\end{aligned} \tag{6}$$

Note that the term $tr(\boldsymbol{\Omega}\boldsymbol{\Omega}_w)$ is positive since it can be interpreted as the expectation of $\mathbf{v}'_t\boldsymbol{\Omega}_w\mathbf{v}_t$, which expectation will be positive with probability 1. In addition, the positivity of $\boldsymbol{\mu}'\boldsymbol{\Omega}_w\boldsymbol{\mu}$ follows from the positive definiteness of $\boldsymbol{\Omega}_w$. Since all three terms in the above equation are non-negative, the variance of the portfolio is higher than the portfolio variance taken at the average portfolio weight $\boldsymbol{\mu}'_w\boldsymbol{\Omega}\boldsymbol{\mu}_w$.

Remark 1. *In the case of non-stochastic weights and* $\mathbf{w}_t = \boldsymbol{\mu}_w, \Omega_w = 0$, *and* $\mathrm{var}(r_{pt+1}) = \boldsymbol{\mu}'_w\boldsymbol{\Omega}\boldsymbol{\mu}_w$. *This result corresponds to the* ex post *tracking error with fixed weights.*

Remark 2. *It also follows that, since* $\mathbf{e}'\mathbf{w}_t = 0$ *for all t,* $\mathbf{e}'\boldsymbol{\mu}_w = 0$ and $\mathbf{e}'\boldsymbol{\Omega}_w\mathbf{e} = 0$. *Thus if there is little variation in* $\boldsymbol{\mu}$ *so that* $\boldsymbol{\mu}$ *is nearly collinear with* $\mathbf{e}$, *the term* $\boldsymbol{\mu}'\boldsymbol{\Omega}_w\boldsymbol{\mu}$ *should be very nearly zero. Thus, if there is little (cross-sectional) variability in* $\boldsymbol{\mu}$ *over the period that the fund is being* *measured, we would expect most of the bias from* $\mu'_w\Omega\mu_w$. *Lawton-Browne (2000) establishes that* $\mu'\Omega_w\mu$ *is very small in the cases she examines.*

This result establishes that calculations based on treating portfolio weights as fixed will, on average, underestimate the *ex post* tracking error over a historical period if the weights are not kept fixed. So if we take a particular fund, compute its monthly rate of return, r_{pt}, and then calculate the tracking error/variance over a period $T(t = 1, T)$, where the weights have not been rebalanced monthly prior to reporting the returns, we should expect underestimation of the actual tracking error.

Having identified the disease, finding the cure seems to be rather hard. If, over the period being analysed, we store the weights ($\mathbf{w}_t$, $t = 1, \ldots, T$), we can estimate μ_w and Ω_w, $\hat{\mu}_w = \Sigma_{t=1}^{T}\mathbf{w}_t/T$ and $\hat{\Omega}_w = 1/T\,\Sigma_{t=1}^{T}\mathbf{w}_t\mathbf{w}'_t - \hat{\mu}_w\hat{\mu}'_w$. Armed with these estimates, we can get a much more accurate measure of TE_{SD} but the analysis is *ex post. Ex ante* analysis would require assessing the type of strategy the manager wishes to indulge in and converting these strategies into parameter estimates so that we might expect quarterly rebalancing to result in errors of a certain magnitude, for example. Such strategy-based estimates could be calculated and would be a useful research contribution.

More simple-minded solutions are already in existence. Planned Sponsors often require that managers limit their turnover or specific exposures. Although these requirements are usually motivated by considerations of transaction costs or concerns of risk/bankruptcies of specific companies, they can also be interpreted as pragmatic ways of reducing Ω_w.

In the above, it might be thought that randomness in the weights might move them so as to reduce the tracking error. In tracking error problems, $\mathbf{e}'\mathbf{w}_t = 0$, and so there may be stochastic realisations of $\mathbf{w}_t$ that make all the weights zero, in which case the tracking error is of course reduced to zero. In the above calculations, it is assumed that $prob(w_{jt} = 0, j = 1, n)$ is zero. That is, mathematically, we exclude the possibility that $\mathbf{w}_t$ is the zero vector. In practical terms, we assume that you will not hold the benchmark in any period.

If the benchmark is cap-weighted, as most are, then over the holding period, its weights will change. Even if the fund being measured just does buy and hold or quarterly rebalancing, there will be a random pattern in the overall weights because the cap-weight of the benchmark changes over time.

This is recognised by Gardner *et al.* (2000: Section 3.1), who distinguish between experienced versus prospective tracking errors. The former is based on the returns of the portfolio versus returns of the benchmark taken over the holding period. The latter takes initial weights, $\mathbf{w}_t$, and computes, *ex ante*, an estimate of $\boldsymbol{\Omega}$, then the *ex ante* TE^2_{SD} is $\mathbf{w}_t'\boldsymbol{\Omega}\mathbf{w}_t$.

We cannot apply the same argument as in Theorem 1 to the relationship between *ex post* and *ex ante* TE_{MAD}s. For the MAD case, we propose Theorem 2.

Theorem 2

If $\mathbf{w}_t$ *that satisfies* $\mathbf{e}'\mathbf{w}_t = 0$ *is stochastic,* ie $\mathbf{w}_t = \boldsymbol{\mu}_w + \mathbf{v}_t$, *where* $\mathbf{v}_t \sim (\mathbf{0}, \boldsymbol{\Omega}_w)$, *then the* ex post *mean absolute deviations of the difference between portfolio returns and benchmark portfolio returns,* $\hat{TE}_{\mathrm{MAD}}$, *can be shown as*

$$\hat{TE}_{\mathrm{MAD}} \leq |\boldsymbol{\mu}_w'\boldsymbol{\mu}| + E(|\mathbf{v}_t'\mathbf{r}_t|) \tag{7}$$

Proof. *Using the law of iterated expectations, we have*

$$\begin{aligned}
\hat{TE}_{\mathrm{MAD}} &= E_{w_t}[E(|r_{pt}||\mathbf{w}_t)] \\
&= E_{w_t}[E(|(\boldsymbol{\mu}_w + \mathbf{v}_t)'\mathbf{r}_t||\mathbf{w}_t)] \\
&= E_{w_t}[E(|\boldsymbol{\mu}_w'\mathbf{r}_t + \mathbf{v}_t'\mathbf{r}_t||\mathbf{w}_t)] \\
&\leq E_{w_t}[|\boldsymbol{\mu}_w'\boldsymbol{\mu}| + E(|\mathbf{v}_t'\mathbf{r}_t||\mathbf{v}_t)] \\
&= |\boldsymbol{\mu}_w'\boldsymbol{\mu}| + E_{v_t}[E(|\mathbf{v}_t'\mathbf{r}_t||\mathbf{v}_t)] \\
&= |\boldsymbol{\mu}_w'\boldsymbol{\mu}| + E(|\mathbf{v}_t'\mathbf{r}_t|) \qquad QED.
\end{aligned}$$

Note that $|\boldsymbol{\mu}_w'\boldsymbol{\mu}|$ can be interpreted as the *ex ante* TE_{MAD}. If the weight, $\mathbf{w}_t$, is not stochastic, then $\mathbf{w}_t = \boldsymbol{\mu}_w$ and $\hat{TE}_{\mathrm{MAD}} = |\boldsymbol{\mu}_w'\boldsymbol{\mu}|$. That is, *ex post* and *ex ante* TE_{MAD}s are the same. In addition, we have the following two remarks for TE_{MAD}.

Remark 3. *It follows that if* $\mathbf{r}_t$ *is not correlated with* $\mathbf{v}_t$, *then for many stocks the term* $E(|\mathbf{v}_t'\mathbf{r}_t|)$ *may be very close to zero. Thus, in this case, we can obtain* $\hat{TE}_{\mathrm{MAD}} \leq |\boldsymbol{\mu}_w'\boldsymbol{\mu}|$.

Remark 4. *If* $E(|\mathbf{v}_t'\mathbf{r}_t|)$ *is not negligible, we cannot decide whether* ex post TE_{MAD} *is larger than* ex ante TE_{MAD}*; that is,* $\hat{TE}_{\mathrm{MAD}} \gtreqless |\boldsymbol{\mu}_w'\boldsymbol{\mu}|$.

Remarks 3 and 4 show that we are unable to prove results similar to Theorem 1. In fact, Remark 3 suggests that *ex post* TE_{MAD} may be smaller than *ex ante* TE_{MAD} when $E(|\mathbf{v}_t'\mathbf{r}_t|)$ is close to zero.

As in the case of TE_{SD}, the magnitude of the components in (7) are not known, and thus we cannot conclude whether calculations with fixed portfolio weights underestimate the *ex post* tracking error over a historical period if the weights are stochastic.

Conclusions

We have observed cases when TE becomes influential in the investment management market. For example, sponsors of defined benefit plans increasingly pay attention to 'risk budgeting' that represents allocating TE across managers of different asset classes; see Gupta *et al.* (1999). Another example is that, last year, Barclays Global Investors Ltd agreed to return back a portion of its management fee to plan sponsor J. Sainsbury PLC Pension Scheme, if the firm exceeded its agreed TE limits.[2]

If TE is used to measure the performance of active funds as in the cases above, the bias we find in this study should be considered. That is, fund managers should allow bias when they begin to make portfolio strategy; the planned TE should be less than the target TE because of the bias.

Unfortunately, the magnitude of the TE bias is not known to the authors. In this issue, Lawton-Browne (2001) presents results which suggest that it will more or less double *ex ante* TE measured on an annual basis. Other calculations the authors have seen with different packages produce much less bias. Thus there appears to be some variation in different investment technologies bias production. In cases where there appears to be evidence of bias-correction, however, no methodology of bias-correction is explained.

Notes

1. Tracking error is defined in different ways in different studies. For example, Pope and Yadav (1994), Lee (1998) and Rudolf *et al.* (1999) defined tracking error as the variance (standard deviation) of the difference between portfolio returns and benchmark returns. On the other hand, Clarke *et al.* (1994) and Roll (1992) defined tracking error as the difference between portfolio returns and the benchmark portfolio returns. In this study, we follow the definition of the former, since it is widely accepted by practitioners.
2. *Pension & Investments,* 28(8), 18, 17th April, 2000.

References

Baierl, G. T. and Chen, P. (2000) 'Choosing Managers and Funds', *Journal of Portfolio Management,* 26(2), 47–53.

Clarke, R. G., Krase, S. and Statman, M. (1994) 'Tracking Errors, Regret and Tactical Asset Allocation', *Journal of Portfolio Management,* Spring, 16–24.

Gardner, D. and Bowie, D., Brooks, M. and Cumberworth, M. (2000) 'Predicted Tracking Errors Fact or Fantasy?' Faculty and Institute of Actuaries, Investment Conference Paper, 25–27 June.
Gupta, F., Prajogi, R. and Stubbs, E. (1999) 'The Information Ratio and Performance', *Journal of Portfolio Management,* Fall, 33–9.
Larsen, G. A. and Resnick, B. G. (1998) 'Empirical Insights on Indexing', *Journal of Portfolio Management,* 25(1), 51–60.
Lawton-Browne, C. L. (2001) 'An Alternative Calculation of Tracking Error', *Journal of Asset Management,* 2 (3), 223–234.
Lee, W. (1998) 'Return and Risk Characteristics of Tactical Asset Allocation under Imperfect Information', *Journal of Portfolio Management,* Fall, 61–70.
Markowitz, H. M. (1959) *Portfolio Selection,* 1st edn, John Wiley, New York.
Pope, P. and Yadav, P. K. (1994) 'Discovering Error in Tracking Error', *Journal of Portfolio Management,* Winter, 27–32.
Roll, R., (1992) 'A Mean/Variance Analysis of Tracking Error', *Journal of Portfolio Management,* 13–22.
Rudolf, M., Wolter, H. and Zimmermann, H. (1999) 'A Linear Model for Tracking Error Minimization', *Journal of Banking and Finance,* 23, 85–103.
Sharpe, W. (1964) 'Capital Asset Prices: A Theory of Capital Market Equilibrium under Conditions of Risk', *Journal of Finance,* 19, 425–42.

4

Performance Clustering and Incentives in the UK Pension Fund Industry

*David Blake**

is Professor of Financial Economics at Birkbeck College in the University of London and Chairman of Square Mile Consultants, a training and research consultancy; Senior Research Associate, Financial Markets Group, London School of Economics; Senior Consultant, UBS Pensions Research Centre, London School of Economics; Research Associate, Centre for Risk and Insurance Studies, University of Nottingham Business School; formerly Director of the Securities Industry Programme at City University Business School and Research Fellow at both the London Business School and the London School of Economics. He was a student at the London School of Economics in the 1970s and early 1980s, gaining his PhD on UK pension fund investment behaviour in 1986. In June 1996 he established the Pensions Institute at Birkbeck College (http://www.pensions-institute.org).

Bruce N. Lehmann

is Professor at the University of San Diego and has published numerous papers in scholarly journals, served on professional associations, mutual fund and scientific advisory boards, and earned many honours and distinctions. He currently edits the Journal of Financial Markets *and serves on the Investment Advisory Board of the University of California Retirement System and Endowment.*

Allan Timmermann

is Professor of Economics at the University of California San Diego and a fellow of the Centre for Economic Policy Research. He is a departmental editor of the Journal of Forecasting *and an associate editor of the* Journal of Business and Economic Statistics *and the* Journal of Economic Dynamics and Control. *Dr Timmermann obtained his PhD from the University of Cambridge and his research interests cover econometric and forecasting methods, particularly in relation to financial markets. His work has been published in a range of journals including the* Journal of Econometrics, Journal of Finance, Review of Economic Studies *and the* Quarterly Journal of Economics.

**Pensions Institute, Birkbeck College, University of London, 7–15 Gresse Street, London W1T 1LL, UK*
Tel: +44 (0) 20 7631 6410; Fax: +44 (0) 20 7631 6416; e-mail: d.blake@bbk.ac.uk

---

Reprinted from 'Performance clustering and incentives in the UK pension fund industry' by David Blake, Bruce N. Lehmann and Allan Timmermann in *Journal of Asset Management*, 3, 2002, pp. 173–194, DOI:10.1057/palgrave.jam.2240073.

Introduction

Despite the vast growth and increased economic importance of the fund-management industry, few studies have considered the effect of incentives and fee structures on fund behaviour. Further, those studies that have been produced have almost exclusively focused on the investment behaviour of US mutual funds, predominantly those invested in US equities.[1] Investment performance by institutions outside the US has been much less intensively researched. This omission is important, since differences in institutional and legal frameworks and, indeed, different investment cultures and fund manager compensation schemes might help to shed additional light on the incentive effects operating in this industry.

The few studies that consider fund-manager behaviour show the importance of incentive effects. In careful empirical studies of the incentives facing US mutual fund managers, Chevalier and Ellison (1997) and Sirri and Tufano (1998) document a non-linear relationship between fund inflows and past relative performance. This relationship, which is particularly strong for young funds, provides different incentives for funds to assume idiosyncratic risk, depending on their past relative performance. Likewise, Brown *et al.* (1996) find that funds experiencing underperformance during the first half of an assessment period (usually a calendar year) have an incentive to load on additional idiosyncratic risk, while outperforming funds tend to 'lock-in' their position and off-load risk, although this finding has recently been questioned by Busse (2001).

A closely related literature, eg Trueman (1994) and Zwiebel (1995), considers the effect of reputation on herding behaviour. Zwiebel shows that, when managers care about their reputation and there is asymmetric information about their ability, managers may abstain from risky investments that could lead to a deterioration in their measured relative performance. Empirical studies such as Chevalier and Ellison (1999) and Hong *et al.* (2000) find that reputation effects can explain the unwillingness of security analysts and mutual fund managers to deviate from the median agent's decision.

This paper contributes to this literature by examining the effect of incentives and fee structures on the cross-sectional distribution of investment performance for a large sample of UK occupational pension funds over the period 1986–94.[2] The data were provided by The WM Company (a key performance measurement service in the UK). As in the US, UK pension-fund managers typically underperform external benchmarks that represent feasible passive investment vehicles. Yet there are some striking differences between the fund management industries in the two countries. UK pension funds face a smaller set of constraints than their US counterparts do. The industry is much more highly concentrated in the UK than in the US, turnover in fund managers is much lower, balanced fund management dominates, there is a smaller range of alternative investment styles, and relative performance evaluation at both the individual fund-manager and fund-management-house (FMH) levels has a more significant impact on investment strategies and outcomes.[3] Since we have data on peer-group benchmarks, the empirical importance of relative performance evaluation can be assessed directly. Remarkably little cross-sectional variation is found in the average total or asset class returns, however adjusted for risk, of the funds in our sample; in the case of equities, the cross-sectional variation in the UK is only about half that of US pension fund managers. Only fund size can account for a non-trivial fraction of this distribution and then only in the case of UK equities. Furthermore, the distributions across asset classes are centred very close to (and slightly below in the case of key asset classes) the corresponding market indices: the underperformance of UK pension fund managers appears to be lower than that of their US counterparts.

Fee structures appear to provide a strong disincentive to undertake active management. UK pension fund managers are set the objective of adding value but their fees are generally related to year-end asset values, not directly to performance. Genuine *ex ante* ability that translates into superior *ex post* performance increases assets under management and, thus, the base on which the management fee is calculated. This incentive, however, is not particularly strong, and active management subjects the manager to non-trivial risks. The incentive is weak because the prospective fee increase is second order, being the product of the *ex post* return from active management and the management fee, and thus around two full orders of magnitude smaller than the base fee itself. Moreover, the *ex post* return from active management of a truly superior fund manager will often be negative and occasionally large as well, resulting in poor performance relative to managers who eschewed active management irrespective of their ability. The probability of relative underperformance large enough to lose the investment mandate is likely to be at least an order of magnitude larger than the proportional management fee. Hence, the potential consequences of underperformance (failure to renew the mandate) arising from poor luck outweighs the prospective benefits from active management (a slightly bigger fee) for all but the most certain security selection or market timing opportunities.

The structure of the paper is as follows. The third section investigates the cross-sectional variation in the performance of UK pension funds. The performance conditional on fund characteristics, such as size and past performance, is investigated in the fourth section, and the fifth section concludes. The next section begins with a brief review of incentives in the UK pension-fund industry.

Incentives and fee structures in the UK pension fund industry

Certain institutional features of the UK pension fund industry affect managerial incentives in important ways. First, UK pension fund managers face perhaps the smallest set of externally imposed restrictions on their investment behaviour of any group of institutional investors anywhere in the world. During the sample period, the funds being managed were, by and large, unconstrained by their liabilities: UK pension funds were running large actuarial surpluses until almost the end. The fund managers are also largely unconstrained in their investment decisions by trustee sponsors who do not interfere in day-to-day operations.[4] They are unconstrained in their choice of investments: unlike many of their counterparts in continental Europe and elsewhere, they are free to invest in almost any class of asset, in any currency denomination and in any amount (although there are statutory limits on self-investment in the sponsoring company and, on grounds of prudence, fund managers would limit the extent of currency mismatch of assets against sterling-denominated liabilities). Unlike their US counterparts, UK pension fund managers faced no substantive regulatory controls or real threat of litigation against imprudent investment behaviour during the sample period (Del Guercio, 1996). These differing sets of restrictions are reflected in different asset allocations: UK pension funds hold a far larger portfolio weight in equities and a lower weight in bonds than do their US or continental European counterparts. The great attraction, therefore, of the WM data set is that, in principle, it enables us to identify the genuine investment skills of a group of fund managers in a way that is not possible with other data sets on investment performance generated under more restrictive conditions.

This investment freedom is moderated somewhat by the second institutional feature, namely the high degree of concentration in the UK fund management industry. Over the sample period, the top five FMHs[5] accounted for 80 per cent of total assets under management (Lambert, 1998). This results in the asset allocations of a large number of pension funds being influenced by a small number of 'house views' on key economic and market conditions. In contrast, the US fund-management industry is considerably less heavily concentrated, with the top five FMHs accounting for just 14 per cent of total assets in 1990 (Lakonishok *et al.*, 1992a: Table 12).

One interesting feature of pension fund management in the UK was that there is rarely a change of FMH, even if there is sometimes a change of mandate (eg requiring a change of benchmark): The average length of a pension fund investment mandate in the UK was 7.25 years over the sample period (Prosser, 1995). This is partly because of the expenses associated with a shift in management. But it is also partly because of reputation. As Kay *et al.* (1994) observe, there are two components to this. The first is trust, that is, confidence in the honesty and integrity of the manager, and the largest FMHs have the most secure reputations in this field. The second is good investment performance which is based on a consistent 'track record'. According to Kay *et al.* (1994) the largest FMHs use their track records to retain existing clients or to attract new clients, rather than to extract higher charges. In addition, UK pension fund trustees tend to place a high value on the service provided by the fund manager. Good service and a good personal relationship between the fund manager and the trustees can compensate for periods of poor investment performance and so also help to retain the mandate. Indeed, one fund manager informed us that fund managers do not get fired for past bad performance, but rather for lack of confidence in future performance that might be signalled, for example, by major changes in personnel or systems, or because major clients begin to leave.

This leads directly to the third institutional feature: the long-term survival of fund managers is determined by their relative performance against their peer group rather than by their absolute performance. Even if all fund managers performed badly in a particular year, managers who appear in the upper quartile would still be regarded as relatively good. No potential new managers will be invited to join the 'beauty contest' for a mandate renewal unless they have enjoyed a good relative performance record over the previous three years. Similarly, managers with persistent poor relative performance will eventually lose their mandates. This has been clearly demonstrated in recent years as the persistent underperformance of some of the larger active FMHs has resulted in major clients switching to index fund managers.[6]

Finally, most UK pension fund managers earn fees related solely to the value of assets under management, and not to their relative performance against either a predetermined benchmark or their peer group (ie there is typically no specific penalty for underperforming and no specific reward for outperforming an explicit benchmark). In the case of balanced management, the fee is proportional to the value of the fund and therefore rises as the fund manager adds value. Specialist mandates, however, tend to be more directly performance related than balanced mandates. The fee in this case involves a value-related component which is designed to cover the fund manager's costs plus a component that is related to the fund's outperformance of a prespecified benchmark.

To get some notion of the size of the fees charged by UK pension fund managers, the fee structures of three major UK fund managers were obtained. Merrill Lynch Investment Management's[7] management fees for balanced, segregated funds were as follows (reported in Kay *et al.*, 1994): for funds up to £50m in value, 0.75 per cent on the first £1m, 0.5 per cent on the next £4m, 0.3 per cent on the next £5m and 0.15 per cent on the next £40m; for funds between £50m and £100m, 0.175 per cent on the first £50m and 0.15 per cent on the next £50m; for funds between £100m and £200m, 0.15 per cent; for funds greater than £200m, negotiable. Gartmore's management fees were as follows: 0.5 per cent on the first £25m, 0.3 per cent on the next £50m, 0.2 per cent thereafter, and the fee was negotiable above £150m. The fees of another large fund management group (which asked not to be identified) were: 0.5 per cent on the first £20m, 0.3 per cent on the next £30m, 0.25 per cent on the next £50m and 0.175 per cent thereafter. So, although the marginal fee is falling, the total fee is weakly performance related because it increases with the value of the fund (in practice, the fee is paid quarterly, depending on the value of the fund at the end of each quarter). Comparable figures for the US reported in Lakonishok *et al.* (1992a: 371) are 0.6 per cent for a $25m account (with an interquartile range of 0.52–0.70 per cent) and 0.53 per cent for a $50m account (with an interquartile range of 0.43–0.56 per cent). Larger funds can, of course, negotiate lower fees (Halpern and Fowler, 1991).

UK pension fund managers therefore face the following incentives:

1. They have an incentive to add value, and they are largely unconstrained in the way in which they do this. The strategic asset allocation is set by the trustees (on the advice of investment or actuarial consultants); however, there are tolerance limits around the SAA,

which can in most cases be renegotiated, so that these limits are flexible and effectively non-enforced.
2. In the short term (during the course of the current mandate), their fee is directly related to the fund value they achieve and not to either their value added or their relative performance against either a predetermined benchmark or their peer group.
3. They have to bear in mind that it is their relative performance against their peer group rather than their absolute performance that determines their long-term survival in the industry.[8]

The unconstrained way in which UK pension funds are permitted to add value under (1) might induce different fund managers to pursue very different investment strategies, and this might, in turn, lead to a wide dispersion in investment performance. In contrast, the weak incentive to add value under (2) and strong incentives under (3) to avoid relative underperformance might cause fund managers to pursue very similar investment strategies (behaviour known as 'herding'), which can result in a narrow distribution of investment performance. The following sections attempt to identify which effect dominates.

The performance of UK pension funds

The data from WM consist of monthly observations on the returns of 306 UK pension funds in eight asset categories[9] covering the period 1986–94. The returns are net of the bid-offer spread, but before management fees are taken into account. The sample is complete in the sense that it contains all the funds with no missing data that maintained the same single, externally appointed FMH throughout the period. The total returns on the portfolios as well as the separate returns within the eight asset classes are examined. As benchmarks for evaluating performance, WM uses both external, independently calculated indices (eg the Financial Times Actuaries (FTA) All-Share Index for UK equities), as well as WM universe indices based on value-weighted portfolios of the population of funds tracked by WM.[10] The latter peer-group indices are commonly used by the industry to assess funds' medium- to long-term relative performance.

To the authors' knowledge, this is the first study to consider herding in the context of a multi-asset portfolio. Data are included on the value of asset holdings as well as returns, in contrast with some earlier studies of US pension funds, where only returns data were available (Christopherson, *et al.,* 1998a, b). Having access to this type of data could make a big difference to the empirical results. For example, Lakonishok *et al.* (1992b) find only weak evidence of herding effects and mainly so for small firm stocks. Commenting on this, Zwiebel (1995: 2) notes that 'herding is more likely over broader investment categories (stocks, bonds, real estate, foreign investments, etc.) than over individual stocks. Lakonishok *et al.* do not test for such broad-based herding.'

Another virtue of the UK study concerns the nature of the benchmarks used to correct for systematic risk. Benchmark inefficiency is a central theme of both the theoretical and empirical literatures on performance evaluation, because of the difficulty in distinguishing benchmark inefficiency from abnormal performance. As an empirical matter, Lehmann and Modest (1987), Grinblatt and Titman (1989) and Elton *et al.* (1993) have found that measured US equity mutual fund performance can depend critically on the benchmark used in the analysis. Elton *et al.* (1993) and Ferson and Schadt (1996) highlight some of the misspecification problems associated with performance measurement that arise when the funds under consideration hold assets, such as international equities and bonds, that are excluded from the benchmark index.[11] The present data set permit some of these issues to be dealt with. Since the structure of the asset allocations of the included pension funds is known, benchmarks that do not suffer from defects of asset coverage can be used. That is, asset-class returns can be compared with suitable asset-class benchmarks in both unconditional and conditional single-index models and with appropriate multiple-index benchmarks that represent all of the different asset categories actually held by the pension funds.

Table 4.1 presents some regularities in average fund performance. Panel A provides key fractiles and the minimum and maximum of the cross-sectional distribution of average total returns on the seven most important asset classes as well as on the total portfolio. The interquartile range runs from 11.47 per cent to 12.59 per cent per year and less than 300 basis points separate the funds in the 5th and 95th percentiles. Certainly there is somewhat greater cross-sectional variability in particular asset classes. For example, the interquartile range for UK equity returns is of the order of 150 basis points and the corresponding 5th–95th percentile range is 400 basis points. The corresponding ranges are larger for international equity returns, with an interquartile range of more than 200 basis points and a 5th–95th percentile range of 450 basis points.

Table 4.1 Fractiles of UK pension fund total and risk-adjusted returns by asset class, 1986–94 (average annual percentages)

	UK equities	**Intl. equities**	**UK bonds**	**Intl. bonds**	**UK Index bonds**	**Cash/ other inv.**	**UK property**	**Total**
A. Total returns								
Minimum	8.59	4.42	6.59	−0.64	5.59	2.67	3.05	7.22
5%	11.43	8.59	9.44	2.18	7.20	5.46	5.07	10.60
10%	11.85	9.03	9.95	7.56	7.81	7.60	6.58	10.96
25%	12.44	9.64	10.43	8.30	7.91	8.97	8.03	11.47
50%	13.13	10.65	10.79	11.37	8.22	10.25	8.75	12.06
75%	13.93	11.76	11.22	13.37	8.45	11.72	9.99	12.59
90%	14.81	12.52	11.70	14.55	8.80	14.20	10.84	13.13
95%	15.46	13.14	12.05	18.15	8.89	16.13	11.36	13.39
Maximum	17.39	14.68	17.23	26.34	10.07	19.73	13.53	15.03
B. Risk-adjusted returns: Equation (1)								
Minimum	−4.59	−6.19	−3.59	−10.08	−2.49	−7.60	−6.72	−4.98
5%	−1.90	−2.17	−0.92	−6.74	−0.95	−4.53	−3.69	−1.77
10%	−1.49	−1.69	−0.42	−1.89	−0.65	−2.76	−2.57	−1.36
25%	−0.85	−0.96	0.07	−1.11	−0.16	−0.97	−0.90	−0.79
50%	−0.15	−0.06	0.44	1.76	0.09	0.31	−0.21	−0.14
75%	0.70	1.07	0.87	4.38	0.28	2.13	0.94	0.39
90%	1.49	1.83	1.34	5.48	0.70	4.68	1.79	0.89
95%	2.14	2.36	1.72	8.36	0.75	10.02	2.31	1.22
Maximum	4.68	4.06	6.89	16.67	1.77	12.67	4.33	3.09

Notes: (i) Panel A shows the fractiles of the cross-sectional distribution of raw returns on individual asset classes as well as on the total portfolios of UK pension funds.
(ii) Panel B shows the fractiles of the cross-sectional distribution of estimates of intercept terms from single-factor Jensen regressions of excess returns within a particular asset class on the excess return on the external benchmark for that asset class.

This comparatively narrow range of cross-sectional variability suggests that any differences in performance ability across the funds in this sample should show up conditionally, since an unconditional distribution with low variability can conceal highly variable distributions once non-trivial conditioning information is taken into account. Panel B of Table 4.1 shows, however, that the requisite variability does not emerge from simple risk-adjustment procedures such as basic Jensen regressions:

$$r_{ijt} - r_{ft} = \alpha_{ijt} + \beta_{ijt}(r_{mjt} - r_{ft}) + \varepsilon_{ijt} \tag{1}$$

where r_{ijt} is the return on the *i*th fund's *j*th asset class in period *t*, r_{ft} is the return on a one-month T-bill, and r_{mjt} is the return on the *j*th external index in period *t*. In this panel, the Jensen α_{ijt} and β_{ijt} are time invariant. As is readily apparent, the shape of the cross-sectional distribution of the alphas is virtually identical to that of raw average returns across funds in each asset class and for the aggregate portfolio. For all asset classes with portfolio weights exceeding 5 per cent and for the overall portfolio, the interquartile ranges of the sample Jensen alphas are within about five percentage points of those of the corresponding average returns.

Furthermore, the performance of the median fund manager is very close to that of the external index (just 15 and 14 basis points, respectively, below in the case of the equity and total portfolios). This suggests not only that the sample of fund managers clustered around the median fund manager, but also that the median fund manager, despite both claiming to be and paid to be an active fund manager, behaves like a closet index matcher. The degree of underperformance by pension fund managers is much greater in the US, 130 basis points in the case of US equities according to Lakonishok *et al.* (1992a: 348).[12,13]

In general, relative ranking would not be expected to change much whether ranked on the basis of average returns, mean-adjusted returns or on conventional Jensen alphas. Consequently, any diligent search for abnormal performance in these funds must consider alternative risk-adjustment procedures. The next subsection provides a detailed examination of the domestic equity portfolios of the funds using Jensen-style regressions that permit time-varying alphas and betas. This focus on the equity component facilitates comparison with the existing academic literature which mainly covers equity mutual funds. In addition, domestic equities is the most important asset class, accounting for more than half of the aggregate pension fund portfolio and for an even greater fraction of its performance. The subsequent subsection reports *ex post* performance measures from basic Jensen regressions for the other asset categories and from a multiple-index Jensen regression for the total portfolio on the grounds that this is likely to be more appropriate for the aggregate portfolio.

UK equity performance against single-index benchmarks

UK equity fund performance is investigated using five versions of Equation (1). The first is the original Jensen regression with time-invariant alphas and betas, which provides performance measures conditional only on differences in unconditional betas. The second follows Ferson and Schadt (1996) by permitting betas to vary over time, allowing for predictable variation in risk exposures and, implicitly, in benchmark returns, on the grounds that managers should not be credited for performance based on changing portfolio weights in the light of costless public information.[14] The third allows for predictable variation in alphas as well, as in Christopherson *et al.* (1998a).[15] The fourth adds the monthly returns on the Hoare-Govett small-cap index to the unconditional Jensen regression, since the value-weighted nature of the UK equity index might bias the alphas. Finally, following Treynor and Mazuy (1966), the squared excess benchmark return was added to the unconditional Jensen regression, since all the above procedures are suspect if managers possess market timing ability. If managers do possess market timing ability, they should earn positive excess returns when benchmark returns are large in absolute value, while selection skills should show up as positive alphas in the absence of benchmark error under plausible assumptions.[16]

The behaviour of the Jensen alphas from these models should differ depending on the nature of the underlying economic environment and the hypothesised market timing ability of managers. If the investment opportunity set is unchanging (that is, if benchmark returns and their first few moments are time-invariant) and managers have no market timing ability, all models using the same benchmark will produce alphas and betas with the same expected values. In particular, the cross-sectional distribution of the alphas should be identical across models, holding the benchmark constant. The interpretation is more problematic if the investment opportunity set is time varying (that is, if the mean, volatility, and, perhaps, higher moments of the benchmark returns exhibit predictable variation). The Jensen alphas and betas will be biased estimates of their unconditional means in this case if fund betas move with the relevant conditional moments of the benchmark return, even if managers possess no market timing ability. Hence, conditioning on public information, as in the second and third models and on the squared excess market return as in the fifth model, can materially alter the distribution of the alphas to the extent that betas are negatively correlated with population alphas. Finally, conditioning on public information might eliminate some of the cross-sectional variation in measured alphas to the extent that fund betas are correlated with conditional market risk premiums and volatilities.

Table 4.2 reports a number of summary statistics describing the cross-sectional distribution of the alphas from these models. Key fractiles of their distribution are provided as well as their maximum and minimum

Table 4.2 UK pension fund performance in UK equities against a variety of benchmarks, 1986–94 (average annual percentages)

	Unconditional alpha	**Conditional alpha (Ferson–Schadt)**	**Conditional alpha (Christopherson *et al.*)**	**Small cap-adjusted**	**Treynor–Mazuy**	**Peer-group adjusted**
Minimum	−4.59	−3.85	−6.54	−4.70	−5.07	−4.19
5%	−1.90	−1.95	−1.61	−1.87	−1.79	−1.35
10%	−1.49	−1.58	−1.18	−1.44	−1.51	−0.92
25%	−0.85	−0.91	−0.44	−0.83	−0.81	−0.33
50%	−0.15	−0.17	0.29	−0.14	−0.07	0.35
75%	0.70	0.58	1.03	0.68	0.74	1.16
90%	1.49	1.36	2.09	1.51	1.60	2.03
95%	2.14	1.90	2.55	2.15	2.06	2.69
Maximum	4.68	3.92	8.13	4.78	4.08	4.62
Range of alpha estimates:						
Positive	140	136	177	139	148	194
(of which significant)	(24)	(13)	(24)	(27)	(21)	(48)
Negative	166	170	129	167	158	112
(of which significant)	(29)	(27)	(12)	(27)	(25)	(13)
Bonferroni bounds						
Minimum t value	−5.18	−5.93	−5.24	−6.90	−5.08	−3.91
(p value)	(<0.0001)	(<0.0001)	(<0.0001)	(<0.0001)	(<0.0001)	(0.0138)
Maximum t value	5.11	3.90	4.14	5.65	4.74	6.35
(p value)	(<0.0001)	(0.0146)	(0.0052)	(<0.0001)	(0.0003)	(<0.0001)
Average alpha estimate	−0.047	−0.127	0.332	−0.022	−0.001	0.459
(t value)	(−0.22)	(−0.57)	(0.66)	(−0.10)	(−0.01)	(4.04)

Note: This table reports the cross-sectional distribution of alpha estimates from Jensen regressions. The unconditional Jensen regression gives the alpha estimate from a regression of the funds' equity excess returns on the excess return on the market index. The conditional Jensen regressions refine the standard equation by allowing the beta (and alpha) to depend linearly on a set of predetermined factors (Ferson and Schadt, 1996; and Christopherson *et al.*, 1998a, respectively). In addition to using excess returns on the market index as a regressor, the small cap regression also includes returns on a small cap index. The Treynor–Mazuy (1966) model uses as regressors an intercept term and the level and squared value of the excess return on the market index. The peer-group model simply subtracts peer-group returns from the pension funds' equity returns. All alphas are in annualised percentage terms. Alpha estimates are counted as being significant provided their coefficients are statistically significant at the 5 per cent critical level.

values and their associated Bonferroni probability values (p values).[17] Also presented are the mean alphas and associated t statistics.[18]

Several regularities emerge from these models. With the exception of the last column of Table 4.2, average performance is economically and statistically negligible, the largest alpha estimate (that for the Christopherson–Ferson–Glassman model) being only 33 basis points annualised. Similarly, the fraction of funds with positive alphas is less than 50 per cent for all models, again apart from the Christopherson–Ferson–Glassman model, for which 58 per cent of the estimates were positive, with just 8 per cent of these significant at the 5 per cent level. In addition, the most extreme outperformer and underperformer had one-sided t statistics with Bonferroni p values well below the 0.0001 level, except for the marginal significance level of 0.015 for the largest outperformer identified by the Ferson–Schadt model. The effect of taking time-varying alphas and betas into account is to reduce or leave unchanged the number of statistically significant positive and negative alpha values. Taken together, and ignoring any concern for benchmark error and survivor bias, there is little evidence of abnormal performance on average in this industry or indeed much evidence of extreme out- or underperformance that is significant at any reasonable level.

The main regularity concerns the shape of the cross-sectional distribution. The annualised interquartile range in each of these models is about 150 basis points, virtually identical to that of raw UK equity returns at 149 basis points. Conditioning on alternative models for beta changes the location of the cross-sectional distribution of raw returns, but leaves its shape virtually unchanged. Pension funds with similar performance by any of these measures also have similar risk exposures. Moreover, any shifts in their betas had sufficiently low correlations with benchmark returns or publicly available conditioning information as to leave the cross-sectional distribution of the *ex post* alphas unchanged.[19] Market timing switches among asset classes do not contribute materially to cross-sectional variation in average equity returns within the UK pension fund industry.

Of course, UK managers are evaluated relative to peer-group benchmarks, not explicitly by any risk-adjustment procedure. WM's performance evaluation methodology is replicated by comparing the UK equity performance with that of the WM2000 UK Equity Index (r^{*}_{mjt})[20]

$$\alpha_{ijt} = r_{ijt} - r^{*}_{mjt} \tag{2}$$

In contrast with the previous methods, the peer-group approach requires no estimation of risk exposures, since it implicitly sets β_{ijt} to unity. Recent empirical evidence (eg Brown *et al.* 1996; and Chevalier and Ellison, 1997) suggests the importance of relative performance evaluation for US equity managers as well. The final column of Table 4.2 reveals that this UK pension fund industry practice significantly alters the appearance of managerial effectiveness. Nearly two-thirds of the funds (mainly the smaller ones)[21] outperformed the relative (value-weighted) equity benchmark, with 48 funds (16 per cent of the total) having relative performance alphas that are significant at the 5 per cent level. Many fewer funds earned negative alphas, and fewer than 15 of these were significant at the 5 per cent level. Average performance was positive: the mean alpha estimate was 0.459 per cent per year with a *t* value of 4.04. Of course, relative performance evaluation only changes the location of the cross-sectional distribution of raw average returns, leaving the shape unchanged.

Finally, this section compares the results of this study with those found by Coggin *et al.* (1993: 1051) for US equity pension fund managers using the Treynor–Mazuy model.[22] A spread between the 10th and 90th percentile is found for UK equities of 3.11 per cent. Coggin *et al.*, in contrast, found a spread between the 10th and 90th percentiles of between 5.84 and 6.03 per cent (depending on the benchmark), almost double that in this sample. As is readily apparent, there is remarkably little cross-sectional variation in annualised total returns in this sample compared with US results (see also Figure 4.1).

Performance in other asset categories and the total portfolio

Comparable analyses were conducted across asset classes with single-asset class benchmarks and the findings obtained were similar to those reported for UK equities, cf Panel B in Table 4.1.[23] That is, the average Jensen alpha sometimes varies across risk-adjustment procedures, but the shape of the cross-sectional distribution of *ex post* performance measures remains largely unchanged and thus very similar to that of raw and mean-adjusted returns. Since data on asset-class-specific benchmarks are available, the multi-factor version of the standard Jensen regression is used to compare the excess total portfolio return of the *i*th fund with the excess returns on the entire set of indices:

$$r_{ipt} - r_{ft} = \alpha_{ip} + \sum_{j=1}^{M} \beta_{ij}(r_{mjt} - r_{ft}) + \varepsilon_{ipt} \tag{3}$$

where M is the number of asset classes for which a benchmark index is available.[24] Hence α_{ip} is the multi-factor analogue of the standard Jensen

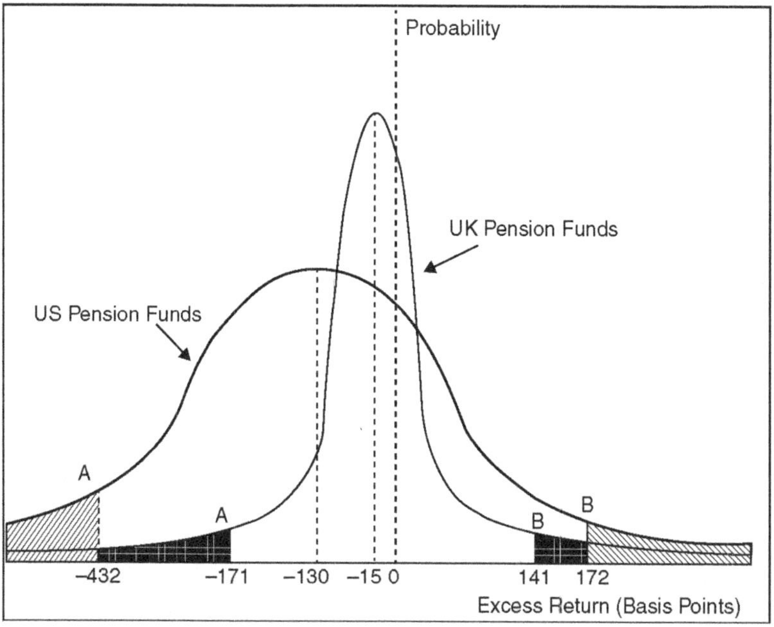

Figure 4.1 The dispersion of excess equity returns of UK and US pension funds
Note: A = 10th percentile; B = 90th percentile.

measure and the potential pitfalls arising from market timing ability parallel those in the single index case.

Overall, UK pension fund managers tended to underperform slightly in the present sample: 138 funds had positive alphas with only nine (3 per cent of the total) significant at the 5 per cent level, and 168 funds had negative alphas, of which six (2 per cent) were similarly significant. Their interquartile range ran from –0.71 per cent to 0.44 per cent, an annualised range (of 115 basis points) that differed from that of the raw returns by only three basis points (cf Table 4.1). The alpha estimate for the equally weighted portfolio was a minuscule –0.11 per cent, with a *t* value of –0.17.

The left tail of the cross-sectional distribution was neither long nor dense, and the Bonferroni *p* value for the most underperforming fund had a marginal significance level of only 0.62. Only the Bonferroni test statistic for the most successful fund was suggestive of abnormal performance, with a p value of less than 0.0001, indicating sharp rejection of the null of no outperforming funds at any conventional level. Of course, this rejection could still reflect benchmark error and survivor bias as well.[25]

Relative performance evaluation for the overall portfolio paralleled that of the equity case: 197 (mainly smaller) funds (64 per cent) outperformed the peer-group benchmark, 41 (13 per cent) significantly so at the 5 per cent level. Average fund performance was quite close to that of the peer-group benchmark, being an economically and statistically negligible 6 basis points below, but underperformed the external benchmark by a more substantial 45 basis points.

Testing and correcting for survivor bias

A potential problem with the data set is the survivor bias induced by the restriction to funds that maintained the same FMH over the whole period, which is nearly two years longer than the average duration of a pension fund management house mandate in the UK.[26] Funds were excluded from the sample supplied to the authors for one of five reasons. First, funds that switched FMHs are excluded from the sample, potentially the most pernicious source of survivor bias. Secondly company takeovers often mean that funds are merged and merged funds are excluded. Thirdly, funds might withdraw themselves from the WM measurement service with no explanation. Fourthly, funds that switched from in-house to external management are eliminated because this constitutes a change in management. Finally some FMHs permit WM to measure only a proportion of the funds in their stable in order to save costs and, occasionally, they will rotate these funds, a practice called 'dynamisation', and such funds are dropped from the sample. The last four sources are often independent of actual performance, so the elimination of funds from the universe often occurs for reasons that do not induce survivor bias.

To address this concern, the value-weighted total returns of the funds in the sample by asset class and in aggregate were compared with the corresponding value-weighted returns of the entire population of funds in the WM universe (1034 at the end of 1994). There was no systematic tendency for the returns in the sample to exceed those in the whole WM universe, either year-to-year or on average: in fact, the average return on the sample of funds was just 6 basis points below the WM universe. If survivor bias was pernicious, one would expect to observe such outperformance, particularly towards the end of the sample as the omitted returns from managers dropped owing to poor performance are subtracted from returns in the whole universe but not from those of the sample.

A final reason why survivor bias does not appear to be an important issue in the sample can be gleaned from a comparison of the evolution of the portfolio weights of the funds in the sample with those in the WM universe. The aggregate asset allocations in the sample and in the WM universe were nearly always within one percentage point of each other for each asset class and for each year,[27] which explains the similarity in the performance of the two groups each year and indicates that both sets of managers followed similar market timing strategies. So the mean returns in the sample do not appear to be affected significantly by survivor bias.

It is possible, however, that survivor bias affects the dispersion of returns. To investigate this possibility, an examination of the asymmetry of the tails of the distribution of performance estimates was conducted. The elimination from the sample of funds with large negative returns will both lower the overall dispersion of returns and lead to the left tail of the distribution of returns being thinner than the right tail. This is evident from Panel A of Table 4.1 in the case of UK equities (the 5–50 per cent range is 1.70 per cent, while the 50–95 per cent range is 2.33 per cent), US equities (the corresponding ranges are 2.06 per cent and 2.49 per cent) and cash/other investments (4.79 per cent and 5.88 per cent). The left tail, however, is thicker than the right tail in the case of UK bonds (1.35 per cent and 1.26 per cent), international bonds (9.19 per cent and 6.78 per cent), UK index bonds (1.02 per cent and 0.67 per cent), UK property (3.68 per cent and 2.61 per cent) and, most significantly, for the portfolio as a whole (1.46 per cent and 1.33 per cent). So, in general, it can be concluded that survivor bias does not appear to have affected dispersion of returns in any important way.

A more formal econometric analysis was also conducted, which allows the likely effect of survivor bias on the Jensen measure to be estimated.[28] The idea is simple: funds whose risk-adjusted performance is large and negative are likely to be excluded from the sample, since these funds are least likely to have their investment mandate renewed. One way to model this effect is by assuming that the sample of funds observed is a subsample of funds that avoided risk-adjusted performance below a certain level, κ. Suppose that the density of the fund-specific performance component, ε_{ijt}, is normal with a mean of zero and a variance of σ_{ij}. Then the density of this component conditional on risk-adjusted performance, $\alpha_{ij} + \varepsilon_{ijt} > \kappa$, is simply:

$$f(\varepsilon_{ijt}|\alpha_{ij} + \varepsilon_{ijt} > \kappa) = \frac{\dfrac{1}{\sigma_{ij}}\phi\left(\dfrac{r_{ijt} - r_{ft} - \alpha_{ij} - \beta_{ijt}(r_{mjt} - r_{ft})}{\sigma_{ij}}\right)}{1 - \Phi\left(\dfrac{\kappa - \alpha_{ij}}{\sigma_{ij}}\right)} \tag{4}$$

where $\phi(.)$ and $\Phi(.)$ are respectively the density and cumulative density functions of a standard normal variable. As a result of this conditioning effect, the mean of the *i*th fund's risk-adjusted performance in the *j*th asset class is no longer a linear function of α_{ij}.

$$E[r_{ijt} - r_{ft} - \beta_{ijt}(r_{mjt} - r_{ft})\,|\,\alpha_{ij} + \varepsilon_{ijt} > \kappa] = \alpha_{ij} + \sigma_{ij}\frac{\phi\left(\dfrac{\kappa - \alpha_{ij}}{\sigma_{ij}}\right)}{1 - \Phi\left(\dfrac{\kappa - \alpha_{ij}}{\sigma_{ij}}\right)} \tag{5}$$

This is clearly a highly non-linear expression in α_{ij}. Under the assumed density of ε_{ijt}, estimation of the parameters involves maximising the log likelihood function:

$$\ln(L_{ij}) = -\frac{T}{2}\{\ln(2\pi) + \ln(\sigma_{ij}^2)\} - \frac{1}{2\sigma_{ij}^2}\sum_{t=1}^{T}[r_{ijt} - r_{ft} - \alpha_{ij} - \beta_{ij}(r_{mjt} - r_{ft})]^2 - \sum_{t=1}^{T}\ln\left[1 - \Phi\left(\frac{\kappa - \alpha_{ij}}{\sigma_{ij}}\right)\right] \tag{6}$$

Although far more involved than ordinary least squares estimation, the log likelihood function can be maximised for a given level of the performance truncation point, κ. This is set to $\kappa = -1$ per cent and $\kappa = -5$ per cent per month, which are reasonable low and high bounds on the point at which risk-adjusted underperformance might expect to lead to a fund being dropped from the sample. If the proportion of funds with performance below κ, is low, then the second term on the right-hand side of (5) will be small and the estimates of risk-adjusted performance will not change significantly.

Results from undertaking this analysis on UK equities and the total portfolio are presented in Table 4.3. When $\kappa = -1$ per cent, survivor bias has two effects on the performance estimates. First, the median fund's

Table 4.3 Fractiles of UK pension funds' truncation-adjusted performance estimates for UK equities and the total portfolio, 1986–94 (average annual percentages)

	UK equity return No censoring	Censoring (per month) −1%	Censoring (per month) −5%	Total return No censoring	Censoring (per month) −1%	Censoring (per month) −5%
Minimum	−4.59	−4.74	−4.60	−4.98	−5.15	−5.00
5%	−1.90	−1.90	−1.90	−1.77	−1.78	−1.77
10%	−1.49	−1.50	−1.49	−1.36	−1.37	−1.36
25%	−0.84	−0.86	−0.84	−0.79	−0.80	−0.79
50%	−0.15	−0.17	−0.15	−0.14	−0.16	−0.16
75%	0.70	0.70	0.70	0.39	0.39	0.39
90%	1.49	1.48	1.49	0.89	0.89	0.89
95%	2.14	2.14	2.14	1.22	1.21	1.22
Maximum	4.68	4.60	4.68	3.09	3.07	3.09

Note: This table shows maximum likelihood estimates of Jensen's alpha based on the model that allows for survivor bias.

performance in UK equities is reduced slightly from −0.15 per cent per annum to −0.17 per cent per annum. For the total portfolio, a similar reduction in the median fund's performance from −0.14 per cent to −0.16 per cent per annum is observed. Second, the worst fund's performance is no longer −4.59 per cent in UK equities but a somewhat larger −4.74 per cent. For the total portfolio, the worst fund's performance is extended from −4.98 per cent to −5.15 per cent per annum. In comparison, censoring at $\kappa = -5$ per cent makes a negligible difference.

Overall, the conclusion that clearly emerges from Table 4.3 is one of robustness of the results with respect to this correction for survivor bias. In particular, the spread between the performance of the bottom 5 per cent and top 5 per cent of funds is remarkably stable and changes by no more than a single basis point for both UK equities and the total portfolio.

Performance and fund characteristics

The preceding results reveal two key features of abnormal performance in the UK pension fund industry. First, a variety of benchmark corrections suggests that few funds have robustly measured extreme abnormal performance. The second feature strikes us as of greater economic significance: the shape of the cross-sectional distribution of average raw total and asset class returns are broadly unaffected by risk adjustment, with even extreme ranges such as the 5th–95th percentile spread virtually unchanged. Cross-sectional variation in risk exposures does not appear to conceal cross-sectional variation in abnormal performance.

Perhaps fund performance is related to other fund attributes. We consider two natural and related candidates: size and past performance. The former might generate diseconomies of scale in asset management due to market impact, while the latter is not readily detectable using the methods of the previous section. If both prove to be related to abnormal performance, separating these effects involves recognising that current size can be related to past performance.

Fund size effects

A finding that larger funds tend to underperform the peer-group would add credence to the often-made claim that size is the anchor of performance. Accordingly, equally weighted portfolios were formed based on quartiles sorted according to the value of assets under management at the beginning of each year, starting with the smallest funds. This procedure generated four time series of portfolio returns for each asset class, the abnormal performance of which is presented in Table 4.4. Panel A suggests that, based on multi-index Jensen regressions, a size effect is present, most clearly for UK equities. The smallest-fund quartile has a positive alpha and the largest a negative alpha, neither of which is significantly different from zero at conventional levels, but the difference between them (0.79 per cent) has a *t* statistic of 3.33 and an associated significance level of less than 0.001.[29] Panel B confirms these results using relative performance measurement. Each portfolio has positive mean excess returns relative to the peer-group benchmark, rising from an economically and statistically insignificant 2.7 basis points per year for the large-fund portfolio to 72 basis points per year for the small-fund portfolio. The remaining asset classes reveal no clear pattern save for international bonds and equities, which suggest a direct, rather than an inverse, relationship between fund size and Jensen alpha.[30] Perhaps most importantly, there is no systematic relationship between fund size and abnormal performance for the aggregate pension fund portfolios.

Nevertheless, the finding of an inverse relationship between fund performance and fund size in UK equities could be an important part of the explanation for mandate retention. UK pension funds hold a very substantial proportion of total issued domestic equities, and large UK funds hold large fractions of their portfolios in UK equities as well. These funds can surely argue that an annual underperformance of the

Table 4.4 UK pension funds' alpha values in different asset categories: quartile-sorted according to fund size, 1986–94 (average annual percentages)

Quartile	**UK equities**	**Intl equities**	**UK bonds**	**Intl bonds**	**Index bonds**	**Cash/ other inv.**	**UK property**	**Intl property**	**Total**
A. Multi-index benchmark: Equation (3)									
I (Smallest)	0.352	−3.189	0.676	−3.989	0.106	0.53	−0.999	NA	−0.315
	(0.91)	(−1.28)	(1.00)	(−1.20)	(0.31)	(0.73)	(−0.98)	NA	(−0.47)
II	0.063	−2.492	0.575	−0.805	−0.344	1.545	−0.384	NA	−0.360
	(0.16)	(−1.13)	(0.92)	(−0.35)	(−0.52)	(1.57)	(−0.36)	NA	(−0.59)
III	0.213	−1.464	1.130	−1.886	0.074	0.764	−0.937	NA	0.110
	(0.68)	(−0.76)	(1.69)	(−0.85)	(0.23)	(0.93)	(−1.15)	NA	(0.21)
IV (Largest)	−0.435	−1.041	0.249	2.247	0.137	0.247	−0.334	NA	−0.268
	(−1.36)	(−0.60)	(0.28)	(0.91)	(0.46)	(0.29)	(−0.26)	NA	(−0.53)
B. Peer-group benchmark: Equation (2)									
I (Smallest)	0.716	−0.421	0.496	−1.631	0.306	0.733	−1.064	−0.396	0.311
	(4.60)	(−0.33)	(1.20)	(−0.60)	(0.89)	(1.07)	(−1.39)	(−0.10)	(1.23)
II	0.456	−0.396	0.298	−1.245	−0.273	1.056	−0.396	−4.356	0.157
	(2.75)	(−0.58)	(0.92)	(−0.73)	(−0.51)	(1.23)	(−0.48)	(−0.64)	(0.88)
III	0.503	0.103	0.737	−1.161	0.287	0.633	−0.794	−0.804	0.422
	(4.36)	(0.51)	(2.68)	(−0.61)	(1.05)	(0.95)	(−1.30)	(−0.18)	(3.69)
IV (Largest)	0.027	0.439	0.175	1.271	0.283	0.702	−0.668	1.920	0.037
	(0.19)	(1.26)	(0.28)	(0.52)	(1.20)	(1.03)	(−1.00)	(0.62)	(0.15)

Note: Based on their size at the beginning of each year, the funds were sorted into quartiles, and four equal-weighted portfolios were formed for the following calendar year corresponding to the smallest group of funds (quartile I), the second smallest group of funds (quartile II), and so forth. This procedure was repeated each calendar year, generating four time series, each with 96 observations. For these portfolios, Jensen regressions were used to estimate the mean of the risk-adjusted returns. These alpha estimates are reported in Panel A in the case of the multi-index benchmark and in Panel B in the case of the peer–group benchmark. The reported figures measure the alpha estimates of the portfolios, with the figures in brackets showing the *t* values based on Newey and West (1987) heteroscedasticity- and autocorrelation-consistent standard errors.

order of 70 basis points reflects the impact of the trading of large funds in a market in which they are important players.

Another possibility is that large funds do not actually underperform relative to smaller ones once management charges are taken into account. To explore this point, management fees based on the major FMHs' commission schedules were calculated. The management fee on a very small fund is of the order of 50 basis points per year while a very large fund would typically be charged 10 or fewer basis points. Hence, the difference in performance of 70 basis points can only be partially explained by differential charges.

Past performance effects

Funds can be small because they have just been established or because they were previously large but have suffered substantial losses. Hence, it is obviously of some interest to ascertain whether it is size itself or whether there is a past-performance component driving the negative relation between fund size and performance in UK equities.[31]

Two approaches were adopted to maintain comparability with both the literature and the evidence given above. In the first, the relation between future and past rankings of relative portfolio returns was examined without adjusting for their correlation with one or more indices, an appropriate approach for investors with the bulk of their wealth invested in a single pension scheme. In the second approach, the persistence of Jensen measures obtained from average asset class returns after correcting for their correlation with the multiple-index benchmark was investigated, a more appropriate method for investors with only a fraction of their wealth invested in a particular pension scheme. In essence, this distinction reflects the difference between the Sharpe and Jensen–Treynor–Black approaches to the measurement of performance.

Tests for persistence in performance used a variant of the approach employed by Hendrick *et al.* (1993). For December of each year, the funds were sorted into four equal-weighted portfolios based on the rank of their abnormal performance measure over the most recent 12-month period. Their performance over the subsequent year was recorded and the procedure was repeated every 12 months. Thus returns are available on four portfolios over 96 months. (The first 12 months of data were used to generate the initial abnormal performance estimate.[32])

Panels A and B of Table 4.5 provide some evidence of persistence in performance but only in respect of peer-group comparisons and then only for UK equities and cash/other investments. Further, this persistence does not extend beyond a one-year horizon. For the multi-index benchmark case, the individual alphas from the quartile-sorted Jensen regressions are insignificant at conventional levels, although the difference between the annualised alphas of the highest and lowest past-performance portfolios for UK equities is 126 basis points. This regularity is also reflected in the peer-group benchmark-adjusted returns, where the corresponding annualised average raw return differential for UK equities is 146 basis points. The sample means are also ordered from largest to smallest across the four quartiles.

Panel C of Table 4.5 provides an alternative characterisation of the persistence of abnormal performance. Zero-net-investment portfolios were formed each December by taking a long position in those funds that had positive alphas over the previous year and a short position in those that had negative alphas, and the performance of these constructed portfolios were tracked over subsequent 12 months, in a manner similar to Brown *et al.* (1992) and Hendricks *et al.* (1993). The results remain consistent with the hypothesis that there is measured persistence in UK equity returns. Once again, the magnitude of the effect with UK equities is modest, of the order of 0.5 per cent annualised.

Of course, fund size partly reflects cumulative past performance, while the previous-year-return measure reflects recent performance. That these two effects are interrelated shows up in portfolio composition: only 15 per cent of the quartile containing the smallest funds were also in the quartile of worst-performing funds, whereas 32 per cent of the largest funds were contained in this quartile. Evidence such as this makes it hard to tell whether size is the anchor of current performance or the result of good previous performance.

In an attempt to disentangle the two effects, single-index Jensen regressions were run for each UK equity portfolio, with the portfolio's own (size-adjusted and/or past-performance-adjusted) quartile return included as an additional regressor. This procedure can be justified on the grounds that the single index regressions omitted some important risk factor and that the betas on the size- and/or past-performance-adjusted quartile portfolios are constant. The results covering the period 1987–94 (96 months) are presented in Table 4.6. One year of data were lost owing to the initial sort. The 5–95 per cent range for the alpha estimates, based on the standard benchmark regression, is 400 basis points from −1.86 to 2.11 per cent. When the funds' size-sorted-quartile portfolio returns were included in the regression, this range fell substantially to 319 basis points. The range only fell to 374 basis points, however, when the corresponding past-performance-sorted portfolios were included. Fund size thus accounts for a non-trivial proportion of the cross-sectional

Table 4.5 UK pension funds' alpha values in different asset categories: quartile-sorted according to previous-year returns, 1986–94 (average annual percentages)

Quartile	UK equities	Intl equities	UK bonds	Intl bonds	Index bonds	Cash/ other inv.	UK property	Intl property	Total
A. Multi-index benchmark: Equation (3)									
I (Highest)	0.574	−1.880	0.771	−1.345	0.216	1.464	−0.953	NA	0.007
	(1.55)	(−0.88)	(1.08)	(−0.48)	(0.68)	(1.79)	(−0.77)	NA	(0.01)
II	0.243	−1.908	0.585	1.761	−0.296	0.315	−0.162	NA	−0.247
	(0.75)	(−0.93)	(0.89)	(0.94)	(−0.46)	(0.51)	(−0.16)	NA	(−0.46)
III	0.071	−1.843	1.017	−0.698	0.081	0.448	−0.983	NA	−0.217
	(0.21)	(−0.77)	(1.90)	(−0.32)	(0.20)	(0.39)	(−0.96)	NA	(−0.38)
IV (Lowest)	−0.688	−2.534	0.261	−4.151	−0.008	0.849	−0.556	NA	−0.373
	(−1.74)	(−1.08)	(0.30)	(−1.67)	(−0.03)	(0.96)	(−0.62)	NA	(−0.59)
B. Peer-group benchmark: Equation (2)									
I (Highest)	1.145	0.264	0.818	−2.572	−0.194	2.366	−0.295	4.092	0.331
	(5.37)	(0.55)	(2.03)	(−0.94)	(−0.32)	(2.42)	(−0.47)	(0.95)	(1.27)
II	0.604	0.068	0.335	1.325	0.275	1.117	−0.597	2.508	0.315
	(4.75)	(0.10)	(1.12)	(0.68)	(1.44)	(2.25)	(−0.80)	(0.77)	(2.29)
III	0.275	0.086	0.367	−1.291	0.184	0.215	−1.129	−0.120	0.211
	(2.32)	(0.08)	(1.15)	(−0.80)	(1.05)	(0.23)	(−1.92)	(−0.03)	(1.55)
IV (Lowest)	−0.313	−0.677	0.187	−0.229	0.331	−0.555	−0.903	1.092	0.069
	(−1.72)	(−1.18)	(0.30)	(−0.12)	(0.98)	(−0.76)	(−1.12)	(−0.33)	(0.30)

C. Zero net investment portfolios									
Multi-index	0.458	1.214	−0.105	0.349	0.015	6.334	−0.009	NA	0.151
	(4.18)	(0.68)	(−0.47)	(1.82)	(1.49)	(1.50)	(−0.03)	NA	(0.85)
Peer-group	0.478	0.257	0.115	−0.219	0.003	2.246	0.094	0.120	0.056
	(5.23)	(0.69)	(1.30)	(−1.24)	(0.33)	(1.10)	(0.30)	(0.82)	(0.49)

Notes: (i) At the end of each calendar year, benchmark-adjusted returns were computed for the assets held by the pension funds in the sample. Based on their mean risk-adjusted returns, the funds were then sorted into quartiles, and four equal-weighted portfolios were formed for the following calendar year corresponding to the best–performing quartile (quartile I), the second best–performing funds (quartile II), and so forth. This procedure was repeated each calendar year, generating four time series, each with 96 observations. For these portfolios, Jensen regressions were used to estimate the mean of the risk-adjusted returns. These alpha estimates are reported in Panel A in the case of the multi-index benchmark and in Panel B in the case of the peer-group benchmark.

(ii) The zero net investment portfolios were based on a similar procedure, except that a single portfolio with long positions in funds that historically had a positive estimate of alpha, and short positions in funds with a negative alpha estimate, were formed so that the net cost of the portfolio equals zero. As in Panels A and B, the reported figures in Panel C measure the alpha estimates of the resulting portfolios, with the figures in brackets showing the t values based on Newey–West (1987) heteroscedasticity- and autocorrelation–consistent standard errors.

Table 4.6 Fractiles of UK pension funds' alpha estimates, correcting for size- and past-performance-sorted quartile effects, 1987–94 (average annual percentages)

	Benchmark only	**Benchmark and size**	**Benchmark and past performance**	**Benchmark, size and past performance**
Minimum	−5.24	−5.18	−5.24	−5.23
5%	−1.86	−1.54	−1.82	−1.70
10%	−1.27	−1.02	−1.29	−1.19
25%	−0.75	−0.54	−0.74	−0.59
50%	−0.04	−0.10	−0.02	−0.10
75%	0.69	0.55	0.70	0.57
90%	1.63	1.31	1.56	1.38
95%	2.11	1.65	1.92	1.84
Maximum	4.62	3.86	4.85	4.73
Range of alpha estimates:				
positive	147	134	148	140
(of which significant)	(30)	(17)	(29)	(25)
negative	159	172	158	166
(of which significant)	(19)	(18)	(27)	(22)
Bonferroni bounds				
Minimum *t* value	−4.74	−3.75	−5.00	−4.67
(*p* value)	(0.0003)	(0.0271)	(<0.0001)	(0.0004)
Maximum *t* value	4.40	3.91	4.31	3.77
(*p* value)	(0.0017)	(0.0144)	(0.0025)	(0.0248)

Note: At the beginning of each year, the funds were sorted into quartiles based on either current size or risk-adjusted performance over the previous year. For the subsequent 12-month period, excess returns on the corresponding equal-weighted-quartile portfolios were computed and the procedure repeated to get monthly time series of excess returns for the period 1987–94. Alpha estimates were computed from regressions of a given fund's excess returns on an intercept, excess returns on the market portfolio, and the excess returns on the quartile-sorted portfolio to which the fund belonged during a given year. The table reports the cross-sectional distribution of these alpha estimates. An estimate is counted as being significant if its coefficient is statistically significant at the 5 per cent critical level.

variation in abnormal performance, while past performance does not. Perhaps size is, after all, the real anchor of performance.

Conclusions

UK pension fund managers have not exploited the investment freedoms given to them by pension plan trustees. Instead, two of the four key regularities documented in this paper – a narrow dispersion of returns around the median fund manager and the slight underperformance of the median fund manager compared with the market average – appear to be the result of the incentive effects of the fee structures, the performance evaluation environment operating, and the degree of concentration in the UK pension fund industry during the sample period. The fee structures provided a very weak incentive to add value, while relative performance evaluation provided a strong incentive to avoid underperforming the median fund manager.[33] At the same time, the incentive to implement independent investment strategies that deviated significantly from that of the median fund manager was severely limited by the highly concentrated nature of the UK fund management industry. The third and fourth key regularities – the outperformance of the median fund manager from the sample of long-standing fund managers compared with the peer-group average (especially in UK equities) and the relative underperformance of large funds – can be explained by a fund size effect. Hence, most managers could point to their above-average performance or to plausible reasons for underperformance. Thus it is perhaps unsurprising that managers were found to produce remarkably little cross-sectional variation in overall *ex post* performance and were generally able to retain their mandates. What is more surprising is how they were able to demand active management fees when their performance clearly indicated that passive management fees would have been more appropriate.

The contrast with the US is striking. The study by Lakonishok *et al.* (1992a) of US equity pension fund managers shows a greater degree of market underperformance (130 basis points per year compared with 15 basis points for UK equity pension fund managers), while the study by Coggin *et al.* (1993) shows that the dispersion of returns on equity funds is twice as high in the US compared with the present findings for the UK (up to 603 basis points for the 10–90 percentile range compared with 311 basis points in the UK). These results are consistent with the low degree of concentration in the US pension fund industry, the greater degree of turnover of fund managers and the much wider range of investment styles compared with the UK.

Acknowledgments

We should like to thank Gordon Bagot and Val Ashmore of The WM Company for advice on interpreting the data used in this study and Juan-Pedro Gómez and seminar participants at the INSEAD conference on institutional investors and financial markets in April 2001 for valuable comments on an earlier draft. The comments of Paul Yates and

Andrew Maclaren of UBS Global Asset Management and three anonymous referees were also very helpful in revising the paper.

Notes

1. Recent examples of studies that also consider US pension funds' behaviour include Lakonishok *et al.* (1992a), Coggin *et al.* (1993) and Christopherson (1998a,b).
2. With a few exceptions (eg Brown *et al.* 1997; Blake *et al.* 1999; Thomas and Tonks, 2000), the UK pension fund industry remains significantly under-researched.
3. See, eg, Lakonishok *et al.* (1992b) for evidence on the US market.
4. Pension or investment consultants (such as Watson Wyatt or Frank Russell) are hired by trustees to help design the investment mandate and interview potential fund managers. But the final decision rests with the trustees. Once the mandate has been awarded, it typically lasts for three years. The trustees can cancel the mandate at any time before this if they are dissatisfied with their fund managers, although in practice the periodic reviewing process gives half a year's lead time.
5. Merrill Lynch Investment (formerly Mercury Asset) Management, UBS Global Asset (formerly Phillips and Drew Fund) Management, Gartmore Pension Fund Managers, Deutsche (formerly Morgan Grenfell) Asset Management and Schroder Investment Management.
6. Eg Barclays Global Investors and Legal & General.
7. At the time the company was named Mercury Asset Management.
8. Further details of the investment environment faced by UK pension funds during the late 1980s and early 1990s are contained in Stevenson (1993) and Blake (1995). See Lakonishok *et al.* (1992a) for a comparative analysis of the incentives operating in the US pension fund industry.
9. UK and international equities, bonds and property and UK index bonds and cash/other investments.
10. The WM universe contains all the funds tracked by WM, including both surviving and non-surviving funds.
11. Elton *et al.* (1993) found that the inclusion of a bond index and a small cap equity index substantially altered the performance in their analysis of a large universe of US mutual funds.
12. While their sample period (1983–90) is similar to the one used in this study (1986–94), these results are not directly comparable, since the data sets do not coincide. The samples, however, do contain five overlapping years, and the market environments in the non-overlapping years would have to be very different to render the comparison invalid.
13. Lakonishok *et al.* found this degree of underperformance using a benchmark of large-cap stocks (S&P500). Christopherson *et al.* (1998b), in contrast, found no evidence of underperformance using investment-style benchmarks such as growth, value, large cap or small cap. Their returns data, however, are equally weighted, as they have no information on fund size, and this will impart an upward bias if, as found here, large funds underperform small funds. Like the present data set, the Lakonishok *et al.* data set is value weighted, suggesting that the finding of greater underperformance by the

median fund manager in the US than in the UK (against a similar aggregate benchmark) is both valid and economically significant.

14. Under the null hypothesis of no market timing ability (that is the ability to switch into (out of) an asset class prior to a rise (fall) in prices in that class (relative to other classes)), this procedure only affects the precision of the selectivity estimates, since the time variation in betas is uncorrelated with the realisations of the index return, making it a component of the residual.
15. As is common in the literature, it is assumed that β_{ijt} in the second set of regressions and both α_{ijt} and β_{ijt} in the third set are linear functions of a vector of predetermined variables, z_{t-1}, which comprises the same instruments used in asset pricing applications: the lagged values of the dividend yield, the T-bill rate and the long-term gilt yield. See Pesaran and Timmermann (1995) for a recent evaluation and references.
16. See, eg, Jensen (1972), Admati *et al.* (1986), Lehmann and Modest (1987), and Grinblatt and Titman (1989).
17. Since the t statistics of these alphas are interdependent and there are more alphas than time series observations, a joint test of their significance cannot be constructed. Moreover, the joint test has low power if a small subset of the alphas differs from zero in the population, as would be expected *a priori* on the hypothesis that abnormal performance is not pervasive. For both reason, p values are reported based on the Bonferroni inequality, which in this case states that the marginal significance level of the largest t statistic in absolute value is less than π when its p value is π/N, where N is the number of t statistics examined simultaneously.
18. Following Fama and MacBeth (1973), the standard error of this average alpha was computed from the time series of returns on the equal-weighted portfolio; the small downward bias associated with the omission of the sample squared Sharpe ratio of the index is ignored, cf Shanken (1992).
19. The cross-sectional variation in the unconditional betas was trivial, as reflected in the interquartile range in sample betas of 0.99–1.01, a range that would be expected if closet index matching were a significant practice. Also, the location of the individual alpha estimates within their cross-sectional distribution proved quite robust across risk-adjustment procedures. For example, using the unconditional and the conditional Jensen procedures, the cross-sectional rank-correlation between the funds' mean (raw) excess returns and their alpha estimates was 0.99 and 0.88, respectively.
20. This is a value-weighted index of all the funds tracked by WM, except for the very large funds, which have their own WM50 index.
21. The effect of fund size on performance is examined below.
22. Their sample period (1983–90) is similar to the one used in this study (1986–94), but not coincident. The 10–90 per cent quantile spread widens to 4.70 per cent for the coincident five-year period 1986–1990, which is still substantially less than the range of around 6 per cent for US pension funds' US equity returns.
23. Versions of time-varying beta models or of Treynor–Mazuy regressions were not fitted here since either approach would greatly increase the number of parameters, straining an already modest-sized sample.
24. Benchmarks were available for UK and international equities and bonds, UK index bonds, cash and UK property, but not for international property over the sample.

25. As noted earlier, the asset class benchmarks might have biases associated with value weighting and asset coverage, country coverage in the case of international securities, and sector coverage in the case of domestic securities.
26. See Brown and Goetzmann (1995), Brown *et al.* (1992), Grinblatt and Titman (1989, 1992), and Malkiel (1995). There is no consensus regarding the magnitude of survivor bias. Malkiel finds that it can account for mean returns of as much as 1.5 per cent per annum, while Grinblatt and Titman (1989) estimate the effect to be somewhat smaller at 0.4 of a per cent year.
27. For example, in 1986 these weights were (for this sample and the WM universe (in brackets) respectively) as follows: UK equities: 54 (54), international equities 22 (22), UK bonds 5 (6), international bonds 3 (4), index bonds 4 (4), cash 4 (4), UK property 8 (6), international property 0 (0).
28. The procedure is similar to methods for dealing with parameter biases introduced by data truncation (Greene, 1999). While the standard procedure assumes, however, that the truncation is based on the value of the independent variable, which in this case would be $r_{ijt} - r_{ft}$, our case is modified by instead assuming that the truncation is determined by low risk-adjusted performance.
29. Lakonishok *et al.* (1992a) also find that smaller funds outperform larger ones.
30. One possible explanation (which it is not possible to test here) lies in the potential economies of scale to information gathering in global asset markets.
31. In contrast, Lehmann and Modest (1987), Grinblatt and Titman (1992), Lakonishok *et al.* (1992a), Hendricks *et al.* (1993) and Brown and Goetzmann (1995) find persistence in the performance of (mainly) the worst-performing mutual funds in the US.
32. On average, each of the four portfolios contained around 80 funds for UK equities, international equities, cash/other investments and total holdings and somewhat fewer funds for the other asset classes.
33. Support for these results can be found in the theoretical literature on agency effects in delegated portfolio management which generates a 'non-incentive' result in the case of linear relative performance evaluation (RPE) contracts (whereby the fund manager's fee is proportional to the excess return above a peer-group benchmark). Such contracts fail to provide managers who are unconstrained in their investment objectives with adequate incentives to search for superior information and hence encourage herding (Dybvig *et al*, 2000, Gómez and Sharma, 2001). While UK pension fund managers do not face explicit RPE contracts, their long-term survival depends on implicit RPE contracts and again these provide an incentive to herd around the median fund manager.

References

Admati, A., Bhattacharya, S., Pfleiderer, P. C. and Ross, S. A. (1986) 'On Timing and Selectivity', *Journal of Finance,* 41, 715–30.

Blake, D. (1995) *Pension Schemes and Pensions Funds in the United Kingdom,* Oxford University Press, Oxford (second edition, 2003).

Blake, D., Lehmann, B. and Timmermann, A. (1999) 'Asset Allocation Dynamics and Pension Fund Performance', *Journal of Business,* 72, 429–61.

Brown, G., Draper, P. and McKenzie, E. (1997) 'Consistency of UK Pension Fund Investment Performance', *Journal of Business Finance and Accounting,* 24, 155–78.

Brown, K. C., Harlow, W. V. and Starks, L. T. (1996) 'Of Tournaments and Temptations: An Analysis of Managerial Incentives in the Mutual Fund Industry', *Journal of Finance,* 51, 85–110.

Brown, S. J. and Goetzmann, W. (1995) 'Performance Persistence', *Journal of Finance,* 50, 679–98.

Brown, S. J., Goetzmann, W. N., Ibbotson, R. and Ross, S. (1992) 'Survivorship Bias in Performance Studies', *Review of Financial Studies,* 5, 553–80.

Busse, J. (2001) 'Another Look at Mutual Fund Tournaments', *Journal of Financial and Quantitative Analysis,* 36, 53–73.

Chevalier, J. and Ellison, G. (1997) 'Risk Taking by Mutual Funds as a Response to Incentives', *Journal of Political Economy,* 105, 1167–200.

Chevalier, J. and Ellison, G. (1999) 'Career Concerns of Mutual Fund Managers', *Quarterly Journal of Economics,* 114, 389–432.

Christopherson, J. A., Ferson, W. E. and Glassman, D. A. (1998a) 'Conditioning Manager Alphas on Economic Information: Another Look at the Persistence of Performance', *Review of Financial Studies,* 11, 111–42.

Christopherson, J. A., Ferson, W. E. and Glassman, D. A. (1998b) 'Conditioning Measures of Performance and Persistence for Pension Funds', in A. H. Chen (ed.) *Research in Finance,* Vol. 16, JAI Press, Stamford, CT, 1–46.

Coggin, T. D., Fabozzi, F. J. and Rahman, S. (1993) 'The Investment Performance of US Equity Pension Fund Managers: An Empirical Investigation, *Journal of Finance,* 48, 1039–55.

Del Guercio, D. (1996) 'The Distorting Effect of Prudent Man Laws on Institutional Equity Investments', *Journal of Financial Economics,* 40, 31–62.

Dybvig, P. H., Farnsworth, H. K. and Carpenter, J. N. (2000) 'Portfolio Performance and Agency', mimeo, Washington University in St Louis.

Elton, E. J., Gruber, M. J., Das, S. and Hlavka, M. (1993) 'Efficiency with Costly Information: A Reinterpretation of Evidence from Managed Portfolios', *Review of Financial Studies,* 6, 1–22.

Fama, E. F. and MacBeth, J. (1973) 'Risk, Return and Equilibrium: Empirical Tests', *Journal of Political Economy,* 81, 607–36.

Ferson, W. F. and Schadt, R. W. (1996) 'Measuring Fund Strategy and Performance in Changing Economic Conditions', *Journal of Finance,* 51, 425–62.

Gómez, J-P. and Sharma, T. (2001) 'Providing Managerial Incentives: Do Benchmarks Matter?', mimeo, Norwegian School of Management.

Greene, W. (1999) *Econometric Analysis,* Prentice-Hall International, London.

Grinblatt, M. and Titman, S. (1989) 'Mutual Fund Performance: An Analysis of Quarterly Portfolio Holdings', *Journal of Business,* 62, 393–416.

Grinblatt, M. and Titman, S. (1992) 'The Persistence of Mutual Fund Performance', *Journal of Finance,* 47, 1977–84.

Halpern, P. and Fowler, I. (1991) 'Investment Management Fees and the Determinants of Pricing and Structure in the Industry', *Journal of Portfolio Management,* Winter, 74–9.

Hendricks, D., Patel, J. and Zeckhauser, R. (1993) 'Hot Hands in Mutual Funds: Short-run Persistence of Relative Performance, 1974–88', *Journal of Finance,* 48, 93–130.

Hong, H., Kubik, J. D. and Solomon, A. (2000) 'Security Analysts' Career Concerns and Herding of Earnings Forecasts', *Rand Journal of Economics,* 31, 121–44.

Jensen, M. C. (1972) 'Optimal Utilization of Market Forecasts and the Evaluation of Investment Portfolio Performance', in G. P. Szego and K. Shell (eds) *Mathematical Methods in Investment and Finance,* North-Holland, Amsterdam, 310–35.

Kay, J., Laslett, R. and Duffy, N. (1994) 'The Competitive Advantage of the Fund Management Industry in the City of London', Subject Report 9, The City Research Project, Corporation of London, London.

Lakonishok, J., Shleifer, A. and Vishny, R. W. (1992a) 'The Structure and Performance of the Money Management Industry', *Brookings Papers: Microeconomics,* 339–91.

Lakonishok, J., Shleifer, A. and Vishny, R. W. (1992b) 'The Impact of Institutional Trading on Stock Prices', *Journal of Financial Economics,* 32, 23–43.

Lambert, E. (1998) 'Herding Instinct', *Pensions Management,* January, 44–5.

Lehmann, B. N. and Modest, D. M. (1987) 'Mutual Fund Performance Evaluation: A Comparison of Benchmarks and Benchmark Comparisons', *Journal of Finance,* 42, 233–65.

Malkiel, B. G. (1995) 'Returns from Investing in Equity Mutual Funds, 1971 to 1991', *Journal of Finance,* 50, 549–72.

Newey, W. K. and West, K. D. (1987) 'A Simple, Positive Semi-Definite Heteroskedasticity- and Autocorrelation-Consistent Covariance Matrix', *Econometrica,* 55, 703–708.

Pesaran, M. H. and Timmermann, A. (1995) 'Predictability of Stock Returns: Robustness and Economic Significance', *Journal of Finance,* 50, 1201–28.

Prosser, D. (1995) 'Segregated Funds: The Big Game Hunt is Over', *Pensions Management,* March, 45–62.

Shanken, J. (1992) 'On the Estimation of Beta Pricing Models', *Review of Financial Studies,* 5, 1–33.

Sirri, E. and Tufano, P. (1998) 'Costly Search and Mutual Fund Flows', *Journal of Finance,* 53, 1589–622.

Stevenson, M. (1993) 'Investment Management Survey', *The Economist,* 27th November.

Thomas, A. and Tonks, I. (2000) 'Equity Performance and Segregated Pension Fund in the UK', Discussion Paper 00/26, Centre for Market and Public Organisation, University of Bristol.

Treynor, J. and Mazuy, F. (1966) 'Can Mutual Funds Outguess the Market?', *Harvard Business Review,* 44, 131–6.

Trueman, B. (1994) 'Analyst Forecast and Herding Behaviour', *Review of Financial Studies,* 7, 97–124.

Zwiebel, J. (1995) 'Corporate Conservatism and Relative Compensation', *Journal of Political Economy,* 103, 1–25.

5

Do Hedge Funds Add Value to a Passive Portfolio? Correcting for Non-Normal Returns and Disappearing Funds

Roy Kouwenberg

received a PhD degree in finance from Erasmus University Rotterdam in 2001, after finishing a thesis on 'Dynamic Asset Liability Management'. After his graduation, he visited the University of British Columbia in Vancouver, where he taught MBA and graduate courses. Roy joined the equity department of AEGON Asset Management NL (AEAM) in August 2001, as a quantitative analyst. At AEAM, he focuses on quantitative models for managing equity portfolios, alternative investment strategies and derivatives. Roy has a position as guest lecturer at the Finance Department of Erasmus University Rotterdam, and he teaches at the Rotterdam School of Management.

AEGON Asset Management NL and Erasmus University Rotterdam, AEGON Plein 20, The Hague, The Netherlands Tel: +31 70 344 8089; Fax: +31 70 344 8442; e-mail: rkouwenberg@aegon.nl

Introduction

Hedge funds have increased their assets under management rapidly in the last few years, partly owing to increasing inflows from large institutional investors such as pension funds and endowment funds. Not surprisingly, hedge funds have also received increasing attention from the academic community. Non-linear factor models and option strategies have been used in the literature to explain hedge fund returns (see Fung and Hsieh, 2001; Agarwal and Naik, 2001; Mitchell and Pulvino, 2001; Amin and Kat, 2002). These papers provide insight into the risk involved in investing in hedge funds, and they are beneficial in developing benchmarks for hedge fund investment styles.

Reprinted from 'Do hedge funds add value to a passive portfolio? Correcting for non-normal returns and disappearing funds' by Roy Kouwenberg in *Journal of Asset Management*, 3, 2003, pp. 361–382, DOI:10.1057/palgrave.jam.2240089.

The literature that dissects the returns of the hedge funds with option-based strategies and non-linear models is very insightful, but it does not address the following simple question: does it make sense for a typical short-sell constrained passive investor to invest a part of his portfolio in hedge funds? Most investors face restrictions on investment strategy that prevent them from replicating hedge fund returns themselves. The simple question above is relevant for most institutional investors, such as pension funds and endowments funds.

The Zurich Hedge Fund Universe (formerly known as the MAR hedge fund database) is used for the empirical investigation, over the period 1995–2000. The database includes a large number of funds that have disappeared over the years, which reduces the impact of survivorship bias. The second section provides more information about the database and the hedge fund return characteristics.

In the third section, Jensen's alpha of hedge funds is measured in order to see whether they added value to an efficient portfolio consisting of the S&P 500, the Nasdaq and cash. As hedge fund return distributions are often skewed and fat-tailed, not only are alphas for passive mean-variance investors (ie Jensen's alpha) calculated, but also alphas for investors with a power utility function. On average, no strong evidence is found that the non-normality of hedge fund returns affects alphas.

Overall, 72 per cent of the hedge funds are found to have a positive alpha (including disappearing funds) and would therefore add value to a passive portfolio. A more advanced investment strategy is also considered as a yardstick for the hedge funds. Suppose an investor can also buy and sell one-month call and put options on the S&P 500, in addition to investing in the S&P 500, the Nasdaq and cash. It is found that this benchmark significantly reduces the alphas of Event-driven funds, Emerging Market funds and Fund of Funds, owing to their exposure to a strategy that sells out-of-the-money put options. Still 70 per cent of the hedge funds have a positive alpha, however.

In the fourth section, the out-of-sample performance persistence of hedge funds is considered. If hedge funds with a positive alpha in the period 1995–97 had been selected, would the period 1998–2000 have been more profitable? The results draw attention to the huge attrition rate in the hedge fund data: out of the sample, more than 30 per cent of the funds disappear from the database. These disappearing funds have significantly lower alphas, returns and Sharpe ratios. The large number of disappearing funds greatly diminishes the odds of selecting a surviving fund with positive performance.

In contrast to most existing literature (Brown *et al.*, 1999; Agarwal and Naik, 2000a,b), some evidence of performance persistence is found:

selecting funds with a good track record, based on alpha, mean return or Sharpe ratio, improves the chance of outperformance in the out-of-sample period. Edwards and Caglayan (2001) also find evidence of performance persistence, but their study does not explicitly deal with the large number of disappearing hedge funds. The final section concludes and summarises the paper.

Hedge fund data

This paper analyses the returns of the funds in the Zurich Hedge Fund Universe (formerly known as the MAR/Hedge database), provided by Zurich Capital Markets. The data start in 1977 and end in November 2000. Overall, there are 2,078 hedge funds in the database and 536 Fund of Funds. Since January 1995, the database also keeps track of funds that disappear. Only the hedge fund data from January 1995 to November 2000 is analysed, as this period is free of survivorship bias. The return data is net of management fees and net of incentive fees.

Fund styles

The funds in the database are classified into eight different investment styles by the provider: Event-driven, Market Neutral, Global Macro, Global International, Global Emerging, Global Established, Sector and Short-sellers. Table 5.1 provides a short description of each of these hedge fund investment styles. As funds can potentially switch style quite easily, some of these styles will now be aggregated into larger categories, with more distinct style descriptions and statistical return properties.

Roughly, the four macro styles can be considered as speculative, involving markets anywhere in the world, and the frequent use of leverage and derivatives. George Soros' Quantum Fund used to be a well-known global macro hedge fund. The styles Global International, Global Established and Global Macro will be merged into one group, denoted 'Global Funds', as these three styles have similar investment style descriptions (see Table 5.1). The Global Emerging funds are treated as a separate category, denoted 'Emerging Markets', as the funds within this style are often unable to short securities in emerging markets. The emerging market funds also have quite different return characteristics, compared with the other global funds.

The Event-driven style focuses on special situations such as mergers and acquisitions (risk arbitrage) and bankruptcy. For example, a risk arbitrage fund buys stocks of a company being acquired and

Table 5.1 Hedge fund styles in the Zurich Hedge Fund Universe

Hedge fund style	Description
Event-driven	Investment style is dominated by special events, such as bankruptcy (distressed securities) or merger and acquisitions activity (risk arbitrage).
Market Neutral	The exposure to market risk is reduced by having offsetting long and short positions. This style includes convertible arbitrage and fixed income arbitrage.
Global Macro	Opportunistic global investment style. Use of leverage and derivative positions is common.
Global International	Funds are focused on economic change around the world, excluding the US. More oriented towards bottom-up stock picking than global macro managers.
Global Emerging	Focus on less mature markets. Short selling is not permitted in many emerging markets, so the managers sometimes hold cash instead or they have to turn to developed markets.
Global Established	Opportunistic investment style, limited to established markets: US, Europe and Japan.
Sector	Funds follow specific economic sectors and/or industries. Many focus on the technology sector.
Short-sellers	These funds borrow stocks and sell them, hoping to buy them back later at lower prices.

simultaneously sells the acquirer. Market Neutral funds tend to hold offsetting long and short positions, financing the purchase of perceived undervalued securities with the sale of securities that are considered expensive. Many funds that try to exploit arbitrage opportunities have a Market Neutral style. An infamous example of a Market Neutral fund is Long Term Capital Management.

The two remaining hedge fund styles in Table 5.1 are quite distinct: Sector funds and Short-sellers. Funds with a Sector style tend to pick stocks within one particular industry or sector, such as technology. Short-sellers only sell stocks short: this style is interesting for long-only investors, who are looking to diversify their portfolio. Finally, the database contains many Fund of Funds: these funds invest in multiple hedge funds, typically with different styles, in order to diversify risk. Fund of Funds are interesting, as they represent the return on an actively managed selection of hedge fund managers. Note that investors in Fund of Funds pay 'double fees': to the Fund of Fund manager and indirectly also to the hedge fund managers that are selected by the Fund of Fund.

Number of funds and attrition rates

An important property of hedge funds is that they tend to come and go very rapidly. There has been an enormous increase in the number of funds: at the beginning of 1995 there were 561 hedge funds in the database, and this number has grown to 1,067 in November 2000. During this period, 1,146 new funds appeared, but 640 funds disappeared. The database does not provide information about the reason for the disappearance of a fund: the fund might simply have stopped reporting its returns, it might have returned its assets to the investors after a period with poor returns, and in some cases the fund might have gone bankrupt.

Table 5.2 provides information about the dynamics of the number of funds in the database. The table shows the total number of funds existing at the beginning of each year, from 1995 to 2000, and the number of new funds and disappearing funds during the year as a percentage of this total. The last column shows the total number of funds alive in November 2000 and the amount of money under management at that time (some funds do not report assets under management, so the figure is biased downward).

During the period 1995–2000, new hedge funds appeared in the database at an average rate of 23 per cent a year, while funds disappeared at a rate of 11 per cent a year. The total reported amount of assets under management (excluding Fund of Funds) increased from 56 billion to 123 billion. The sub-period 1995–98 is characterised by strong growth of the number of funds and the amount under management. In 1999 and 2000, the trend reversed: the amount under management stabilised, and the number of funds decreased slightly. It is remarkable that of the 561 funds present in the database in January 1995, only 296 (53 per cent) were still present at the end in November 2000.

Hedge fund returns

Table 5.3 presents information about the individual hedge fund returns. First, the mean return, volatility, Sharpe ratio, minimum return and maximum drawdown were computed for each fund with a particular style and with at least 12 monthly observations. Table 5.3 displays the cross-sectional average, median and standard deviation of these statistics over the funds within each style.

The Event-driven funds have an average Sharpe ratio of 1.23, and a median Sharpe ratio of 0.90. Hence, the distribution is quite skewed towards the right: there are a few very successful Event-driven funds

Table 5.2 Number of hedge funds, Jan 1995–Nov 2000

Hedge fund style	1995	1996	1997	1998	1999	2000	Funds and assets end of 2000 ($)
Event-driven							
No. of funds, beginning of year	75	90	115	135	138	131	134
% New	+25	+31	+30	+12	+12	+7	17,736m
% Disappeared	5	−3	−12	−10	−17	−5	
Market Neutral							
No. of funds, beginning of year	157	180	228	291	318	323	286
% New	+26	+36	+36	+27	+18	+4	42,603m
% Disappeared	−11	−9	−8	−18	−16	−15	
Global Funds							
No. of funds, beginning of year	255	271	352	436	484	482	418
% New	+16	+35	+24	+20	+17	+5	57,279m
% Disappeared	−10	−6	−3	−7	−17	−18	
Emerging Markets							
No. of funds, beginning of year	29	36	57	90	109	103	91
% New	+24	+58	+58	+27	+17	+8	2,670m
% Disappeared	−0	−0	−0	−6	−23	−19	
Sector							
No. of funds, beginning of year	26	38	57	86	103	125	119
% New	+46	+50	+53	+31	+38	38	6,788m
% Disappeared	−0	−0	−2	−12	−17	−17	
Short-sellers							
No. of funds, beginning of year	19	14	18	22	23	21	19
% New	+5	+36	+22	+9	+13	+10	1,500m
% Disappeared	−32	−7	−0	−5	−22	−19	
All hedge funds combined							
No. of funds, beginning of year	561	639	827	1,050	1,175	1,185	1,067
% New	+22	+37	+32	+22	+18	+6	121,876m
% Disappeared	−9	−6	−5	−10	−18	−16	
Fund of Funds							
No. of funds, beginning of year	217	236	281	329	335	348	332
% New	+20	+25	+23	+14	+14	+9	32,761m
% Disappeared	−11	−6	−6	−12	−10	−14	

Table 5.3 Hedge fund statistics, Jan 1995–Nov 2000

Hedge fund style	**Mean return (%)**	**Standard deviation (%)**	**Sharpe ratio**	**Minimum return (%)**	**Maximum drawdown (%)**
Event-driven					
Mean	13.7	14.2	1.17	−10.8	−17.5
Median	13.0	10.1	0.96	−7.0	−11.7
Standard deviation	11.2	14.2	1.26	10.9	19.6
Market Neutral					
Mean	14.0	12.2	1.25	−8.2	−13.2
Median	12.4	8.7	0.86	−5.7	−7.7
Standard deviation	15.7	12.3	1.77	8.8	16.0
Global Funds					
Mean	20.4	23.4	0.75	−14.8	−24.5
Median	19.3	19.1	0.77	−12.9	−18.2
Standard deviation	20.8	16.5	0.91	11.1	21.5
Emerging Markets					
Mean	6.3	30.4	0.18	−25.2	−44.6
Median	8.9	25.6	0.13	−21.0	−36.2
Standard deviation	22.7	17.8	0.74	18.5	36.3
Sector					
Mean	32.4	35.1	0.85	−18.9	−32.5
Median	30.7	33.0	0.88	−16.0	−27.1
Standard deviation	23.6	20.9	0.67	12.2	23.2
Short-sellers					
Mean	11.6	33.3	0.27	−25.0	−40.7
Median	11.6	29.0	0.16	−19.5	−34.9
Standard deviation	17.7	16.8	0.62	17.3	28.4
Fund of Funds					
Mean	11.6	11.3	0.92	−8.2	−14.5
Median	12.2	9.7	0.81	−6.6	−10.4
Standard deviation	10.0	7.9	1.08	7.1	16.5

with Sharpe ratios above 2. On average, funds with this style tend to combine relatively low volatility (average 12.7 per cent, median 8.9 per cent) with reasonable mean returns (average 13.9 per cent, median 12.8 per cent). The results for Market Neutral funds are similar, with an average return of 14.0 per cent a year and a median Sharpe ratio of 0.86.

Sector funds have a median Sharpe ratio of 0.88, similar to the Event-driven and Market Neutral funds, but the underlying returns are quite different. The mean return of the Sector funds is very high (30.4 per cent on average), and the volatility too (35.1 per cent on average). Hence, the underlying investment strategy of the Sector funds is quite risky. This might be expected, as many Sector funds focus on the volatile technology sector.

The group of Global funds also follows quite risky strategies (average volatility of 23.4 per cent), which are compensated by relatively high mean returns (average of 20.4 per cent), resulting in an average Sharpe ratio of 0.75. Global hedge funds focus on absolute returns and often have an opportunistic investment style with frequent use of leverage, and hence it is not surprising that the returns are quite volatile. Short-sellers have a similar risky profile, but with lower mean returns (an average of 11.6 per cent).

Emerging Markets funds are an outlier in the hedge fund universe: they had relatively poor returns in the period 1995–2000: the average return was 6.3 per cent, combined with above average volatility of 30.4 per cent and a maximum drawdown of –44.6 per cent. Obviously, this results in a low median Sharpe ratio of 0.13. Note that Emerging Markets funds tend to pick stocks in developing countries, and therefore these funds probably suffered severely from the Asian crisis following the collapse of the Thai Baht in 1997. Furthermore, in 1998 the emerging markets were shocked by the Russian bond default.

Fund of Funds have relatively low risk on average, similar to Event-driven and Market Neutral funds: the average volatility is 11.3 per cent and the maximum drawdown is only –14.5 per cent on average. The median of the Mean Return is 11.6 per cent, and the median Sharpe ratio is 0.81. Hence, the diversification benefits of Fund of Funds seem to compensate the 'double fees': an investor in a Fund of Fund pays fees to the Fund of Fund manager and, indirectly, to the underlying hedge fund managers.

Correlation with stock and bond markets

Table 5.4(a) provides information about the correlation of hedge fund returns with the following market indices: the MSCI World Index,

Table 5.4 Hedge fund return correlation with indices (average), Jan 1995–Nov 2000

(a)							(b)					
Hedge fund style	**MSCI World**	**S&P 500**	**Nasdaq**	**Russell 2000**	**MSCI Emerging**	**SB World Bond Index**	**Put selling**	**Call selling**	**MKT**	**HML**	**SMB**	**UMD**
Event-driven	0.34	0.32	0.35	0.42	0.35	−0.08	0.26	−0.12	0.36	−0.24	0.27	0.07
Market Neutral	0.14	0.14	0.17	0.19	0.14	−0.07	0.09	−0.10	0.16	−0.12	0.13	0.09
Global Funds	0.39	0.37	0.44	0.46	0.37	−0.02	0.21	−0.14	0.43	−0.34	0.26	0.17
Emerging Markets	0.50	0.46	0.45	0.50	0.60	−0.15	0.29	−0.16	0.43	−0.32	0.27	0.15
Sector	0.43	0.40	0.55	0.56	0.43	−0.01	0.28	−0.08	0.50	−0.46	0.37	0.29
Short-sellers	−0.38	−0.34	−0.50	−0.49	−0.34	−0.01	−0.25	0.12	−0.45	0.48	−0.35	−0.22
Fund of Funds	0.41	0.37	0.46	0.50	0.45	−0.13	0.25	−0.16	0.45	−0.35	0.33	0.22

the S&P 500, the Nasdaq, the Russell 2000 (US small caps), the MSCI Emerging Markets Index and the Salomon Brothers World Government Bond Index. Market-neutral funds have relatively low correlation with these market indices (average of about 0.14), corresponding to the investment style.

The other hedge fund styles have a correlation of up to 0.50 with the indices. As might be expected, Emerging Markets funds have a relatively high correlation with the MSCI Emerging Market Index (0.60) and Sector funds have relatively high exposure to the Nasdaq (0.55). The returns of Short-sellers are negatively correlated with all stock market indices, as might be expected. Fund of Funds have an average correlation of up to 0.50 with the stock market.

Interestingly, most fund returns have a higher average correlation with US small caps (Russell 2000) than with the S&P 500. This seems to indicate that hedge funds prefer stock picking in the broad market, including stocks of medium-size and small firms.

Correlation with option strategies

Many hedge funds follow dynamic investment strategies and, as a result, their exposure to the market can vary through time, in some cases depending on the return of the equity market. The results in Table 5.4(a) only describe the average exposure to the market. Fung and Hsieh (2001) and Mitchell and Pulvino (2001) show that the returns of some hedge fund styles are correlated with option strategies. The correlation of hedge fund returns with simple option investment strategies that are well known and not too difficult to replicate for most investors will be investigated.

First, a strategy is considered that sells a 1-month put option on the S&P 500 with an exercise price 5 per cent below the current index value and repeats this every month. Similarly, the returns of a strategy that sells a 1-month call option on the S&P 500 with an exercise price 5 per cent above the current index value are constructed. Table 5.4(b) shows that, on average, funds with an Event-driven style, Global funds, Emerging Market funds, Sector funds and Fund of Funds have a positive exposure to the put selling strategy, with average correlation ranging from 0.21 to 0.29. The exposure to the call selling strategy is small and negative on average for most hedge fund styles.

Finally, Table 5.4(b) shows the correlation of the hedge fund returns with the Fama and French factors (MKT, HML, SMB) and a momentum factor (UMD). The market factor, MKT, represents the value-weighted return of the overall US stock market. The value factor, HML, represents the return of a portfolio that is long stocks with high book to market and short stocks with low book to market. The size factor, SMB, represents the difference in returns between small stocks and big stocks (in terms of market capitalisation).

Most hedge funds tend to have negative exposure on average to the value factor, indicating that they might have a preference for glamour stocks over value stocks (except for Short-sellers). Most funds have a small positive exposure to the momentum factor. Sector funds have the highest correlation on average with the momentum factor, which can probably be explained by the momentum-driven technology sector.

Surviving and disappearing funds

The return characteristics of disappearing funds are now compared with surviving funds, in order to find some clues about why funds might drop out of the database. There are a number of potential reasons. First, funds might disappear from the database because they have been quite successful in growing the assets under management, and they have no need to attract new investors. Secondly, funds might disappear from the database after poor performance, in some cases leading to closure of the fund (returning the assets to the investors), or even bankruptcy. Finally, fund managers can stop reporting because of other reasons, not related to the returns of the fund.

Table 5.5 shows the average Mean Return, Volatility, Sharpe ratio, Minimum Return and Maximum Drawdown of surviving funds (still in the database at November 2000) and disappearing funds. The third row shows the difference in the average statistics between disappearing and surviving funds; an asterisk denotes significance at the 5 per cent level. It is apparent from the second column of Table 5.5 that disappearing firms tend to have significantly lower mean returns than surviving funds. The risk of disappearing funds, represented by the volatility, the minimum return and the maximum drawdown, tends to be higher too, except for the relatively small styles Sector and Short-sellers.

Overall, disappearing funds tend to have lower Sharpe ratios. It is therefore concluded that it is plausible that most funds disappear from the database because of relatively poor performance.

Alpha measurement

So far, this paper has focused solely on the return characteristics of hedge funds. This section tries to measure the added value of an

Table 5.5 Hedge fund statistics: Surviving vs disappearing funds, Jan 1995–Nov 2000

Hedge fund style	**Mean return (%)**	**Standard deviation (%)**	**Sharpe ratio**	**Minimum return (%)**	**Maximum drawdown (%)**
Event-driven					
Surviving funds	13.9	12.4	1.38	–10.4	–16.5
Disappearing funds	13.2	18.9	0.64	–12.1	–20.2
Difference	–0.7	6.5*	–0.74*	–1.7	–3.8
Market Neutral					
Surviving funds	16.4	11.2	1.56	–7.5	–11.6
Disappearing funds	10.1	13.7	0.74	–9.4	–15.9
Difference	–6.3*	2.5*	–0.82*	–1.9*	–4.3*
Global Funds					
Surviving funds	21.8	22.9	0.87	–14.4	–24.0
Disappearing funds	17.7	24.3	0.52	–15.7	–25.5
Difference	–4.1*	1.4	–0.35*	–1.3	–1.4
Emerging Markets					
Surviving funds	13.1	29.2	0.40	–23.6	–39.2
Disappearing funds	–6.8	32.8	–0.26	–28.4	–55.0
Difference	–20.0*	3.5	–0.66*	–4.8	–15.8*
Sector					
Surviving funds	35.6	37.9	0.88	–19.8	–34.6
Disappearing funds	25.6	29.1	0.80	–17.1	–28.0
Difference	–10.0*	–8.8*	–0.08	2.7	6.7
Short-sellers					
Surviving funds	13.6	34.7	0.36	–27.9	–43.0
Disappearing funds	7.3	30.3	0.07	–18.3	–35.6
Difference	–6.2	–4.4	–0.29	9.6	7.4
Fund of Funds					
Surviving funds	13.5	10.7	1.11	–7.7	–13.4
Disappearing funds	7.7	12.5	0.53	–9.3	–16.9
Difference	–5.7*	1.9*	–0.58*	–1.6*	–3.5*

*Significance at the 5% level.

Note: significance only tested for difference between surviving and disappearing funds.

investment in hedge funds for a passive investor, holding a portfolio of stocks and bonds. In the last two decades, hedge funds gained in popularity with pension funds, insurance companies and endowment funds. These institutions typically invest a small fraction of their portfolio in hedge funds, in order to diversify their portfolio. The diversification benefits of an investment in hedge funds arise due to the perceived low correlation with the bond market and the stock market (see Table 5.4). Moreover, hedge funds focus on absolute returns and seem to provide an attractive risk/return trade-off (see Table 5.3).

Most investors in hedge funds face short-sale constraints on their portfolio: they tend to hold only long positions. Insurance companies, pension funds and endowment funds typically have additional restrictions on their investment policy: they often have to track a predefined benchmark closely. Hence, most investors will have difficulty replicating a hedge fund strategy, if it involves short positions, leverage and large positions in the (OTC) derivative markets. As a result, non-linear factor models and models with dynamic trading strategies might not be suited to measure the performance of a hedge fund from the point of view of a typical constrained investor, such as a pension fund.

In this paper, the aim is to measure the added value of an investment in hedge funds for a passive investor. Hence, Jensen's alpha could be applied, regressing the hedge fund returns on a number of passive benchmark portfolios. Jensen's alpha, however, does not take the non-normality of hedge fund return distributions into account. This aspect is important, as the dynamic investment strategies of hedge funds tend to lead to skewed and fat-tailed return distributions (eg selling put options). Therefore, alphas for investors with a power utility function are also calculated, taking the non-normality of hedge fund returns into account. Moreover, straightforward put and call selling strategies on the S&P 500 are used as additional benchmarks for the hedge fund returns.

Alpha measurement for passive investors

Following Cumby and Glen (1990) and Chen and Knez (1996), it is assumed that investors choose a portfolio from a universe of N assets with returns r_{it}, for $i = 1, 2, \ldots, N$. In addition, it is supposed that the expected returns and the covariance matrix of the returns are constant according to uninformed investors (given the information available to them). Hence, as a result, all uninformed investors will choose a portfolio with constant weights.

Let r_{bt} denote the return on a portfolio that is mean-variance efficient from the point of view of an uninformed investor. From Roll (1977), it follows that the return on each asset can be written as follows:

$$r_{it} = \beta_j r_{bt} + \varepsilon_{it}, \text{ with } \beta_j = \operatorname{cov}(r_{jt}, r_{bt}) / \sigma_b^2 \tag{1}$$

where σ_b^2 is the variance of the mean-variance efficient portfolio, the beta β_j is constant and $\mathrm{E}[\varepsilon_{it}] = 0$, according to the uninformed investor.

In order to test whether a hedge fund with return r_{at} could add value to the constant portfolio of an uninformed investor, Jensen's alpha can be estimated (Jensen, 1968). The alpha is the intercept α_a in a regression of the hedge fund's return on the benchmark:

$$r_{at} = \alpha_a + \beta_a r_{bt} + \varepsilon_{at} \tag{2}$$

If the alpha of a hedge fund is positive, each uninformed mean-variance investor will add the fund to his optimal portfolio.

A serious drawback of Jensen's alpha is its reliance on mean-variance efficiency. Grinblatt and Titman (1989, 1994) show that Jensen's alpha can be interpreted as a weighted average of the fund returns:

$$\alpha_a = \sum_{t=1}^{T} w_t r_{at}, \quad \text{with} \sum_{t=1}^{T} w_t = 1 \quad \text{and} \quad \sum_{t=1}^{T} w_t r_{bt} = 0 \tag{3}$$

where w_t is the marginal utility that an uninformed mean-variance investor assigns to his optimal portfolio at time t.

Mean-variance analysis unfortunately ignores the skewness and the potential fat tails of a return distribution. Owing to the nature of hedge fund investment strategies, the returns often have option-like features (see Fung and Hsieh, 2001; Agarwal and Naik, 2001; Mitchell and Pulvino, 2001), leading to a non-normal return distribution. Hence, performance measurement based on mean-variance preferences could be misleading.

Instead, it is assumed that the preferences of the uninformed investor are described by a power utility function (4):

$$U(W_t) = \frac{1}{\gamma} W_t^{\gamma}, \quad \text{with } \gamma < 1 \tag{4}$$

where W_t is the wealth of the investor.

Investors with a power utility function and $\gamma < -1$ have preference for positive skewness and dislike fat tails. The performance of a hedge fund from the perspective of a passive investor with a power utility function can be computed with the weighting function (3), where the weights are the scaled marginal utilities of the power investor:

$$w_t = (W_t^*)^{\gamma-1} / \sum_{j=1}^{T} (W_j^*)^{\gamma-1} \tag{5}$$

where W_t^* is the wealth level of uninformed power investor at time t, if he chooses an optimal passive portfolio to maximise his expected utility.

Let α_a^γ denote the alpha of a hedge fund, from the point of view of an uninformed investor with a power utility function and risk aversion parameter γ. If α_a^γ is positive, the investor will add the hedge fund to his optimal passive portfolio. Whether hedge funds indeed have positive alphas will be examined later. First, it will be investigated whether investors with power utility assign lower alphas to hedge funds than do investors with mean-variance preferences, owing to the skewness and fat tails of the return distribution.

It is assumed that the indices in Table 5.4 are representative for the investment opportunity of passive short-sell constrained investors. The efficiency of these indices was tested using alpha regressions, and it was found that S&P 500 and the Nasdaq were efficient in the period from 1995 to 2000. Hence, from now on the S&P 500 and the Nasdaq will be used as benchmarks for calculating hedge fund alphas. Later, monthly put and call selling strategies on the S&P 500 will also be added to the benchmark set.

Non-normality and alpha

Table 5.6 shows the average alpha of hedge funds from the perspective of a mean-variance investor (2nd column) and an investor with power utility with $\gamma = -5$ (3rd column),[1] using the S&P 500 and Nasdaq as a benchmark set. If the hedge fund return distribution is normal, there should be no difference between the two alphas. If the distribution is non-normal, the difference can be positive or negative, depending on whether the fund returns are positively skewed or negatively skewed and whether the tails are thin or thick.

Table 5.6 Hedge fund alpha and normality I, Jan 1995–Nov 2000

Hedge fund style	Alpha MV (%)	Alpha power (%)	Skewness	Kurtosis	Rejects normality (%)
Event-driven					
Mean	0.35*	0.29*	−0.68	7.18	68
Median	0.46	0.43	−0.56	5.70	
Standard deviation	0.96	0.99	1.29	5.39	
Market Neutral					
Mean	0.58*	0.57*	−0.60	7.28	52
Median	0.51	0.51	−0.32	4.48	
Standard deviation	1.37	1.34	1.68	7.69	
Global Funds					
Mean	0.59*	0.60*	−0.20	5.09	47
Median	0.48	0.49	−0.19	4.14	
Standard deviation	1.71	1.75	1.02	3.46	
Emerging Markets					
Mean	−0.68*	−0.86*	−0.99	8.44	66
Median	−0.47	−0.49	−0.62	5.12	
Standard deviation	2.17	2.33	1.76	8.59	
Sector					
Mean	1.29*	1.31*	−0.17	4.53	39
Median	1.11	1.19	−0.13	3.70	
Standard deviation	1.93	1.81	0.91	2.90	
Short-sellers					
Mean	1.64*	1.84*	−0.38	5.85	50
Median	1.57	1.66	−0.21	4.48	
Standard deviation	1.12	1.32	1.00	3.44	
Fund of Funds					
Mean	0.18*	0.16*	−0.52	6.22	55
Median	0.28	0.27	−0.27	4.69	
Standard deviation	0.97	1.04	1.22	4.60	

*Significance at the 5% level.
Note: significance only tested for the mean alpha based on mean-variance preferences and power utility.

Columns 4 and 5 of Table 5.6 show the average skewness and kurtosis of the hedge fund returns, and column 6 shows the percentage of funds that rejects a normal distribution (at 5 per cent significance). On average, hedge funds return distributions tend to have negative skewness and excess kurtosis. Still, about 40–50 per cent of the funds do not reject a normal distribution, so the shape of the return distribution tends to vary quite strongly among funds. The degree and proportion of non-normality is relatively high for Event-driven funds, Market Neutral funds, Emerging Market funds and Fund of Funds.

In general, the difference between the mean-variance alpha and the alpha based on power utility is rather small in Table 5.6. This suggests that the non-normality of hedge fund returns does not have a major and uniform impact on the portfolios of passive investors. Table 5.7 provides more details: funds within each style have been sorted on skewness (positive or negative) and kurtosis (larger than 4 or not). Table 5.7 shows the number of funds within each group, the average mean-variance alpha, the average power alpha and the difference between the alphas. A star denotes a significant difference at the 5 per cent level.

Table 5.7 shows that power investors assign significantly lower alphas than mean-variance investors to Event-driven funds, Market Neutral funds, Emerging Market funds and Fund of Funds with negative skewness and kurtosis greater than 4. Note, however, that the majority of funds do not belong to the unfavourable category with negative skewness and large kurtosis. This explains why on average there is not that much difference between hedge fund alphas based on mean-variance preferences and power utility. It is concluded that hedge fund returns are often not normally distributed; however, on average, this non-normality does not have a significant effect on the alphas, and hence on the portfolios of passive investors. From now on, only alphas based on power utility will be used for further analysis.

Hedge fund alphas

If the absolute level of the alphas in Table 5.6 is considered, the Short-sellers stand out with an average alpha of 1.84 per cent (22.1 per cent annualised). The Sharpe ratio of the Short-sellers in Table 5.3 is quite unattractive, but in a portfolio context the negative exposure of these funds to the equity market provides great diversification benefits. Second best in terms of alpha are the Sector funds with an average alpha of 1.31 per cent (15.7 per cent annualised). Event-driven funds have an average alpha of 0.35 per cent (4.2 per cent annualised), Market Neutral funds 0.58 per cent (7.0 per cent annualised), Global funds 0.60 per cent (7.2 per cent annualised) and Fund of Funds 0.16 per cent (1.9 per cent annualised). Emerging Markets funds are a negative outlier again, with an average alpha of −0.86 (−10.3 per cent annualised).

Table 5.7 Hedge fund alpha and normality II, Jan 1995–Nov 2000

Hedge fund style	Skew < 0 kurt > 4	Skew ≥ 0 kurt > 4	Skew < 0 kurt ≤ 4	Skew ≥ 0 kurt ≤ 4	All funds
Event-driven					
Funds (% of total)	99 (57)	27 (16)	22 (12)	25 (14)	173
Alpha Power (%)	0.14	0.58	0.12	0.75	0.29
Alpha MV (%)	0.24	0.61	0.10	0.72	0.35
Difference (%)	–0.09*	–0.03	0.02	0.03	–0.06*
Market Neutral					
Funds (% of total)	185 (42)	77 (17)	91 (21)	89 (20)	442
Alpha Power (%)	0.24	1.21	0.35	0.94	0.58
Alpha MV (%)	0.29	1.18	0.33	0.89	0.57
Difference (%)	–0.04*	0.03	0.03	0.06*	–0.01
Global Funds					
Funds (% of total)	214 (35)	106 (17)	149 (25)	138 (23)	607
Alpha Power (%)	0.08	1.16	0.18	1.42	0.60
Alpha MV (%)	0.08	1.17	0.18	1.38	0.59
Difference (%)	0.00	–0.01	0.00	0.04	0.01
Emerging Markets					
Funds (% of total)	69 (53)	16 (12)	25 (19)	19 (15)	129
Alpha Power (%)	–1.45	0.62	–0.62	–0.24	–0.86
Alpha MV (%)	–1.18	0.62	–0.51	–0.16	–0.68
Difference (%)	–0.27*	0.00	–0.11	–0.08	–0.18*
Sector					
Funds (% of total)	36 (24)	26 (18)	49 (33)	37 (25)	148
Alpha Power (%)	0.45	1.98	0.98	2.12	1.31
Alpha MV (%)	0.26	1.89	0.91	2.37	1.29
Difference (%)	0.18	0.09	0.07	–0.26	0.02
Short-sellers					
Funds (% of total)	10 (38)	6 (23)	7 (27)	3 (12)	26
Alpha Power (%)	1.58	1.95	1.97	2.20	1.84
Alpha MV (%)	1.44	1.79	1.70	1.85	1.64
Difference (%)	0.13	0.16	0.27	0.35	0.20*
Fund of Funds					
Funds (% of total)	196 (44)	80 (18)	95 (21)	77 (17)	448
Alpha Power (%)	–0.12	0.48	0.18	0.54	0.16
Alpha MV (%)	–0.06	0.46	0.12	0.57	0.18
Difference (%)	–0.07*	0.02	0.06*	–0.03	–0.02

*Significance at the 5% level.
Note: significance only tested for the difference between MV alpha and power alpha.

Table 5.8 compares the average alpha of surviving funds with the alpha of disappearing funds. In general, the average alpha of disappearing funds is significantly lower than the alpha of surviving funds. The same holds for the percentage of funds with a positive alpha. This

Table 5.8 Hedge fund alphas: Surviving vs disappearing funds, Jan 1995–Nov 2000

Hedge fund style	Alpha (%)	Alpha > 0 (%)
Event-driven		
Surviving funds	0.40	84
Disappearing funds	0.03	50
Disappearing–surviving	0.37*	−34
Market Neutral		
Surviving funds	0.81	89
Disappearing funds	0.20	60
Disappearing–surviving	−0.60*	−29
Global Funds		
Surviving funds	0.75	78
Disappearing funds	0.30	55
Disappearing–surviving	−0.45	−23
Emerging Markets		
Surviving funds	−0.14	49
Disappearing funds	−2.23	16
Disappearing–surviving	−2.09*	−34
Sector		
Surviving funds	1.54	83
Disappearing funds	0.82	70
Disappearing–surviving	−0.72*	−13
Short-sellers		
Surviving funds	1.86	100
Disappearing funds	1.80	88
Disappearing–surviving	−0.06	−13
Fund of Funds		
Surviving funds	0.38	83
Disappearing funds	−0.30	52
Disappearing–surviving	−0.68*	−31

*Significance at the 5% level.
Note: significance only tested for the difference in average alpha between disappearing and surviving funds.

confirms the earlier conclusion that hedge firms tend to disappear from the database after relatively poor performance. In the next section, it will be investigated whether investors can reduce the odds of selecting bad and disappearing funds.

Table 5.9 shows the percentage of funds with positive and negative alphas, and the percentage funds with significantly positive, significantly negative and insignificant alphas. The row for 'Model 1' shows results for the passive benchmark set (S&P 500 and Nasdaq), while the second row 'Model 2' contains results for the extended benchmark set

Table 5.9 Hedge fund models and alpha, Jan 1995–Nov 2000

Hedge fund style	Alpha	Alpha > 0 & sign (%)	Alpha < 0 & sign (%)	Alpha insign (%)	Alpha > 0 (%)	Alpha ≤ 0 (%)
Event-driven						
Model 1	0.30	40	2	58	75	25
Model 2	0.23	36	5	59	71	29
Market Neutral						
Model 1	0.58	41	3	56	78	22
Model 2	0.56	40	4	56	78	22
Global Funds						
Model 1	0.60	23	4	73	70	30
Model 2	0.61	22	6	72	69	31
Emerging Markets						
Model 1	−0.86	6	8	86	38	62
Model 2	−1.14	6	20	74	33	67
Sector						
Model 1	1.31	31	1	68	79	21
Model 2	1.20	32	5	63	77	23
Short-sellers						
Model 1	1.84	42	0	58	96	4
Model 2	1.88	35	0	65	96	4
Fund of Funds						
Model 1	0.16	29	4	68	73	27
Model 2	0.13	28	6	65	69	31

with option selling strategies. For now the first benchmark set will be concentrated on.

Short-sellers stand out again: 96 per cent of the funds have a positive alpha, and 42 per cent have a significantly positive alpha. About 75 per cent of the Event-driven and Market Neutral funds have a positive alpha, and 40 per cent also have a significantly positive alpha. Global funds, Sector funds and Fund of Funds have at least 70 per cent positive alphas, but with less significance (between 23 per cent and 31 per cent).

The average alpha of each hedge fund style in Table 5.8 is significantly positive at the 5 per cent level, except for Emerging Markets (significantly negative). These results are in sharp contrast to the alphas of mutual funds reported in the literature. Malkiel (1995) finds that US mutual funds had an average annuahsed alpha of −3.2 per cent in the period 1971–91. Brown and Goetzmann (1995), Gruber (1996) and Carhart (1997) also find that mutual fund alphas are either negative or insignificant. The present results are in line with the hedge fund literature: Ackermann *et al.* (1999), Brown *et al.* (1999) and Edwards and Caglayan (2001) find that hedge funds have significantly positive Jensen alphas.

Alphas with option selling strategies

The hedge fund alphas with the second benchmark set will now be considered, including the put and call option selling strategies on the S&P 500 (in addition to the S&P 500 itself, the Nasdaq and cash). The option selling strategies have non-linear returns and are better suited for explaining the dynamic hedge fund strategies, while most investors can still replicate these strategies quite easily. Table 5.9 compares the average alpha for the two benchmark sets, denoted by model 1 (without options) and 2 (with options), for each hedge fund style.

The inclusion of option selling strategies in the benchmark set leads to significantly lower alphas for the Event-driven funds, Emerging Markets funds, Sector funds and Fund of Funds. Apparently the performance of these funds can be explained to some extent by the option selling strategies. Table 5.10 shows the average adjusted R^2 of both benchmark sets (models) in the Jensen alpha regressions, for each hedge fund style. Moreover, columns 3–6 show the percentage of funds with significant positive and significant negative exposure to each of the benchmark factors.

The Event-driven funds, Emerging Market funds and Fund of Funds have the highest proportion of significantly positive exposure to out-of-the-money put selling (between 20 per cent and 32 per cent). The call selling strategy is less significant and mainly has a negative sign, indicating that some funds buy out-of-the-money call options. The Jensen regressions with the option selling strategies have higher adjusted R2 on average, compared with the regressions without option strategies.

It is concluded that the simple put and call selling strategies, which are available to most investors, have quite some incremental power in explaining hedge fund returns. The inclusion of these strategies in the benchmark set leads to lower hedge fund alphas. It should be stressed, however, that the average alpha of each hedge fund style is still significantly positive (except Emerging Markets). Moreover, the R2 are below 50 per cent on average for the regressions with option selling strategies. Hence, the simple put and call selling strategies still leave most of the hedge return variation unexplained.

Table 5.10 Hedge fund models R^2 and significance of coefficients, Jan 1995–Nov 2000

Hedge fund style	R^2 (%)	S&P (%) +/−	NSD (%) +/−	Put (%) +/−	Call (%) +/−
Event-driven					
Model 1	22	20/5	29/1		
Model 2	27	8/7	32/1	32/3	1/12
Market Neutral					
Model 1	14	11/5	21/5		
Model 2	19	7/9	24/5	14/5	3/16
Global Funds					
Model 1	26	27/9	50/6		
Model 2	33	20/9	50/6	8/7	2/11
Emerging Markets					
Model 1	26	31/5	29/1		
Model 2	33	12/4	31/1	29/5	0/12
Sector					
Model 1	46	17/22	61/7		
Model 2	49	12/21	60/7	12/6	5/9
Short-sellers					
Model 1	47	35/12	8/69		
Model 2	50	27/8	8/77	8/19	12/4
Fund of Funds					
Model 1	34	19/6	56/3		
Model 2	40	12/16	58/3	24/4	1/17

Fund selection rules

The empirical results so far have included every fund in the database with at least 12 monthly observations. In practice, investors will typically require some track record of good performance before they will consider investing in a fund. This section attempts to replicate the fund selection process of investors, to see whether the selected funds also deliver outperformance out of sample, after correcting for survivorship bias and look-ahead bias.

Methodology

The entire sample period, January 1995 to November 2000, is split up into two sub-periods: the selection period from January 1995 to December 1997, and the evaluation period from January 1998 to November 2000. It is assumed that an investor is considering investing in a hedge fund (or Fund of Fund) in December 1997. The investor can select all funds that are in the database at December 1997; however, he will only consider funds with a certain track record. A limit of at least 12 months of available data at December 1997 is applied (and, alternatively, a limit of at least 36 months of data). Next, the investor will make a distinction between funds that met a certain performance criterion in the selection period and funds that failed to meet the criterion. A fund's alpha, Sharpe ratio and mean return are used as performance criteria.

To test whether funds with a good track record in the selection period also deliver outperformance in the out-of-sample period January 1998 to November 2000, it is checked whether a fund meets the performance criteria in the out-of-sample period. Out-of-sample funds can also disappear from the database, however, and as a result many have insufficient observations to calculate performance. If these disappearing funds were ignored, the results would suffer from so-called look ahead bias, as surviving funds tend to perform better than disappearing funds. To solve this problem, disappearance of a fund is treated as a third performance category in the out-of-sample period. Next, a two by three contingency table of fund performance in the selection period versus fund performance in the out-of-sample period is constructed. A xi-square test is applied to see whether the selection rule resulted in significantly different odds of selecting winners and losers in the out-of-sample period.

Results with the alpha criterion

As a first selection rule, funds that have at least 12 months of data up to December 1997 are considered. As a performance criterion, the fund's alpha is used: the sample is split up into funds with positive alpha and negative alpha over the selection period. In the out-of-sample period 1998–2000, the funds are assigned to three performance groups: funds either disappear from the sample, they survive with a negative alpha or they survive with a positive alpha. Table 5.11 shows the results in a contingency table, together with the *p*-value of the xi-square test.

First, Event-driven funds are considered: of the funds with a positive alpha in the selection period, about 21 per cent disappear from the database out of sample, 28 per cent of the funds survive with a negative alpha, while 52 per cent of the funds survive with a positive alpha. Note that the 52 per cent surviving funds with consecutive positive alphas in Table 5.11 is much less impressive than the unconditional 75 per cent

Table 5.11 Alpha persistence, model 1 (S&P 500 and Nasdaq)

Hedge fund style	Positive alpha 1998–2000	Negative alpha or zero 1998–2000	Disappears 1998–2000	Total
Event-driven				
Positive alpha 1995–97	53 (52%)	28 (28%)	21 (21%)	102 (85%)
Negative alpha 1995–97	6 (33%)	6 (33%)	6 (33%)	18 (15%)
Total 1995–97	59 (49%)	34 (28%)	27 (23%)	120, p=0.21
Market Neutral				
Positive alpha 1995–97	103 (52%)	25 (13%)	70 (35%)	198 (85%)
Negative alpha 1995–97	12 (34%)	1 (3%)	22 (63%)	35 (15%)
Total 1995–97	115 (49%)	26 (11%)	92 (40%)	233, p=0.00
Global Funds				
Positive alpha 1995–97	119 (47%)	50 (20%)	86 (34%)	255 (71%)
Negative alpha 1995–97	41 (38%)	22 (21%)	42 (40%)	105 (29%)
Total 1995–97	160 (44%)	72 (20%)	128 (36%)	360, p=0.40
Emerging Markets				
Positive alpha 1995–97	5 (15%)	16 (49%)	12 (36%)	33 (53%)
Negative alpha 1995–97	5 (17%)	13 (45%)	11 (38%)	29 (47%)
Total 1995–97	10 (16%)	29 (47%)	23 (37%)	62, p=0.95
Sector				
Positive alpha 1995–97	20 (43%)	5 (11%)	22 (47%)	47 (75%)
Negative alpha 1995–97	11 (67%)	3 (19%)	2 (13%)	16 (25%)
Total 1995–97	31 (49%)	8 (13%)	24 (38%)	63, p=0.05
Short-sellers				
Positive alpha 1995–97	10 (63%)	1 (6%)	5 (31%)	16 (89%)
Negative alpha 1995–97	0 (0%)	1 (50%)	1 (50%)	2 (11%)
Total 1995–97	10 (56%)	2 (11%)	6 (33%)	18, p=NA
Fund of Funds				
Positive alpha 1995–97	115 (51%)	56 (25%)	53 (24%)	224 (78%)
Negative alpha 1995–97	17 (27%)	17 (27%)	28 (45%)	62 (22%)
Total 1995–97	132 (46%)	73 (26%)	81 (28%)	286, p=0.00

Note: *p*-value for the xi-square test reported in the last column.

of Event-driven funds that had a positive alpha in Table 5.9. The difference is mainly due to the large number of disappearing funds in the 36 month out-of-sample period, and due to the fact that hedge fund performance was relatively weak in the period 1998–2000.

Next, Event-driven funds with a negative alpha in the selection period are considered: about 33 per cent disappear from the database out of sample, 33 per cent of these funds survive with a negative alpha, while only 33 per cent survive with a positive alpha. These results are worse than for the funds with positive alpha in the selection period, but the xi-square test shows that the difference is insignificant. In the case of Market Neutral funds there are more observations, and the difference is significant: it can be concluded that selecting Market Neutral funds with a positive alpha in the selection period improved the odds of survival and a positive alpha in the out-of-sample period.

For Global funds, similar results are shown in Table 5.11, although with less significance ($p = 0.40$). Emerging Markets funds mainly stand out owing to their appalling performance: only 16 per cent of the funds survive out of sample. About 63 per cent of the Short-sellers have positive alphas both in and out of sample, which is quite high, but there are not enough funds to establish significance. Sector funds show significant signs of performance reversal: funds with positive alphas in the selection period tend to disappear more often out of sample, and tend to underperform more frequently. The Fund of Funds results in Table 5.10 show significant evidence of performance persistence: Fund of Funds with positive alphas in the selection period tend to perform better out of sample.

Performance persistence if the track record requirement in the selection period is raised from 12 months to 36 months has also been estimated (results available on request). As a result of the longer required track record, the proportion of disappearing funds decreases out of sample. The odds of selecting an Event-driven or Market Neutral fund that survives out of sample with a positive alpha are now 55 per cent, if confined to funds with positive alphas in the 36 month selection period. For Fund of Funds, the odds of selecting funds with consecutive positive alphas are also 55 per cent, while the odds are 48 per cent for Global Funds.

Table 5.12 shows the results for the alphas estimated with the extended model, including the option selling strategies. In this case, the percentage of funds with consecutive positive alphas in the selection period and the out-of-sample period decreases for the Event-driven funds, Global Funds and Fund of Funds. The odds of selecting

Table 5.12 Alpha persistence, model 2 (S&P 500, Nasdaq and Option Selling Strategies)

Hedge fund style	Positive alpha 1998–2000	Negative alpha or zero, 1998–2000	Disappears 1998–2000	Total
Event-driven				
Positive alpha 1995–97	50 (46%)	34 (32%)	24 (22%)	108 (90%)
Negative alpha 1995–97	3 (25%)	6 (50%)	3 (25%)	12 (10%)
Total 1995–97	53 (44%)	40 (33%)	27 (23%)	120, p=0.32
Market Neutral				
Positive alpha 1995–97	104 (51%)	28 (14%)	73 (36%)	205 (88%)
Negative alpha 1995–97	9 (32%)	0 (0%)	19 (68%)	28 (12%)
Total 1995–97	113 (49%)	28 (12%)	92 (40%)	233, p=0.00
Global Funds				
Positive alpha 1995–97	130 (44%)	67 (22%)	102 (34%)	299 (83%)
Negative alpha 1995–97	18 (30%)	17 (28%)	26 (43%)	61 (17%)
Total 1995–97	148 (41%)	84 (23%)	128 (36%)	360, p=0.13
Emerging Markets				
Positive alpha 1995–97	4 (11%)	18 (50%)	14 (39%)	36 (58%)
Negative alpha 1995–97	5 (19%)	12 (46%)	9 (35%)	26 (42%)
Total 1995–97	9 (15%)	30 (48%)	23 (37%)	62, p=0.67
Sector				
Positive alpha 1995–97	23 (43%)	9 (17%)	22 (41%)	54 (86%)
Negative alpha 1995–97	6 (67%)	1 (11%)	2 (22%)	9 (14%)
Total 1995–97	29 (46%)	10 (16%)	24 (35%)	63, p=0.40
Short-sellers				
Positive alpha 1995–97	11 (69%)	0 (0%)	5 (31%)	16 (89%)
Negative alpha 1995–97	1 (50%)	0 (0%)	1 (50%)	2 (11%)
Total 1995–97	12 (67%)	0 (0%)	6 (33%)	18, p=NA
Fund of Funds				
Positive alpha 1995–97	110 (45%)	68 (28%)	65 (27%)	243 (85%)
Negative alpha 1995–97	15 (35%)	12 (28%)	16 (37%)	43 (15%)
Total 1995–97	125 (44%)	80 (28%)	81 (28%)	286, p=0.31

Note: p-value for the xi-square test reported in the last column.

a consistent winner drop below 50 per cent, except for Market-neutral funds and Short-sellers. In conclusion: some evidence of performance persistence is found. Overall, however, the proportion of hedge funds with positive alpha in the out-of-sample period 1998–2000 is quite low, owing to the large number of disappearing funds.

These results are in line with Edwards and Caglayan (2001), who report evidence of performance persistence in hedge fund returns over one-year and two-year periods. Edwards and Caglayan (2001), however, do not investigate the impact of disappearing funds. Brown et al. (1999) do not find evidence of performance persistence in offshore hedge fund returns over the period 1995–2001. Agarwal and Naik (2000a,b) find performance persistence, but the result is driven mainly by repeat losers. The present approach differs from these previous studies, as it explicitly deals with the large number of disappearing funds and applies a long performance evaluation period of three years.

Results with Sharpe ratio criterion

The performance criterion is now changed to the Sharpe ratio, using a 36-month track record requirement (results for a 12-month period are similar and available on request). In the 36-month selection period from 1995 to 1997, a hedge fund is designated a winner if its Sharpe ratio is above the median for its style and a loser if its Sharpe ratio is below the median. In the out-of-sample period 1998–2000, funds either disappear, or they are classified as winner or loser, depending on whether their Sharpe ratio is above the median of the surviving funds. Table 5.13 displays the resulting contingency tables for each hedge fund style.

Table 5.13 shows strong evidence of performance persistence on the basis of the Sharpe ratio for Event-driven funds, Market Neutral funds, Global funds and Fund of Funds. If a fund that was a winner in the 36-month selection period is chosen out of sample the odds are lower that the fund disappears from the database. Moreover, winners in the selection period also have higher odds of becoming winners out of sample (regardless of whether conditioned on survival or not). It should be pointed out that Event-driven, Market Neutral, Global funds and Fund of Funds constitute about 90 per cent of the entire database, so these results are quite general.

Short-sellers also seem to display performance persistence. However, there are not enough funds to establish significance. Emerging Markets

Table 5.13 Sharpe ratio persistence, with 36-month track record requirement

Hedge fund style	Sharpe ratio winner 1998–2000	Sharpe ratio loser 1998–2000	Disappears 1998–2000	Total
Event-driven				
Sharpe ratio Winner 1995–97	29 (51%)	19 (33%)	9 (16%)	57 (50%)
Sharpe ratio Loser 1995–97	17 (29%)	28 (48%)	13 (22%)	58 (50%)
Total 1995–97	46 (40%)	47 (41%)	22 (19%)	115, p=0.06
Market Neutral				
Sharpe ratio Winner 1995–97	42 (40%)	36 (34%)	28 (26%)	106 (50%)
Sharpe ratio Loser 1995–97	28 (26%)	35 (33%)	43 (41%)	106 (50%)
Total 1995–97	70 (33%)	71 (33%)	71 (33%)	212, p=0.05
Global Funds				
Sharpe ratio Winner 1995–97	65 (42%)	49 (31%)	42 (27%)	156 (50%)
Sharpe ratio Loser 1995–97	39 (25%)	55 (35%)	63 (40%)	157 (50%)
Total 1995–97	104 (33%)	104 (33%)	105 (34%)	313, p=0.00
Emerging Markets				
Sharpe ratio Winner 1995–97	10 (34%)	10 (34%)	9 (31%)	29 (49%)
Sharpe ratio Loser 1995–97	9 (30%)	10 (33%)	11 (37%)	30 (51%)
Total 1995–97	19 (32%)	20 (34%)	20 (34%)	59, p=0.89
Sector				
Sharpe ratio Winner 1995–97	5 (17%)	13 (43%)	12 (40%)	30 (50%)
Sharpe ratio Loser 1995–97	14 (47%)	7 (23%)	9 (30%)	30 (50%)
Total 1995–97	19 (32%)	20 (33%)	21 (35%)	60, p=0.04
Short-sellers				
Sharpe ratio Winner 1995–97	5 (56%)	0 (0%)	4 (44%)	9 (50%)
Sharpe ratio Loser 1995–97	1 (11%)	6 (67%)	2 (22%)	9 (50%)
Total 1995–97	6 (33%)	6 (33%)	6 (33%)	18, p=NA
Fund of Funds				
Sharpe ratio Winner 1995–97	70 (52%)	43 (32%)	22 (16%)	135 (50%)
Sharpe ratio Loser 1995–97	32 (24%)	60 (44%)	43 (32%)	135 (50%)
Total 1995–97	102 (38%)	103 (38%)	65 (24%)	270, p=0.00

Note: p-value for the xi-square test reported in the last column.

funds do not show any sign of persistence, while Sector funds stand out in Table 5.13 with significant performance reversal. A performance persistence test with the mean return (relative to the peer group) as performance criterion was also done. Again strong evidence of performance persistence for Event-driven funds, Market Neutral funds, Global funds and Fund of Funds was found. As the results are similar to those based on the Sharpe ratio, they have been omitted to save space.

Conclusions

This paper investigates whether hedge funds can add value to the portfolio of an uninformed, passive investor. This simple question is relevant for most institutional investors, such as pension funds and endowments funds, which have been boosting the growth of the hedge fund industry. Jensen's alpha is applied to measure the performance of hedge funds: if a fund has a positive alpha, then a passive mean-variance investor would add the fund to his portfolio. Mean-variance preferences, however, are not appropriate for evaluating hedge funds, as they tend to have non-normal return distributions. Therefore, alphas for a passive investor with power utility are also measured, taking the skewness and fat tails of the return distribution into account.

The results show that hedge funds have significantly positive alphas on average, except for Emerging Market funds. The difference between alphas assigned to hedge funds by mean-variance investors and investors with power utility is quite small. The non-normality of the return distribution is most pronounced for Event-driven and Market Neutral funds, Emerging Markets funds and Fund of Funds. Within these styles, funds with negative skewness and excess kurtosis tend to have significantly lower alphas based on power utility than based on mean-variance preferences. Of all hedge funds, however, 59 per cent have a return distribution without these two unpleasant characteristics: in those cases non-normality does not have a significant impact on the alpha of the funds, and hence on the portfolio of the passive investor.

In order to capture some of the non-normalities in the hedge fund returns, a benchmark set that includes put and call option contracts on the S&P 500 (5 per cent out-of-the-money options with 1-month maturity) was also used. These contracts are rolled over every month after expiration. Most investors can implement the strategies quite easily with exchange-listed option contracts. It is found that 32 per cent of the Event-driven funds have significant exposure to a put-selling strategy, 29 per cent of the Emerging Market Funds and 24 per cent of the Fund of Funds. The average alphas of these hedge fund styles are reduced by about 20 per cent, after including the option strategies in the benchmark set. On average, however, alphas are still significantly positive for all hedge fund styles (except Emerging Markets). Moreover, the R^2s are below 50 per cent on average for the alpha regressions with option selling strategies. Hence, most of the hedge fund return variation remains unexplained.

Next, the performance persistence of hedge funds is tested over a three-year period, correcting for the large number of disappearing funds. Overall the results in Tables 5.11, 5.12 and 5.13 show evidence of performance persistence. Unfortunately though, the chance of selecting a surviving winning fund is reduced considerably by the large number of disappearing funds. An investor that randomly selected a fund with a positive alpha in the selection period and a track record of at least 12 months would have had about a 50 per cent chance of drawing a surviving fund with a positive alpha in the following 36-month out-of-sample period.

The good news, however, is that selecting winning funds with a 36-month track record and above-median Sharpe ratio increased the chance of selecting a surviving fund with an above-median Sharpe ratio in the out-of-sample period from 27 per cent to 44 per cent on average. Similar results were found with selection rules that use alpha and a 12-month track record. Hence, it is concluded that it pays to select funds with a track record of good past performance, in order to avoid poor performance out of sample.

Overall, the majority hedge funds have positive alphas, and therefore seem to add value to the portfolio of passive investors. The non-normality of hedge fund return distributions does not affect this result. The probability of selecting a fund with a positive alpha over a longer horizon is reduced severely, however, by the large number of disappearing funds. During the last three years of this sample, the average yearly rate of fund disappearance was about 15 per cent. It is not known why funds disappear from the database, but it is known that disappearing funds underperform surviving funds significantly.

In the author's opinion, more research into the reasons and the frequency of hedge fund disappearance from the available databases is essential before definite conclusions about the added value of investing in hedge funds can be reached.

Acknowledgments

The author would like to thank: INQUIRE Europe for financial support; Zurich Capital Markets for providing the hedge fund data; Greg Newton and Richard Oberuc for their help with obtaining access to the Zurich Hedge Fund universe; Altaf Kassam of Goldman Sachs Equity Derivatives Research for providing S&P 500 options data; Cees Dert for finding time to provide thorough comments on the paper. Many thanks to Arjan Berkelaar, Mark Carhart, Kevin Chang, Stuart Doole, Bart Dowling, Audrey Kaplan, Thierry Post, Mika Toikka, Bill Ziemba, colleagues at AEGON and participants of the INQUIRE Europe seminar for their feedback.

Note

1. Results are robust to changes in the risk aversion parameter γ.

References

Ackermann, C., McEnally, R. and Ravenscraft, D. (1999) 'The Performance of Hedge Funds: Risk, Return and Incentives', *Journal of Finance*, 54, 833–74.
Agarwal, V. and Naik, N. (2000a) 'On Taking the Alternative Route: Risks, Rewards and Performance Persistence of Hedge Funds', *Journal of Alternative Investments*, 2, 6–23.
Agarwal, V. and Naik, N. (2000b) 'Multi-Period Performance Persistence of Hedge Funds', *Journal of Financial and Quantitative Analysis*, 35, 327–42.
Agarwal, V. and Naik, N. (2001) 'Characterizing Hedge Fund Risks with Buy-and-Hold and Option-Based Strategies', Working Paper, London Business School.
Amin, G. S. and Kat, H. M. (2002) 'Hedge Fund Performance 1990–2000: Do the Money Machines Add Value', *Journal of Financial and Quantitative Analysis*.
Brown, S. J. and Goetzmann, W. N. (1995) 'Performance Persistence', *Journal of Finance*, 50, 679–98.
Brown, S. J., Goetzmann, W. N. and Ibbotson, R. G. (1999) 'Offshore Hedge Funds: Survival and Performance', *Journal of Finance*, 50, 679–98.
Carhart, M. (1997) 'On Persistence in Mutual Fund Performance', *Journal of Finance*, 50, 679–98.
Chen, Z. and Knez, P. J. (1996) 'Portfolio Performance Measurement: Theory and Applications', *Review of Financial Studies*, 9, 511–55.
Cumby, R. E. and Glen, J. D. (1990) 'Evaluating the Performance of International Mutual Funds', *Journal of Finance*, 45, 497–521.
Edwards, F. R. and Caglayan, M. O. (2001) 'Hedge Fund Performance and Manager Skill', Working Paper, Columbia University.
Fung, W. and Hsieh, D. A. (2001) 'The Risk in Hedge Fund Strategies: Theory and Evidence from Trend Followers', *Review of Financial Studies*, 14, 313–41.

Grinblatt, M. and Titman, S. (1989) 'Portfolio Performance Evaluation: Old Issues and New Insights', *Review of Financial Studies*, 2, 393–421.
Grinblatt, M. and Titman, S. (1994) 'A Study of Mutual Fund Returns and Performance Evaluation Techniques', *Journal of Financial and Quantitative Analysis*, 29, 419–44.
Gruber, M. J. (1996) 'Another Puzzle: The Growth in Actively Managed Mutual Funds', *Journal of Finance*, 51, 783–810.
Jensen, M. C. (1968) 'The Performance of Mutual Funds in the Period 1945–64', *Journal of Finance*, 23, 389–416.
Malkiel, B. G. (1995) 'Returns from Investing in Equity Mutual Funds 1971 to 1991', *Journal of Finance*, 50, 1249–90.
Mitchell, M. and Pulvino, T. (2001) 'Characteristics of Risk and Return in Risk Arbitrage', *Journal of Finance*, 56, 2135–75.

6.1
The Performance of Value and Momentum Investment Portfolios: Recent Experience in the Major European Markets

*Ron Bird**

is an Emeritus Professor from the Australian National University where he taught from 1973 to 1989. In 1999, he joined the Finance and Economics School at the University of Technology, Sydney. In the interim, he held the following private sector positions: directing Towers Perrin's asset consulting business in the Asia region; several management positions at Westpac Investment Management; co-founder of GMO's fund management operations in Australia. He remained an academic consultant to GMO until the end of 2002, at which time he took up a similar role with MIR Investment Management.

Jonathan Whitaker

is currently working as a research analyst with GT Capital in Melbourne having previously been a research associate in the Finance and Economics School at the University of Technology, Sydney. He holds an honours degree in physics from UTS and a Masters in Statistics from the University of New South Wales. He held a number of positions in medical physics before taking up his current position.

**School of Finance and Economics, University of Technology, Sydney, PO Box 123, Broadway, NSW 2007, Australia*
Tel: +612 9514 7716; Fax: +612 9514 7711; e-mail: ron.bird@uts.edu.au

Introduction

Over the last 25 years there have been numerous studies that have identified various market anomalies, many of which have given rise to a new quantitative investment strategy. This paper concentrates on the two most prolific of these strategies: value investing and momentum

Reprinted from 'The performance of value and momentum investment portfolios: Recent experience in the major European markets' by Ron Bird and Jonathan Whitaker in *Journal of Asset Management*, 4, 2003, pp. 221–246, DOI:10.1057/palgrave.jam.2240105. With kind permission from Palgrave Macmillan Ltd.

investing, whose performance is evaluated in the major European markets over the interesting period from January 1990 to June 2002. The first decade of the sample period was characterised by a consistently rising market, with the European markets rising on average by 12.5 per cent per annum but this period was followed by a rapid (still on-going) market correction, with the European markets falling on average by 12 per cent per annum over the first two and a half years of the new millennium.[1]

In the first section of this paper the authors briefly outline the history of the two investment techniques under evaluation and the past evidence with respect to their performance. They then proceed to provide a broad outline of the methods and data employed in this study. Thereafter the authors outline the findings which verify the on-going success of a number of alternative implementations of these two strategies. The paper concludes with some summary comments.

Existing evidence on value and momentum investing

As indicated above, the focus of this paper is to evaluate the recent performance of value and momentum investing in the major European markets. Before turning to the empirical findings, the authors survey in this section the nature and performance record of both of these two approaches to investing.

Value investing

The foundations of value investing date back to Graham and Dodd (1934) who suggested that analysts extrapolate past earnings growth too far out into the future and by so doing drive the price of the stock of the better performing firms to too high a level. The Graham and Dodd hypothesis is that firms who have experienced and who are currently experiencing high earnings growth are unlikely to be able to sustain it over extended time periods. When the earnings growth of such a firm reverts back towards some industry/economy-wide mean, it will fall well short of the unrealistic expectations that have been built into current prices and give rise to a downward correction in its stock price. A similar story also applies to a firm that has been performing poorly, whose share price has been driven down too far and which subsequently mean-reverts when the fundamentals of the firm begin to pick up.

A number of valuation multiples have been used to provide insights into possible mispricings due to these unrealistic expectations. For example, a high (low) price-to-earnings or market-to-book multiple is taken as indicative that the firm's stock is expensive (cheap). Value (or contrarian) investment strategies have been developed using such multiples where stocks are ranked in accordance to their multiple values and the investment portfolio is tilted towards the cheaper stocks and away from the expensive stocks. Although such strategies have been in use since the writings of Graham and Dodd, it is only in the last 25 years that academics have devoted time to both measuring and providing explanations for their apparent success. Basu (1977) evaluated earnings-to-price as the value criterion; Rosenberg *et al.* (1985) investigated price-to-book; Chan *et al.* (1991) studied cash flow-to-price, while Lakonishok *et al.* (1994), Dreman and Berry (1995) and Bernard *et al.* (1997) all evaluated several value criteria.

A consistent finding in these papers has been that value investing is a profitable investment strategy not only in the USA but also in most of the other major markets (Arshanapalli *et al.*, 1998; Rouwenhorst, 1999). The debate then goes as to whether the excess returns associated with a value strategy represent a market anomaly (Lakonishok *et al.*, 1994) or whether they simply represent a premium for taking on extra investment risk (Fama and French, 1993). A third possible explanation is that the value premium is simply a reward for taking on the greater business risk associated with holding a disproportionate amount of out-of-favour stocks in one's portfolio. According to this third explanation, the greater return to value investment would be an equilibrium (permanent) outcome although still appearing an anomaly within the narrowly defined objective function assumed in classical economic models.

Irrespective of the source of the extra returns from value investing, they seem to exist and persist across almost all of the major world markets. Not surprisingly, this outcome has attracted an increasing number of investment managers to integrate this form of investing into their process. One particular downside to value investing that has been identified in recent studies is that the majority (typically around 55 per cent) of the so-called cheap stocks do not outperform the market (Bird and Gerlach, 2003), the reason being that the multiples used to identify value stocks are by their nature very crude. For example, the market may expect a firm that has been experiencing poor earnings performance for several years to continue to do so for many more years, and this will cause the firm to have a low (say) price-to-earnings multiple. Of course, if the earnings do revert upwards in the immediate future the market will revise the firm's stock price upwards and the low price-to-earnings multiple would have been reflective of a cheap stock. On the other hand, the market might have been right in its expectations and the firm's profitability may never improve and so it does not prove to be cheap. Indeed, the firm's fundamentals might even worsen and so investing in this firm on the basis of its price-to-earnings multiple would prove a very bad investment.

Momentum investing

Momentum investing basically involves investing on the basis of a past trend with many investment managers including some component of this form of investment in their process. Momentum investing comes in various guises and in this study we evaluate two of the most common: price momentum and earnings momentum.

Price momentum

Price momentum investing represents the simplest outworking of the technical analysts' motto that the trend is your friend. The suggestion being that recent trends in returns will be maintained into the future and so an investment approach that favours stocks that have realised high returns in recent times will outperform the market. The usual justification for such a strategy being that the performance of both markets and individual stocks is largely driven by market sentiment which itself follows trends.

Empirical tests of whether stocks prices move randomly or follow some predictable patterns date back over 100 years.[2] The early tests largely concentrated on the correlation between relatively short-term price movements and found limited evidence of mean-reversion (see Elton *et al.*, 2003: 411). In more recent times DeBondt and Thaler (1985, 1987) found that price movements overreact over extended time periods and subsequently mean-revert; the implication being that the best performing stocks over the last three to five years will tend to realise poor subsequent performance. This behaviour is similar to that previously discussed with respect to value investing, and it may well be that such investment opportunities are better identified using valuation multiples rather than some measure of long-term market performance.

Although the findings discussed above suggest that there is some mean-reversion in both short-term and long-term price movements, the majority of the interest in recent years has been in the continuance of medium-term price movements. It is the work in this area that has given rise to what has become known as (price) momentum investing. Jegadeesh and Titman (1993) when evaluating US stocks found that the relative return on stocks over a 3–12 months period is highly correlated with their relative returns over the previous 3–12 months. Many authors subsequently confirmed these findings with perhaps the most comprehensive being Jegadeesh and Titman's update of their original study (Jegadeesh and Titman, 2001). The evidence on price momentum is not limited to the USA. The most extensive international studies were conducted by Rouwenhorst (1998), who found that price momentum strategies also performed well in other developed markets and also many of the emerging markets.

The strength of the findings with respect to price momentum provided the impetus for a number of authors to try and provide an explanation for the empirical findings, with investment risk being the most obvious candidate. A consistent finding, however, was that applying the traditional risk controls (CAPM, Fama–French three factor model) actually increases momentum returns (Grundy and Martin, 2001; Chopra *et al.*, 1992; Jegadeesh and Titman, 2001; and Rouwenhorst, 1998). Other attempts to attribute momentum to illiquidity, data snooping and the like have also failed to meet with much success. Indeed, the outperformance of simple price momentum strategies remains so much a mystery that Fama has identified this as the one outstanding anomaly in market behaviour (Fama, 1998). The authors propose that a most likely explanation for the continued success of momentum trading is that it is a consequence of information signals being correlated over time (good news is more likely to follow good news) and the fact the market tends to underreact to new information (see Kadiyala and Rau, 2001, and Soffer and Walther, 2000). Such conditions create the environment for extended trends in price movement, especially in a positive direction, at a time when management is actively manipulating information flows (see, for example, Richardson *et al.*, 2000).

Earnings momentum

As indicated above, a likely contributing factor to price momentum is the fact that information signals are correlated over time (ie good news is more likely to be followed by more good news). Reported earnings is a prime suspect as the major source of information to which prices react. As a consequence, a number of writers have studied the market reaction to several forms of earnings momentum. A very early study in this area was conducted by Ball and Brown (1968), who evaluated the share price reaction to a change in a firm's earnings from one reporting period to the next and found that such changes did result in a consistent movement in share price. Evidence of a post announcement earnings drift has also been found, which suggests that investment strategies based on earnings momentum would be rewarded.

From evaluating the price response to earnings announcements, writers then turned to undertaking similar analyses and obtained similar findings using the earnings forecasts undertaken by equity analysts as the information source. These forecasts not only have the advantage of occurring earlier in the information cycle, but also are updated more frequently than reported earnings and so are more in tune with an investment strategy that is rebalanced on a monthly basis. It is for these reasons that the two earnings momentum criteria that we apply in this study for rankings stocks and forming portfolios are both based on the analysts' earnings forecasts, ie:

- Agreement measures the direction of changes in analysts' earnings forecasts over a short time period. It was first studied by Givoly and Lakonishok (1979) and is commonly used by a number of managers as part of their investment process;
- Forecast revisions measure the change in the magnitude of the analysts' earnings forecasts over a short time period. It has been evaluated by a number of writers including Chan *et al.* (1996) and is also used by a number of managers as part of their process.

Data and method

The data

In the following section the authors report on the performance of both value and price momentum investing when applied in several European countries: France, Germany, Italy, The Netherlands, Spain, Switzerland and the UK. The analysis was conducted over the period from January 1990 to June 2002, using accounting data obtained from the Worldscope database, return data provided by GMO Woolley and data on analyst's earnings forecasts provided by I/B/E/S. The only companies excluded from the sample were financial sector stocks and stocks with a negative book value. The average number of companies included in the database for each country is reported in Table 6.1.1.

Forming portfolios

Under both value and momentum investing, the stocks are ranked on the basis of some criterion with these rankings then being used as the

Table 6.1.1 Sample size by country

	Average	Maximum	Minimum
United Kingdom	1,081	1,274	730
France	376	454	376
Germany	332	515	230
Italy	129	147	108
Switzerland	127	162	108
Netherlands	97	115	75
Spain	78	99	57
Combined	2,219	2,533	1,641

basis for forming investment portfolios. The four criteria used by the authors are:

- Book-to-market (bm)
- Dividend yield (divvy)
- Earnings yield (epsy)
- Sales-to-price (sales price)

The first of these measures is a stock measure based on valuations while the other three relate current price to some flow measure that captures some activity of the firm. In each case, the lowest ranked stocks are the most expensive stocks and the highest ranked stocks are the cheapest stocks.

Two different measures of price momentum were also used to form the portfolios:

- 6-month price momentum (pmS)
- 12-month price momentum (pmL)

These two options were chosen as previous studies have shown that the best results from forming price momentum portfolios are obtained when the classification period for ranking stocks lies somewhere between 6 and 12 months. With price momentum, the bottom ranked stocks are those that have realised the lowest return over the measurement period (often referred to as the 'losers'), while the top ranked stocks are those that have realised the highest return (referred to as the 'winners'). The expectation being that the winners will continue to outperform the losers over the next several months.

Finally, two measures of earnings momentum were used, each based on analysts' earnings forecasts:

- Agreement (agree)
- Forecast revisions (fcr)

Agreement is measured by the quantity of analyst earnings revisions over a 2-month period – upward revisions minus downward revisions divided by the total number of revisions. A forecast revision is measured by the percentage change in the consensus analysts' earnings forecast over a two-month period.[3] Although both measures are based on analysts' forecasts, the former picks up on the fact that analysts tend to herd when making these revisions and so provides a measure of the strength of the signal relating to this herding behaviour while the second measure picks up on the magnitude of the signal. In the case of both criteria, stocks that have high rankings are expected to do much better than those with low rankings.

The procedure that the authors follow is to rank stocks at the beginning of each month based on each of the eight criteria outlined above. For example, each stock within each country (say France) is ranked on the basis of its book-to-market. Assume that there are 100 stocks with five portfolios to be formed. Then the 20 stocks with the lowest book-to-market values are included in the quintile one (most expensive) portfolio, the next 20 stocks ranked by book-to-market in the quintile two portfolio and so on. The resulting portfolios are (partially) rebalanced monthly and assumed to be held over holding periods that vary from 1 month to 48 months. With a 1-month holding period, the portfolios are totally rebalanced each month but with (say) a 12-month holding period, effectively one-twelfth of the portfolio is rebalanced each month, which means selling the stocks acquired 12 months ago and replacing them with the currently preferred stocks.

Besides following the procedure described above to build portfolios within countries, the authors also pool all of the stocks and build a combined portfolio incorporating all the available stocks from the seven markets. When all the stocks are then ranked in accordance with the procedures described above, there will be a tendency for the portfolios to reflect the relative valuations across the seven markets. For example, if French stocks are relatively cheap when measured by book-to-market, then they are likely to have a disproportionate weighting in the cheap portfolio that will be reflected in the returns on that portfolio. In order to minimise the impact of any country bias on the combined portfolios, the authors also form these portfolios on a country-corrected basis. The country-corrected value for the particular criterion being used (eg book-to-market) is calculated for each stock in each country by deducting the average value for the criterion across all the stocks in the country from the actual value for that criterion for each stock. For example, country-corrected book-to-market for all French stocks in a particular month is determined by deducting the average book-to-market for all French stocks for that month from each stock's book-to-market. Each stock is ranked across all countries in accordance with these country-corrected values. The portfolio formed from following this approach is described as a country-corrected portfolio and the returns, country-corrected returns.

Determining the returns on the portfolios

The end objective is to measure the performance of the portfolios formed following one of the approaches described above. The authors calculate several returns, each of which is described below:[4]

1. Equally weighted return – these are returns on equally weighting each stock within each portfolio.
2. Market weighted returns – these are the returns obtained by weighting each stock in each portfolio on the basis for its contribution to the market capitalisation of the portfolio.
3. Size-adjusted equally weighted returns – in this case each stock is equally weighted within each portfolio but the returns used to calculate the portfolio returns are not the actual stock returns for each month, but rather the size-adjusted returns obtained by subtracting the return of the portfolio composed of stocks that fall in the same size-decile portfolio from the stock's actual return. (See La Porta *et al.*, 1997, for a detailed discussion of the calculation of size-adjusted returns.)
4. Size-adjusted market weighted returns – each stock is held in each portfolio in proportion to its market capitalisation with portfolio returns being calculated using the size-adjusted returns that are calculated using the method described above.

As well as calculating the monthly returns for each portfolio, the authors also calculate a p-value as a test of the significance of these returns. These p-values are calculated using the Newey–West measure of variance that corrects for serial correlation (Newey and West, 1987).

Finally, the authors collect the following characteristics for each portfolio:

- The portfolio's average book-to-market value as a measure of its valuation level
- The portfolio's six-month price momentum as a measure of its recent market performance
- The relative trading volume of the stocks in the portfolio over the previous month as a measure of its liquidity
- The decile ranking of the market capitalisation of the stocks in the portfolio

The findings

The authors begin their analysis of how value and momentum strategies performed over the sample period by examining the performance of the four value criteria across the combined sample of the stocks in the seven countries and then evaluating the value criteria at the individual country level. Attention is then turned to conducting the same analysis applying both the two price momentum and two earnings momentum criteria.

Individual value strategies across all markets

Table 6.1.2 shows the absolute returns realised by applying the four value criteria to the pooled sample of stocks drawn from all seven markets. The immediate impression that one gains from reviewing this table is that some of the value criteria have been a lot more successful than others in separating what prove to be the cheap from the expensive stocks. Those criteria that disappoint are dividend yield and the earnings yield while sales-to-price and particularly book-to-market work well. Indeed, the authors would suggest that sales-to-price and book-to-market are purer measures of value as they are more difficult to manipulate than the other criteria. Hence the authors will concentrate on sales-to-price and book-to-market as the value criteria throughout the remainder of the discussions.

The evidence suggests that sorting stocks by book-to-market adds value over periods of up to three years, which is consistent with previous experience for US stocks (see Lakonishok *et al.*, 1994). For example, the first quintile portfolio composed of expensive stocks returns 0.61 per cent per month over a three-year holding period with there being

Table 6.1.2 Equally weighted returns (per cent per month) across value portfolios created using four criteria and with differing holding periods (combined markets, January 1990 to June 2002)

Panel 1: Sorting by book-to-market

Holding period	bm1	bm2	bm3	bm4	bm5	bm5 – bm1
1 month	0.633	0.589	0.553	0.592	1.175	0.542
	0.291	0.154	0.112	0.108	0.01	0.277
3 months	0.529	0.562	0.624	0.722	1.334	0.805
	0.366	0.165	0.071	0.045	0.006	0.121
6 months	0.427	0.578	0.646	0.792	1.542	1.115
	0.456	0.134	0.052	0.02	0.005	0.058
9 months	0.532	0.756	0.844	0.997	1.88	1.348
	0.353	0.047	0.01	0.003	0.002	0.031
12 months	0.507	0.773	0.894	1.059	2.002	1.495
	0.375	0.041	0.006	0.001	0.001	0.021
24 months	0.546	0.762	0.887	1.202	2.077	1.531
	0.333	0.05	0.009	0.001	0.001	0.013
36 months	0.614	0.825	0.956	1.309	2.206	1.591
	0.265	0.032	0.004	0	0.001	0.013
48 months	0.443	0.684	0.746	1.119	1.7	1.257
	0.417	0.078	0.023	0.004	0.004	0.02

Panel 2: Sorting by dividend yield

Holding period	divy1	divy2	divy3	divy4	divy5	divy5 – divy1
1 month	0.531	0.727	0.777	0.76	0.771	0.241
	0.402	0.041	0.038	0.047	0.137	0.555
3 months	0.7	0.791	0.834	0.713	0.755	0.055
	0.297	0.024	0.023	0.056	0.13	0.907
6 months	0.883	0.806	0.849	0.696	0.776	–0.107
	0.239	0.014	0.015	0.054	0.105	0.859
9 months	1.135	1.002	1.074	0.872	0.954	–0.181
	0.156	0.002	0.002	0.017	0.041	0.788
12 months	1.229	1.047	1.138	0.897	0.953	–0.275
	0.141	0.001	0.001	0.016	0.037	0.702
24 months	1.081	1.009	1.162	1.167	1.042	–0.04
	0.169	0.004	0.001	0.005	0.017	0.953
36 months	1.009	1.054	1.247	1.472	1.098	0.089
	0.157	0.002	0	0.004	0.011	0.882
48 months	0.73	0.821	0.989	1.264	0.891	0.161
	0.305	0.018	0.003	0.013	0.03	0.791

(continued)

Table 6.1.2 Continued

Panel 3: Sorting by earnings yield

Holding period	epsy1	epsy2	epsy3	epsy4	epsy5	epsy5 – epsy1
1 month	0.369	0.705	0.697	0.838	0.959	0.59
	0.571	0.08	0.04	0.018	0.023	0.112
3 months	0.543	0.709	0.746	0.874	0.923	0.38
	0.419	0.071	0.025	0.013	0.024	0.374
6 months	0.773	0.681	0.742	0.9	0.915	0.142
	0.287	0.071	0.02	0.006	0.02	0.793
9 months	1.109	0.811	0.92	1.101	1.096	–0.013
	0.147	0.03	0.004	0.001	0.005	0.983
12 months	1.256	0.835	0.96	1.133	1.08	–0.176
	0.112	0.024	0.002	0	0.006	0.78
24 months	1.535	0.847	0.937	1.093	1.117	–0.418
	0.076	0.025	0.006	0.001	0.006	0.567
36 months	1.566	0.908	0.965	1.123	1.336	–0.23
	0.039	0.015	0.004	0	0.002	0.644
48 months	1.215	0.709	0.738	0.852	1.188	–0.027
	0.078	0.059	0.034	0.006	0.01	0.947

Panel 4: Sorting by sales-to-price

Holding period	sales price1	sales price2	sales price3	sales price4	sales price5	sales price5 – sales price1
1 month	0.479	0.689	0.8	0.742	0.869	0.391
	0.363	0.054	0.028	0.069	0.072	0.149
3 months	0.491	0.737	0.809	0.791	0.98	0.49
	0.341	0.037	0.025	0.046	0.047	0.083
6 months	0.498	0.725	0.796	0.824	1.182	0.683
	0.313	0.031	0.02	0.03	0.033	0.069
9 months	0.706	0.899	0.967	1.051	1.429	0.723
	0.15	0.007	0.004	0.005	0.016	0.096
12 months	0.769	0.94	1.004	1.092	1.473	0.705
	0.117	0.005	0.003	0.003	0.018	0.135
24 months	0.817	0.928	0.983	1.131	1.677	0.86
	0.106	0.009	0.006	0.004	0.018	0.132
36 months	0.964	0.972	1.022	1.167	1.857	0.892
	0.054	0.006	0.003	0.001	0.019	0.183
48 months	0.801	0.757	0.756	0.874	1.6	0.799
	0.11	0.035	0.028	0.012	0.038	0.216

Notes: The first line in each cell is the monthly returns while the second line reports the *p*-value calculated using the Newey-West measure of variance corrected for serial correlation. For example, the top left hand cell in Panel 1 shows that the first quintile of book-to-market realised a monthly return of 0.633 per cent with a *p*-value of 0.291.

a smooth transition in returns across the other quintile portfolios with the fifth quintile portfolio composed of cheap stocks returning 2.20 per cent over the same holding period. For all holding periods in excess of 9 months, the difference between the returns on the cheap and expensive portfolios is highly significant. The sorting of stocks by sales-to-price produces portfolios whose returns are equally regular and long-lived as are those for the book-to-market portfolios, even though they suggest a value strategy which is slightly less profitable.

In order to gain greater insights into the reasons why these two criteria might give rise to a profitable value strategy the authors examined several characteristics of the resulting portfolios and these are reported in Table 6.1.3. The characteristics of both sets of portfolios are quite distinctive – the cheap book-to-market portfolios comprised relatively small and cheap (by book-to-market) stocks that have experienced poor recent market performance and a relatively low trading volume; the cheap sales-to-price portfolios comprised stocks that have experienced poor recent market performance on a relatively low trading volume but which are, on average, neither small nor cheap.

Table 6.1.3 Characteristics of book-to-market and sales-to-price portfolios (combined markets, January 1990 to June 2002)

Book-to-market				
Portfolio	**Book-to-market**	**6-month price momentum (per cent per month)**	**Volume (proportion of total)**	**Size (decile rank)**
bm1	0.0933	2.3887	0.2126	6.8255
bm2	0.2409	1.3565	0.2155	6.745
bm3	0.4143	0.7897	0.2548	6
bm4	0.6957	0.3507	0.212	4.9664
bm5	1.4211	−0.8508	0.105	2.9765
Book-to-market				
Portfolio	**Book-to-market**	**6-month price momentum (per cent per month)**	**Volume (proportion of total)**	**Size (decile rank)**
sales price1	0.2928	1.4622	0.2672	6.2181
sales price2	0.3486	1.2984	0.3712	6.1409
sales price3	0.5005	0.8808	0.2527	5.1007
sales price4	0.5646	0.3246	0.0545	4.2383
sales price5	0.4382	0.0385	0.0544	5.3188

The characteristics presented in Table 6.1.3 would suggest the possibility that, especially in the case of the book-to-market portfolios, size and illiquidity considerations might mitigate against being able to extract much of the potential added value highlighted in Table 6.1.2. In order to throw more light on this possibility, we also report the performance of each of the portfolios first measured on a market weighted basis (Table 6.1.4) and then on a market-weighted and size-adjusted basis (Table 6.1.5). The overall effect of market weighting the stocks within the portfolio is to lower the impact of the smaller stocks on portfolio returns. Therefore, it is not surprising to find from an examination of Table 6.1.4 that the spread in the returns across the various portfolios is lower than they were when returns were calculated for equally weighted portfolios. The introduction of size-adjusted returns as reported in Table 6.1.5 does not, however, result in any further erosion of the outperformance of the cheaper stocks, with the spread between the returns on the cheap and expensive portfolios remaining at around 7 per cent per annum over a 36-month holding period in the case of book-to-market portfolios and almost 5 per cent per annum in the case of sales-to-price portfolios. The optimal holding period for the value portfolios would appear to be somewhere between 24 months and 36 months, over which time the spread between the returns on the cheap and expensive portfolios has maximum statistical significance.

The final issue to examine when investigating the application of value investing across the whole population of stocks is whether the way in which the rankings from the various countries have been combined introduces country positions that impact on the performance of the portfolios. In order to gain insights into this possibility, the authors produce country-corrected portfolios following the procedure described in the previous section, and report the returns on these country-corrected portfolios in Table 6.1.6. The effect of correcting for country bias results in a slight erosion in the performance of the portfolios, especially in the case of those formed using sales-to-price over the longer holding periods. It does seem, however, that the vast majority of the potential added value from implementing a value strategy during this period would have been due to stock selection rather than country bets.

The conclusion the authors draw from the discussion to date is that a value strategy based on either book-to-market or sales-to-price performed well if executed over the major European markets during the period from January 1990 to June 2002. This is a particularly interesting period as it contains a 10-year period when there was a boom in stock prices followed by a 2+ year correction period. Indeed, an analysis of

Table 6.1.4 Market-weighted returns (per cent per month) for book-to-market and sales-to-price portfolios (combined markets, January 1990 to May 2002)

Panel 1: Sorting by book-to-market

Holding period	bm1	bm2	bm3	bm4	bm5	bm5 – bm1
1 month	0.657	0.865	0.877	0.822	1.129	0.471
	0.117	0.01	0.005	0.029	0.009	0.329
3 months	0.639	0.812	0.857	0.865	1.103	0.464
	0.111	0.012	0.005	0.013	0.011	0.318
6 months	0.629	0.812	0.865	0.838	1.115	0.486
	0.1	0.008	0.002	0.014	0.007	0.259
9 months	0.805	1.008	1.046	1.017	1.345	0.54
	0.038	0.001	0	0.002	0	0.191
12 months	0.768	1.006	1.029	1.032	1.328	0.559
	0.05	0.001	0	0.002	0	0.153
24 months	0.724	0.947	1.04	1.041	1.379	0.654
	0.073	0.004	0	0.002	0	0.054
36 months	0.738	0.898	1.008	1.044	1.352	0.614
	0.061	0.008	0.001	0.002	0	0.055
48 months	0.67	0.774	0.865	0.899	1.137	0.467
	0.093	0.029	0.004	0.011	0.001	0.136

Panel 2: Sorting by sales-to-price

Holding period	sales price1	sales price2	sales price3	sales price4	sales price5	sales price5 – sales price1
1 month	0.546	0.765	0.917	0.944	1.109	0.564
	0.193	0.009	0.005	0.009	0.005	0.014
3 months	0.554	0.803	0.906	0.97	1.015	0.461
	0.174	0.007	0.004	0.004	0.008	0.057
6 months	0.534	0.754	0.786	1	1.034	0.5
	0.179	0.009	0.011	0.002	0.004	0.037
9 months	0.725	0.94	0.948	1.201	1.2	0.475
	0.074	0.001	0.002	0	0.001	0.047
12 months	0.737	0.947	0.904	1.178	1.153	0.416
	0.074	0.001	0.003	0	0.001	0.073
24 months	0.668	0.9	0.934	1.149	1.151	0.483
	0.128	0.002	0.005	0.001	0.002	0.036
36 months	0.756	0.834	0.908	1.043	1.16	0.404
	0.079	0.006	0.004	0.002	0.002	0.07
48 months	0.695	0.73	0.751	0.87	0.991	0.296
	0.11	0.024	0.02	0.012	0.01	0.198

Table 6.1.5 Market-weighted and size-adjusted returns (per cent per month) for book-to-market and sales-to-price portfolios (combined markets, January 1990 to June 2002)

Panel 1: Sorting by book-to-market

Holding period	bm1	bm2	bm3	bm4	bm5	bm5 – bm1
1 month	–0.028	0.18	0.188	0.151	0.442	0.47
	0.887	0.157	0.372	0.491	0.19	0.329
3 months	–0.016	0.158	0.197	0.215	0.45	0.466
	0.935	0.239	0.316	0.291	0.155	0.316
6 months	0.013	0.195	0.245	0.226	0.49	0.477
	0.942	0.14	0.203	0.245	0.1	0.272
9 months	0.008	0.21	0.245	0.219	0.54	0.531
	0.964	0.109	0.2	0.273	0.055	0.2
12 months	–0.009	0.225	0.246	0.252	0.534	0.543
	0.962	0.079	0.192	0.214	0.045	0.169
24 months	–0.081	0.137	0.228	0.232	0.551	0.632
	0.664	0.228	0.173	0.246	0.016	0.067
36 months	–0.102	0.052	0.16	0.198	0.478	0.58
	0.573	0.621	0.307	0.324	0.034	0.076
48 months	–0.028	0.07	0.158	0.196	0.411	0.44
	0.872	0.468	0.268	0.331	0.055	0.171

Panel 2: Sorting by sales-to-price

Holding period	sales price1	sales price2	Sales price3	sales price4	sales price5	sales price5 – sales price1
1 month	–0.135	0.08	0.238	0.263	0.427	0.562
	0.505	0.688	0.084	0.038	0.009	0.015
3 months	–0.092	0.145	0.255	0.317	0.364	0.455
	0.662	0.426	0.062	0.008	0.037	0.062
6 months	–0.074	0.134	0.171	0.387	0.42	0.495
	0.729	0.435	0.192	0.001	0.015	0.041
9 months	–0.063	0.14	0.153	0.406	0.402	0.466
	0.775	0.411	0.268	0.001	0.013	0.052
12 months	–0.034	0.165	0.125	0.401	0.374	0.409
	0.876	0.339	0.373	0.002	0.016	0.08
24 months	–0.135	0.091	0.126	0.339	0.341	0.476
	0.546	0.584	0.366	0.01	0.023	0.04
36 months	–0.089	–0.009	0.064	0.193	0.316	0.405
	0.684	0.953	0.676	0.135	0.026	0.071
48 months	–0.006	0.027	0.049	0.164	0.289	0.295
	0.977	0.841	0.753	0.216	0.04	0.201

Table 6.1.6 Market-weighted returns (per cent per month) for country-corrected book-to-market and sales-to-price portfolios (combined markets, January 1990 to June 2002)

Panel 1: Sorting by country-corrected book-to-market

Holding period	bm1	bm2	bm3	bm4	bm5	bm5 – bm1
1 month	0.803	0.771	0.743	0.836	1.163	0.36
	0.056	0.027	0.017	0.016	0.006	0.411
3 months	0.86	0.708	0.72	0.844	1.169	0.308
	0.035	0.033	0.015	0.01	0.003	0.466
6 months	0.805	0.682	0.725	0.901	1.181	0.375
	0.043	0.033	0.01	0.003	0.001	0.341
9 months	0.957	0.865	0.942	1.112	1.426	0.468
	0.016	0.007	0.001	0	0	0.213
12 months	0.928	0.867	0.925	1.116	1.423	0.495
	0.02	0.007	0.001	0	0	0.172
24 months	0.82	0.844	1.003	1.101	1.439	0.619
	0.052	0.012	0.001	0.001	0	0.069
36 months	0.805	0.796	1.002	1.102	1.398	0.593
	0.06	0.019	0.001	0.001	0	0.099
48 months	0.798	0.642	0.843	0.923	1.172	0.374
	0.072	0.061	0.005	0.006	0	0.297

Panel 2: Sorting by country-corrected sales-to-price

Holding period	sales price1	sales price2	sales price3	sales price4	sales price5	sales price5 – sales price1
1 month	0.748	0.87	0.578	0.902	1.473	0.725
	0.04	0.027	0.085	0.007	0	0.001
3 months	0.72	0.872	0.603	0.965	1.407	0.686
	0.038	0.021	0.071	0.003	0	0.001
6 months	0.798	0.846	0.586	0.846	1.36	0.563
	0.015	0.019	0.079	0.006	0	0.003
9 months	0.98	1.047	0.736	1.055	1.57	0.59
	0.002	0.004	0.027	0.001	0	0.002
12 months	0.953	1.064	0.685	1.085	1.503	0.55
	0.003	0.004	0.041	0	0	0.003
24 months	1.005	0.967	0.614	1.125	1.334	0.329
	0.003	0.011	0.09	0.001	0.001	0.059
36 months	1.014	0.975	0.564	1.122	1.2	0.185
	0.002	0.011	0.119	0	0.002	0.254
48 months	0.866	0.881	0.469	0.943	1.025	0.159
	0.011	0.023	0.208	0.005	0.01	0.316

the returns on the value portfolios confirm the authors' expectations that the value strategy struggled during the former period but strongly came into its own during the correction period. The other finding that is worth noting is that the authors have confirmed that despite the outperformance of value portfolios during this period, the majority of cheap (top quinitile) stocks underperform the market. Applying a one-year holding period the authors found that on average only 46 per cent of their value stocks as ranked by book-to-market, outperformed the market – which is consistent with previous evidence on this same issue for other markets (Bird and Gerlach, 2003).

Value strategies across each European market

The authors conducted the same analysis at the individual country level as was conducted at the combined level, and found in general that value investing performed well in each country. It should be noted, however, that the sample size for some of the countries, such as Italy, the Netherlands, Spain and Switzerland, is likely to mitigate against the possibility of finding significant results in countries. The findings for each country are reported in Table 6.1.7, where stocks are sorted by book-to-market with the returns being in local currency and calculated for equally weighted portfolios. The book-to-market criterion produces a positive spread between the returns on the cheap and expensive portfolios varying from around 5 per cent per annum for Spanish and Swiss markets to as much as 25 per cent per annum for the UK market. The strongest results in terms of statistical significance were in the larger markets (UK, France and Germany) plus Italy. In each country there is a fairly smooth transition in returns across the quintile portfolios, with a differentiation in the return between the bottom and top quintile. The overall findings provide confirmation that the outperformance previously seen at the combined level was mainly due to stocks selection within the seven markets.

The stocks have very similar characteristics across the seven countries – with the cheap portfolios on average being composed of stocks that are relatively small and illiquid with poor recent market performance (ie 6-month price momentum). The performance of the book-to-market strategy for the seven countries where portfolios are formed on a market capitalisation basis are reported in Table 6.1.8. These results, which correct to a certain extent for the small-cap bias and, to a lesser extent, for the lower liquidity, indicate that performance remains strong in both the UK and France but has significantly eroded in Germany. In

Table 6.1.7 Equally weighted returns (per cent per month) for book-to-market portfolios (individual markets, January 1990 to June 2002)

Holding period	bm1	bm2	bm3	bm4	bm5	bm5 – bm1
Panel 1: German stocks sorted by book-to-market						
12 months	−0.376	0.019	0.198	0.213	0.28	0.656
	0.532	0.96	0.524	0.49	0.501	0.226
24 months	−0.59	0.07	0.313	0.357	0.421	1.011
	0.302	0.854	0.304	0.235	0.267	0.019
36 months	−0.508	0.134	0.382	0.461	0.481	0.989
	0.339	0.713	0.198	0.135	0.189	0.01
Panel 2: French stocks sorted by book-to-market						
12 months	0.867	1.124	1.25	1.315	2.716	1.849
	0.259	0.02	0.003	0.001	0	0.022
24 months	1.101	1.194	1.304	1.667	2.697	1.596
	0.131	0.014	0.003	0.001	0	0.019
36 months	1.279	1.369	1.486	2.04	2.76	1.482
	0.073	0.007	0.001	0.001	0	0.015
Panel 3: Italian stocks sorted by book-to-market						
12 months	0.808	1.003	0.945	1.903	1.733	0.925
	0.229	0.084	0.129	0.019	0.021	0.062
24 months	0.996	1.076	1.141	1.984	1.72	0.724
	0.137	0.09	0.084	0.009	0.022	0.065
36 months	1.241	1.368	1.473	2.198	1.939	0.698
	0.066	0.034	0.023	0.002	0.01	0.053
Panel 4: Netherlands stocks sorted by book-to-market						
12 months	0.987	1.073	1.079	1.074	1.538	0.551
	0.076	0.018	0.007	0.011	0.011	0.274
24 months	0.994	1.022	1.243	1.229	1.518	0.525
	0.088	0.039	0.004	0.004	0.011	0.253
36 months	1.048	1.3	1.401	1.325	1.778	0.73
	0.076	0.007	0.001	0.003	0.004	0.131
Panel 5: Spanish stocks by book-to-market						
12 months	1.105	1.406	1.623	1.511	1.532	0.428
	0.082	0.013	0.002	0.008	0.007	0.181
24 months	1.297	1.5	1.666	1.429	1.576	0.28
	0.049	0.01	0.003	0.013	0.009	0.383
36 months	1.748	1.836	2.054	1.746	2.244	0.496
	0.005	0	0	0.001	0.001	0.365

(*continued*)

Table 6.1.7 Continued

Holding period	bm1	bm2	bm3	bm4	bm5	bm5 – bm1
Panel 6: Swiss stocks by book-to-market						
12 months	0.99	0.967	0.945	1.187	1.199	0.209
	0.065	0.054	0.073	0.022	0.015	0.52
24 months	1.013	1.012	1.04	1.254	1.413	0.4
	0.068	0.052	0.057	0.029	0.005	0.177
36 months	1.136	1.177	1.164	1.417	1.537	0.402
	0.043	0.027	0.034	0.014	0.002	0.158
Panel 7: United Kingdom stocks by book-to-market						
12 months	0.674	0.842	0.995	1.081	2.3	1.626
	0.332	0.08	0.012	0.006	0.025	0.095
24 months	0.555	0.726	0.943	1.215	2.293	1.738
	0.431	0.136	0.024	0.009	0.021	0.057
36 months	0.579	0.745	0.947	1.258	2.481	1.902
	0.407	0.113	0.015	0.005	0.029	0.068

Table 6.1.8 Market-weighted returns (per cent per month) for book-to-market portfolios (individual markets, January 1990 to June 2002)

Holding period	bm1	bm2	bm3	bm4	bm5	bm5 – bm1
Panel 1: German stocks sorted by book-to-market						
12 months	0.381	0.741	0.821	0.952	0.735	0.354
	0.553	0.103	0.019	0.018	0.065	0.517
24 months	0.529	0.699	0.963	0.947	0.911	0.383
	0.416	0.122	0.012	0.018	0.026	0.466
36 months	0.805	0.891	1.103	1.141	1.066	0.262
	0.189	0.033	0.002	0.003	0.01	0.594
Panel 2: French stocks sorted by book-to-market						
12 months	1.074	1.194	1.113	1.063	1.745	0.671
	0.031	0.007	0.013	0.021	0.002	0.111
24 months	1.066	1.207	1.269	1.047	1.717	0.651
	0.043	0.013	0.003	0.038	0.002	0.081
36 months	1.051	1.383	1.34	1.313	1.854	0.804
	0.054	0.008	0.001	0.02	0.001	0.011
Panel 3: Italian stocks sorted by book-to-market						
12 months	0.993	1.641	1.318	1.193	1.192	0.198
	0.183	0.014	0.04	0.072	0.136	0.721
24 months	1.195	1.76	1.447	1.269	1.289	0.094
	0.098	0.017	0.033	0.067	0.123	0.858
36 months	1.426	1.888	1.719	1.551	1.647	0.221
	0.049	0.009	0.011	0.021	0.043	0.676

(continued)

Table 6.1.8 Continued

Holding period	bm1	bm2	bm3	bm4	bm5	bm5 – bm1
Panel 4: Netherlands stocks sorted by book-to-market						
12 months	0.711	1.312	1.394	1.462	0.789	0.077
	0.315	0	0.001	0.003	0.215	0.9
24 months	0.943	1.262	1.382	1.438	0.874	−0.069
	0.16	0.001	0.001	0.002	0.148	0.894
36 months	0.942	1.456	1.521	1.446	1.256	0.314
	0.157	0	0.001	0.006	0.03	0.534
Panel 5: Spanish stocks by book-to-market						
12 months	0.936	1.432	1.607	1.697	1.769	0.833
	0.135	0.002	0.001	0.004	0.007	0.111
24 months	1.218	1.262	1.537	1.676	1.663	0.445
	0.063	0.012	0.002	0.003	0.014	0.388
36 months	1.588	1.511	1.706	1.885	1.879	0.291
	0.012	0.001	0	0	0.004	0.573
Panel 6: Swiss stocks by book-to-market						
12 months	0.962	1.407	1.393	1.542	1.418	0.456
	0.022	0	0.005	0.003	0.01	0.3
24 months	0.818	1.488	1.281	1.608	1.499	0.681
	0.065	0	0.007	0.007	0.009	0.126
36 months	0.797	1.463	1.269	1.709	1.48	0.683
	0.074	0.001	0.012	0.007	0.012	0.1
Panel 7: United Kingdom stocks by book-to-market						
12 months	0.711	0.768	0.874	0.972	1.405	0.694
	0.092	0.01	0.006	0.009	0.001	0.149
24 months	0.476	0.661	0.953	0.972	1.443	0.967
	0.293	0.041	0.004	0.011	0	0.037
36 months	0.446	0.491	0.955	0.898	1.403	0.957
	0.338	0.144	0.003	0.016	0	0.044

the smaller markets, the success of the value strategies has if anything strengthened in both Spain and Switzerland, but has been severely eroded in both Italy and the Netherlands with the portfolios being formed using market value weights.

In general, the previous favourable finding with respect to the performance of value investing across a combination of the major European market during our sample period transcends to the individual countries, although it suffers somewhat from the smaller sample size in some markets. There is a similar trend across the various markets with respect to the success rate at the individual stock level – 46 per cent of all cheap (top quintile) outperform their market over a 12-month holding period in France, Switzerland and the UK, while this figure is slightly higher (47 per cent) in the other four markets, confirming at the country level that value strategies outperform despite the fact that the majority of cheap value stocks underperform.

Price momentum strategies across all markets

Momentum is the second form of investment strategy evaluated in this paper. In this sub-section the authors consider price momentum where stocks are ranked and portfolios formed on the basis of a stock's returns over a prior period. In this study 6-month and 12-month periods have been chosen as the prior periods, on the basis that they incorporate the range over which other authors have found strong continuation in market returns.

Table 6.1.9 shows the returns on the portfolios formed applying these two momentum criteria. Highlighting the immediacy of this strategy, the performance tends to be very good, realising sizable and significant added value over holding periods of 3 months or less. The 6-month strategy continues to maintain good performance for holding periods of up to 9 months, with the past winners (top quintile) outperforming the losers (bottom quintile) by in excess of 7 per cent over this holding period. In the case of the 12-month strategy, the optimum holding period is less than 6 months with the outperformance of past winners over past losers being around 4 per cent over a 6-month holding period. In both cases the short-term added value quickly reverses itself and becomes negative over periods beyond 24 months for the 6-month strategy and beyond 12 months for the 12-months strategy.

The characteristics of the price momentum portfolios are reported in Table 6.1.10. The typical winning (top quintile) portfolio is composed of stocks which are expensive, of above average size and very heavily traded. In contrast, the losing portfolio (bottom quintile) is composed of cheap stocks, which are relatively small and have been experiencing low turnover. As most of the potential added value is with the winning stocks, there seems little reason to be concerned with potential problems in implementing the strategy in terms of being able to acquire the desired stocks. The market weighted returns will, however, still be of interest, because other writers have found that correcting for any size bias actually increases the performance. These market-weighted returns, as reported in Table 6.1.11, indicate that the potential performance of a price momentum strategy is slightly lower in the case of market weighted portfolios (compared to equally weighted portfolios) over holding periods of up to 3 months but much greater for holding periods

Table 6.1.9 Equally weighted returns (per cent per month) across momentum portfolios created using 6- and 12-month price momentum (combined markets, January 1990 to June 2002)

Panel 1: Sorting by 6-month price momentum

Holding period	pmS1	pmS2	pmS3	pmS4	pmS5	pmS5 – pmS1
1 month	0.209	0.239	0.563	0.884	1.599	1.39
	0.754	0.542	0.077	0.005	0.002	0.014
3 months	0.317	0.319	0.698	0.896	1.509	1.192
	0.643	0.41	0.029	0.004	0.001	0.032
6 months	0.536	0.365	0.754	0.919	1.392	0.856
	0.472	0.326	0.014	0.001	0.001	0.162
9 months	0.743	0.677	0.952	1.097	1.503	0.761
	0.281	0.079	0.002	0	0	0.148
12 months	0.979	0.738	1.002	1.092	1.403	0.424
	0.171	0.044	0.001	0	0.001	0.441
24 months	1.325	0.962	1.064	1.024	1.105	–0.219
	0.059	0.011	0.001	0.001	0.012	0.655
36 months	1.571	1.077	1.168	1.034	1.044	–0.528
	0.022	0.003	0	0.001	0.014	0.244
48 months	1.285	0.854	0.922	0.835	0.817	–0.468
	0.061	0.018	0.006	0.01	0.056	0.298

Panel 2: Sorting by 12-month price momentum

Holding period	pmL1	pmL2	pmL3	pmL4	pmL5	pmL5 – pmL1
1 month	0.146	0.157	0.53	1.038	1.668	1.522
	0.82	0.676	0.088	0.001	0.001	0.003
3 months	0.387	0.292	0.608	0.99	1.547	1.16
	0.559	0.444	0.051	0.001	0.001	0.029
6 months	0.725	0.391	0.654	0.946	1.367	0.642
	0.323	0.281	0.026	0.001	0.002	0.302
9 months	1.182	0.678	0.863	1.051	1.363	0.181
	0.12	0.055	0.003	0	0.002	0.779
12 months	1.416	0.79	0.925	1.042	1.206	–0.21
	0.068	0.019	0.001	0	0.007	0.749
24 months	1.586	1.064	1.028	0.995	0.938	–0.647
	0.027	0.003	0.001	0.002	0.039	0.217
36 months	1.893	1.158	1.108	1.013	0.876	–1.017
	0.017	0.001	0	0.001	0.043	0.095
48 months	1.536	0.909	0.872	0.83	0.695	–0.84
	0.018	0.004	0.001	0.004	0.043	0.092

Table 6.1.10 Characteristics of price momentum portfolios (combined markets, January 1990 to June 2002)

6-months price momentum				
Portfolio	**Book-to-market**	**6-month price momentum (per cent per month)**	**Trading volume (proportion of total)**	**Size (decile rank)**
pmS1	0.6174	−5.768	0.1696	3.9698
pmS2	0.4536	−1.3652	0.1253	5.3826
pmS3	0.4192	0.6272	0.1327	5.8993
pmS4	0.3742	2.6466	0.2235	6.2852
pmS5	0.3212	7.783	0.3489	5.9966
12-months price momentum				
Portfolio	**Book-to-market**	**6-month price momentum (per cent per month)**	**Trading volume (proportion of total)**	**Size (decile rank)**
pmL1	0.7043	−3.9803	0.177	3.6544
pmL2	0.4865	−0.732	0.1092	5.2215
pmL3	0.4304	0.697	0.1292	5.9732
pmL4	0.3702	2.1305	0.2252	6.4396
pmL5	0.279	5.7852	0.3594	6.3624

beyond 3 months. For example the returns of the losing portfolio under a 6-month strategy for a 9-month holding period are now around 1.4 per cent, while that for the winning portfolio is around 12 per cent. Further, this 10 per cent differential is maintained beyond holding periods in excess of 12 months, which highlights that forming market weighted portfolios extends the productive life of a price momentum strategy. The authors would suggest that the findings largely support those of previous writers, that any attempt to control for size biases actually improves the performance of price momentum portfolios. Another point that can be noted from the findings is that the majority of the added value from the market weighted price momentum strategies comes from shorting the losing stocks.

In obtaining the results reported above, the authors simply pooled the stocks. Thus, the portfolio of winners (losers) will be overrepresented with stocks from those markets where the market returns were greatest (smallest). In order to control for any country bias the authors also ranked the stocks across all the markets on a country-corrected basis. The results for the country-corrected portfolios are reported in Table 6.1.12. Again the evidence is a little mixed, with the country-corrected

Table 6.1.11 Market-weighted returns (per cent per month) for price momentum portfolios (combined markets, January 1990 to June 2002)

Panel 1: Sorting by 6-month price momentum

Holding period	pmS1	pmS2	pmS3	pmS4	pmS5	pmS5 – pmS1
1 month	0.436	0.734	0.895	0.825	0.952	0.517
	0.501	0.075	0.004	0.009	0.021	0.345
3 months	0.115	0.748	0.894	0.865	1.013	0.898
	0.86	0.058	0.002	0.004	0.008	0.083
6 months	−0.067	0.631	0.849	0.94	1.03	1.097
	0.914	0.1	0.003	0.001	0.004	0.025
9 months	0.154	0.754	1.005	1.102	1.259	1.106
	0.794	0.048	0	0	0.001	0.016
12 months	0.279	0.744	1.007	1.055	1.153	0.875
	0.626	0.049	0	0	0.002	0.043
24 months	0.601	0.847	1.003	0.981	0.944	0.343
	0.233	0.018	0.001	0.001	0.019	0.264
36 months	0.762	0.931	0.978	0.906	0.879	0.117
	0.086	0.005	0.001	0.003	0.029	0.578
48 months	0.655	0.779	0.842	0.787	0.764	0.109
	0.143	0.021	0.007	0.014	0.058	0.568

Panel 2: Sorting by 12-month price momentum

Holding period	pmL1	pmL2	pmL3	pmL4	pmL5	pmL5 – pmL1
1 month	0.159	0.514	0.875	0.894	1.029	0.87
	0.812	0.252	0.008	0.002	0.023	0.163
3 months	−0.043	0.512	0.795	0.917	1.053	1.096
	0.947	0.252	0.009	0.001	0.014	0.073
6 months	0.084	0.498	0.761	0.904	1.009	0.925
	0.893	0.248	0.011	0	0.014	0.114
9 months	0.472	0.801	0.949	1.042	1.098	0.626
	0.42	0.052	0.001	0	0.009	0.265
12 months	0.602	0.839	0.97	1.009	0.985	0.384
	0.273	0.032	0.001	0	0.023	0.464
24 months	0.852	0.916	1.033	0.98	0.825	−0.027
	0.064	0.011	0.001	0.001	0.066	0.94
36 months	0.989	1.011	1.015	0.924	0.779	−0.21
	0.016	0.003	0.001	0.002	0.073	0.441
48 months	0.846	0.844	0.83	0.821	0.684	−0.162
	0.041	0.014	0.008	0.008	0.112	0.508

Table 6.1.12 Market-weighted returns (per cent per month) for country-corrected price momentum portfolios (combined markets, January 1990 to June 2002)

Holding period	pmS1	pmS2	pmS3	pmS4	pmS5	pmS5 – pmS1
Panel 1: Sorting by 6-month country corrected price momentum						
1 month	0.176	0.837	0.721	1.004	0.97	0.794
	0.772	0.042	0.024	0.002	0.02	0.119
3 months	0.005	0.713	0.795	0.872	1.14	1.136
	0.994	0.065	0.007	0.003	0.004	0.018
6 months	–0.026	0.662	0.796	0.895	1.112	1.137
	0.964	0.077	0.004	0.001	0.002	0.01
9 months	0.198	0.773	0.961	1.079	1.314	1.115
	0.715	0.034	0.001	0	0	0.01
12 months	0.318	0.759	0.986	1.062	1.169	0.85
	0.548	0.037	0	0	0.002	0.032
24 months	0.667	0.862	0.982	0.991	0.938	0.272
	0.154	0.014	0.001	0.001	0.017	0.283
36 months	0.821	0.897	0.962	0.94	0.866	0.045
	0.046	0.007	0.001	0.002	0.028	0.786
48 months	0.71	0.75	0.825	0.801	0.749	0.04
	0.09	0.025	0.009	0.011	0.056	0.782
Panel 2: Sorting by 12-month country-corrected price momentum						
1 month	0.087	0.393	0.821	0.815	1.229	1.143
	0.892	0.394	0.005	0.006	0.005	0.073
3 months	–0.141	0.416	0.764	0.828	1.26	1.401
	0.825	0.325	0.006	0.003	0.002	0.026
6 months	0.076	0.423	0.753	0.86	1.116	1.04
	0.899	0.302	0.006	0.001	0.005	0.068
9 months	0.492	0.701	0.958	1.019	1.166	0.674
	0.38	0.08	0.001	0	0.004	0.213
12 months	0.601	0.776	0.982	0.986	1.044	0.443
	0.251	0.043	0	0	0.012	0.372
24 months	0.863	0.912	1.028	0.943	0.852	–0.01
	0.049	0.01	0	0.002	0.045	0.974
36 months	0.986	0.972	0.998	0.925	0.788	–0.198
	0.012	0.003	0	0.002	0.057	0.398
48 months	0.863	0.822	0.815	0.791	0.706	–0.157
	0.03	0.015	0.007	0.012	0.088	0.458

portfolios performing slightly better over holding periods of up to 3 months but slightly worse over longer holding periods. The authors' general finding is that removing the country bias has little effect on the performance of the price momentum portfolios, however, suggesting that all the added value is coming from stock selection rather than as a consequence of introducing any country bias.

Price momentum strategies across each European market

The next step in the analysis is to examine the performance of the price momentum strategies on a country-by-country basis. Table 6.1.13 shows the performance of the 6-month strategy over several holding periods based on market weighting the stocks within the portfolios. Consistent with the findings for the combined markets, a combination of 6-month momentum with a 9-month holding period performs very well in all but the French and Spanish markets. In the other five markets, a long-short portfolio of winners and losers would have returned upwards of 9 per cent over a 9-month holding period, but even in the French and Spanish markets there exists some added value potential and a smooth gradation in returns across the quintile portfolios. Indeed, the strength

Table 6.1.13 Market-weighted returns (per cent per month) for 6-month price momentum portfolios (individual markets, January 1990 to June 2002)

Holding period	pmS1	pmS2	pmS3	pmS4	pmS5	pmS5 – pmS1
Panel 1: German stocks sorted by price momentum						
6 months	–0.793	0.26	0.502	0.601	0.819	1.612
	0.272	0.533	0.122	0.022	0.036	0.004
9 months	–0.606	0.435	0.669	0.831	1.028	1.633
	0.371	0.291	0.038	0.001	0.011	0.001
12 months	–0.571	0.47	0.706	0.82	0.913	1.484
	0.392	0.243	0.03	0.002	0.023	0.002
Panel 2: French stocks sorted by price momentum						
6 months	0.566	0.615	0.888	1	0.928	0.363
	0.304	0.133	0.014	0.002	0.022	0.389
9 months	0.851	0.796	1.083	1.188	1.117	0.266
	0.115	0.044	0.001	0	0.007	0.486
12 months	0.899	0.911	1.116	1.149	1.142	0.243
	0.1	0.023	0.001	0	0.007	0.523
Panel 3: Italian stocks sorted by price momentum						
6 months	0.434	0.665	0.8	0.779	1.159	0.724
	0.534	0.261	0.163	0.151	0.101	0.183
9 months	0.616	0.863	1.023	1.081	1.382	0.765
	0.347	0.135	0.081	0.046	0.052	0.119
12 months	0.722	0.995	1.076	1.237	1.368	0.645
	0.259	0.084	0.061	0.027	0.056	0.167

(continued)

Table 6.1.13 Continued

Holding period	pmS1	pmS2	pmS3	pmS4	pmS5	pmS5 – pmS1
Panel 4: Netherlands stocks sorted by price momentum						
6 months	0.376	0.695	1.369	1.165	1.186	0.81
	0.568	0.077	0	0	0.006	0.164
9 months	0.447	0.863	1.468	1.364	1.299	0.852
	0.511	0.027	0	0	0.003	0.159
12 months	0.432	0.951	1.46	1.338	1.27	0.838
	0.517	0.012	0	0	0.005	0.158
Panel 5: Spanish stocks by price momentum						
6 months	0.447	0.546	0.773	0.711	0.716	0.269
	0.526	0.324	0.136	0.112	0.152	0.598
9 months	0.794	0.828	0.975	1.168	1.08	0.286
	0.215	0.109	0.039	0.005	0.027	0.522
12 months	0.885	0.893	1.105	1.178	1.073	0.189
	0.146	0.073	0.016	0.004	0.025	0.651
Panel 6: Swiss stocks by price momentum						
6 months	0.757	0.646	0.802	1.302	1.475	0.718
	0.102	0.123	0.031	0.001	0.002	0.135
9 months	0.759	0.765	1.128	1.454	1.617	0.858
	0.097	0.072	0.002	0	0.001	0.053
12 months	0.858	0.836	1.132	1.445	1.477	0.619
	0.051	0.043	0.002	0	0.001	0.112
Panel 7: United Kingdom stocks by price momentum						
6 months	−0.393	0.503	0.794	0.859	1.142	1.535
	0.583	0.245	0.009	0.005	0.001	0.015
9 months	−0.15	0.538	0.856	0.997	1.313	1.462
	0.821	0.208	0.003	0.001	0	0.011
12 months	−0.135	0.467	0.79	0.903	1.141	1.277
	0.835	0.281	0.007	0.002	0.002	0.022

of the finding across the individual markets is consistent with the previous evidence, which confirms that the added value from price momentum is largely attributable to the performance of price momentum within the individual markets.

Earnings momentum strategies across all markets

The authors' two measures of earnings momentum are based upon analysts forecasts: the first being based on the volume of analysts changing their forecast about a firm's earnings in a particular direction (agreement) over a 2-month period and the second based on the magnitude of the change in the average forecast by the analysts (forecast revision) over a 2-month period. Table 6.1.14 shows the returns from both of these strategies where the portfolios are formed on an equally weighted basis.

Table 6.1.14 Equally weighted returns (per cent per month) for earnings momentum portfolios (combined markets, January 1990 to June 2002)

Panel 1: Sorting by Agreement

Holding period	agree1	agree2	agree3	agree4	agree5	agree5 – agree1
1 month	–0.168	0.383	0.521	0.992	1.302	1.471
	0.708	0.372	0.242	0.014	0.001	0
3 months	0.007	0.483	0.402	1.032	1.164	1.157
	0.987	0.24	0.349	0.011	0.003	0
6 months	0.151	0.539	0.481	0.915	1.032	0.881
	0.724	0.17	0.264	0.018	0.005	0
9 months	0.437	0.757	0.829	1.086	1.148	0.711
	0.295	0.045	0.112	0.004	0.002	0
12 months	0.53	0.784	0.971	1.08	1.136	0.606
	0.197	0.036	0.108	0.004	0.002	0
24 months	0.658	0.853	1.018	0.953	1.027	0.368
	0.123	0.027	0.07	0.014	0.006	0
36 months	0.773	0.927	0.955	1.033	0.986	0.213
	0.051	0.013	0.048	0.005	0.007	0.004
48 months	0.538	0.706	0.665	0.802	0.754	0.216
	0.172	0.052	0.15	0.029	0.041	0.001

Panel 2: Sorting by Forecast Revision

Holding period	fcr1	fcr2	fcr3	fcr4	fcr5	fcr5 – fcr1
1 month	0.13	0.434	0.801	1.046	0.642	0.512
	0.793	0.25	0.027	0.004	0.137	0
3 months	0.226	0.532	0.794	0.945	0.643	0.416
	0.626	0.149	0.024	0.01	0.144	0
6 months	0.271	0.563	0.773	0.9	0.731	0.46
	0.547	0.11	0.024	0.008	0.099	0
9 months	0.617	0.768	1.008	1.072	0.937	0.32
	0.177	0.025	0.004	0.001	0.038	0.001
12 months	0.656	0.801	1.1	1.068	0.983	0.327
	0.139	0.018	0.005	0.001	0.032	0.011
24 months	0.755	0.848	1.007	0.983	0.945	0.19
	0.09	0.019	0.008	0.005	0.041	0.152
36 months	0.857	0.916	0.981	0.986	0.959	0.102
	0.037	0.009	0.006	0.004	0.024	0.313
48 months	0.615	0.666	0.74	0.764	0.719	0.103
	0.123	0.054	0.04	0.028	0.086	0.213

The results for the portfolios formed using agreement (agree) as the criterion proved to be particularly strong, especially for periods of up to 12 months. There is a smooth transition in the returns realised across the quintile portfolios with the difference in the performance between the low and high momentum portfolios being 7.5 per cent per annum and highly significant. The performance of the portfolios based on the magnitude of the forecast revisions (fcr) are much weaker and less consistent across the quintile portfolios although they still give rise to an outperformance of 4 per cent per annum over a 12-month holding period.

Again, the authors tracked the characteristics of the portfolios formed on the two criteria (see Table 6.1.15). In the case of agreement, the stocks that most analysts have been revising upwards prove to be slightly above average in terms of both size and valuation (as measured by book-to-market) with good recent market performance on fairly average volume. The characteristics of the favoured portfolio by forecast revisions are similar but slightly less extreme than those for agreement. Given that the authors found that the size bias in the case of price momentum actually was detrimental to overall performance, they also

Table 6.1.15 Characteristics of earnings momentum portfolios (combined markets, January 1990 to June 2002)

Agreement

Portfolio	Book-to-market	6-month price momentum (per cent per month)	Trading volume (proportion of total)	Size (decile rank)
agree1	0.4635	−0.9404	0.2723	4.9732
agree2	0.3785	0.2401	0.2075	6.7416
agree3	0.3954	0.6218	0.0957	4.2886
agree4	0.409	1.2033	0.1935	4.8893
agree5	0.3216	2.3806	0.231	6.3658

Forecasts revisions

Portfolio	Book-to-market	6-month price momentum (per cent per month)	Trading volume (proportion of total)	Size (decile rank)
mag1	0.4464	−0.3386	0.2507	5.3893
mag2	0.3917	0.3154	0.1283	5.6376
mag3	0.3996	0.8682	0.168	4.9027
mag4	0.3592	1.4107	0.1524	5.6779
mag5	0.3791	1.3008	0.3006	5.7483

investigated the impact on the earnings momentum findings of forming portfolios using market weights. The results are reported in Table 6.1.16. In contrast to the findings for the price momentum portfolios, the separation in the returns for the earnings momentum portfolios are lower where the portfolios are market-weighted, rather than equally

Table 6.1.16 Market-weighted returns (per cent per month) for earnings momentum portfolios (combined markets, January 1990 to June 2002)

Panel 1: Sorting by Agreement

Holding period	agree1	agree2	agree3	agree4	agree5	agree5 – agree1
1 month	0.345	0.611	0.813	1.047	1.202	0.858
	0.41	0.063	0.05	0.002	0	0.004
3 months	0.418	0.717	0.519	0.989	1.098	0.68
	0.288	0.027	0.133	0.004	0	0.012
6 months	0.483	0.739	0.516	0.87	0.981	0.498
	0.209	0.019	0.128	0.005	0.001	0.045
9 months	0.684	0.931	0.664	1.03	1.13	0.446
	0.063	0.004	0.059	0.001	0	0.036
12 months	0.655	0.93	0.574	1.025	1.116	0.461
	0.069	0.004	0.124	0.001	0	0.017
24 months	0.672	0.886	0.583	0.944	1.062	0.39
	0.072	0.01	0.134	0.004	0.001	0.005
36 months	0.692	0.872	0.553	0.907	0.966	0.275
	0.058	0.01	0.138	0.005	0.002	0.013
48 months	0.588	0.75	0.458	0.793	0.823	0.234
	0.109	0.03	0.222	0.02	0.013	0.005

Panel 2: Sorting by Forecast Revision

Holding period	fcr1	fcr2	fcr3	fcr4	fcr5	fcr5 – fcr1
1 month	0.724	0.609	1	1.073	0.808	0.083
	0.068	0.08	0.003	0.001	0.011	0.656
3 months	0.712	0.735	0.862	0.928	0.785	0.073
	0.031	0.027	0.004	0.003	0.021	0.484
6 months	0.693	0.748	0.826	0.898	0.797	0.104
	0.04	0.02	0.004	0.002	0.015	0.094
9 months	0.906	0.938	1.011	1.067	0.957	0.051
	0.006	0.003	0	0	0.003	0.322
12 months	0.858	0.953	0.96	1.039	0.94	0.082
	0.011	0.003	0.001	0	0.003	0.065
24 months	0.86	0.911	0.901	0.983	0.897	0.037
	0.015	0.009	0.003	0.001	0.008	0.327
36 months	0.841	0.884	0.85	0.921	0.861	0.02
	0.016	0.011	0.005	0.003	0.01	0.52
48 months	0.717	0.752	0.749	0.779	0.746	0.029
	0.043	0.036	0.02	0.018	0.03	0.262

weighted. In the case of the agreement portfolios, the added value remains significant but is reduced from 7.5 per cent per annum to 5.7 per cent per annum over a 12-month holding period. In the case of the forecast revision portfolios, however, any potential added value almost entirely disappears.[5] It would appear that the volume of analysts revising their forecasts is much more related to future price movements than is the magnitude of their average revision.

As with the other criteria, when applied across all the countries, it could be that some of the added value is coming from biasing the portfolios towards particular markets rather than from stock selection. In order to evaluate this possibility, the authors also ranked stocks and formed portfolios on a country-corrected basis. Although not reported here, the returns on these portfolios were almost identical to those reported in Table 6.1.14 (equally weighted) and Table 6.1.16 (market weighted), which suggests that almost all the added value was coming from stock selection across the various markets.

Earnings momentum strategies across each European market

The authors evaluated the performance of earnings momentum as measured by agreement at the individual country level, the findings are reported in Table 6.1.17. The markets in which agreement would seem to have worked best as the criterion for forming portfolios are France, Spain, Switzerland and the UK. A long-short portfolio across each of these four markets returns between 6 per cent per annum and 8 per cent per annum over a 12-month holding period, which would appear to be optimum for investment strategies based upon agreement. In the case of the other three markets, an earnings momentum strategy based on agreement would appear to hold out some potential worthy of further consideration, especially when one considers the option of combining an earnings momentum strategy with some other strategy.

Summary and concluding comments

The objective of this paper has been to undertake a thorough evaluation of the performance of value and momentum investment across the major European markets over the period from January 1990 to June 2002, a major motivation being to extend our knowledge of the performance of such strategies across a widening range of markets and over different time periods. Such knowledge enables one to obtain a better

Table 6.1.17 Market-weighted returns (per cent per month) for earnings momentum portfolios (agree) (individual markets, January 1990 to June 2002)

Holding period	agree1	agree2	agree3	agree4	agree5	agree5 – agree1
Panel 1: German stocks sorted by Agreement						
6 months	0.254	0.645	0.084	0.086	0.843	0.59
	0.675	0.139	0.811	0.861	0.064	0.062
12 months	0.555	0.857	0.212	0.115	0.863	0.308
	0.314	0.041	0.554	0.823	0.066	0.254
24 months	0.696	0.903	0.396	0.298	0.803	0.107
	0.19	0.033	0.245	0.573	0.108	0.666
Panel 2: French stocks sorted by agreement						
6 months	0.516	0.811	0.733	1.108	1.297	0.78
	0.368	0.079	0.114	0.016	0.003	0.019
12 months	0.859	1.067	1.078	1.204	1.446	0.586
	0.122	0.024	0.015	0.01	0.001	0.048
24 months	1.034	0.977	1.03	1.112	1.342	0.308
	0.07	0.057	0.021	0.022	0.003	0.159
Panel 3: Italian stocks sorted by agreement						
6 months	0.83	1.064	0.84	1.355	1.192	0.361
	0.176	0.039	0.023	0.011	0.004	0.437
12 months	1.177	1.185	1.036	1.257	1.347	0.17
	0.05	0.027	0.005	0.01	0.002	0.679
24 months	1.116	1.174	1.099	1.131	1.396	0.281
	0.055	0.024	0.01	0.04	0.002	0.315
Panel 4: Netherlands stocks sorted by agreement						
6 months	0.83	1.064	0.84	1.355	1.192	0.361
	0.176	0.039	0.023	0.011	0.004	0.437
12 months	1.177	1.185	1.036	1.257	1.347	0.17
	0.05	0.027	0.005	0.01	0.002	0.679
24 months	1.116	1.174	1.099	1.131	1.396	0.281
	0.055	0.024	0.01	0.04	0.002	0.315
Panel 5: Spanish stocks by agreement						
6 months	0.562	0.925	1.304	1.114	1.265	0.703
	0.403	0.074	0.03	0.055	0.02	0.041
12 months	0.938	1.483	1.413	1.614	1.551	0.613
	0.106	0.004	0.01	0.004	0.004	0.018
24 months	1.243	1.462	1.44	1.525	1.624	0.381
	0.048	0.008	0.013	0.007	0.006	0.097

(continued)

Table 6.1.17 Continued

Holding period	agree1	agree2	agree3	agree4	agree5	agree5 – agree1
Panel 6: Swiss stocks by agreement						
6 months	0.45	0.65	0.8	0.896	1.289	0.839
	0.398	0.2	0.103	0.108	0.024	0
12 months	0.864	0.953	0.976	1.095	1.335	0.47
	0.116	0.071	0.056	0.046	0.019	0.003
24 months	1.132	1.044	1.078	1.201	1.189	0.057
	0.053	0.062	0.044	0.034	0.041	0.634
Panel 7: United Kingdom stocks by agreement						
6 months	0.427	0.62	0.72	0.658	0.868	0.441
	0.258	0.05	0.077	0.048	0.005	0.056
12 months	0.498	0.726	0.635	0.901	1.011	0.513
	0.16	0.025	0.154	0.003	0.001	0.006
24 months	0.441	0.678	0.494	0.821	0.898	0.457
	0.249	0.055	0.294	0.011	0.004	0.002

understanding of market behaviour and potential anomalies that can in turn give rise to superior investment management strategies.

The authors' general finding is that value and momentum strategies would have performed well over the period studied both if applied across the combination of all markets evaluated and, in most instances, at the individual market level. Of the various criteria used to form value portfolios, both book-to-market and sales-to-price performed well and generated added value when applied over holding periods of up to 36 months. The stocks favoured had a small capitalisation bias which, when controlled, resulted in a reduction in, but far from complete erosion of, the added value associated with these implementations of a value strategy. The momentum strategies also meet with a high level of success, although this was confined to much shorter holding periods. Again there was a small-cap bias in the well performing momentum portfolios, with attempts to control for this bias resulting in even greater added value in the case of price momentum, although it did erode, but far from completely remove, the added value from the earnings momentum portfolios.

Of course most studies raise more questions than they can answer. In the case of this paper, one obvious question stems from the fact that the authors have limited their evaluation of value and momentum to only ranking stocks and forming portfolios based on a single criterion. A number of writers have found that using multiple criteria to form portfolios can result in even better performance. An obvious extension, then, is to evaluate portfolios composed on multiple criteria (eg two value criteria or a value criterion with a momentum criterion).

A second challenge is to determine how best to tackle the dilemma of all value investors – the fact that the majority of stocks in which they invest underperform the market. This suggests that the combination of some quality measure with the value criteria has the potential of improving the hit rate from value investing which would translate into a significant increase in added value. Finally, there is the complex issue as to why value and momentum strategies continue to add value, especially as they are well known and easy to implement. As suggested earlier, the success of value strategies is possibly easier to understand as it may just be a premium to compensate for the discomfort associated with holding value stocks. Momentum is a bit more difficult to understand as it seems just another outworking of the market under-reacting to new information, which is one aspect of market behaviour for which the authors are still seeking an explanation.

Acknowledgments

The authors wish to thank GMO Woolley, a London-based quantitative investment manager who kindly supplied the fundamental and return data for this study. They would also like to thank Thomson Financial for providing the analysts' forecast data, available through I/B/E/S.

Notes

1. These returns are based upon the S&P Europe 350 index measured in British pounds.
2. The first comprehensive work undertaken in this area was by Bachelier (1900).
3. The forecast at each point in time is calculated for a constant 12-month period. For example, if it is 6 months from the end of the next financial year, the 12-month forecast is calculated as one-half the one-year forecast and one-half the two-year forecast.
4. When forming portfolios within one country, the returns on the portfolio are calculated in local currency. Where the portfolios are formed across all seven countries, the returns are all calculated in British pounds.
5. Although not reported here, the findings for the market-weighted size-adjusted portfolios are almost identical as those for the market-weighted portfolios.

References

Arshanapalli, B., Coggin, T. and Doukas, J. (1998) 'Multifactor Asset Pricing Analysis of International Value Investment Strategies', *The Journal of Portfolio Management*, 24, 4.

Bachelier, L. (1900) 'Theory of Speculation', reprinted in *The Random Character of Stock Market Prices*, P. Cootner (Ed.), (1964), MIT Press, Cambridge, MA.

Ball, R. and Brown, P. (1968) 'An empirical evaluation of accounting income numbers', *Journal of Accounting Research*, 6, 2.

Basu, S. (1977) 'Investment Performance of Common Stocks in Relation to Their Price Earnings Ratios: A Test of the Efficient Market Hypothesis', *Journal of Finance*, 32, 3.

Bernard, V., Thomas, J. and Wahlen, J. (1997) 'Accounting-based Stock Price Anomalies: Separating Market Inefficiencies From Risk', *Contemporary Accounting Research*, 14, 2.

Bird, R. and Gerlach, R. (2003) *A Bayesian Approach to Enhancing a Value Strategy: Evidence from the US, UK and Australia*, UTS Working Paper.

Chan, L., Hamao, Y. and Lakonishok, J. (1991) 'Fundamentals and Stock Returns in Japan', *Journal of Finance*, 46, 5.

Chan, L., Jegadeesh N. and Lakonishok, J. (1996) 'Momentum Strategies', *Journal of Finance*, December, 51, 5.

Chopra, N., Lakonishok, J. and Ritter, J. (1992) 'Measuring Abnormal Performance: Do Stocks Overreact?' *Journal of Financial Economics*, 31, 2.

DeBondt, W. and Thaler, R. (1985) 'Does the Stock Market Overreact?' *Journal of Finance*, 40, 3.

DeBondt, W. and Thaler, R. (1987) 'Further Evidence on Investor Overreaction and Stock Market Seasonality,' *Journal of Finance*, 42, 3.

Dreman, D. and Berry, M.A. (1995) 'Analysts' Forecasting Errors and Their Implications for Security Analysis', *Financial Analysts Journal*, May–June, 51, 3.

Elton, E., Gruber, M., Brown, S. and Goetzman, W. (2003) *Modern Portfolio Theory and Investment Analysis*, 6th edition, John Wiley & Sons, New York.

Farma, E. (1998) 'Market Efficiency, Long-Term Returns and Behavioral Finance', *Journal of Financial Economics*, 39, 3.

Fama, E. and French, K. (1993) 'Common Risk Factors in the Returns on Stocks and Bonds,' *Journal of Financial Economics*, 33, 1.

Givoly, D. and Lakinishok, J. (1979) 'The Information Content of Financial Analysts' Forecasts of Earnings', *Journal of Accounting and Economics*, 1, 3.

Graham, B. and Dodd, D. (1934) *Security Analysis*, McGraw Hill, New York.

Grundy, B. and Martin, S. (2001) 'Understanding the Nature of the Risks and the Source of Rewards to Momentum Investing', *Review of Financial Studies*, 14, 1.

Jegadeesh, N. and Titman, S. (1993) 'Returns to Buying Winners and Losers: Implications for Stock Market Efficiency', *Journal of Finance*, 48, 1.

Jegadeesh, N. and Titman, S. (2001) 'Profitability of Momentum Strategies: An Evaluation of Alternative Explanations', *Journal of Finance*, 56, 2.

Kadiyala, P. and Rau, P. (2001) *It's All Under-Reaction*, Purdue University Working Paper.

Lakonishok, J., Shleifer, A. and Vishny, R. (1994) 'Contrarian Investment, Extrapolation and Risk,' *Journal of Finance*, 49, 5.

La Porta, R., Lakonishok, J., Shleifer, A. and Vishny, R. (1997) 'Good News for Value Stocks: Further Evidence on Market Efficiency', *Journal of Finance*, 52, 2.
Newey, W. and West, N. (1987) 'A Simple Positive Semi-Definite, Heteroskedasticity and Autocorrelation Consistent Covariance Matrix', *Econometrica*, 55, 3.
Richardson, S., Teoh, S. and Wysocki, P. (2002) 'The Walkdown to Beatable Analyst Forecasts: The Role of Equity Issuance and Inside Trading Incentives', University of Pennsylvania Working Paper.
Rosenberg, B., Reid, K. and Lanstein, R. (1985) 'Persuasive Evidence of Market Inefficiency', *Journal of Portfolio Management*, 11, 3.
Rouwenhorst, K. (1998) 'International Momentum Strategies', *Journal of Finance*, 53, 1.
Rouwenhorst, K. (1999) 'Local Return Factors and Turnover in Emerging Markets', *Journal of Finance*, 54, 4.
Soffer, L. and Walther, B. (2000) *Return Momentum, Return Reversals and Earnings Surprise*, Northwestern Graduate School of Management Working Paper.

6.2
The Performance of Value and Momentum Investment Portfolios: Recent Experience in the Major European Markets Part 2

*Ron Bird**

is an Emeritus Professor from the Australian National University where he taught from 1973 to 1989. In 1999, he joined the Finance and Economics School at the University of Technology, Sydney. In the interim, he held the following positions: practice leader of Towers Perrin's asset consulting business in the Asian region; in charge of quantitative funds management at Westpac Investment Management; co-founder of GMO's fund management operations in Australia. He remained an academic consultant to GMO until the end of 2002, at which time he took up a similar position with MIR Investment Management.

Jonathan Whitaker

is currently working as a portfolio analyst with GE Consumer Finance Australia and New Zealand, having previously been a research associate in the Finance and Economics School at the University of Technology, Sydney. He holds an honours degree in physics from UTS and a Masters in statistics from the University of New South Wales. Prior to his career in finance, Jonathan held positions in medical physics and scientific research.

**School of Finance and Economics, University of Technology Sydney, PO Box 123, Broadway, NSW 2007, Australia. Tel: +612 9514 7716; Fax: +612 9514 7711; e-mail: ron.bird@uts.edu.au*

Introduction

Numerous writers over the last 25 years have documented the success of value and momentum investment strategies when applied over a wide selection of markets. In a paper in the December 2003 issue of this Journal, it was established that a number of simple implementations of

---

Reprinted from 'The performance of value and momentum investment portfolios: Recent experience in the major European markets Part 2' by Ron Bird and Jonathan Whitaker in *Journal of Asset Management*, 5, 2004, pp. 157–175, DOI:10.1057/palgrave.jam.2240136. With kind permission from Palgrave Macmillan Ltd.

these strategies performed particularly well across the major European markets during the period from January 1990 to June 2002. The purpose of this paper is to extend the previous analysis and examine strategies which combine value and momentum strategies within one portfolio. Indeed, there are reasons to think that such a combination will produce very attractive portfolios, and it is the intention in this paper to evaluate alternative ways of exploiting this investment opportunity.

The next section of this paper briefly introduces value and momentum investing and their performance history. The third section provides a broad outline of the methods and data employed in this study. The fourth section outlines the findings, which confirm the potential of combining value and momentum criteria when selecting investment portfolios and, in particular, illustrates how this might best be done. The paper concludes with some summary comments.

Value and momentum investing

As indicated above, the focus of this paper is on the opportunities presented by building portfolios using combinations of value and momentum portfolios within the major European markets over the period from January 1990 to June 2002. Before the empirical findings are discussed, however, a brief introduction is provided to both approaches to investing, including a review of the findings in the previous paper based on the same European data (Bird and Whitaker, 2003).

Value investing

It was Graham and Dodd (1934) who first suggested that analysts extrapolate past earnings growth too far out into the future and, by so doing, drive the price of the stock of the better-performing firms to too high a level and that of the poorly performing stocks to too low a level. A number of valuation criteria (price-to-book, price-to-earnings, price-to-sales and so on) have been used to identify mispriced stocks and so form the basis for choosing portfolios designed to exploit the resulting investment opportunities. This approach to investing became known as either value investing, because of its focus on investing in 'cheap' stocks and avoiding 'expensive' stocks, or contrarian investing, as it meant forming portfolios which are atypical of those being held more generally by investors at a particular time.

Numerous authors have found that strategies based on value criteria are capable of adding value (eg Rosenberg *et al.*, 1985; Chan *et al.*, 1991; Arshanapalli *et al.*, 1998; Rouwenhorst, 1999; Lakonishok *et al.*, 1994).

The previous paper evaluated several value criteria for choosing stocks and came to the following conclusion:

> 'a value strategy based on either book-to-market or sales-to-price performed well if executed over the major European markets during the period from January 1990 to June 2002. This is a particularly interesting period as it contains a 10-year period when there was a boom in stock prices followed by a 2+ year correction period. Indeed, an analysis of the returns on the value portfolios confirms the authors' expectations that the value strategy struggled during the former period but strongly came into its own during the correction period.'

Momentum investing

Momentum investing basically involves choosing stocks on the basis of a past trend typically in stock prices or some precursor of movement in prices such as earnings. As will be seen, momentum stocks tend to display a number of the characteristics of 'growth' stocks (high valuation ratios, immediate past and expected future earnings growth and so on), and so momentum investing can be regarded as a simple implementation of growth investing. This (and the previous) paper considers two types of momentum: price momentum and earnings momentum.

Price momentum

Price momentum investing involves favouring stocks that have performed relatively well in the more recent past while avoiding those that have performed relatively poorly. The usual justification for such a strategy being that the performance of both markets and individual stocks is largely driven by market sentiment which itself follows trends.

A number of studies in the last decade have identified strong continuation in performance based upon a stock's performance over the prior three to 12 months (Jegadeesh and Titman, 1993, 2001; Rouwenhorst, 1998). The previous paper came to the following conclusion relating to the performance of a price momentum strategy over the sample period:

> 'The six-month (price) momentum strategy continues to maintain good performance for holding periods of up to 9 months ... In the 12-month strategy the optimal holding period is less than 6 months ... Consistent with the findings in the combined markets, a combination of 6-month price momentum with a 9-month holding period perform very well in all but the French and Spanish markets.'

Earnings momentum

A second form of momentum that has been evaluated is earnings momentum, with the many writers evaluating the relationship between the information provided by reported earnings or analyst's earnings forecast and future investment returns. A very early study in this area was conducted by Ball and Brown (1968), who substantiated that prices do react to the announcement of unexpected earnings and also provided early evidence of a post-announcement earnings drift. Subsequently, writers identified a correlation between many aspects of the information provided by analysts with future stock returns, thus confirming the importance to the market of information relating to earnings (see, for example, Givoly and Lakonishok, 1979; Chan *et al.*, 1991; Womack, 1996). These forecasts have the advantage over reported earnings of occurring earlier in the information cycle and being updated more frequently and so are more in tune with an investment strategy that is rebalanced on a regular basis.

The previous paper came to the following conclusion with respect to the use of earnings momentum as an investment signal over the sample period:

> 'The results for portfolios formed using agreement as the criterion proved to be particularly strong, especially for (holding) periods of up to 12 months ... portfolios based on the magnitude of the earnings revision are much weaker and less consistent ...'

Interplay between value and momentum

The previous paper concluded that there were a number of individual implementations of both value and momentum investing which performed very successfully in the major European markets over the period from January 1990 to June 2002. This paper turns attention to the possibility of realising even better returns by combining value and momentum within a single investment strategy. In response to a perceived cyclicality in stock performance, a number of studies have attempted to identify factors which predict periods of outperformance by growth stocks and by value stocks (see, for example, Asness *et al.*, 2000). In general, the authors of these studies would claim a fair degree of success, with macroeconomic factors (eg yield spreads) and valuation factors (eg value spreads relative to growth spreads) seemingly having predicted power. It is proposed that the findings in these studies and those of others suggest that there are many stocks which go through a value/momentum cycle and that this cycle is closely tied to the economic cycle, with the rewards to momentum investing being largely pro-cyclical and those to value investing being largely counter-cyclical. The fact that the present sample encompasses sustained periods of both positive and negative market performance enables this proposition to be evaluated.

There has been much reference in the finance literature to the apparent conundrum where some stocks underreact to information whereas others overreact. Momentum and value investing are very much part of this phenomenon, with underreaction to individual pieces of information being an important characteristic of trends in price behaviour that lead to momentum profits, while an overreaction to a series of similar announcements (eg good news) is an important contributor to the excesses in pricing which eventually give rise to the conditions for value investing to succeed. It can be expected that the value and momentum criteria are well placed to capture the cyclical nature of stock performance, as suggested in the papers by Barberis *et al.* (1998) and Hong and Stein (1999). This paper first confirms these expectations by examining the correlation between the returns from value and momentum strategies and then evaluates alternative means of exploiting the resulting investment opportunities.

Data and method

Data

The following section presents the findings on the combination of both value and price momentum investing when practised across the following European markets both individually and in combination: France, Germany, Italy, the Netherlands, Spain, Switzerland and the UK. The analysis was conducted over the period from January 1990 to June 2002 using accounting data obtained from the Worldscope database, return data provided by GMO Woolley and data on analyst's earnings forecasts provided by I/B/E/S. The only companies excluded from the sample were financial sector stocks and stocks with a negative book value. The average number of companies included in the database for each country is reported in Table 6.2.1.

Criteria for ranking stocks

Under both value and momentum investing, the stocks are ranked on the basis of some criterion with these rankings being used as the basis for forming investment portfolios. This paper restricts the analysis to

Table 6.2.1 Sample size by country

	Average	Maximum	Minimum
United Kingdom	1,043	1,235	654
France	366	495	219
Germany	375	597	207
Italy	165	155	93
Switzerland	135	151	113
Netherlands	118	146	83
Spain	82	109	48
Combined	2,284	2,682	1,448

those criteria which performed best in the previous study of the same markets. The criteria used are as follows:

Value criterion:	Book-to-market (bm)
Price momentum criterion:	6-month (return) momentum (pm)
Earnings momentum:	Agreement (agree)[1]

For each criterion, the lowest ranked stocks are the ones expected to perform worst and the highest ranked stocks are those expected to perform best.

In this paper, a second earnings momentum measure not previously considered is introduced: dispersion in the analysts' forecasts (dis), as measured by the standard deviation of the forecasts at any point in time. Dispersion provides no information on the direction of the signal, and so it is not used as a standalone criterion for forming portfolios but rather used in combination with other criteria. It is felt that low dispersion is an indication of the strength of the signal from the other criteria, which suggests that stocks with low dispersion will do much better than those with high dispersion, other factors being held constant.

Forming portfolios

The focus of this paper is on forming portfolios using a combination of criteria, and this is achieved in two different ways:

1. The stocks are ranked separately on the basis of two criteria, and then portfolios are formed on the basis of the intersections of the two sets of rankings. For example, one portfolio could be composed of the stocks from the bottom quartile (quartile one) of book-to-market and the bottom quartile from sales-to-price, another portfolio would be composed of stocks from quartile one of book-to-market and quartile

two of sales-to-price and so on. In this case, 16 portfolios are formed which again are rebalanced monthly with holding periods for stocks of between one month and 48 months.

2. Again, the stocks are ranked on the basis of two separate criteria, but in this case separate portfolios are formed using each criterion and then half the funds are effectively invested in one portfolio and half in the other. Assume the two criteria are book-to-market and sales-to-price, and two sets of portfolios are produced formed into deciles. Ten portfolios are then formed by combining the bottom decile book-to-market portfolio with the bottom decile sales-to-price portfolio, the next lowest book-to-market portfolio with the next lowest sales-to price portfolio, and so on.

In addition, following the procedures described above to build portfolios within countries, all the stocks are also pooled and a combined portfolio is built, incorporating all the available stocks across the seven markets. When all the stocks are ranked in accordance with the procedures described above, there will be a tendency for the portfolios to reflect the relative valuations across the seven markets. For example, if French stocks appear relatively cheap to those in the other markets when measured by book-to-market, they are likely to have a disproportionate weighting in the cheap portfolio, and this will be reflected in the returns on that portfolio. In order to minimise the impact of any country bias on the combined portfolios, these portfolios are also formed on a country corrected basis by ranking stocks using the country corrected value for the particular criterion being used (eg book-to-market) for each stock, which involves, each month, deducting the average value for the criterion across all the stocks in the country from the actual value for that criterion for each stock. For example, country corrected book-to-market for all French stocks in a particular month is determined by deducting from each stock's book-to-market the average book-to-market for all French stocks for that month. Each stock from the seven countries is then ranked in accordance with these country corrected values and country corrected portfolios formed, which are then used as the basis for calculating the country corrected returns.

Determining the returns on the portfolios

The end objective is to measure the performance of the portfolios formed following one of the approaches described above. Several returns are calculated, each of which is described below:[2]

1. Equally weighted returns – these are obtained by equally weighting each stock within each portfolio.

2. Market weighted returns – these are obtained by weighting each stock in each portfolio on the basis of its contribution to the market capitalisation of the portfolio.
3. Size-adjusted equally weighted returns – in this case each stock is equally weighted within each portfolio but the returns used to calculate the portfolio returns are not the actual stock returns for each month but rather the size-adjusted returns obtained by subtracting from the stock's actual return, the mean return of all the stocks that fall in the same size-quintile portfolio.[3]
4. Size-adjusted market weighted returns – each stock is held in each portfolio in proportion to its market capitalisation with portfolio returns being calculated using the size-adjusted returns calculated using the method described above.

As well as calculating the monthly returns for each portfolio, the study also calculates a p value as a test of the significance of those returns. These p values are calculated using the Newey-West measure of variance that corrects for serial correlation.

Finally, the following characteristics were collected for each portfolio:

1. The portfolio's average book-to-market value as a measure of its valuation level
2. The portfolio's six-month price momentum as a measure of its recent market performance
3. The relative trading volume of the stocks in the portfolio over the previous month as a measure of its liquidity
4. The decile ranking of the market capitalisation of the stocks in the portfolio.

Findings

The previous paper examined the performance of 12 criteria for forming value or momentum portfolios in the major European markets over the period from January 1990 to June 2002 (Bird and Whitaker, 2003). The overall finding was that value, price momentum and earnings momentum all performed particularly well over this sample period. More disturbing evidence in relation to the value portfolios was also found, however, which suggests that (i) the criteria used often have low discriminatory power in that they select many stocks that underperform, and (ii) they are effectively devoid of any market timing resulting in extended periods of underperformance. The focus of this paper is on determining the extent to which these deficiencies can be overcome and so performance can be improved by simply using a combination of value and momentum criteria, rather than a single criterion, to form portfolios. As will be seen, investment strategies benefit not only from encompassing criteria which add value in their own right but also from combining criteria which produce the best performance at different times in the market cycle.

Combining value and price momentum strategies

Perhaps the most interesting option to consider is just how value and momentum investing will work in combination. The key consideration when combining different investment streams is to identify strategies which both contribute added value in their own right but also deliver added value that has a low correlation with the added value from other well-performing strategies. The correlations were evaluated between the added value from the best value strategy (book-to-market), the two best momentum strategies (six-month and agreement) and dispersion assuming a 12-month holding period. The findings are reported in Table 6.2.2 for the bottom and top quintiles under each criterion.[4]

The observed correlations reported in Table 6.2.2 are very pleasing from an investment perspective, as they suggest that the added value from the winning stocks by price momentum (pm5) are negatively correlated with the added value from investing in the cheap stocks under the value strategy (bm5). Similarly, the returns of the losing stocks by price momentum are negatively correlated with the returns of the expensive stocks by the value measures. These findings provide a strong *a priori* case for assuming that an investment strategy where portfolios are built using some combination of book-to-market with price momentum will perform very well.[5]

Table 6.2.3 presents the returns on equally weighted portfolios formed using both book-to-market and six-month price momentum assuming various holding periods. The returns reported in this table provide a myriad of interesting findings, including the suggestion that the best strategy would have been to go short expensive losers and long cheap losers (rather than cheap winners). This is consistent with the work of Lee and Swaminathan (2000) and Swaminathan and Lee (2000), who suggest that expensive losing stocks are early into their negative momentum cycle, while cheap losing stocks are late into this stage of the cycle, to the extent that they will soon turn around and start generating good returns. It is also consistent with the findings of Asness (1997), who found that book-to-market was especially good at

Table 6.2.2 Correlations between the monthly market weighted excess returns of portfolios formed using value and price momentum criterion and holding for 12 months (combined markets, January 1990 to June 2002)

	pm1	**pm5**	**agree1**	**agree5**	**dis1**	**dis5**	**bm1**	**bm5**
pm1	1	−0.73701	−0.41301	−0.8825	−0.02466	0.09150	−0.24349	0.80151
pm5	−0.73701	1	0.40676	0.69092	0.25292	−0.12509	0.65354	−0.74022
agree1	−0.41301	0.40676	1	0.44396	−0.14646	0.09046	0.31575	−0.67301
agree5	−0.8825	0.69092	0.44396	1	0.17799	−0.20843	0.43272	−0.88088
dis1	−0.02466	0.25292	−0.14646	0.17799	1	−0.78249	0.65065	−0.28675
dis5	0.09150	−0.12509	0.09046	−0.20843	−0.78249	1	−0.48822	0.32585
bm1	−0.24349	0.65354	0.31575	0.43272	0.65065	−0.48822	1	−0.6540
bm5	0.80151	−0.74022	−0.67301	−0.88088	−0.28675	0.32585	−0.6540	1

Table 6.2.3 Equally weighted returns (per cent per month) across portfolios created using the intersection of book-to-market and 6-month price momentum (combined markets, January 1990 to June 2002)

	Losers	pm2	pm3	Winners	Winners – Losers
Panel 1: Book-to-market and 6-month price momentum over 6-month holding period					
Expensive	−0.623	0.129	0.652	1.429	2.052
	0.346	0.777	0.124	0.016	0
bm2	−0.321	0.317	0.817	1.465	1.786
	0.570	0.351	0.006	0	0
bm3	−0.057	0.521	0.855	1.296	1.354
	0.915	0.121	0.005	0	0
Cheap	1.625	0.947	1.148	1.169	−0.456
	0.107	0.009	0	0.001	0.617
Cheap–Expensive	2.249	0.818	0.495	−0.260	1.792
	0.010	0.017	0.198	0.632	0.001
Panel 2: Book-to-market and 6-month price momentum over 12-month holding period					
Expensive	−0.218	0.392	0.773	1.291	1.509
	0.728	0.376	0.063	0.024	0
bm2	0.138	0.597	0.928	1.449	1.311
	0.789	0.060	0.001	0	0
bm3	0.374	0.791	1.053	1.424	1.050
	0.428	0.014	0	0	0
Cheap	2.174	1.315	1.409	1.571	−0.603
	0.052	0	0	0	0.567
Cheap–Expensive	2.393	0.922	0.636	0.281	1.790
	0.014	0.007	0.079	0.604	0.001
Panel 3: Book-to-market and 6-month price momentum over 24-month holding period					
Expensive	0.281	0.552	0.730	0.906	0.624
	0.637	0.202	0.084	0.121	0.007
bm2	0.399	0.689	0.840	1.046	0.646
	0.407	0.036	0.010	0.007	0.001
bm3	0.718	0.880	1.016	1.192	0.474
	0.117	0.009	0.002	0.001	0.025
Cheap	2.423	1.511	1.448	1.484	−0.939
	0.040	0.001	0	0	0.383
Cheap–Expensive	2.142	0.959	0.718	0.578	1.203
	0.043	0.008	0.024	0.220	0.008

differentiating between winning stocks, and price momentum was particularly good at differentiating between expensive stocks.

Table 6.2.4 replicates the analysis reported in Table 6.2.3, but agreement is used as the momentum measure in place of price momentum. Unlike the case with price momentum, agreement does a good job of

Table 6.2.4 Equally weighted returns (per cent per month) across portfolios created using both book-to-market and agreement (combined markets, January 1990 to June 2002)

	Losers	agree2	agree3	Winners	Winners – Losers
Panel 1: Book-to-market and agreement over 6-month holding period					
Expensive	−0.177	0.290	0.506	0.957	1.134
	0.763	0.611	0.360	0.066	0
bm2	0.062	0.432	0.681	0.860	0.798
	0.880	0.221	0.110	0.012	0
bm3	0.175	0.437	0.728	0.961	0.786
	0.656	0.231	0.047	0.004	0
Cheap	0.535	0.748	1.268	1.213	0.678
	0.243	0.119	0.012	0.002	0
Cheap–Expensive	0.712	0.458	0.762	0.256	1.390
	0.182	0.381	0.117	0.599	0.009
Panel 2: Book-to-market and agreement over 12-month holding period					
Expensive	0.114	0.411	0.697	0.955	0.841
	0.843	0.438	0.211	0.062	0
bm2	0.447	0.626	0.777	0.975	0.529
	0.255	0.071	0.058	0.004	0
bm3	0.537	0.700	0.899	1.146	0.609
	0.151	0.036	0.010	0	0
Cheap	0.968	1.002	2.266	1.459	0.490
	0.025	0.023	0.041	0	0
Cheap–Expensive	0.854	0.591	1.569	0.503	1.344
	0.098	0.197	0.132	0.274	0.009
Panel 3: Book-to-market and agreement over 24-month holding period					
Expensive	0.283	0.422	0.642	0.774	0.491
	0.622	0.423	0.259	0.129	0
bm2	0.478	0.667	0.630	0.881	0.403
	0.245	0.062	0.125	0.013	0.001
bm3	0.661	0.856	0.846	1.078	0.417
	0.089	0.016	0.020	0.002	0
Cheap	1.121	1.220	1.977	1.472	0.351
	0.011	0.004	0.026	0	0.006
Cheap–Expensive	0.838	0.798	1.335	0.698	1.189
	0.077	0.042	0.101	0.103	0.015

differentiating across the whole range of value including the cheap stocks. In this case, the best performing portfolio is composed of cheap winners that outperform the worst performing portfolio (expensive losers) by almost 1.4 per cent per month over holding periods of up to 12 months. Although this added value is somewhat lower than that added by the combination of book-to-market with price momentum (see Table 6.2.3), there is evidence to suggest that the potential added value from the book-to-market/agreement combination extends over a longer holding period than is the case from the book-to-market/price momentum combination.

Table 6.2.5 presents the characteristics of the portfolios that are formed using the intersection of book-to-market with both price momentum and agreement. In both cases, the better-performing portfolios are composed of much smaller stocks than are the poorly performing portfolios. In order to investigate the possibility that the findings simply reflect a small capitalisation bias, Table 6.2.6 reports the size-adjusted, market weighted returns for the book-to-market/price momentum combination and Table 6.2.7 the size-adjusted, market weighted returns for the book-to-market/agreement combination. The success of these strategies are slightly diminished but far from removed by calculating returns in this way. Further, the previous somewhat unexpected finding that the cheap portfolio of losers produced the best performance is no longer the case, which suggests that it was largely a size-driven phenomenon. On the basis of market weighted and size-adjusted returns, the best portfolio outperforms the worst portfolio by about 1.2 per cent per month over holding periods of up to 12 months where price momentum is used as the momentum criterion and by about 0.9 per cent per month where agreement is used as the momentum criterion. As was previously the case when independent price momentum portfolios and independent agreement portfolios were analysed, it is found that price momentum works better than agreement when used in combination with a value criterion.

The combined strategies discussed above involve forming portfolios based on the intersection of a value and a momentum criterion. As discussed in the third section, however, another way of drawing on the strengths of both strategies would be to form separate value and momentum portfolios and then allocate a portions of one's investment funds to each. Table 6.2.8 reports the performance of just such an investment strategy where half the funds are allocated to the value portfolio and half to the momentum portfolio (based on price momentum in

Table 6.2.5 Characteristics of combinations of book-to-market with 6-month price momentum and agreement (combined markets, January 1990 to June 2002)

Portfolio	Book-to-market	6-month price momentum (% p.a.)	Trading volume (% of total)	Size (ave. decile rank)	Average no. of stocks in portfolio
Book-to-market with 6-month price momentum					
Exp., losers	0.1159	−4.5176	0.0493	5.6745	83.1007
bm1, pm2	0.1199	−0.4866	0.0406	6.9362	100.5436
bm1, pm3	0.1209	1.9751	0.0569	7.3389	114.8591
bm1, pm4	0.1141	7.4745	0.0763	6.8624	154.5436
bm2, pm1	0.3066	−4.5829	0.0459	5.2987	90.3557
bm2, pm2	0.3068	−0.5397	0.0465	6.5671	114.1946
bm2, pm3	0.3028	1.8789	0.0689	6.8691	125.0470
bm2, pm4	0.2950	6.2202	0.1004	6.4161	123.5034
bm3, pm1	0.5707	−4.7769	0.0509	4.4732	113.1141
bm3, pm2	0.5548	−0.5584	0.0592	5.5134	121.9128
bm3, pm3	0.5497	1.8674	0.0858	5.9664	117.3826
bm3, pm4	0.5494	6.1860	0.1086	5.4094	100.6309
Cheap, losers	1.3516	−5.7600	0.0492	2.5034	166.5705
bm4, pm2	1.1729	−0.4909	0.0354	3.5302	116.3893
bm4, pm3	1.1356	1.9493	0.0421	3.6980	95.7517
Cheap, winners	1.1132	6.7611	0.0841	3.5638	74.3423
Book-to-market with agreement					
Exp., losers	0.1183	0.5319	0.0499	6.5503	74.9664
bm1, agree2	0.1149	1.4791	0.0268	6.9664	97.8054
bm1, agree3	0.1123	2.5012	0.0603	5.5235	81.1879
bm1, agree4	0.1129	3.1729	0.0615	7.2919	110.5436
bm2, agree1	0.2905	−0.3661	0.0792	6.0638	84.4295
bm2, agree2	0.2886	0.7492	0.0386	6.7919	93.3154
bm2, agree3	0.2880	1.5692	0.0514	4.7718	86.1208
bm2, agree4	0.2849	2.3136	0.0667	6.8389	100.7315
bm3, agree1	0.5237	−0.9087	0.1224	5.4228	98.1074
bm3, agree2	0.5097	0.2113	0.0475	6.0168	90.9262
bm3, agree3	0.5199	0.9436	0.0564	3.6779	88.1745
bm3, agree4	0.5105	1.7083	0.0791	6.2013	87.3758
bm4, agree1	1.0861	−2.0790	0.0927	3.5772	107.0336
bm4, agree2	1.1001	−0.8844	0.0386	4.3121	82.5705
bm4, agree3	1.1495	−0.3720	0.0645	2.2483	109.1074
Cheap, winners	1.0271	0.8211	0.0642	4.6275	65.9060

Table 6.2.6 Size-adjusted and market weighted returns (per cent per month) across portfolios created using both book-to-market and 6-month price momentum (combined markets, January 1990 to June 2002)

	Losers	pm2	pm3	Winners	Winners – Losers
Panel 1: Book-to-market and 6-month price momentum over 6-month holding period					
Expensive	–0.786	–0.103	0.241	0.399	1.185
	0.009	0.580	0.204	0.147	0.008
bm2	–0.614	0.038	0.285	0.521	1.136
	0.043	0.844	0.161	0.006	0.003
bm3	–0.379	0.202	0.412	0.200	0.578
	0.263	0.374	0.063	0.399	0.182
Cheap	–0.166	0.130	0.577	0.448	0.614
	0.676	0.632	0.043	0.171	0.222
Cheap–Expensive	0.620	0.233	0.336	0.049	1.234
	0.109	0.446	0.335	0.915	0.019
Panel 2: Book-to-market and 6-month price momentum over 12-month holding period					
Expensive	–0.668	–0.042	0.203	0.261	0.929
	0.019	0.798	0.257	0.305	0.009
bm2	–0.503	0.066	0.271	0.461	0.964
	0.069	0.718	0.181	0.011	0.007
bm3	–0.385	0.146	0.373	0.249	0.634
	0.212	0.503	0.103	0.271	0.078
Cheap	0.044	0.143	0.517	0.477	0.433
	0.907	0.583	0.037	0.080	0.347
Cheap–Expensive	0.712	0.185	0.313	0.216	1.145
	0.084	0.501	0.277	0.592	0.019
Panel 3: Book-to-market and 6-month price momentum over 24-month holding period					
Expensive	–0.374	0.016	0.080	–0.014	0.359
	0.125	0.922	0.648	0.953	0.163
bm2	–0.305	0.110	0.187	0.168	0.473
	0.071	0.464	0.278	0.269	0.051
bm3	–0.084	0.176	0.331	0.259	0.343
	0.711	0.368	0.137	0.224	0.216
Cheap	0.340	0.275	0.427	0.428	0.088
	0.277	0.225	0.077	0.100	0.822
Cheap–Expensive	0.714	0.259	0.348	0.442	0.802
	0.056	0.296	0.221	0.282	0.068

Table 6.2.7 Size-adjusted and market weighted returns (per cent per month) across portfolios created using both book-to-market earnings momentum (agree) (combined markets, January 1990 to June 2002)

	Losers	agree2	agree3	Winners	Winners – Losers
Panel 1: Book-to-market and earnings momentum (agree) over 6-month holding period					
Expensive	−0.282	−0.125	−0.041	0.437	0.719
	0.175	0.502	0.840	0.042	0.002
bm2	−0.117	0.160	0.141	0.182	0.299
	0.541	0.336	0.350	0.432	0.279
bm3	0.089	0.140	0.095	0.280	0.191
	0.648	0.485	0.717	0.248	0.343
Cheap	0.070	0.519	0.536	0.559	0.488
	0.808	0.053	0.035	0.069	0.084
Cheap–Expensive	0.352	0.644	0.577	0.121	0.840
	0.382	0.107	0.133	0.780	0.063
Panel 2: Book-to-market and earnings momentum (agree) over 12-month holding period					
Expensive	−0.272	−0.033	−0.078	0.323	0.594
	0.155	0.863	0.703	0.108	0.001
bm2	−0.030	0.229	0.101	0.231	0.260
	0.869	0.130	0.469	0.246	0.242
bm3	0.021	0.148	0.217	0.325	0.304
	0.917	0.488	0.362	0.181	0.054
Cheap	0.157	0.374	0.466	0.659	0.502
	0.543	0.124	0.048	0.027	0.025
Cheap–Expensive	0.428	0.407	0.544	0.336	0.930
	0.252	0.281	0.162	0.425	0.029
Panel 3: Book-to-market and earnings momentum (agree) over 24-month holding period					
Expensive	−0.231	−0.091	−0.241	0.158	0.389
	0.218	0.631	0.259	0.432	0.008
bm2	−0.134	0.141	0.003	0.171	0.305
	0.261	0.315	0.981	0.297	0.036
bm3	0.071	0.189	0.214	0.397	0.326
	0.696	0.342	0.314	0.089	0.012
Cheap	0.179	0.380	0.431	0.632	0.452
	0.478	0.097	0.062	0.015	0.033
Cheap–Expensive	0.411	0.471	0.673	0.473	0.863
	0.231	0.175	0.084	0.229	0.016

Table 6.2.8 Size-adjusted and market weighted returns (per cent per month) across portfolios created by combining both book-to-market (50 per cent) and agreement (50 per cent) (combined markets, January 1990 to June 2002)

Panel 1: Book-to-market with price momentum

Holding period	Exp. losers	bm2, pm2	bm3, pm3	bm4, pm4	bm5, pm5	bm6, pm6	bm7, pm7	bm8, pm8	bm9, pm9	Cheap winners	Exp. losers – Cheap winners
6 mth	–0.751	–0.213	–0.027	0	0.101	0.140	0.216	0.154	0.335	0.529	1.281
	0.018	0.168	0.806	0.998	0.512	0.293	0.154	0.134	0.042	0	0.001
12 mth	–0.566	–0.192	–0.023	0.014	0.098	0.141	0.217	0.136	0.338	0.453	1.019
	0.048	0.179	0.828	0.910	0.507	0.301	0.180	0.213	0.015	0	0.001
24 mth	–0.320	–0.096	0.012	0.033	0.098	0.148	0.211	0.059	0.274	0.324	0.644
	0.181	0.452	0.899	0.751	0.448	0.262	0.160	0.569	0.010	0.009	0.010

Panel 2: Book-to-market with agreement

Holding period	Exp. losers	bm2, ag2	bm3, ag3	bm4, ag4	bm5, ag5	bm6, ag6	bm7, ag7	bm8, ag8	bm9, ag9	Cheap winners	Exp. losers – Cheap winners
6 mth	–0.240	–0.091	0.046	0.074	–0.052	0.021	0.128	0.111	0.313	0.416	0.656
	0.163	0.361	0.519	0.486	0.676	0.808	0.259	0.368	0.084	0.018	0.022
12 mth	–0.280	–0.069	0.075	0.094	–0.048	–0.067	0.130	0.145	0.317	0.412	0.692
	0.082	0.450	0.291	0.308	0.659	0.505	0.284	0.210	0.057	0.010	0.009
24 mth	–0.240	–0.101	0.031	0.041	–0.036	–0.088	0.095	0.087	0.319	0.394	0.634
	0.117	0.282	0.702	0.606	0.711	0.460	0.406	0.438	0.021	0.005	0.010

Panel 1 and on agreement in Panel 2). Again, such a way of implementing a combined strategy produces good investment returns, especially for holding periods of up to 12 months. In order to facilitate a comparison of the various combined strategies, Table 6.2.9 presents the difference in the performance of the best and worst portfolio in each case over various holding periods. It can be seen that enhancing a book-to-market strategy with an agreement strategy results in only a small improvement over using book-to-market as the sole criterion for forming portfolios. When price momentum is used as the momentum criterion, however, it can be seen that it enhances the performance of a book-to-market strategy by between 0.3 per cent and 0.5 per cent per month for holding periods of up to 12 months. There is little to choose between the option of forming portfolios using the intersection of the value with price momentum criteria or allocating an equal amount of funds to separate value and momentum portfolios – the former generating slightly higher returns over longer holding periods but the latter producing slightly less volatile returns.[6]

Although the potential of combining a value and a momentum investment strategy has been established, and book-to-market and six-month price momentum have been identified as the best criteria for implementing such a strategy over the sample period, the question remains as to whether further improvements can be gained from introducing additional criteria into the analysis. Undoubtedly, the most interesting potential inclusion into a strategy is dispersion, which was found in unreported results to add significantly to the performance of strategies based on either price momentum or earnings momentum (see Ackert and Athananassakos, 1997; Dische, 2002; Ciconne, 2003). With this in mind, the previous analysis is extended to build portfolios based on three criteria: book-to-market, six-month price momentum and dispersion. Table 6.2.7 reported on the performance of 16 portfolios created when splitting stocks into quintiles based on the first two of these of criteria. The stocks included in each of these 16 portfolios are now further divided on the basis of whether each stock falls into the top or bottom 50 per cent of stocks when ranked on the basis of dispersion. For example, one might have (say) 150 stocks in the portfolio consisting of cheap winners, and each of these 150 stocks will be further divided into a portfolio of cheap winners with high dispersion and cheap winners with low dispersion. The end result is that 32 separate portfolios will now be formed, and so it can be judged whether the addition of the new criterion adds to the performance of the strategies as reported in Table 6.2.7.

Table 6.2.9 Comparing the performance calculated using market weighted and size-adjusted returns between the best and worst ranking portfolios formed by book-to-market and price momentum with those formed by book-to-market and agreement (per cent per month) (combined markets, January 1990 to June 2002)

Holding period	Book-to-market alone (top and bottom deciles)	Book-to-market with price momentum		Book-to-market with agreement	
		Intersection (top and bottom quintiles	50/50 (top and bottom deciles)	Intersection (top and bottom quintiles	50/50 (top and bottom deciles)
6 mths	0.736	1.234	1.281	0.840	0.656
	0.166	0.019	0.001	0.063	0.022
12 mths	0.836	1.145	1.019	0.930	0.692
	0.112	0.019	0.001	0.029	0.009
24 mths	0.898	0.802	0.644	0.863	0.634
	0.077	0.068	0.010	0.016	0.010

The findings reported in Table 6.2.10 highlight the added performance attributable to supplementing book-to-market and price momentum with dispersion. The ability of dispersion to differentiate between the cheap winning stocks and expensive losing stocks results in an increase in the returns on a long/short portfolio of around 0.9 per cent per month over a six-month holding period and 0.8 per cent per month over a 12-month holding period when compared with the same strategies implemented in the absence of dispersion (see Table 6.2.7). In the case of both holding periods, the entire incremental added value resulting by adding the dispersion criterion comes from the ability of dispersion to differentiate between the expensive winning stocks. It also seems that the majority of the added value from running a long/short portfolio based on value and momentum is due to the difference in the performance of the cheap winning portfolio and the expensive losing portfolio incorporating those stocks, where there is relatively large disagreement between the analysts as to the future earnings prospects of the company (ie high dispersion). Information on the characteristics of these portfolios is reported in Table 6.2.11. The separation of the expensive losing portfolios on the basis of their dispersion produces two portfolios which have similar characteristics with the exception that the low dispersion portfolio is slightly less liquid than the high dispersion portfolio. The two cheap winning portfolios separated by dispersion also are fairly similar with the low dispersion portfolio again being slightly less liquid but also composed of smaller capitalisation stocks. The other point worth noting is that there is high level of consensus in the analysts' earnings forecasts in the majority of cases (almost two-thirds) for the expensive losing stocks. The reverse is the case, however, with respect to the cheap winning stocks, which suggests that the analyst community in general have yet to come to terms with the future prospects of companies which have most likely experienced a relatively recent turnaround in performance.

In order to determine whether the performance was sourced by stock selection or the country bets created as a consequence of the stock selection process, the results reported in Table 6.2.10 are also repeated but with the returns calculated on a country corrected basis. A reduction in added value of between 25 per cent and 30 per cent was found as a result of correcting for the country bets, which confirms that the majority of the added value is attributable to stock selection, which is examined in closer detail in the next sub-section of the paper.

Table 6.2.10 Size-adjusted and market weighted returns (per cent per month) across selected portfolios created by combining value, earnings momentum and dispersion (combined markets, January 1990 to June 2002)

	Expensive losers (1)	Cheap winners (2)	(2)–(1)
Holding period: 6 months			
High dispersion (1)	−1.311	0.319	1.630
	0.006	0.351	0.016
Low dispersion (2)	−0.597	0.328	0.925
	0.042	0.280	0.047
(2)–(1)	0.714	0.009	1.639
	0.050	0.979	0.012
Holding period: 12 months			
High dispersion (1)	−1.309	0.376	1.685
	0.004	0.168	0.006
Low dispersion (2)	−0.422	0.322	0.744
	0.109	0.241	0.104
(2)–(1)	0.887	−0.054	1.632
	0.018	0.877	0.011
Holding period: 24 months			
High dispersion (1)	−0.999	0.374	1.373
	0.006	0.198	0.012
Low dispersion (2)	−0.042	0.081	0.122
	0.856	0.748	0.734
(2)–(1)	0.957	−0.293	1.079
	0.003	0.396	0.028

Table 6.2.11 Characteristics of combinations of selected book-to-market with 6-month price momentum portfolios further differentiated by dispersion (combined markets, January 1990 to June 2002)

Portfolio	Book-to-market	6-month price momentum (% p.a.)	Trading volume (% of total)	Size (ave. decile rank)	Average no. of stocks in portfolio
Expensive losers with high dispersion	0.1141	−4.2633	0.0345	5.4295	20.0671
Expensive losers with low dispersion	0.1109	−4.1234	0.0118	5.5772	32.7785
Cheap winners with high dispersion	0.9724	5.9145	0.0539	4.7987	32.7919
Cheap winners with low dispersion	0.9383	5.5418	0.0208	3.3716	16.0268

Combining value and price momentum at the country level

The discussion to date has identified that a strategy of creating portfolios by combining value (using book-to-market as the criterion) and momentum (using six-month price momentum as the criterion) and then applying dispersion as a third criterion produced very good performance at the aggregate level during the period of this study. The same strategy was applied to the seven individual markets, and the findings are reported in Table 6.2.12.[7]

It proves that the strategy has worked well in all seven markets, but particularly in the UK, Germany, the Netherlands and Switzerland, with Spain being the only market where the added value could be regarded as marginal. In the case of the Netherlands and France, the use of dispersion has turned a marginal value/momentum strategy into a very profitable strategy, while the use of dispersion has made a positive contribution to performance in all the markets, with the exception of Germany. The source of the added value attributable to dispersion is sometimes mixed owing to its ability to differentiate expensive losing stocks (the UK and Spain), in other cases it is able to differentiate cheap winning stocks (France and Italy) while, in the case of the Netherlands, dispersion proves effective in differentiating between both types of stocks.

Summary and concluding comments

The previous paper reported that both value and price momentum investment portfolios, when formed on the basis of a single criterion (eg book-to-market, six-month price momentum), performed well in the major European markets over the period from January 1990 to June 2002. The focus of this paper is on extending the analysis to evaluating portfolios that have been formed on the basis of combinations of value and momentum criteria. A major motivation is to extend existing knowledge of the performance of such strategies across a wider range of markets and time periods and thus contribute to a better understanding of market behaviour and potential anomalies, which can then give rise to superior investment management strategies.

The two major findings from the analysis covering the major European markets during the 1990s and early 2000s are summarised below:

- Value portfolio based on book-to-market could be significantly improved by combining it with a momentum strategy, particularly price momentum.

Table 6.2.12 Size-adjusted and market weighted returns (per cent per month) across selected portfolios created by combining value, earnings momentum and dispersion (individual markets, January 1990 to June 2002)

	Expensive losers (1)	Cheap winners (2)	(2)–(1)
UK: 12-month holding period			
High dispersion (1)	−1.686	0.592	2.279
	0.001	0.056	0.001
Low dispersion (2)	−0.828	0.595	1.423
	0.020	0.059	0.011
(2)–(1)	0.858	0.002	2.281
	0.016	0.993	0.001
Germany: 12-month holding period			
High dispersion (1)	−1.604	0.833	2.436
	0.002	0.072	0.001
Low dispersion (2)	−1.912	0.699	2.611
	0.015	0.055	0.013
(2)–(1)	−0.309	−0.134	2.303
	0.566	0.865	0.001
France: 12-month holding period			
High dispersion (1)	−0.701	−0.022	0.679
	0.062	0.946	0.182
Low dispersion (2)	−0.601	0.840	1.441
	0.246	0.236	0.280
(2)–(1)	0.100	0.862	1.541
	0.877	0.100	0.122
Italy: 12-month holding period			
High dispersion (1)	0.110	−0.381	−0.490
	0.788	0.254	0.457
Low dispersion (2)	−0.203	1.098	1.301
	0.373	0.043	0.041
(2)–(1)	−0.313	0.720	0.989
	0.445	0.286	0.110
Netherlands: 12-month holding period			
High dispersion (1)	−1.065	−0.080	0.985
	0.050	0.795	0.099
Low dispersion (2)	−0.479	0.557	1.036
	0.097	0.125	0.053
(2)–(1)	0.586	0.637	1.622
	0.355	0.099	0.034
Spain: 12-month holding period			
High dispersion (1)	−0.630	0.197	0.827
	0.037	0.564	0.105
Low dispersion (2)	−0.368	0.031	0.399
	0.212	0.929	0.449
(2)–(1)	0.262	−0.166	0.661
	0.619	0.771	0.253
Switzerland: 12-month holding period			
High dispersion (1)	−0.184	0.291	0.475
	0.498	0.296	0.210
Low dispersion (2)	−0.345	0.799	1.144
	0.160	0.015	0.012
(2)–(1)	−0.161	0.508	0.983
	0.649	0.291	0.025

- The addition of dispersion to a value/momentum strategy resulted in further enhancements to performance at the level of the individual markets and the aggregate of these markets.

Perhaps the most interesting findings come from the analysis of the combined value/momentum portfolios. It has been identified that the added value from a value strategy tends to be negatively correlated with the added value from price momentum and that both tend to be related to the market (and economic) cycle. This all suggests that many stocks also go through a cycle not dissimilar to that proposed by Lee and Swaminathan, where the price of a typical stock will first trend in one direction beyond its fair value and then reverse and trend in the opposite direction, again overshooting fair value. Of course, not all stocks behave in this way, nor does a particular stock always behave in this way. A profitable strategy, however, will be feasible, provided sufficient stocks are behaving in this way at any point in time and the criteria used are able to identify enough of these stocks at an appropriate point in their cycle.

The better-performing value strategies tended to produce portfolios composed of relatively small and less traded stocks. The performances of these portfolios, however, were only slightly eroded when stocks were held in proportion to their market capitalisations and returns calculated on a size-adjusted basis. In contrast, the better-performing enhanced momentum portfolios (eg price momentum with dispersion) are composed of relatively large and highly liquid stocks, and their performance actually improved when calculated on a market weighted basis. As a consequence, when value and momentum are combined within the one strategy, the resulting portfolios are composed of stocks that are quite liquid, although still slightly below average in terms of market capitalisation. Further, the annual turnover of the better-performing strategies tends to fall between 50 per cent and 75 per cent, which suggests that transactions costs will only erode a small proportion of the potential added value when implementing these strategies.

Of course, most studies open up as many questions as they can answer. In the case of this paper, one obvious question is whether one can obtain even better performance by forming portfolios using even more convoluted combinations of criteria. Some strategies based on two, or even three, criteria work particularly well as the basis for forming portfolios, as each strategy not only adds value in its own right but also complements the other through the market cycle. The best of all the one-by-one combinations evaluated for forming portfolios across all the major European markets would appear to be book-to-market with price momentum. Dispersion also provides a good basis for further enhancing such a one-by-one strategy. Many fund managers use more than three criteria within their investment strategy, and it is not surprising that there are good reasons, both conceptual and empirical, to consider more criteria in the portfolio construction process.

As discussed above, the challenge for any criteria is to provide the basis for identifying the correct stocks at the appropriate time in their cycle. This has always been a particular problem in forming value portfolios, as the majority of stocks chosen by the commonly used criteria underperform the market over reasonable holding periods, such as 12 months (Bird and Gerlach, 2003). The use of other criteria such as price momentum and dispersion are likely to have gone some way towards solving these problems by, for example, keeping a 'cheap' stock out of the portfolio until a more appropriate time. Indeed, price momentum would seem to offer some promise in timing the entry of a stock into a value portfolio. Further, recent studies have found that a combination of some quality measure with the value criteria has the potential of improving the proportion of value stock that outperforms, which translates into a significant increase in added value.

Finally, there is the complex issue as to why do value and momentum strategies continue to add value, especially as they are well known and easy to implement. As suggested earlier, the success of value strategies is possibly easier to understand, as it may just be a premium to compensate for the discomfort associated with holding value stocks. The success of momentum is a bit more difficult to understand as it seems just another outworking of the market underreacting to new information, which is one aspect of market behaviour for which an explanation is still being sought.

Acknowledgments

The authors gratefully acknowledge the contribution of Thomson Finance for providing the I/B/E/S earnings per share data as part of their programme to encourage academic research, and also GMO Woolley, a London-based quantitative investment manager, who kindly supplied much of the other data used in this study.

Notes

1. With agreement stocks are ranked on the basis of earnings revisions by analysts over the previous two-month period – upward revisions minus

downward revisions divided by the total number of revisions – with a low (high) ranking indicative of a large number of negative (positive) revisions.
2. When forming portfolios within one country, the returns on the portfolio are calculated in local currency. Where the portfolios are formed across all seven countries, the returns are all calculated in British pounds.
3. For a detailed discussion of the calculation of size-adjusted returns, see La Porta *et al.* (1997)
4. Combinations of value were evaluated with the three measures of momentum (price momentum, agreement and dispersion), but findings are reported only for the first two of these momentum criteria. It was proved that dispersion does a great job in differentiating expensive stocks, with low dispersion expensive stocks performing quite well, and value also performs well differentiating high dispersion stocks with cheap high dispersion stocks performing quite well. While the use of dispersion was found to enhance a value strategy, however, it did less well than either price momentum or dispersion.
5. These expectations are also supported by the present findings when the timing of outperformance of the value and momentum strategies was evaluated. The value portfolio did little better than break even during the 1990s, with all the added value coming during the post-January 2000 period. In the case of the momentum strategies, all their added value came during the 1990s, with this strategy actually underperforming the market in the period since January 2000. These finds are consistent with the findings of studies on style timing, which found that momentum investing performed best in periods of strong economic growth, while value performed best during periods of economic weakness.
6. Although the findings are not reported in this paper, the performance of this strategy actually increased to about 1.25 per cent per month when the portfolios were formed on a country corrected basis, suggesting that the country bias introduced without the correction actually detracts from performance.
7. For the three larger markets (UK, Germany and France), the results reported are for a 4 (book-to-market) × 4 (six-month price momentum) × 2 (dispersion), which results in 32 portfolios being formed. However, the sample size was too small to apply this to the other markets, where a 3 × 2 × 2 analysis was used.

References

Acker, L. and Athanassakos, G. (1997) 'Prior Uncertainty, Analyst Bias, and Subsequent Abnormal Performance', *Journal of Financial Research,* 20, 483–502.

Arshanapalli, B., Coggin, T. and Doukas, J. (1998) 'Multifactor Asset Pricing Analysis of International Value Investment Strategies', *Journal of Portfolio Management,* Summer, 23, 79–87.

Asness, C. (1997) 'The Interaction of Value and Momentum Strategies', *Financial Analysts Journal,* March/April, 26, 50–60.

Asness, C., Friedman, J., Krail, R. and Liew, M. (2000) 'Style Timing: Value versus Growth', *Journal of Portfolio Management,* 26, 50–60.

Babaris, N., Shleifer, A. and Vishny, R. (1998) 'A Model of Investor Sentiment', *Journal of Finance.*

Ball, R. and Brown, P. (1968) 'A Empirical Evaluation of Accounting Income Numbers', *Journal of Accounting Research,* 6, 159–78.

Bird, R. and Gerlach, R. (2003) 'A Bayesian Approach to Enhancing a Value Strategy: Evidence from the US, UK and Australia', University of Technology, Sydney, Working Paper.

Bird, R. and Whitaker, J. (2003) 'The Performance of Value and Momentum Investment: Portfolios: Recent Experience in the Major European Markets', *Journal of Asset Management*, 4, 221–46.

Chan, L., Hamao, Y. and Laknoishok, J. (1991) 'Fundamentals and Stock Returns in Japan', *Journal of Finance*, 46, 1739–64.

Ciconne, S. (2003) 'Forecast Dispersion and Error versus Size, Book-to-market Ratio and Momentum: A Comparison of Anomalies from 1992 to 2001', *Journal of Asset Management*, 3, 333–44.

Dische, A. (2002) 'Dispersion in Analyst Forecasts and the Profitability of Earnings Momentum', *European Financial Management*, 8, 211–28.

Givoly, D. and Lakonishok, J. (1979) 'The Information Content of Financial Analysts' Forecasts of Earnings', *Journal of Accounting and Economics*, 1, 165–78.

Graham B. and Dodd, D. (1934) *Security Analysis*, McGraw-Hill, New York.

Hong, H. and Stein, J. (1999) 'A Unified Theory of Underreaction, Momentum Trading and Overreaction in Asset Markets', *Journal of Finance*, December, 54, 2143–83.

Jegadeesh, N. and Titman, S. (1993) 'Returns to Buying Winners and Losers: Implications for Stock Market Efficiency', *Journal of Finance*, 48, 65–91.

Jegadeesh, N. and Titman, S. (2001) 'Profitability of Momentum Strategies: An Evaluation of Alternative Explanations', *Journal of Finance*, 56, 699–720.

Lakonishok, J., Schleifer, A. and Vishny, R. (1994) 'Contrarian Investment, Extrapolation and Risk', *Journal of Finance*, 49, 1541–78.

La Porta, R., Lakonishok, J., Schleifer, A. and Vishny, R. (1997) 'Good News for Value Stocks: Further Evidence on market Efficiency', *Journal of Finance*, 52, 859–75.

Lee, C. and Swaminathan, B. (2000) 'Price Momentum and Volume Trading', *Journal of Finance*, 55, 2143–83.

Rosenberg, B., Reid, K. and Lanstein, R. (1985) 'Persuasive Evidence of Market Inefficiency', *Journal of Portfolio Management*, 11, 9–17.

Rouwenhorst, K. (1998) 'International Momentum Strategies', *Journal of Finance*.

Rouwenhorst, K. (1999) 'Local Return Factors and Turnover in Emerging Markets', *Journal of Finance*, 54, 1439–64.

Swaminathan, B. and Lee, C. (2000) 'Do Stock Prices Overreact to Earnings News?' Cornell Graduate School of Management Working Paper.

Womack, K. (1996) 'Do Brokerage Analysts' Recommendations Have Information Value?', *Journal of Finance*, 51, 137–67.

7

Cointegration Portfolios of European Equities for Index Tracking and Market Neutral Strategies

*Christian L. Dunis**
is Professor of Banking and Finance at Liverpool John Moores University, and Director of its Centre for International Banking, Economics and Finance (CIBEF). He is also a consultant to asset management firms and an Editor of the European Journal of Finance. He has published widely in the field of financial markets analysis and forecasting, and has organised the annual Forecasting Financial Markets Conference since 1994.

Richard Ho
is an associate researcher at the Centre for International Banking, Economics and Finance of Liverpool John Moores University (CIBEF). Richard holds a MSc in International Banking and Finance from Liverpool John Moores University.

**CIBEF – Centre for International Banking, Economics and Finance, JMU, John Foster Building, 98 Mount Pleasant, Liverpool L3 5UZ, UK*
Tel: +44 (0)20 7228 6126; e-mail: cdunis@totalise.co.uk

Introduction

Financial markets are highly interdependent and for many decades portfolio managers have scrutinised the comovements between markets. It is regrettable, however, that traditional quantitative portfolio construction still heavily relies on the analysis of correlations for modelling the complex interdependences between financial assets. Admittedly, the application of the concept of correlation has been improved and, over the last ten years, following the generalised use of the JP Morgan (1994)

Reprinted from 'Cointegration portfolios of European equities for index tracking and market neutral strategies' by Christian L. Dunis and Richard Ho in *Journal of Asset Management*, 6, 2005, pp. 33–52, DOI:10.1057/palgrave.jam.2240164. With kind permission from Palgrave Macmillan Ltd.

RiskMetrics approach, quantitative portfolio managers have made increasing use of conditional correlations.

Yet, if correlations are indeed time varying, their many changes across time make them a difficult tool to use in practice when managing quantitative portfolios, as the frequent rebalancing they imply may be very costly. Correlation and cointegration are somewhat related concepts, but the key distinction between them is that correlation reflects short-run comovements in returns, while cointegration measures long-run comovements in prices.

Accordingly, the main motivation for this paper is to gauge the benefits of less frequent portfolio rebalancing through the use of the concept of cointegration, which relies on the long-term relationship between time series, and thus assets, to devise quantitative European equities portfolios in the context of two applications: a classic index tracking strategy and a long/short equity market neutral strategy.

When index tracking portfolios are constructed on the basis of returns analysis, ie correlation, it is necessary to rebalance them frequently to keep them in line with the benchmark index to be tracked. Yet, if the allocations in a portfolio are designed such that the portfolio tracks an index, the portfolio should be cointegrated with the index: in the short run the portfolio might deviate from the index, but they should be tied together in the longer run. Optimal cointegration portfolios, as they rely on the long-run trends between asset prices, should therefore not require as much rebalancing.

Market neutral strategies have become popular among investment managers, particularly since the end of the stock market bull run in 2000, as their key characteristic is that, if constructed and implemented properly, the underlying stock market behaviour does not affect the results of the portfolio. In other words, returns generated by an equity market neutral portfolio should be independent of the general stock market returns. A long/short equity market neutral strategy consists in buying a portfolio of attractive stocks, the long portion of the portfolio, and selling a portfolio of unattractive stocks, the short portion of the portfolio. The spread between the performance of the longs and the shorts provides the value added of this investment strategy and, here again, the frequency of rebalancing is a key element in the final performance.

Data are used from the Dow Jones EUROStoxx50 index and its constituent stocks from 4th January, 1999, to 30th June, 2003, to construct cointegration portfolios of European equities, implementing in turn index tracking and long/short equity market neutral strategies: the results show that the designed portfolios are strongly cointegrated with the benchmark and indeed demonstrate good tracking performance; in the same vein, the long/short market neutral strategy generates steady returns under adverse market circumstances but, contrary to expectations, does not minimise volatility.

The rest of the paper is organised as follows. The second section briefly reviews the literature on common trends in equity markets and cointegration-based trading strategies. The third section describes the techniques and investment strategies retained for this study, while the fourth section documents the data used and the construction of the cointegration portfolios. The estimation results are presented in the fifth section, and the final section closes this paper with a summary of the conclusions.

Literature review

Since the seminal work of Engle and Granger (1987), cointegration has emerged as a powerful technique for investigating common trends in multivariate time series, providing a sound methodology for modelling both long-run and short-run dynamics in a system.

Although models of cointegrated financial time series are now relatively common, their importance for quantitative porfolio optimisation has remained very limited until now, because the traditional starting point for portfolio construction since Markowitz (1952, 1959) is a correlation analysis of returns, whereas cointegration is based on the raw price, rate or yield data: any decision based on long-term common trends in the price data is excluded in standard risk-return modelling.

Recent research on stock market linkages has emphasised finding common stochastic trends for a group of stock markets through testing for cointegrating relationships. Using monthly and quarterly data for the period January 1974 to August 1990 and the Johansen (1988) test for multiple cointegration, Kasa (1992) investigates whether there are any common stochastic trends in the equity markets of the US, Japan, the UK, Germany and Canada. The results indicate the presence of a single common trend driving these countries' stock markets. Corhay *et al.* (1993) study whether the stock markets of different European countries display a common long-run trend. They use static regression models and a VAR-based maximum likelihood framework, which provides empirical evidence of common stochastic trends among five important European stock markets over the period 1975–1991. Masih and Masih (1997) underline the growing leading role of the US market following the 1987 crash.

Meanwhile, Choudhury (1997) analyses the long-run relationships between six Latin American stock markets and the US market using weekly data for the period January 1989 to December 1993. The cointegration tests indicate the presence of a long-run relationship between the six Latin American indices with and without the US index. Other studies looking at linkages across developing countries include Cheung and Mak (1992), Chowdhury (1994), Garrett and Spyrou (1994), Ng (2002) and Dunis and Shannon (2004).

Yet, these papers focus primarily on stock market linkages. Closer to the preoccupation with optimal portfolio construction, Cerchi and Havenner (1988) and Pindyck and Rothemberg (1992) underline that an equity index is by definition a weighted sum of its constituents, so that there should be a sufficiently large basket of component equities which is cointegrated with the index, provided index weights are reasonably stable across time. Alexander and Dimitriu (2002) build index tracking and market neutral cointegration portfolios for domestic US equities based on the Dow Jones Industrial Average index with daily data from January 1990 to December 2001 whereas, using 12 years of daily data from January 1990 to March 2002, Qiu (2002) devises a cointegration-based portfolio of international bonds from eight different countries to replicate the 13-country JP Morgan global government bond index. Finally, using the same EUROStoxx50 index and constituent series as the present authors do, but with daily data from September 1998 to July 2002, Burgess (2003) develops cointegration-based strategies for hedging a given equity position or implementing statistical arbitrage trading opportunities.

Methodology and investment strategies

Cointegration models

The issues of common trends and the interdependence of financial markets have come under increased scrutiny in recent years, following Engle and Granger (1987), who point out that a linear combination of two or more non-stationary series may be stationary: if such a stationary linear combination exists, the non-stationary time series are said to be cointegrated. The stationary linear combination is called the cointegrating equation and may be interpreted as a long-run equilibrium relationship between the variables. Thus, cointegration of stock markets means there is a long-run relationship between them: if Y and X are $I(1)$ time series and are cointegrated so that $u = Y - \alpha - \beta x$ is $I(0)$, then, in the long run, Y and X do not drift apart, since u has a constant mean, which is zero. Hence, $Y = \alpha + \beta X$ can be interpreted as an equilibrium or long-run relationship between these markets, and u is referred to as the error-correction term (ECT), since it gives the 'error' value in $Y = \alpha + \beta X$ and so is the deviation from equilibrium which, in the long run, is zero.

Engle and Granger (1987) and Engle and Yoo (1987) propose a two-step estimation method, where the first step consists of estimating a long-run equilibrium relationship, and the second is the estimation of the dynamic error-correction relationship using lagged residuals. Holden and Thompson (1992) claim that this two-step approach has the advantage that the estimation of the two steps is quite separate, so that changes in the dynamic model do not enforce re-estimation of the static model obtained in the first step. As such, it offers a tractable modelling procedure.

Alexander (1999) suggests nevertheless that the problem of uniqueness arises when there are more than two variables included in the model, ie the possibility of more than one cointegrating vector between the selected variables according to the choice of dependent variable. In the circumstances, the well-documented Johansen (1988) method for multiple cointegration allows testing for a number of cointegrating vectors at the same time. It relies on estimating a vector autoregression (VAR) model in differences, such as

$$\begin{aligned}\mathbf{\Delta}X_t = \mu + \Gamma_1\mathbf{\Delta}X_{t-1} + \Gamma_2\mathbf{\Delta}X_{t-2} + \ldots + \Gamma_{p-1}\mathbf{\Delta}X_{t-p-1} \\ + \mathbf{\Pi}X_{t-p-1} + BZ_t = u_t \end{aligned} \quad (1)$$

where X is an $(m \times 1)$ matrix of $I(1)$ variables, Z is an $(s \times 1)$ matrix of $I(0)$ variables, the Γ_j and $\mathbf{\Pi}$ are $(m \times m)$ matrices of unknown parameters, and B is an $(m \times s)$ matrix of unknown parameters. M is the number of variables in X, and p is the maximum lag in the equation, which is a VAR model. If $\mathbf{\Pi}$ has zero rank, no stationary linear combination can be identified and the variables in X_t are not cointegrated. The number of lags to be included within the model is determined by minimizing Akaike's error criterion.

In the current applications, however, the choice of the dependent variable is completely obvious, ie the EUROStoxx50 index for the index tracking application and the ad hoc artificial 'long' and 'short' benchmarks for the long/short equity market neutral strategy. There is therefore no doubt as to what the endogenous variable in the cointegration equation should be and which cointegrating vector one should be looking for, so the original Engle and Granger (1987) approach can also be applied to estimate cointegration equations such as

$$Y_t = \alpha + \beta X_t + u_t \tag{2}$$

where Y_t and X_t are cointegrated time series, and therefore the residual series and tracking error u_t is stationary.

It is worth noting that, with a large number of stocks, there may be no alternative to using Equation (2), for technical reasons: indeed, multicollinearity may occur, in which case least squares estimates are unbiased, but their variances are large and may be far from the true value. This can be solved using ridge regression (Hoerl and Kennard, 1970a, b), where, by adding a degree of bias to the regression estimates, it is hoped that the net effect will be to give more reliable ones.

Index tracking

The first investment strategy selected in this paper is a classic index tracking strategy which aims to replicate the benchmark in terms of returns and volatility, using cointegration rather than correlation. This allows us to make use of the full information contained in stock prices and base the portfolio weights on the long-run behaviour of stocks.

As with traditional correlation-based portfolio construction, the selection of the stocks to be included in the cointegration portfolio is 'exogenous', so to speak. Obviously, the quality of the index tracking will highly depend on the stock selection, and several alternative combinations should be tried out before choosing the final tracking portfolio.

Then, portfolio weights are determined over the chosen in-sample period by the coefficients of the cointegration equation between the log price of the market index and the portfolio stocks log prices as exogenous variables.

$$\log(\mathrm{STOXX}_t) = a_0 + \sum_{k=1}^{n} a_k \log(P_{k,t}) + \varepsilon_t \tag{3}$$

where STOXX_t is the EUROStoxx50 index and $P_{k,t}$ is the price of the constituent stock P_k at time t, the series STOXX_t and $P_{k,t}$ are cointegrated, and therefore the residual series, ie the tracking error, ε_t is stationary.

Using log prices has the advantage that the tracking error ε_t is in return format and the a_k coefficients are portfolio weights: they need to be normalised, however, to sum up to one to give the percentage weight of each selected stock in the index tracking portfolio. The index tracking portfolio daily returns are computed as the weighted sum of the daily returns of its constituent stocks.

Long/short equity market neutral strategy

As underlined by Lederman (1996) and Jelicic and Munro (1999), market neutral strategies are often considered by fund managers as state-of-the-art investment strategies. They actually include many different complex trading strategies in the bond and equity markets, and it is beyond the scope of this paper to review them all. This paper concentrates exclusively on long/short equity market neutral strategies.

Long/short equity investment can be traced back to the late 1940s and the A. W. Jones investment partnership that bought and shorted stocks. It was later refined by N. Tartaglia at Morgan Stanley in the late 1980s. It was not until recently, however, that long/short equity strategies gained any real institutional appeal. In fact, these strategies have really become popular among investment managers since the stock market downturn in 2000, because their key characteristic is that, if constructed and implemented properly, the underlying stock market behaviour should not affect the results of the portfolio. In other words, returns generated by an equity market-neutral portfolio should be independent of the general stock market returns.

A long/short equity market neutral strategy consists in buying a portfolio of attractive stocks, the long portion of the portfolio, and selling a portfolio of unattractive stocks, the short portion of the portfolio. The spread between the performance of the longs and the shorts provides the value added of this investment strategy which seeks to provide a return in excess of the risk-free rate. The strategy is not a pure enhanced cash strategy because of the significantly higher risk and return expectations of the strategy, but it is an absolute return investment approach, hence its frequent description as a 'double alpha' strategy.

Indeed, there are two primary sources of return to a long/short equity neutral strategy. The first component is the 'long' portfolio, where the investor is a buyer of stocks: in this 'long' portfolio, the investor profits when the stocks in the portfolio rise in price, on average, and loses when the stock prices fall.[1] The second component is the 'short' portfolio, where the long/short equity investor borrows stocks from another investor and then sells the stocks to generate the short portfolio (note the self-financing aspect of the long/short strategy): in this 'short' portfolio, the investor profits when the prices of the constituent stocks fall, on average, and loses when these stocks rise in price.

In practice, the construction of both 'long' and 'short' portfolios derives from the index tracking strategy: only this time the aim is to devise two cointegrating portfolios to track two benchmarks, a benchmark 'plus' and a benchmark 'minus' constructed by adding to (respectively, subtracting from) the main benchmark daily returns an annual excess return of x per cent (equally distributed on the daily returns). The two cointegration equations tested are

$$\log(\text{STOXX}_t^+) = a_0 + \sum_{k=1}^{n} a_k \log(P_{k,t}^+) + \varepsilon_t^+ \tag{4}$$

where STOXX_t^+ is the EUROStoxx50 'plus' index devised as a benchmark for the 'long' portfolio, and $P_{k,t}^+$ is the price of the constituent stock P_k^+ at time t, the series STOXX_t^+ and $P_{k,t}^+$ are cointegrated, and therefore the residual series ε_t^+ is stationary.

$$\log(\text{STOXX}_t^-) = a_0 + \sum_{k=1}^{n} a_k \log(P_{k,t}^-) + \varepsilon_t^- \tag{5}$$

where STOXX_t^- is the EUROStoxx50 'minus' index devised as a benchmark for the 'short' portfolio and $P_{k,t}^-$ is the price of the constituent stock P_k^- at time t, the series STOXX_t^- and $P_{k,t}^-$ are cointegrated and therefore the residual series ε_t^- is stationary.

Clearly, the choice of the annual excess return to construct the two 'long' and 'short' cointegrated portfolios is critical. If, as mentioned before, there is a good reason to expect *a priori* that a sufficiently large basket of component equities will be cointegrated with the reference market index, this may not be true in the case of ad hoc benchmarks, such as those created for the 'long' and 'short' portfolios. The satisfaction of the cointegration tests in (4) and (5) is therefore essential, but it can be reasonably expected that the larger the annual excess return chosen, the more difficult it will be to satisfy these tests.

Overall, the long/short equity market neutral strategy consists of buying the 'long' portfolio and selling the 'short' portfolio. The global portfolio daily returns are computed as the sum of the daily returns of the 'long' and 'short' portfolios (multiplied by -1 for the 'short' portfolio), where the daily returns of each of these portfolios is the weighted sum of the daily returns of their constituent stocks. In other words, the strategy returns depend on the spread between the benchmarks tracked.

Finally, as the 'long' and 'short' portfolios are both highly correlated with the reference stock market benchmark, and assuming that each tracking error is not correlated with the market, one would expect a low correlation of their difference with the market benchmark, a key characteristic of a market neutral strategy.

Data and portfolio construction

Data

The data used in this paper are the Dow Jones EUROStoxx50 index and its constituent stocks as at 30th June, 2003. The databank spans 4th January, 1999, to 30th June, 2003, four and a half years of data with 1,084 readings in total. It was obtained from the Yahoo financial website (www.finance.yahoo.co.uk). The advantage of taking this stock index is that it covers a panel of international stocks from different European countries, all denominated in a common currency, the euro. Yet, as rightly mentioned by Burgess (2003), the slightly non-synchronous closing times of the different European stock markets would induce distortions in a true trading environment, but, for this paper, it is deemed that these closing prices are good enough and serve well the purpose of demonstrating the use of cointegration portfolios.

The 50 stocks listed in the EUROStoxx50 index, their ticker symbols and their weights in the index as at 30th June, 2003, are given in Appendix 1.

A log transformation is applied to both the benchmark and the underlying stocks, as this ensures that the cointegration equation coefficients can be interpreted as portfolio weights and because, if the level variables are cointegrated, so will be their logarithms. Traditional ADF tests are performed for the EUROStoxx50 index and its constituent time series to confirm that they are all non-stationary.[2]

Portfolio construction

For both applications, an initial in-sample portfolio is constructed initially for the period from January 1999 to December 2001, and it is progressively expanded monthly until June 2003: the initial portfolio (P0) is constructed over the period from January 1999 to December 2001 and simulated out-of-sample in January 2002 as the first tracking portfolio (P1), then the second tracking portfolio is constructed over the period from January 1999 to January 2002 and simulated out-of-sample in February 2002 (P2), the third tracking portfolio is constructed using data from January 1999 to February 2002 and simulated out-of-sample in March 2002 (P3), and so on. Therefore 18 out-of-sample portfolios (P1–P18) are obtained.

The initial portfolio P0 is based on three years of daily data, and the coefficients of the cointegration regression are subsequently re-estimated monthly using the Johansen (1988) test procedure (see Appendix 2 for an example). The first cointegration tracking portfolio (P1) is simulated from 2nd to 31st January, 2002, using estimation data from 4th January, 1999, to 28th December, 2001, to determine portfolio weights. The last tracking portfolio (P18) is simulated from 2nd to 30th June, 2003, using data from 4th January, 1999, to 30th May, 2003, to estimate portfolio weights.

To build the index tracking portfolio, it is first necessary to apply a stock selection procedure: for the purpose of diversification, one initially applies the simplest stock selection criterion available, ie the weight of the stocks in the index at the moment of the portfolio construction to construct P0 portfolios containing 5, 10, 15 and 20 constituent stocks that are most highly cointegrated with the EUROStoxx50 index as at 28th December, 2001. Only relative weights are subsequently modified.

The cointegration equation then allows portfolio weights to be determined, using the regression coefficients and normalizing their sum to 1. There is no specific constraint: both long and short positions are allowed.

The stationarity of the tracking error in each regression is then tested with a traditional ADF test, the more stationary the tracking error, the greater the cointegration between the benchmark and the constructed portfolio.

The final stage is the computation and analysis of portfolio results. To gauge portfolio performance, for each tracking portfolio, annualised returns (using portfolio returns, estimated as the first difference in portfolio log prices), annualised volatility, excess returns, information ratio,[3] Sharpe ratio[4] and correlation of the tracking portfolio returns with the index returns are calculated.

This paper devises cointegration portfolios as described above for three different applications: (1) a simple index tracking; (2) the same, but with different rebalancing frequencies; and (3) a long/short market neutral strategy.

Simple index tracking methods

Cointegrated portfolios are constructed, tracking the EUROStoxx50 index, which contain respectively 5, 10, 15 and 20 stocks.

Different rebalancing frequencies

To investigate whether the stock selection method is responsible for potential weight instability, alternative stock selection methods are used, also based on price ranking criteria. To reduce turnover, each portfolio is kept constant for three-month, six-month and one-year investment periods. The initial strategy based on monthly rebalancing is subsequently referred to as RM, while the quarterly, semi-annual and annual rebalancing strategies are denoted by RQ, RSA and RA, respectively. Note that an important difference between the initial stock selection method and the alternative ones proposed here will be associated transaction costs.

Long/short equity market neutral

An extension for exploiting the tracking potential of cointegrated portfolios is to replicate 'plus' and 'minus' benchmarks by creating 'long' and 'short' portfolios. Yet many different 'plus' and 'minus' benchmarks can be devised on the back of the EuroStoxx50 index, leading to alternative tracking portfolios.

Concerning the 'constrained' long/short strategy, one needs to construct two new *artificial* benchmarks by adding/subtracting an annualised return of x per cent uniformly from the daily returns of the EuroStoxx50 index. (For instance, to construct the 'EuroStoxx50–5 per cent' artificial benchmark, one needs to subtract 0.01984 per cent, ie 5 per cent/252, assuming a 252-day trading year, from the EuroStoxx50 daily returns and then find a cointegration relationship between this new benchmark and some of the stocks available.) The methodology for an artificial 'EuroStoxx50 plus' benchmark is obviously similar.

Having ensured that the portfolios pass the cointegration test, one then computes the weights exactly as with the simple index tracking strategy. The long/short portfolio manager gets the sum of the return of the 'long' portfolio and the return (multiplied by –1) of the 'short' portfolio (in fact, less the borrowing cost of the 'short' portfolio, as he/she needs to borrow to 'buy' the stocks of the 'short' portfolio before selling them, and one therefore subtracts 4 per cent p.a. from the 'short' portfolio return to reflect borrowing costs).

Nine combinations of artificial benchmarks are used in order to implement different long/short equity market neutral portfolios: (1) 'plus' 2.5 per cent vs 'minus' 2.5 per cent; (2) 'plus' 2.5 per cent vs 'minus' 5 per cent; (3) 'plus' 2.5 per cent vs 'minus' 10 per cent; (4) 'plus' 5 per cent vs 'minus' 2.5 per cent; (5) 'plus' 5 per cent vs 'minus' 5 per cent; (6) 'plus' 5 per cent vs 'minus' 10 per cent; (7) 'plus' 10 per cent vs 'minus'

2.5 per cent; (8) 'plus' 10 per cent vs 'minus' 5 per cent; and (9) 'plus' 10 per cent vs 'minus' 10 per cent.

Results and performance analysis

This section presents only some of the results obtained for the three strategies followed, ie the simple index tracking, the different rebalancing frequency and the long/short equity market neutral strategies. Complete results are available from the authors upon request.

Simple index tracking

The actual stocks contained in the different tracking portfolios are given in Appendix 3. Table 7.1 documents the in-sample results of the tracking portfolios compared with the benchmark, and Table 7.2 documents the out-of-sample results of the tracking portfolios compared with the benchmark.

The overall conclusion is that, over an 18-month period where the benchmark lost 24.62 per cent, all tracking portfolios produced better

Table 7.1 In-sample results for EuroStoxx50 and tracking portfolios (January 1999–December 2001)

Portfolio	Annualised return (%)	Annualised volatility (%)	Correlation with benchmark	Information ratio	Sharpe ratio
Benchmark	5.33	23.71	–	0.23	0.06
5 stocks	86.58	91.34	0.21	0.95	0.90
10 stocks	13.05	49.02	0.13	0.27	0.18
15 stocks	19.18	34.30	0.48	0.56	0.44
20 stocks	29.71	45.33	0.44	0.66	0.57

Table 7.2 Out-of-sample results for EuroStoxx50 and tracking portfolios (January 2002–June 2003)

Portfolio	Annualised return (%)	Annualised volatility (%)	Correlation with benchmark	Information ratio	Sharpe ratio
Benchmark	−24.62	34.01	–	−0.72	−0.84
5 stocks	0.23	38.33	0.65	0.01	−0.10
10 stocks	41.75	77.37	0.06	0.54	0.49
15 stocks	−6.28	31.23	0.79	−0.20	−0.33
20 stocks	−9.45	37.28	0.75	−0.25	−0.36

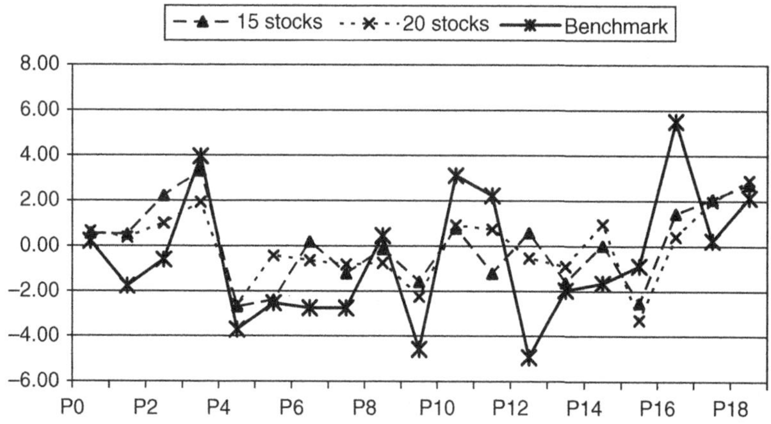

Figure 7.1 Sharpe ratio for EuroStoxx50 and two tracking portfolios (January 2002–June 2003)

out-of-sample returns and risk-adjusted returns. The portfolio comprising ten stocks registers the best performance, but it is also the least correlated with the benchmark.

Figure 7.1 shows that the Sharpe ratios for the 15-stock and 20-stock tracking portfolios are less volatile compared with the benchmark.

Different rebalancing frequencies

The results of the simple index tracking show that the ten-stock tracking portfolio has the best performance out-of-sample. As all tracking errors are stationary throughout the whole period, this portfolio is selected to compare its results when using different rebalancing strategies, monthly (RM), quarterly (RQ), semi-annually (RSA) and annually (RA).

As can be seen from Table 7.3, all portfolios with ten stocks using different rebalancing frequencies have a better performance than the benchmark. In terms of volatility, all tracking portfolios show a higher volatility than the EuroStoxx50 index. Using monthly and quarterly rebalancing produces similar annualised returns of about 42 per cent. The ten-stock tracking portfolio with quarterly rebalancing has the best overall performance, with the highest information ratio and a 0.18 correlation with the benchmark.

It is concluded that quarterly rebalancing is better than monthly rebalancing, especially if transaction costs are included (see Appendix 4 for the weights profiles): true, an important difference between the

Table 7.3 Out-of-sample results for EuroStoxx50 and ten-stock tracking portfolios with various rebalancing frequencies (January 2002–June 2003)

Portfolio	Annualised return (%)	Annualised volatility (%)	Correlation with benchmark	Information ratio	Sharpe ratio
Benchmark	−24.62	34.01	–	−0.72	−0.84
10 (RM)	41.75	77.37	0.06	0.54	0.49
10 (RQ)	42.33	57.21	0.18	0.74	0.67
10 (RSA)	9.90	56.58	0.13	0.18	0.10
10 (RA)	−21.98	48.03	0.25	−0.46	−0.54

rebalancing strategies is transaction costs, which will be lower, the lower the rebalancing frequency retained. Still, with estimated round-trip transaction costs of 12 basis points (b.p.) for the EuroStoxx50 index, and about twice as much for its component stocks in the cash market, these costs are not such a major drawback for the more active strategies.[5]

Long/short equity market neutral

Table 7.4 compares ten-stock tracking portfolios obtained by adding to and subtracting from the benchmark returns an annual excess return of −2.5 per cent, −5 per cent, −10 per cent, +2.5 per cent, +5 per cent and +10 per cent, respectively.

In general, long/short strategies produce better results than the benchmark except for the three strategies replicating the benchmark minus 2.5 per cent which produce very negative performance. Yet, contrary to what one would expect, the long/short strategies do not minimise volatility: annualised volatility is generally higher than the benchmark. The long/short combination 'plus 5 per cent/minus 5 per cent' has the best out-of-sample performance, with a Sharpe ratio of 1.35 compared with −0.84 for the EuroStoxx50 index during this 18-month period.

Still, Table 7.4 shows the out-of-sample results with the benefit of hindsight. In fact, fund managers do not have the benefit of hindsight and would have traded the 'best portfolio' at the end of each calibration period.

Table 7.5 shows that the combination 'plus 5 per cent/minus 5 per cent' has the highest in-sample Sharpe ratio at 0.43 against 0.06 for the EuroStoxx50 index.

Table 7.4 shows that, after 18 months, the combination 'plus 5 per cent/minus 5 per cent' was still the best strategy. In real life, however, as fund managers do not know the future, they would probably have modified their choice of long/short combination every three or six months.

Table 7.4 Average out-of-sample results for ten-stock long/short portfolios (January 2002–June 2003)

	Benchmark	+2.5%/ −2.5%	+2.5%/ −5%	+2.5%/ −10%	+5%/ −2.5%	+5%/ −5%	+5%/ −10%	+10%/ −2.5%	+10%/ −5%	+10%/ −10%
Annualised return (%)	−24.62	−486.75	81.15	37.21	−384.15	183.74	139.80	−368.26	199.64	155.69
Annualised volatility (%)	34.01	179.63	96.83	84.00	206.63	132.92	119.56	285.72	239.65	225.66
Correlation with benchmark	–	−0.17	0.20	0.18	−0.13	0.20	0.18	−0.05	0.18	0.17
Information ratio	−0.72	−2.71	0.84	0.44	−1.86	1.38	1.17	−1.29	0.83	0.69
Sharpe ratio	−0.84	−2.73	0.80	0.40	−1.88	1.35	1.14	−1.30	0.82	0.67

Table 7.5 In-sample results for ten-stock long/short portfolios (January 1999–December 2001)

	Benchmark	+2.5%/ −2.5%	+2.5%/ −5%	+2.5%/ −10%	+5%/ −2.5%	+5%/ −5%	+5%/ −10%	+10%/ −2.5%	+10%/ −5%	+10%/ −10%
Annualised return (%)	5.33	4.25	5.92	7.35	5.75	7.42	8.85	78.94	80.61	82.04
Annualised volatility (%)	23.71	5.67	10.54	21.87	4.85	7.97	18.36	1761.45	1762.00	1763.34
Correlation with benchmark	-	0.19	0.23	0.26	−0.14	0.08	0.21	0.03	0.03	0.03
Information ratio	0.23	0.75	0.56	0.34	1.19	0.93	0.48	0.04	0.05	0.05
Sharpe ratio	0.06	0.04	0.18	0.15	0.36	0.43	0.26	0.04	0.04	0.04

It is unlikely that they would leave their portfolio using the same long/short portfolio mix for more than a year.

Accordingly, it is assumed in the following that investment managers manage their long/short portfolios using three-month and six-month rebalancing frequencies.

Long/short neutral strategies rebalancing every six months

Table 7.6 shows that for the out-of-sample period from January 2002 to June 2002, the combination 'plus 2.5 per cent/minus 10 per cent' produced the best Sharpe ratio at 0.58. Unfortunately, in January 2002, a fund manager would have used the results from Table 7.5 to set up his/her trading strategy using the combination 'plus 5 per cent/minus 5 per cent': six months later, in June 2002, this strategy had produced a Sharpe ratio of –0.58, still superior to the –1.69 achieved by the EuroStoxx50 index.

If one uses the results from Table 7.6 with the combination 'plus 2.5 per cent/minus 10 per cent' for the following six months, Table 7.7 shows that for the following six-month out-of-sample period from July 2002 to December 2002, the retained strategy produces a Sharpe ratio of –0.23 (still far superior to the –1.13 of the EuroStoxx50 index), whereas the best Sharpe ratio for that period is provided by the combination 'plus 10 per cent/minus 5 per cent' with a Sharpe ratio of 2.36.

Using the results from Tables 7.5–7.7, one can simulate the trading performance of a fund manager rebalancing his/her portfolio every six months. Starting from January 2002 to June 2002, he/she would have traded the combination 'plus 5 per cent/minus 5 per cent' (ie the best in-sample combination), then, from July 2002 to December 2002, the combination 'plus 2.5 per cent/minus 10 per cent' (ie the best strategy between January 2002 and June 2002) and, from January 2003 to June 2003, the combination 'plus 10 per cent/minus 5 per cent' (ie the best strategy between July 2002 and December 2002).

The trading simulation with semi-annual rebalancing yields a Sharpe ratio of 1.03 compared with 1.35 for the best single out-of-sample long/short strategy chosen from the in-sample optimisation (see Table 7.8). This is still far superior to the –0.84 achieved by the EuroStoxx50 index over the same 18-month period.

Long/short neutral strategies rebalancing every three months

A similar approach to that adopted for the six-month rebalancing is used, but this time a trading strategy is assumed whereby the fund manager changes the structure of his/her portfolio every three months (see Appendix 5). Starting from January 2002 to March 2002, a fund

Table 7.6 Out-of-sample results for ten-stock long/short portfolios (January 2002–June 2002)

	Benchmark	+2.5%/ −2.5%	+2.5%/ −5%	+2.5%/ −10%	+5%/ −2.5%	+5%/ −5%	+5%/ −10%	+10%/ −2.5%	+10%/ −5%	+10%/ −10%
Annualised return (%)	−34.52	−22.43	−2.04	19.52	−34.59	−14.21	7.36	−700.02	−679.63	−658.07
Annualised volatility (%)	22.75	22.93	30.22	26.75	25.15	31.50	26.96	136.57	141.33	135.30
Correlation with benchmark	–	−0.08	−0.14	−0.16	−0.07	−0.13	−0.16	−0.21	−0.19	−0.19
Information ratio	−1.52	−0.98	−0.07	0.73	−1.38	−0.45	0.27	−5.13	−4.81	−4.86
Sharpe ratio	−1.69	−1.15	−0.20	0.58	−1.53	−0.58	0.12	−5.16	−4.84	−4.89

Table 7.7 Out-of-sample results for ten-stock long/short portfolios (July 2002–December 2002)

	Benchmark	+2.5%/ −2.5%	+2.5%/ −5%	+2.5%/ −10%	+5%/ −2.5%	+5%/ −5%	+5%/ −10%	+10%/ −2.5%	+10%/ −5%	+10%/ −10%
Annualised return (%)	−47.67	−424.38	14.90	−28.25	−116.57	322.70	279.55	514.72	954.00	910.85
Annualised volatility (%)	45.88	198.76	142.41	143.31	280.82	238.67	238.89	402.84	402.90	402.40
Correlation with benchmark	–	−0.05	0.31	0.28	0.03	0.33	0.31	0.16	0.32	0.31
Information ratio	−1.04	−2.14	0.10	−0.20	−0.42	1.35	1.17	1.28	2.37	2.26
Sharpe ratio	−1.13	−2.16	0.08	−0.23	−0.43	1.34	1.15	1.27	2.36	2.25

Table 7.8 Out-of-sample trading simulation of successive optimal long/short portfolio combinations rebalanced every six months and EuroStoxx50 (January 2002–June 2003)

	Long/short strategies	**EuroStoxx50**
Annualised return (%)	124.07	–24.62
Annualised volatility (%)	116.55	34.01
Correlation with benchmark	0.19	–
Information ratio	1.06	–0.72
Sharpe ratio	1.03	–0.84

Table 7.9 Out-of-sample trading simulation of successive optimal long/short portfolio combinations rebalanced every three months and EuroStoxx50 (January 2002–June 2003)

	Long/short strategies	**EuroStoxx50**
Annualised return (%)	90.45	–24.62
Annualised volatility (%)	122.79	34.01
Correlation with benchmark	0.18	–
Information ratio	0.74	–0.72
Sharpe ratio	0.70	–0.84

manager would have traded the combination 'plus 5 per cent/minus 5 per cent' (ie the best in-sample combination), then from April 2002 to June 2002, the combination 'plus 2.5 per cent/minus 5 per cent' (ie the best strategy between January and March 2002), then from July 2002 to September 2002, the combination 'plus 2.5 per cent/minus 10 per cent' (ie the best strategy between April and June 2002), then from October 2002 to December 2002, the combination 'plus 10 per cent/minus 5 per cent' (ie the best strategy between July and September 2002), then from January 2003 to March 2003, the combination 'plus 10 per cent/minus 10 per cent' (ie the best strategy between September and December 2002) and, finally, from April 2003 to June 2003, the combination 'plus 10 per cent/minus 5 per cent' (ie the best strategy between January and March 2003).

This trading simulation with quarterly portfolio rebalancing produces a Sharpe ratio of 0.70 compared with 1.03 for the six-month rebalancing and 1.35 for the best single out-of-sample long/short strategy chosen from the in-sample optimisation. Here again, this trading strategy yields a much better Sharpe ratio than the –0.84 achieved by the EuroStoxx50 index over the same 18-month period (see Table 7.9).

Transaction costs

When analysing the performance of the index tracking strategy, transaction costs will obviously be lower, the lower the rebalancing frequency retained. This is an even more important issue in the case of long/short market neutral strategies, as these entail trading two tracking portfolios, and the self-financing feature offered by the short sale generally implies a leverage of 2:1 and thus double transaction costs. Still, with at most eight round trips in total for quarterly rebalancing and four for semi-annual rebalancing, the transaction costs involved (192 b.p. and 96 b.p., respectively) are minimal compared with the annualised returns, before transaction costs, of the long/short strategies achieved in the trading simulations.

Concluding remarks

The main motivation for this paper was to demonstrate the benefits arising from the use of the concept of cointegration, which relies on the long-term relationship between time series, and thus assets, to devise quantitative European equities portfolios in the context of two applications: a classic index tracking strategy and a long/short equity market neutral strategy. Indeed, its key characteristics, ie a mean-reverting tracking error (ie stationary residuals from the cointegration equation), enhanced portfolio weight stability over time and the full use of the information contained in stock prices, allow for the flexible design of various investment strategies in equity markets, from index tracking to long/short market neutral.

Clearly, the results suffer from some of the simplifying assumptions adopted. First, it was arbitrarily chosen to select at most 20 of the 50 stocks in the EuroStoxx50 index: a larger equity basket would probably have led to better results for the index tracking application. Secondly, the simplest stock selection criterion available are applied, ie the weight of the stocks in the index at the moment of the portfolio construction: the quality of the benchmark tracking highly depends on the stock selection procedure and much improvement could be achieved in this respect. Finally, the slightly non-synchronous closing times of the different European stock markets would induce distortions in a true trading environment, but closing prices serve well the purpose of demonstrating the use of cointegration portfolios.

Yet, the results are quite impressive. Over the 18-month out-of-sample period from January 2002 to June 2003, where the EuroStoxx50 index lost 24.62 per cent, all tracking portfolios produce much better returns and risk-adjusted returns, with less volatile Sharpe ratio profiles than those of the benchmark.

Strategies based on correlation would require rebalancing portfolios frequently. In contrast, cointegration-based portfolios require less frequent turnover: an analysis of alternative rebalancing frequencies shows that a quarterly portfolio update appears preferable to monthly, semi-annual or annual reallocations.

Furthermore, the tracking capabilities offered by cointegration make it possible to track different benchmarks and thus to implement long/short equity market neutral strategies. Most of the long/short combinations analysed in this paper produce better out-of-sample results and risk-adjusted results than the EuroStoxx50 benchmark, albeit at the cost of higher volatility, which may be linked to the smaller number of stocks included in the 'long' and 'short' portfolios. Two trading simulations with quarterly and semi-annual rebalancing show that, during the adverse market conditions of the January 2002 to June 2003 out-of-sample period, the selected long/short combinations would have attracted Sharpe ratios of 1.03 and 0.70, respectively, against –0.84 for the EuroStoxx50 index. These results are seen to be robust to the introduction of transaction costs.

Overall, the main conclusion from this research is that cointegration portfolios add economic value for investors and fund managers. In the circumstances, the results should go some way towards convincing a growing number of quantitative fund managers to experiment beyond the bounds of correlation analysis for portfolio construction.

Notes

1. Note that, if there are no such constraints imposed on the 'long' and 'short' portfolios, both are likely to include some short equity positions.
2. These results and descriptive statistics are not reproduced here to conserve space. They are available from the authors upon request.
3. The information ratio is simply the average annualised return of an investment strategy divided by its average annualised volatility.
4. The Sharpe ratio was computed as the average annualised return of an investment strategy minus the risk-free rate (assumed at 4 per cent p.a.) divided by the average annualised volatility.
5. Assuming that each time the entire portfolio is reshuffled, which is not the case in this application, monthly rebalancing implies at most 12 round trips per year or 288 b.p., quarterly rebalancing four round trips or 96 b.p., semi-annual rebalancing two round trips or 48 b.p., whereas annual rebalancing entails only one round trip or 24 b.p. For trading costs assumptions, see www.interactive-brokers.com and Bessimbinder (2003).

References

Alexander, C. (1999) 'Optimal Hedging Using Co-integration', *Philosophical Transactions of the Royal Society, London,* Series A, 357, 2039–58.

Alexander, C. and Dimitriu, A. (2002) 'The Cointegration Alpha: Enhanced Index Tracking and Long-Short Equity Market Neutral Strategies', ISMA Discussion Papers in Finance 2002–08, ISMA Centre, University of Reading.

Bessimbinder, H. (2003) 'Trade Execution Costs and Market Quality after Decimalization', *Journal of Financial and Quantitative Analysis,* 38(4), 747–77.

Burgess, A. N. (2003) 'Using Cointegration to Hedge and Trade International Equities', in Dunis, C., Laws, J. and Naïm, P. (eds), *Applied Quantitative Methods for Trading and Investment,* John Wiley, Chichester, 41–69.

Cerchi, M. and Havenner, A. (1988) 'Cointegration and Stock Prices', *Journal of Economic Dynamics and Control,* 12, 333–46.

Cheung, Y. L. and Mak, S. C. (1992) 'A Study of the International Transmission of Stock Market Fluctuation between the Developed Markets and Asian Pacific Markets', *Applied Financial Economics, 2,* 43–7.

Choudhury, T. (1997) 'Stochastic Trends in Stock Prices: Evidence from Latin American Markets', *Journal of Macroeconomics,* 19, 285–304.

Chowdhury, A. R. (1994) 'Stock Market Interdependencies: Evidence from the Asian NIE's', *Journal of Macroeconomics,* 16, 629–51.

Corhay, C. A., Tourani Rad, A. and Urbain, J.P. (1993) 'Common Stochastic Trends in European Stock Markets', *Economics Letters,* 42, 385–90.

Dunis, C. L. and Shannon, G. (2004) 'Emerging Markets of South-East and Central Asia: Do they Still Offer a Diversification Benefit?', Working Paper, CIBEF, Liverpool John Moores University (www.cibef.com).

Engle, R. F. and Granger, C. W. J. (1987) 'Co-integration and Error Correction: Representation, Estimation and Testing', *Econometrica,* 55(2), 251–76.

Engle, R. F. and Yoo, B. S. (1987) 'Forecasting and Testing in Co-integrated Systems', *Journal of Econometrics,* 35, 143–59.

Garrett, I. and Spyrou, S. (1994) 'Common Stochastic Trends In Emerging Equity Markets', http://les1.man.ac.uk/af/Staff/Academic/I_Garrett/Research/.

Hoerl, A. E. and Kennard, R. W. (1970a) 'Ridge Regression: Biased Estimation for Nonorthogonal Problems', *Technometrics,* 12, 55–67.

Hoerl, A. E. and Kennard, R. W. (1970b) 'Ridge Regression: Application to Nonorthogonal Problems', *Technometrics,* 12, 69–82.

Holden, K. and Thompson, J. (1992) 'Co-integration: An Introductory Survey', *British Review of Economic Issues,* 14, 1–55.

Jelicic, D. and Munro, J. (1999) 'Market Neutral Investing', *Derivatives Use, Trading & Regulations, 5,* 209–22.

Johansen, S. (1988) 'Statistical Analysis of Cointegration Vectors', *Journal of Economic Dynamics and Control,* 12, 231–54.

JP Morgan (1994) *RiskMetrics Technical Document,* Morgan Guaranty Trust Company, New York.

Kasa, K. (1992) 'Common Stochastic Trends in International Stock Markets', *Journal of Monetary Economics,* 29, 95–124.

Lederman, J. (1996) *Market Neutral, State-of-the-Art Strategies for Every Market Environment,* Irwin Professional Publishing, Chicago.

Markowitz, H. M. (1952) 'Portfolio Selection', *Journal of Finance,* 7, 77–91.

Markowitz, H. M. (1959) *Portfolio Selection, Efficient Diversification of Investments*, John Wiley, New York.
Masih, A. M. and Masih, R. (1997) 'Dynamic Linkages and the Propagation Mechanism Driving Major International Stock Markets: An Analysis of the Pre- and Post-Crash Eras', *Quarterly Review of Economics and Finance*, 37, 859–86.
Ng, H. T. (2002) 'Stock Market Linkages in South-East Asia', *Asian Economic Journal*, 16, 353–77.
Pindyck, R. S. and Rothemberg, J. J. (1992) 'The Comovement of Stock Prices', *Quarterly Journal of Economics*, 108, 1073–103.
Qiu, H. I. (2002) 'Devising a Cointegration-Based International Bond Portfolio', Working Paper, CIBEF, Liverpool John Moores University.

Appendix 1: Stock in Dow Jones EUROStoxx50 as at 30th June, 2003 (in descending order according to their weight in EUROStoxx50 index)

Company	ISIN	Market sector	Float factor[a]	Adjusted weight (%)
TOTAL FINA ELF	FR0000120271	Energy	1.00	8.03
ROYAL DUTCH PETROLEUM	NL0000009470	Energy	1.00	7.83
NOKIA	FI0009000681	Technology	1.00	6.10
TELEFONICA	ES0178430E18	Telecommunications	0.94	4.12
ENI	IT0003132476	Energy	0.65	3.19
SIEMENS	DE0007236101	Technology	0.93	3.16
UNILEVER NV	NL0000009348	Food & Beverage	1.00	3.14
BNP	FR0000131104	Banks	0.94	3.11
BCO SANTANDER CENTRAL HIS	ES0113900J37	Banks	1.00	2.81
AVENTIS	FR0000130460	Healthcare	0.87	2.80
BCO BILBAO VIZCAYA ARGENT	ES0113211835	Banks	1.00	2.46
DEUTSCHE TELEKOM	DE0005557508	Telecommunications	0.57	2.45
DEUTSCHE BANK R	DE0005140008	Banks	0.95	2.29
E.ON	DE0007614406	Utilities	0.87	2.28
DAIMLERCHRYSLER	DE0007100000	Automobiles	0.81	2.21
ASSICURAZIONI GENERALI	IT0000062072	Insurance	0.86	2.09
GROUPE SOCIETE GENERALE	FR0000130809	Banks	1.00	2.05
CARREFOUR SUPERMARCHE	FR0000120172	Noncyclical Goods & Services	0.80	1.99
ABN AMRO	NL0000301109	Banks	0.89	1.91

(*Continued*)

Company	ISIN	Market sector	Float factor[a]	Adjusted weight (%)
SANOFI SYNTHELABO	FR0000120578	Healthcare	0.56	1.90
ING GROEP	NL0000303600	Insurance	0.88	1.87
PHILIPS ELECTRONICS	NL0000009538	Cyclical Goods & Services	1.00	1.85
FRANCE TELECOM	FR0000133308	Telecommunications	0.43	1.82
BASF	DE0005151005	Chemicals	0.91	1.78
L'OREAL	FR0000120321	Noncyclical Goods & Services	0.47	1.78
AXA UAP	FR0000120628	Insurance	0.82	1.58
GROUPE DANONE	FR0000120644	Food & Beverage	0.95	1.52
UNICREDITO ITALIANO	IT0000064854	Banks	0.69	1.51
TELECOM ITALIA	IT0001127429	Telecommunications	0.45	1.51
TIM	IT0001052049	Telecommunications	0.44	1.39
FORTIS	BE0003801181	Financial Services	0.89	1.37
REPSOL YPF	ES0173516115	Energy	0.82	1.33
VIVENDI UNIVERSAL	FR0000127771	Media	1.00	1.31
AIR LIQUIDE	FR0000120073	Chemicals	1.00	1.23
ENDESA	ES0130670112	Utilities	0.95	1.13
ENEL	IT0003128367	Utilities	0.32	1.01
SUEZ	FR0000120529	Utilities	0.93	1.00
ALLIANZ	DE0008404005	Insurance	0.74	0.90
AEGON	NL0000301760	Insurance	0.88	0.87
SAINT GOBAIN	FR0000125007	Construction	1.00	0.87
BAYER	DE0005752000	Chemicals	0.94	0.86
LVMH MOET HENNESSY	FR0000121014	Cyclical Goods & Services	0.46	0.82
RWE	DE0007037129	Utilities	0.76	0.82
SAN PAOLO IMI	IT0001269361	Banks	0.86	0.78
ALCATEL	FR0000130007	Technology	0.93	0.73
LAFARGE	FR0000120537	Construction	1.00	0.69
VOLKSWAGEN	DE0007664005	Automobiles	0.69	0.65
MUENCHENER RUECKVER R	DE0008430026	Insurance	0.62	0.58
AHOLD	NL0000331817	Noncyclical Goods & Services	1.00	0.29
BAYERISCHE HYPO & VEREINS	DE0008022005	Banks	0.63	0.23

[a]The free float factor is the percentage of shares remaining after the block ownership and restricted shares adjustments are applied to the total number of shares. One has: strategic shareholding (%) = number of shares classified as strategic/total number of shares outstanding free float (%) = 100% – strategic shareholding (%).

Appendix 2: Johansen (1988) cointegration test

Sample(adjusted): 6 716
Included observations: 711 after adjusting endpoints
Trend assumption: Linear deterministic trend
Series: LOG_STOXX LOG_FR_12027 LOG_NL_RD LOG_FI_870737 LOG_IT_ENI LOG_DE_723610 LOG_FR_13110 LOG_ES_SAN LOG_FR_13046 LOG_ES_BBVA LOG_DE_555750 Lags interval (in first differences): 1 to 4
Unrestricted cointegration rank test

Hypothesised No. of CE(s)	Eigenvalue	Trace statistic	5% critical value	1% critical value
None**	0.104080	310.8791	277.71	293.44
At most 1	0.086735	**232.7369**	233.13	247.18
At most 2	0.052139	168.2288	192.89	204.95
At most 3	0.040202	130.1564	156.00	168.36
At most 4	0.036513	100.9820	124.24	133.57
At most 5	0.032318	74.53538	94.15	103.18
At most 6	0.028475	51.17799	68.52	76.07
At most 7	0.017255	30.63820	47.21	54.46

*(**) denotes rejection of the hypothesis at the 5% (1%) level

1 Cointegrating Equation(s): Log likelihood 20651.38

Normalised cointegrating coefficients (std err. in parentheses)

LOG_ STOXX	LOG_ FR_12027	LOG_ NL_RD	LOG_ FI_870737	LOG_ IT_ENI	LOG_ DE_723610	LOG_ FR_13110
1.000000	0.445615	−0.813099	−0.072151	0.942272	−0.133696	−0.093449
	(0.10463)	(0.11559)	(0.03832)	(0.13883)	(0.04958)	(0.08731)

Appendix 3: Stocks contained in various tracking portfolios

Company	ISIN	Market Sector
5 stocks tracking portfolio		
TOTAL FINA ELF	FR0000120271	Energy
ROYAL DUTCH PETROLEUM	NL0000009470	Energy
NOKIA	FI0009000681	Technology
ENI	IT0003132476	Energy
SIEMENS	DE0007236101	Technology
10 stocks tracking portfolio		
TOTAL FINA ELF	FR0000120271	Energy
SIEMENS	DE0007236101	Technology

(Continued)

Company	ISIN	Market Sector
BNP	FR0000131104	Banks
AVENTIS	FR0000130460	Healthcare
BCO BILBAO VIZCAYA ARGENT	ES0113211835	Banks
DEUTSCHE TELEKOM	DE0005557508	Telecommunications
DEUTSCHE BANK R	DE0005140008	Banks
DAIMLERCHRYSLER	DE0007100000	Automobiles
ASSICURAZIONI GENERALI	IT0000062072	Insurance
ABN AMRO	NL0000301109	Banks
15 stocks tracking portfolio		
TOTAL FINA ELF	FR0000120271	Energy
ROYAL DUTCH PETROLEUM	NL0000009470	Energy
NOKIA	FI0009000681	Technology
ENI	IT0003132476	Energy
SIEMENS	DE0007236101	Technology
BNP	FR0000131104	Banks
BCO SANTANDER CENTRAL HIS	ES0113900J37	Banks
AVENTIS	FR0000130460	Healthcare
BCO BILBAO VIZCAYA ARGENT	ES0113211835	Banks
DEUTSCHE TELEKOM	DE0005557508	Telecommunications
DEUTSCHE BANK R	DE0005140008	Banks
E.ON	DE0007614406	Utilities
DAIMLERCHRYSLER	DE0007100000	Automobiles
ASSICURAZIONI GENERALI	IT0000062072	Insurance
ABN AMRO	NL0000301109	Banks
20 stocks tracking portfolio		
TOTAL FINA ELF	FR0000120271	Energy
ROYAL DUTCH PETROLEUM	NL0000009470	Energy
NOKIA	FI0009000681	Technology
ENI	IT0003132476	Energy
SIEMENS	DE0007236101	Technology
BNP	FR0000131104	Banks
BCO SANTANDER CENTRAL HIS	ES0113900J37	Banks
AVENTIS	FR0000130460	Healthcare
BCO BILBAO VIZCAYA ARGENT	ES0113211835	Banks
DEUTSCHE TELEKOM	DE0005557508	Telecommunications
DEUTSCHE BANK R	DE0005140008	Banks
E.ON	DE0007614406	Utilities
DAIMLERCHRYSLER	DE0007100000	Automobiles
ASSICURAZIONI GENERALI	IT0000062072	Insurance
ABN AMRO	NL0000301109	Banks
ING GROEP	NL0000303600	Insurance
PHILIPS ELECTRONICS	NL0000009538	Cyclical Goods & Services
BASF	DE0005151005	Chemicals
L'OREAL	FR0000120321	Noncyclical Goods & Services
REPSOL YPF	ES0173516115	Energy

Appendix 4: Portfolio weights in ten-stocking tracking portfolios

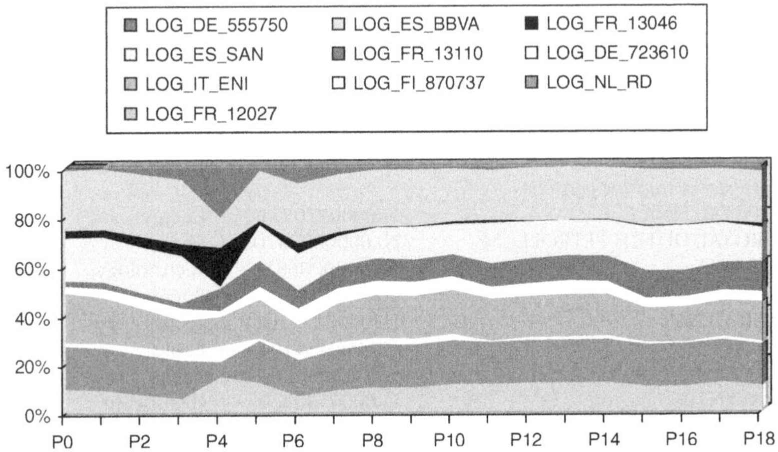

Figure 7A4.1 Portfolio weights in ten-stock tracking portfolio with monthly rebalancing

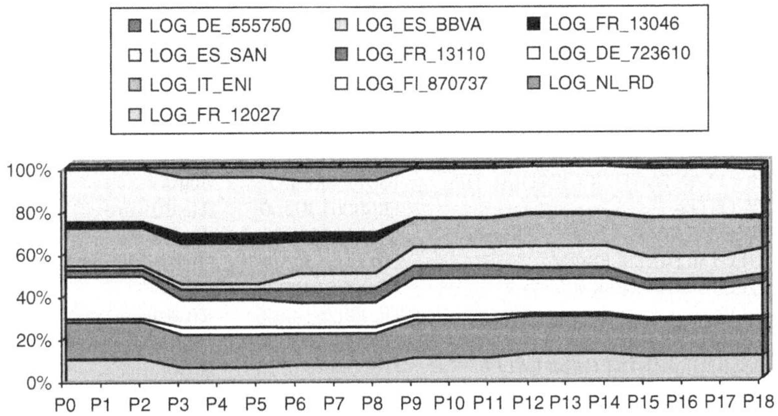

Figure 7A4.2 Portfolio weights in ten-stock tracking portfolio with quarterly rebalancing

Appendix 5: Out-of-sample results for ten-stock long/short portfolios with quarterly rebalancing

Table A5.1 Out-of-sample results for ten-stock long/short portfolios (January–March 2002)

	Benchmark	+2.5%/ −2.5%	+2.5%/ −5%	+2.5%/ −10%	+5%/ −2.5%	+5%/ −5%	+5%/ −10%	+10%/ −2.5%	+10%/ −5%	+10%/ −10%
Annualised return %	3.94	−31.83	−6.58	−10.46	−37.75	−12.50	−16.37	−1348.00	−1322.75	−1326.62
Annualised volatility, %	20.52	12.80	17.25	18.37	13.50	17.35	18.21	234.22	236.47	235.93
Correlation with benchmark	–	0.13	0.14	0.16	0.11	0.12	0.14	−0.23	−0.04	0.04
Information ratio	0.19	−2.49	−0.38	−0.57	−2.80	−0.72	−0.90	−5.76	−5.59	−5.62
Sharpe ratio	0.00	−2.80	−0.61	−0.79	−3.09	−0.95	−1.12	−5.77	−5.61	−5.64

Table A5.2 Out-of-sample results for ten-stock long/short portfolios (April–June 2002)

	Benchmark	+2.5%/ –2.5%	+2.5%/ –5%	+2.5%/ –10%	+5%/ –2.5%	+5%/ –5%	+5%/ –10%	+10%/ –2.5%	+10%/ –5%	+10%/ –10%
Annualised return, %	–72.98	–13.02	2.5	49.50	–31.44	–15.91	31.09	–52.04	–36.52	10.48
Annualised volatility, %	24.97	33.05	43.19	35.14	36.81	45.64	35.72	38.91	46.20	34.66
Correlation with benchmark	–	–0.29	–0.41	–0.47	–0.24	–0.38	–0.45	–0.19	–0.34	–0.42
Information ratio	–2.92	–0.39	0.06	1.41	–0.85	–0.35	0.87	–1.34	–0.79	0.30
Sharpe ratio	–3.08	–0.52	–0.03	1.29	–0.96	–0.44	0.76	–1.44	–0.88	0.19

Table A5.3 Out-of-sample results for ten-stock long/short portfolios (July–September 2002)

	Benchmark	+2.5%/ −2.5%	+2.5%/ −5%	+2.5%/ −10%	+5%/ −2.5%	+5%/ −5%	+5%/ −10%	+10%/ −2.5%	+10%/ −5%	+10%/ −10%
Annualised return, %	−121.08	−834.1	−104.6	−187.6	−233.8	495.7	412.7	710.34	1439.81	1356.80
Annualised volatility, %	53.48	190.7	87.76	94.86	360.9	258.2	263.9	563.18	461.60	465.98
Correlation with benchmark	–	0.03	−0.01	−0.07	0.07	0.03	−0.01	0.09	0.05	0.02
Information ratio	−2.26	−4.37	−1.19	−1.98	−0.65	1.92	1.56	1.26	3.12	2.91
Sharpe ratio	−2.34	−4.39	−1.24	−2.02	−0.66	1.90	1.55	1.25	3.11	2.90

Table A5.4 Out-of-sample results for ten-stock long/short portfolios (October–December 2002)

	Benchmark	+2.5%/ −2.5%	+2.5%/ −5%	+2.5%/ −10%	+5%/ −2.5%	+5%/ −5%	+5%/ −10%	+10%/ −2.5%	+10%/ −5%	+10%/ −10%
Annualised return, %	25.73	−14.70	134.39	131.09	0.63	149.7	146.42	319.11	468.19	464.90
Annualised volatility, %	38.28	206.1	197.06	191.76	200.8	219.1	213.92	242.51	344.20	338.82
Correlation with benchmark	–	−0.14	0.64	0.63	0.00	0.63	0.63	0.24	0.60	0.60
Information ratio	0.67	−0.07	0.68	0.68	0.00	0.68	0.68	1.32	1.36	1.37
Sharpe ratio	0.58	−0.09	0.66	0.66	−0.02	0.67	0.67	1.30	1.35	1.36

Table A5.5 Out-of-sample results for ten-stock long/short portfolios (January–March 2003)

	Benchmark	+2.5%/ −2.5%	+2.5%/ −5%	+2.5%/ −10%	+5%/ −2.5%	+5%/ −5%	+5%/ −10%	+10%/ −2.5%	+10%/ −5%	+10%/ −10%
Annualised return, %	−58.30	−1977	17.74	1.39	−1975	20.06	3.70	−1869.2	125.39	109.03
Annualised volatility, %	40.94	620.80	129.6	108.39	617.0	146.7	125.66	624.16	227.79	207.20
Correlation with benchmark	–	−0.26	0.34	0.34	−0.25	0.34	0.33	−0.20	0.34	0.33
Information ratio	−1.42%	−3.18	0.14	0.01	−3.20	0.14	0.03	−2.99	0.55	0.53
Sharpe ratio	−1.52%	−3.19	0.11	−0.02	−3.21	0.11	0.00	−3.00	0.53	0.51

8

Emerging Markets of South-East and Central Asia: Do They Still Offer a Diversification Benefit?

*Christian L. Dunis**

is Professor of Banking and Finance at Liverpool John Moores University, School of Accounting, Finance and Economics, and Director of CIBEF

Gary Shannon

is an Associate Researcher with CIBEF

**Centre for International Banking, Economics and Finance (CIBEF), JMU, John Foster Building, 98 Mount Pleasant, Liverpool L3 5UZ, UK. E-mail: cdunis@totalise.co.uk*

Introduction

The benefits to the domestic investor from diversifying internationally have been documented widely; see, for example, Grubel (1968), Levy and Sarnat (1970), Lessard (1973), Solnik (1974) and Solnik and Noetzlin (1982). A belief widely held by academics and practitioners is that a portfolio should be well diversified to maximise potential risk-adjusted performance.

Modern portfolio theory advocates the idea that investors should diversify, as this increases the efficient frontier of their portfolio. Yet, if the correlation between the returns of the equity markets considered increases, the risk exposure of the portfolio (all else being constant) will start to increase and, at a certain point, international diversification will no longer be beneficial. The wide recognition that market volatility is time varying should have led to the acceptance that

Reprinted from 'Emerging markets of South-East and Central Asia: Do they still offer a diversification benefit?' by Christian L. Dunis and Gary Shannon in *Journal of Asset Management*, 6, 2005, pp. 168–190, DOI:10.1057/palgrave.jam.2240174. With kind permission from Palgrave Macmillan Ltd.

correlations are time varying too: this is unfortunately not yet the case, and analysing average correlations over successive periods may suggest that international diversification is still beneficial, when in fact it is not.

The growing integration of the world economy may have raised the integration and efficiency of individual stock markets thus leading to a reduction in exposure to individual event risk. Integration, however, may have come at the cost of taking away the diversification benefit of international investment.

Many papers have examined the evolution of correlation among a group of countries over time; see, among others, Kaplanis (1988), Koch and Koch (1991) and Longin and Solnik (1995). Most studies, however, have looked at the independence of stock markets in isolation without taking into account the volatility changes that may occur as a result of the markets becoming less independent.

The motivation for this paper is therefore to check whether, despite the growing world economic integration and progressive lifting of capital controls, emerging markets still offer international investors a valuable diversification benefit.

The study covers the emerging markets of Indonesia, the Philippines, Malaysia, Korea, Taiwan, China and India over the period 31st August, 1999, to 29th August, 2003 (a period with 1,044 observations characterised by both bull and bear stock markets), with the US, the UK and Japan as the reference 'established' markets.

The aim is to present the dynamics of these various markets and see whether emerging market returns show any linkages with these developed markets using various state-of-the-art techniques: multivariate cointegration and vector autoregression models (VARs) with the analysis of variance decomposition (VDC), time-varying correlations with Kalman filter models and the computation of conditional variances and covariances to devise optimal investment portfolios.

Overall, the results indicate that international diversification into the emerging equity markets considered was beneficial for a US investor during the period under study. Furthermore, it is shown that a portfolio optimised during the in-sample period and containing emerging market stocks from the countries considered outperformed a portfolio consisting purely of US stocks over the following out-of-sample period 1st Septermber, 2003, to 5th July, 2004.

The rest of this paper is organised as follows. The second section presents a short review of some articles relevant to this research;

it also looks at why international diversification may be beneficial and the risks associated with emerging markets. The third section documents the data used while the fourth section briefly describes the techniques retained for this study. The fifth section presents the estimation results and offers a comparison with those from previous studies. The final section closes this paper with a summary of the conclusions.

Literature review

Markowitz (1952) and Tobin (1958) were the pioneering advocates of the benefits of domestic portfolio diversification, suggesting that, if certain stocks were not perfectly correlated, a reduction in the overall risk of a portfolio could possibly be achieved by combining these stocks. Grubel (1968) was the first to assess the benefits of international diversification, which stimulated a series of further studies that can be regrouped according to the approach used.

Market correlation

A prerequisite for international diversification is that individual stock market returns have a degree of independence. Earlier studies such as Grubel (1968) and Levy and Sarnat (1970) used simple cross-country correlations when assessing whether the performance of stock markets have some common trend. These cross correlations can be continuously monitored by international money managers, and positions can be altered accordingly.

Grubel (1968) showed that, because of the low correlations of foreign stocks with US stocks, US investors could achieve higher rates of return for a given level of portfolio variance by expanding their portfolio to include foreign stocks from ten other mostly developed countries. These results were supported by Levy and Sarnat (1970). Solnik (1996) demonstrates, for instance, that with approximately 40 securities equally spread among major US and European stock markets, US investors can reduce their risk exposure by at least 50 per cent when compared with a portfolio consisting of only US stocks.

The general consensus is that correlations between emerging and developed stock markets are generally on the increase; see, among others, Divecha *et al.* (1992) and Ng (2002). Bekaert and Harvey (1997) find that capital market liberalisations often increase the correlation between local market returns and the world market but do not drive up local market volatility. In addition, Longin and Solnik (1995) note that volatility is contagious and international correlation increases during periods of high stock market volatility.

In summary, if some emerging markets have seen a substantial increase in correlation between their returns and those of developed stock markets, this could lead to an increase in portfolio risk for international portfolio managers. This is not to say, however, that all emerging markets would no longer be beneficial to international investors, as they could switch investments into different emerging markets that had a sufficiently low correlation to developed markets.

Cointegration

The issues of common trends and the interdependence of financial markets have come under increased scrutiny in recent years, following the seminal work on cointegration by Engle and Granger (1987) who point out that a linear combination of two or more non-stationary series may be stationary: if such a stationary linear combination exists, the non-stationary time series are said to be cointegrated. The stationary linear combination is called the cointegrating equation and may be interpreted as a long-run equilibrium relationship among the variables. Thus, cointegration of stock markets means there is a long-run relationship between them: if Y and X are $I(1)$ time series and are cointegrated so that $u = Y - \alpha - \beta x$ is $I(0)$, then, in the long run, Y and X do not drift apart, since u has a constant mean, which is zero. Hence $Y = \alpha + \beta x$ can be interpreted as an equilibrium or long-run relationship between these markets, and u is referred to as the error-correction term (ECT), since it gives the 'error' value in $Y = \alpha + \beta x$ and so is the deviation from equilibrium which, in the long run, is zero.

Recent research on stock market linkages has thus emphasised finding common stochastic trends for a group of stock markets through testing for cointegrating relationships. Using monthly and quarterly data for the period January 1974 to August 1990 and the Johansen (1988) test for multiple cointegration, Kasa (1992) investigates whether there are any common stochastic trends in the equity markets of the US, Japan, UK, Germany and Canada. The results indicate the presence of a single common trend driving these countries' stock markets.

Corhay *et al.* (1993) study whether the stock markets of different European countries display a common long-run trend. They used static regression models and a VAR-based maximum likelihood framework, which provided empirical evidence of common stochastic trends among five important European stock markets over the period 1975–91.

Meanwhile, Choudhury (1997) analyses the long-run relationships between six Latin American stock markets and the US market, using weekly data for the period January 1989 to December 1993. The cointegration tests indicate the presence of a long-run relationship between the six Latin American indices with and without the US index.

Other studies looking at linkages across developing countries include Cheung and Mak (1992), Chowdhury (1994), Garrett and Spyrou (1994) and Ng (2002).

Cointegration tests, however, cannot show whether the stock markets have become more integrated. This is because cointegration tests assume the time invariance of the cointegrating relationship. Hence, they cannot detect whether stock markets may be gradually moving towards greater integration.

Time-varying parameter models

Following Haldane and Hall (1991), who use a time-varying parameter model to test whether the relationship of sterling with the dollar and deutschmark has strengthened over the period 1976–89, Serletis and King (1997) adopt this methodology to analyse the convergence of the European Union stock markets of Belgium, Denmark, France, Germany, Greece, Ireland, Italy, the Netherlands, Spain and the UK, using quarterly data from 1971Q1 to 1992Q1. They find that the link between EU stock markets has been strengthening, but that convergence is still in the process of being achieved.

Finally, Ng (2002) investigates whether any linkages exist between the stock returns of Indonesia, Malaysia, the Philippines, Singapore and Thailand, using monthly closing stock prices over the period 1988–97. He splits the period into two (1988–92 and 1993–97) and estimates the correlations for the two periods. He then examines whether a long-term relationship exists between any of these markets using the Johansen test for multiple cointegration and estimates a time-varying parameter model for the South-East Asian stock markets to analyse the trend of integration across those markets. He finds that there was no evidence of a cointegrating relationship across the ASEAN stock markets over the period 1988–97. The correlation analysis indicates, however, that the ASEAN stock markets have become more closely linked in the second period 1993–97. The time-varying parameter model indicates that the Indonesian, Filipino and Thai stock markets all show a trend towards closer linkage with the Singaporean stock market. In contrast, the Malaysian stock market starts off relatively closely linked with the stock market of Singapore but becomes less closely linked to it over the period under study.

International diversification and emerging markets

The main reason given for international diversification is the fact that returns in two individual stock markets may be sufficiently independent to provide a benefit to the international investor. International diversification can lead to a reduction in systematic risk because it reduces domestic market exposure that cannot be diversified otherwise.

Yet an argument against international diversification in emerging markets is that they show a higher vulnerability to individual event risk with a particular sensitivity to political rather than economic considerations (see the impact of President Yeltsin's health on Russian markets in 1996–99) and to the fallout from external events (see the 'domino effect' of the South-East Asian crisis in 1997–98).

Another argument against international diversification is that currency risk may more than offset the reduction in portfolio risk. Solnik and Noetzlin (1982) indicate that the contribution made by exchange rate risk to the overall risk carried by an international portfolio is very small. Gruber *et al.* (2002) state that the return on a foreign investment expressed in the home currency is affected by the return on the foreign assets and the change in the exchange rate between the foreign and home country. Jorion (1989) insists that the contribution of currency to total risk of a well-diversified portfolio is insignificant. In any case, the exchange risk of a foreign investment may be hedged for most currencies by utilising future, forward or option contracts.

Overall, the literature confirms the evidence of an international diversification benefit. However, it also indicates that emerging and developed stock markets have become more closely integrated, thus the benefit of international diversification may be diminishing. More often than not, previous studies have either looked at the benefits of international diversification empirically, using simple cross-country correlations, or researched the integration of emerging and developed stock markets without further development of their findings. Looking at simple cross-country correlations can mislead investors, because most of the time it is the average correlation over the time period that is considered. This may cause problems, because the average correlation over the period may suggest that international diversification is beneficial, when in fact it is not. This is because the correlation has changed over time and eroded this benefit away. The wide recognition that market volatility is time varying should have led to the acceptance that correlations are time varying too: this is unfortunately not yet the case. Also, just looking at the integration of stock markets via the existence of long-term relationships, without further development of the findings, does not actually provide any direct evidence as to whether international diversification is beneficial. Numerous elements need to be taken into account when assessing whether international diversification is beneficial: for example, closer integration between two stock markets may be matched by a reduction in volatility, implying that the diversification benefit has not been eroded away.

Overall, instead of weekly or monthly data, which many studies have tended to use, this study uses daily data, as it is more likely to capture potential interactions between stock markets. This choice also recognises the fact that successful fund management has become more 'active' in recent years. In addition, various techniques are used, including the Johansen test for multiple cointegration and VAR models, time-varying parameter models based on the Kalman filters or the computation of conditional variances and covariances. Furthermore, the non-synchronous problem associated with stock markets is explicitly taken into account when tests using appropriate time lags are performed.

Data and descriptive statistics

Databank

The data used for this study are daily closing prices for the stock markets of Indonesia, the Philippines, Malaysia, Korea, Taiwan, China, India, Japan, the US and the UK. The in-sample data period under study is from 31st August, 1999 to 29th August, 2003. The total number of observations for each market is 1,044. This period covers major economic events and both a peak and a trough of global markets, with sentiment swinging wildly on both sides.

The databank is taken from the Morgan Stanley Capital International (MSCI) website (www.msc.com). The stock markets of Japan, Taiwan and Korea are opened for all or a portion of the day on Saturday. MSCI drops these entries, so as to provide consistency across all markets. When stock markets are closed owing to national holidays or severe weather conditions, the index is assumed to remain at its level of the previous day. This approach, however, would affect the test results, because a stock market will then show zero return on that day. To counter this problem, linear interpolation is used (for other possible approaches for filling missing data, refer to Dunis and Karalis (2003)). The returns of all indices are denominated in US dollars.

Table 8.1 reports the opening and closing times of the various stock markets considered. It also reports the market capitalisation rank of each stock market: important information when performing various estimations, especially time-varying parameter models and VDCs.

The selected markets are generally operating in different time zones with different opening and closing times: returns on a given calendar day may thus represent a return realised over different real time periods. It is therefore important to know the operating hours of one market relative to another when performing tests, and taking this into account implies applying appropriate lagged values where necessary.

Unit roots and descriptive statistics

First, the hypothesis that each country's stock index contains a unit root (ie that stock prices are non-stationary processes) is tested. The procedure suggested by Phillips and Perron (1998) is used as it is more robust to heteroscedasticity and autocorrelation of unknown form than the traditional ADF test.

A trend was employed for all ten series, as they seemed from the graphs to be either trending upwards or downwards. The test was performed on

Table 8.1 Opening and closing times of the stock markets under study

Stock Market	**Location of stock exchange**	**Local time**	**Time variation with GMT**	**Time relative to GMT**	**Market cap ranking**
China	Beijing	09.30–15.00	+8	01.30–07.00	5
India	Bombay	10.00–15.30	+5.50	04.30–10.00	8
Indonesia	Jakarta	09.30–12.00	+7	02.30–05.00	9
		13.30–16.00		06.30–09.00	
Japan	Tokyo	09.00–11.00	+9	00.00–02.00	2
		12.30–15.00		03.30–06.00	
South Korea	Seoul	07.30–08.30	+9	22.30–23.30	6
		09.00–16.00		00.00–07.00	
Malaysia	Kuala Lumpur	09.00–12.30	+8	01.00–04.30	7
		14.30–17.00		06.30–09.00	
Philippines	Manila	09.00–14.30	+8	01.00–06.30	10
Taiwan	Formosa	09.00–13.30	+8	01.00–05.30	4
UK	London	08.00–16.30	0	08.00–16.30	3
US	New York	09.30–16.30	–5	14.30–21.30	1

Source: International Finance Corporation (1998); BARRA Market capitalisation ranking is defined by the total amount of the various securities (bonds, debentures, and stocks) issued by corporations.

the levels and also the first differences. Overall, the Phillips–Perron test indicates that all series are non-stationary in level, but stationary when first differenced,[1] which is in agreement with the literature. The log returns of daily stock prices are therefore used for the analysis. It is nevertheless maintained that, on the basis that the series are non-stationary in their levels, there is a chance that they may be cointegrated. The descriptive statistics for the log returns of all ten stock markets retained are reported in Table 8.2.

All series are non-normally distributed, as shown by the Jarque–Bera statistic, which is again consistent with the literature on the distribution of stock market returns following Fama (1965).

Methodology

Cointegration models

Engle and Granger (1987) propose a two-step estimation method, where the first step consists of estimating a long-run equilibrium relationship and the second is the estimation of the dynamic error-correction relationship using lagged residuals. Holden and Thompson (1992) claim that this two-step approach has the advantage that the estimation of the two steps is quite separate, so that changes in the dynamic model do not enforce re-estimation of the static model obtained in the first step. As such, it offers a tractable modelling procedure. However, Alexander (1999) suggests that the problem of uniqueness arises when there are more than two variables included in the model, ie the possibility of more than one cointegrating vector between the selected variables according to the choice of dependent variable.

This is why, although the choice of dependent variable is reasonably obvious in the current application (ie an 'established' stock market), the well documented Johansen (1988) method is selected for multiple cointegration, which allows testing for a number of cointegrating vectors at the same time. It relies on estimating a VAR model in differences, such as

$$\begin{aligned}\Delta X_t = \mu + \Gamma_1 \Delta X_{t-1} + \Gamma_2 \Delta X_{t-2} \\ + \ldots + \Gamma_{p-1} \Delta X_{t-p-1} \\ + \prod X_{t-p-1} + BZ_t = u_t\end{aligned} \tag{1}$$

where X is an $(m \times 1)$ matrix of $I(1)$ variables, Z is an $(s \times 1)$ matrix of $I(0)$ variables, the Γ_j and Π are $(m \times m)$ matrices of unknown parameters,

Table 8.2 Descriptive statistics of log returns of ten stock markets

	China	India	Indonesia	Japan	Korea	Malaysia	Philippines	Taiwan	UK	US
Mean (p.a.)	−19.04	−2.18	−7.93	−10.61	−0.38	0.58	−25.29	−10.30	−9.55	−7.30
Maximum (daily)	11.02	7.05	13.77	5.77	9.18	4.64	21.97	7.39	5.26	5.61
Minimum (daily)	−10.97	−7.32	−19.95	−7.16	−12.17	−6.97	−8.15	−10.94	−5.27	−6.16
Std. dev (p.a)	32.32	26.53	38.81	23.27	39.84	18.30	26.49	32.18	20.95	21.47
Skewness	0.14	−0.45	−0.32	−0.04	−0.22	−0.34	3.24	0.07	−0.11	0.19
Kurtosis	6.63	5.23	9.79	4.09	4.79	7.26	41.74	4.42	4.57	4.33
Jarque–Bera	575	251	2021	52	148	808	67054	89	109	83
Probability	0	0	0	0	0	0	0	0	0	0
Observations	1043	1043	1043	1043	1043	1043	1043	1043	1043	1043

Note: Mean and standard deviation figures are annual averages while the maximum and minimum values are daily figures.

and B is an $(m \times s)$ matrix of unknown parameters. M is the number of variables in X, and p is the maximum lag in the equation, which is a VAR model. If Π has zero rank, no stationary linear combination can be identified, and the variables in X_t are not cointegrated. The number of lags to be included within the model is determined by minimising Akaike's error criterion.

Variance decomposition analysis

This study uses VDC, which can either be modelled in a VAR or vector error correction model (VECM), depending on whether the variables are cointegrated.

An argument that naturally arises in the context of a VAR is whether one should use levels or first differences in the VAR. Clearly, if the variables are stationary in their levels, this is not an issue. The difficulty arises, however, when the variables need to be differenced to get a stationary process. Granger and Newbold (1974) and Phillips (1986) stress that stationary data should be used, since non-stationary data can lead to spurious regression results. Further, Toda and Yamamoto (1995) noted that conventional asymptotic theory is, in general, not applicable to hypothesis testing in level VARs if the variables are integrated. Taking this into account this study uses stationary variables, whether they need to be differenced or not.

Another issue is whether an unrestricted VAR should be used where the variables in the VAR are cointegrated. There is a body of literature that supports the use of a VECM, or cointegrating VAR, in this situation, as the cointegrating vectors bind the long-run behaviour of the variables. Thus the VECM is expected to produce results in the VDC analysis that more accurately reflect the relationship between the variables than the standard unrestricted VAR. However, Naka and Tufte (1997) note that it is not clear that imposing the cointegrating vector improves performance at all horizons. Furthermore, Engle and Yoo (1987), Clements and Hendry (1995) and Hoffman and Rasche (1996) all show that an unrestricted VAR is superior (in terms of forecast variance) to a restricted VECM at short horizons when the restriction is true. Because of the short-term nature of the VDC analysis (up to ten trading days), the use of first differenced unrestricted VARs is chosen.

Finally, it has been shown that the VDC-based Cholesky factor can change dramatically if one alters the ordering of the variables in a VAR. As a result, it is chosen to order the model variables according to market capitalisation, the largest market coming first in the VAR.[2]

Time-varying parameter models with Kalman filter

Most time series analysis techniques assume fixed parameters, but in reality financial data are often time-dependent and parameters are more likely to change over time than remain constant. The Kalman filter technique overcomes the problem of fixed parameters by allowing them to vary with time. This modelling technique is chosen instead of ordinary least squares (OLS) rolling regressions and weighted least squares (WLS) models because of its superior capability to estimate the dynamics of the underlying factor sensitivities. In a typical application, state space models focus on a set of *m* state variables which change over time. In most cases, the signal will not be directly observable, being subject to systematic distortion as well as contamination by 'noise'. Further details of the model and estimation procedure can be found in Harvey (1981) and Hamilton (1994).

The following generic model is assumed in the estimation process

$$Y_t = \alpha + \beta_t X_t + \varepsilon_t \tag{2}$$

$$\beta_t = \beta_{t-1} + \eta_t \tag{3}$$

where Y_t is the dependent variable at time t (typically an emerging market return in this application), α is a stochastic constant included in order to account for any potentially omitted variable, β_t is the time-varying coefficient, X_t is the vector of explanatory variables at time t (in this case, an 'established' stock market return with the appropriate time lag to take into account the time differences mentioned above[3]) and ε_t and η_t are uncorrelated error terms.

This study thus follows Haldane and Hall (1991) and Serletis and King (1997) in a different context, along the lines of Ng (2002), who uses monthly data to check in a similar fashion whether emerging stock markets have become more closely linked with developed stock markets.

Portfolio optimisation with conditional covariance matrix

This study uses portfolio optimisation to investigate whether international diversification is still beneficial for a US investor. The stock markets of Indonesia, the Philippines, Malaysia, Korea, Taiwan, China and India will only be selected for possible inclusion within the US portfolio if they satisfy the condition that, based on the results of the time-varying parameter model, they did not show an increase in integration with the US stock market for the review period. Following this market selection, an optimal portfolio is computed at end August 2003 which is then simulated over the subsequent out-of-sample period 1st September, 2003, to 5th July, 2004.

The portfolio optimisation of Markowitz (1959) that is used requires expected returns and the full covariance matrix of the selected assets as inputs. Traditionally, it is implemented using the unconditional covariance matrix which does not take into account the occurrence through time of events in the selected stock markets and effectively yields meaningless (and thus risky) allocations: which investor or fund manager would implement an allocation that is identical whether a given market has fallen by say 15 per cent over the past week or 100 weeks ago? Accordingly, the traditional approach is modified to include the conditional covariance matrix as at end August 2003. Following JP Morgan (1994) RiskMetrics approach (which is deemed a satisfactory GARCH model specification for this purpose), the conditional variance is computed as

$$\sigma^2_{X,t} = \lambda\sigma^2_{X,t-1} + (1-\lambda)R^2_{X,t} \tag{4}$$

where $\sigma^2_{X,t}$ is the conditional variance of asset X at time t, $R^2_{X,t}$ is its squared return at time t and λ is a decay factor equal to 0.94 for daily data. Conditional covariances are calculated as

$$\sigma_{XY,t} = \lambda\sigma_{XY,t-1} + (1-\lambda)R_{X,t}\,R_{Y,t} \tag{5}$$

where $\sigma_{XY,t}$ is the conditional covariance at time t, and $R_{X,t}$ and $R_{Y,t}$ are the returns on assets X and Y respectively at time t.[4] The expected returns used in this calculation are those for the period 30th August, 2002 to 29th August, 2003, the last year of the in-sample period.

Estimation results and out-of-sample simulation

Correlation analysis

The (unconditional) correlations between the various stock markets for the period 31st August, 1999, to 29th August, 2003 are computed and the results compared with those obtained by Divecha *et al.* (1992) for the period 1986–91 in order to gauge the degree of segmentation and the integration of these markets over time. This is done in Tables 8.3–8.5.

As can be seen from Table 8.5, there does not seem to have been a general increase in correlations, as suggested by some studies, between emerging and developed stock markets. Table 8.5 shows that the UK stock market has seen a fall in correlation with all the

Table 8.3 Correlation of log returns from Divecha *et al.* (February 1986 to March 1991)

	DLCHIN	DLINDIA	DLINDO	DLJAP	DLKOREA	DLMAL	DLPHIL	DLTAI	DLUK	DLUS
DLCHIN	1									
DLINDIA	−0.160	1								
DLINDO	0.150	0.030	1							
DLJAP	−0.020	−0.160	−0.160	1						
DLKOREA	−0.050	0.400	0.070	0.370	1					
DLMAL	0.230	0.040	0.470	0.300	0.180	1				
DLPHIL	0.250	−0.100	0.470	0.230	0.200	0.330	1			
DLTAI	0.330	−0.050	0.370	0.250	−0.010	0.500	0.330	1		
DLUK	0.110	−0.050	0.090	0.470	0.270	0.670	0.190	0.210	1	
DLUS	0.330	−0.140	0.140	0.250	0.220	0.700	0.240	0.230	0.670	1

Table 8.4 Correlation of log returns (31st August, 1999 to 29th August, 2003)

	DLCHIN	**DLINDIA**	**DLINDO**	**DLJAP**	**DLKOREA**	**DLMAL**	**DLPHIL**	**DLTAI**	**DLUK**	**DLUS**
DLCHIN	1									
DLINDIA	0.183	1								
DLINDO	0.131	0.086	1							
DLJAP	0.332	0.176	0.156	1						
DLKOREA	0.387	0.282	0.157	0.0391	1					
DLMAL	0.227	0.166	0.156	0.209	0.238	1				
DLPHIL	0.149	0.112	0.134	0.158	0.187	0.194	1			
DLTAI	0.251	0.209	0.125	0.246	0.416	0.181	0.108	1		
DLUK	0.122	0.107	0.049	0.101	0.170	0.026	0.034	0.093	1	
DLUS	0.077	0.056	0.009	0.069	0.102	–0.007	–0.009	0.072	0.423	1

Table 8.5 Changes in correlation of log returns

	DLCHIN	DLINDIA	DLINDO	DLJAP	DLKOREA	DLMAL	DLPHIL	DLTAI	DLUK	DLUS
DLCHIN	1									
DLINDIA	0.343	1								
DLINDO	−0.019	0.056	1							
DLJAP	0.352	0.0336	0.316	1						
DLKOREA	0.437	−0.118	0.087	0.021	1					
DLMAL	−0.003	0.126	−0.314	−0.092	0.058	1				
DLPHIL	−0.101	0.212	−0.336	−0.072	−0.013	−0.136	1			
DLTAI	−0.079	0.259	0.245	−0.004	0.426	−0.319	−0.222	1		
DLUK	0.012	0.157	−0.041	−0.369	−0.1	−0.644	−0.156	−0.117	1	
DLUS	−0.253	0.196	−0.131	−0.181	−0.118	−0.707	−0.249	−0.158	−0.247	1

emerging stock markets under study except China and India, whereas the US has seen its correlation fall with all these markets except India. The situation of Japan is more mixed: if its market returns correlation with China, India, Korea and Indonesia has increased over the review period, it has dropped with the Philippines, Malaysia and Taiwan. In any case, it is worth noting that the unconditional correlation coefficient only measures the average correlation over a given data period. Thus, if there has been an increase in correlation in the most recent period, this may not be reflected in the unconditional correlation computed here.

Cointegration analysis

As the Phillips–Perron test indicated that all the time series contained a unit root, the next step was to test for cointegration. The tests are broken up into six separate models with three of the models containing four stock price indices and the other three models containing five stock price indices. This procedure allows an established market to be grouped with emerging markets from the same geographical area. The models are as follows: respectively, UK, US and Japan with Indonesia, Philippines and Malaysia and then, respectively, UK, US and Japan with Korea, China, India and Taiwan. As such, each established stock market is included in two separate models: one with all the Central Asian emerging stock markets and the other with the South-East Asian emerging stock markets considered in this study.

The Johansen test is used for multiple cointegration as it allows testing for a number of cointegrating vectors. Johansen and Juselius (1990) and Lütkepohl *et al.* (2001) are also followed; these authors give preference to the trace test over the maximum eigenvalue test, if both tests contradict each other. The results indicate that there exists, at most, a single cointegrating vector in each of the models (see Appendix 1). All markets considered exhibit a common stochastic trend (ie there is a long-run relationship between these stock markets). At first sight, this could suggest that diversification across these markets may no longer be beneficial for international investors. If cointegration is a useful tool for testing the existence of a long-run relationship over a given period, however, it cannot test for a gradual move towards or away from a closer relationship. It would therefore be wrong to conclude from the cointegration analysis that international diversification is no longer beneficial. Other tools must be implemented to see whether the stock markets considered have become more closely linked over time.

Variance decomposition

VDC separates the variation in one market into component shocks in the other markets. Overall, the VDC results in Appendixes 2–4 show that South-East Asian markets are not very responsive to foreign shocks (with less than 8 per cent of their forecast error variance explained by other markets), Malaysia being the most reactive. On the contrary, Central Asian markets are very sensitive to foreign shocks (ie over 10 per cent of the variance explained by foreign markets), with Korea most responsive (over 30 per cent), followed by China and Taiwan.

Finally, owing to the different time zones, the results show that markets tend to respond to US and UK market shocks the next day, whereas they mostly respond to Japanese shocks on the same day. This is corroborated by the analysis of impulse response functions (not reproduced here to conserve space, but available from the authors upon request). In any case, although interesting, VDC analysis does not allow one to conclude over the evolution through time of the links between the stock markets considered.

Time-varying parameter models with Kalman filter

Figures 8.1–8.6 show the trend of the β coefficient of each emerging market against each 'established' market (a 15-day rolling average of the

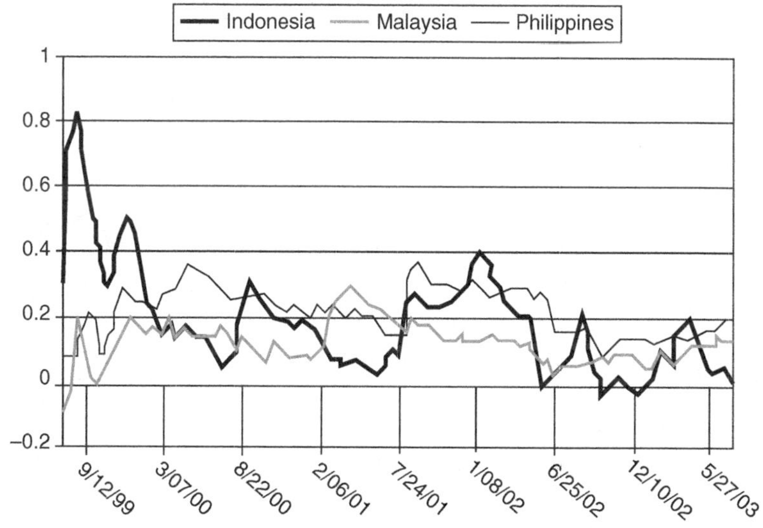

Figure 8.1 Kalman model for South-East Asia with UK as the 'established' market

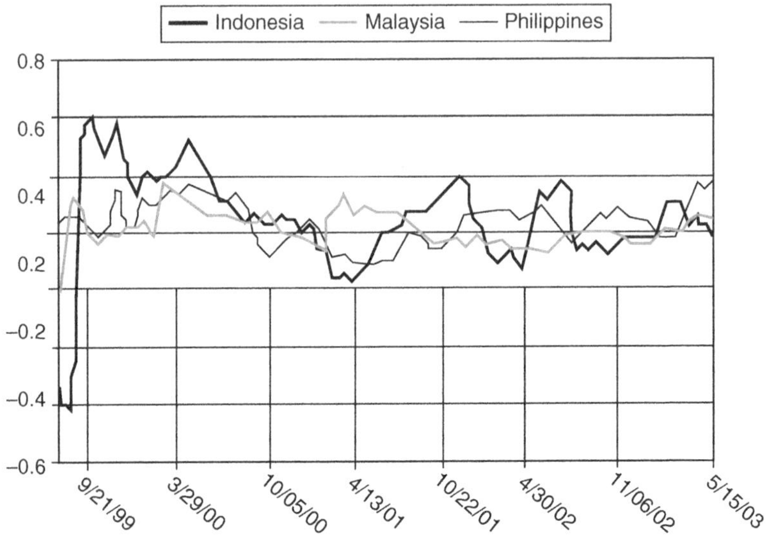

Figure 8.2 Kalman model for South-East Asia with US as the 'established' market

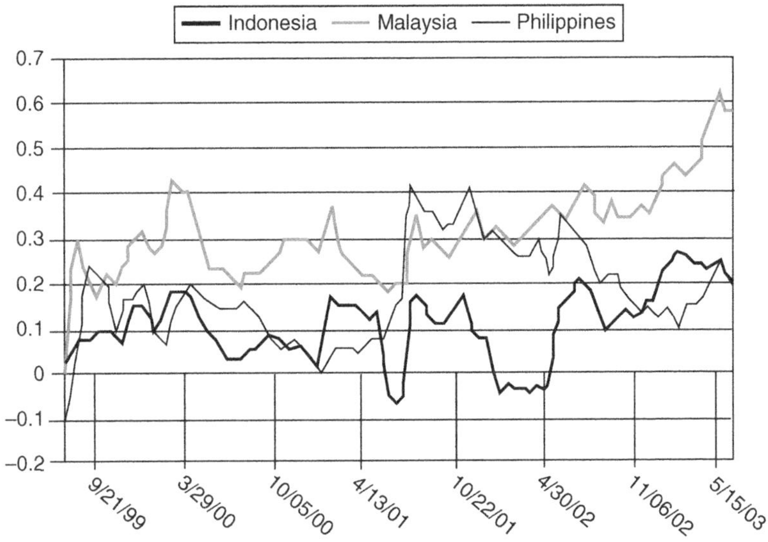

Figure 8.3 Kalman model for South-East Asia with Japan as the 'established' market

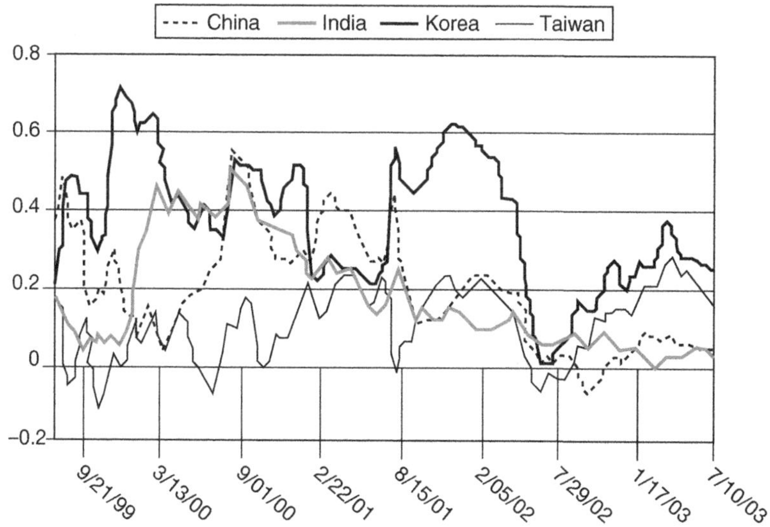

Figure 8.4 Kalman model for Central Asia with UK as the 'established' market

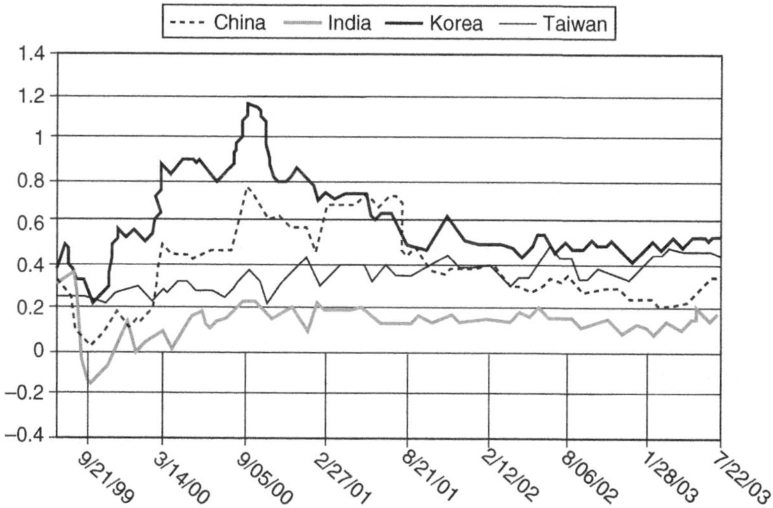

Figure 8.5 Kalman model for Central Asia with US as the 'established' market

Kalman filter results is used to detect more easily the underlying trend). As before, markets have been grouped by regions.

Looking from a UK perspective, and despite the volatility across time of the β coefficients, Figures 8.1 and 8.4 show a much weaker link of

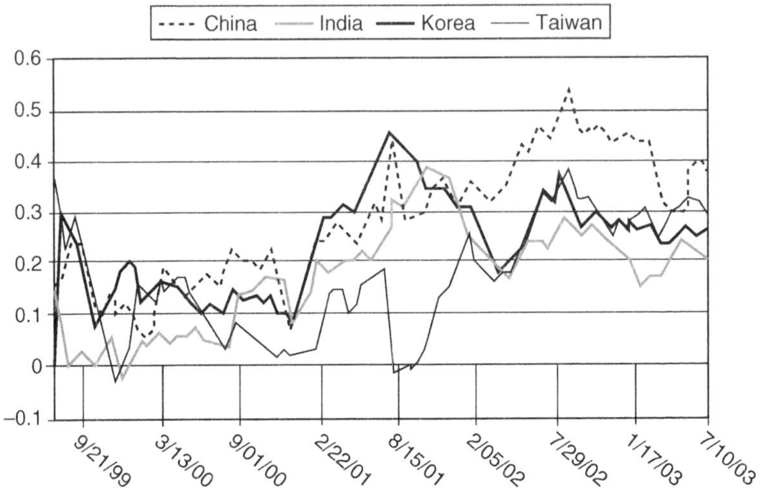

Figure 8.6 Kalman model for Central Asia with Japan as the 'established' market

Indonesia with the UK stock market, with β declining from 0.8 at the end of 1999 to about 0.1 on average in 2002–03. This weaker link is also observable for Central Asian markets, with the exception of Taiwan.

From a US perspective, Figures 8.2 and 8.5 show a general decline, from their peak in 2000, of the links to the US stock market of Indonesia, China, Taiwan and Korea (with, in this latter case, β dropping from levels above 1 to about 0.5 in 2003).

Finally, Figures 8.3 and 8.6 show a general uptrend in integration of the South-East Asian and Central Asian markets with the Japanese stock market.

Overall, the results of our time-varying models for the US and UK indicate that most emerging stock markets have seen their level of integration stay steady or decline over the review period, implying that the benefits from international diversification may not have been eroded away. Conversely, the results obtained for the links between Japan and the stock markets of South-East and Central Asia considered here would lead to a much more cautious conclusion.

Optimal investment portfolios with conditional covariances

In order to gauge more precisely the benefits from diversification into the emerging stock markets considered, the traditional Markowitz approach is used, modified for conditional variances and covariances, to find the optimal emerging markets portfolio for a US investor. The stocks considered for allocation within the investment portfolio are those of Malaysia, Indonesia, India and Taiwan. These markets have been selected for possible inclusion because, in recent times, they have seen their integration (ie their β coefficient) decline or stay steady with the US stock market. Furthermore, VDC analysis indicates that these markets explain most of their own forecast error variance: even though its time-varying β coefficient indicates that Korea has become less closely linked with the US stock market, foreign markets explain over 30 per cent of Korea's forecast error variance, and it is therefore not considered for inclusion within a US investor's portfolio.

Over the review period, the results show that there is indeed an international diversification benefit for a US investor wishing to minimise risk. Without any constraints on maximum holdings, US investors should hold 6 per cent, 52 per cent, 6 per cent and 36 per cent of their wealth in the Indian, Malaysian, Taiwanese and US markets respectively.[5] The optimal portfolio can be seen in Table 8.6.

Still, the analysis above is conducted with the benefit of hindsight, ie with the knowledge of the true conditional covariance matrix over the optimisation period. In real life, an investor would not know the future conditional covariance matrix when making his/her allocation. Accordingly, to gain a true insight as to whether this diversification benefit would be obtained in the real world, the authors assess the out-of-sample performance of the portfolio constructed over the review period during the subsequent period 1st September, 2003, to 5th July, 2004. The out-of-sample performance can be seen in Table 8.7.

Table 8.6 Optimal portfolio for a US investor (30th August, 2002 to 29th August, 2003)

Country	**India**	**Malaysia**	**Taiwan**	**US**	**Optimal portfolio**
Investment weight (%)	6	52	6	36	100
Annualised return (%)	33.28	5.34	18.34	9.06	9.06
Annualised risk (%)	21.47	9.08	22.95	11.40	7.38

Table 8.7 Portfolio out-of-sample performance (1st September, 2003 to 5th July, 2004)

	Optimal portfolio	**US**
Annualised return (%)	10.73	11.25
Annualised risk (%)	9.57	10.87
Sharpe ratio	1.12	1.03

The US portfolio containing emerging stocks performs better than a portfolio consisting of only domestic US stocks. The Sharpe ratio for the diversified portfolio is 1.12, compared with 1.03 for the pure US portfolio.

Overall, this analysis proves that, over the period and for the emerging markets considered, international diversification is still beneficial for a US investor. Most US investors, however, would never allocate such a high percentage of their portfolio in India, Malaysia and Taiwan. Taking this into account three portfolios are computed for a US investor with overseas investment limits of 15 per cent, 20 per cent and 25 per cent, and their out-of-sample performance is analysed (see Tables 8.8–8.11).

Table 8.8 US portfolio with 15 per cent limit on funds invested abroad (30th August, 2002 to 29th August, 2003)

Country	India	Malaysia	Taiwan	US	Optimal portfolio
Investment weight (%)	1	12	2	85	100
Annualised return (%)	33.28	5.34	18.34	9.06	9.06
Annualised risk (%)	21.47	9.08	22.95	11.40	9.93

Table 8.9 US portfolio with 20 per cent limit on funds invested abroad (30th August, 2002 to 29th August 2003)

Country	India	Malaysia	Taiwan	US	Optimal portfolio
Investment weight (%)	2	16	2	80	100
Annualised return (%)	33.28	5.34	18.34	9.06	9.06
Annualised risk (%)	21.47	9.08	22.95	11.40	9.48

Table 8.10 US portfolio with 25 per cent limit on funds invested abroad (30th August, 2002 to 29th August, 2003)

Country	India	Malaysia	Taiwan	US	Optimal portfolio
Investment weight (%)	2	20	3	75	100
Annualised return (%)	33.28	5.34	18.34	9.06	9.06
Annualised risk (%)	21.47	9.08	22.95	11.40	9.07

Table 8.11 Out-of-sample performance for the three diversified portfolios (1st August, 2003 to 5th August, 2004)

	Portfolio (15% limit)	Portfolio (20% limit)	Portfolio (25% limit)	US
Annualised return (%)	11.14	11.13	11.12	11.25
Annualised risk (%)	10.37	10.04	9.77	10.87
Sharpe ratio	1.07	1.11	1.14	1.03

Again all the portfolios containing emerging markets stocks perform better than a portfolio consisting of only domestic US stocks. The portfolio with a 25 per cent limit on foreign investment provides the best out-of-sample performance.

Conclusion

This paper has tried to check whether, despite the growing world economic integration and progressive lifting of capital controls, the emerging stock markets of South-East and Central Asia still offer international investors a diversification benefit.

It was seen that there is evidence of a cointegrating relationship across the markets considered. This is in agreement with previous studies, such as Cheung and Mak (1992), who found a cointegrating relationship between the Asian-Pacific emerging markets (with the exception of Korea and Taiwan, which were relatively closed at the time) and the US market. Despite this long-run relationship, a short-term correlation analysis indicates that, generally, the emerging and developed markets under review have become less closely linked in the period 1999–2003 than previously, which contrasts with Ng (2002), although he used an earlier period and monthly data.

A subsequent VDC analysis showed that South-East Asian markets are not very responsive to foreign shocks from the UK, the US and Japan, contrary to Central Asian markets, with Korea and China the most reactive.

Time-varying parameter models were also used: they indicate that, except for Taiwan, all the emerging markets considered show a general decline in linkage, over the review period, with the UK stock market. The same analysis points to a general uptrend in integration of the South-East Asian and Central Asian markets with the Japanese stock market, whereas the links to the US stock market of most emerging markets appear to have dropped from their peak levels of 2000.

With these findings and using conditional variances and covariances, the paper proceeded to optimise an international portfolio for a US-based investor. The results indicate that this portfolio would include some emerging stocks under study, ie international diversification is beneficial: in-sample, over the period 30th August, 2002, to 29th August, 2003, this 'optimal' portfolio has an annualised risk of 7.38 per cent, as opposed to 11.40 per cent for a pure domestic US portfolio, while both portfolios produce the same return. Simulated out-of-sample over the period 1st September, 2003, to 5th August, 2004, it yields a Sharpe ratio of 1.12, compared with 1.03 for the pure domestic US porfolio. More realistic constraints were then introduced with limits on funds invested in emerging markets: the results still clearly indicate that, over the period considered, international diversification in selected markets of South-East and Central Asia was indeed beneficial for a US investor.

Notes

1. Detailed results are not reproduced here to conserve space. They are available from the authors upon request.
2. The choice of market capitalisation (rather than the time difference of the stock markets) relies on the fact that international investors prefer, all other things being equal, more liquid markets to less liquid ones.
3. A lag of one day is therefore used for both the US and UK stock markets, and no lag for the Japanese market as it closes ahead of all the other markets, except Taiwan (see Table 8.1).
4. Note that, with Equations (4) and (5), one can also compute a time-varying $\beta_t = \sigma_{XY,t}/\sigma^2_{X,t}$. Not surprisingly, these time-varying β_t, not reproduced here to conserve space, are different from the time-varying β_t generated with the Kalman filter approach, but their trends over the review period are similar, which is what is important for the present purpose (see below).
5. The allocation computed for 28th August, 2003 is actually selected rather than that for 29th August, 2003, as the latter gives an investment weighting of only 1 per cent to Indonesia.

References

Alexander, C. (1999) 'Optimal Hedging using Co-integration', *Philosophical Transactions of the Royal Society*, London, Series A 357, 2039–58.

Bekaert, G. and Harvey, C. (1997) 'Emerging Equity Market Volatility', *Journal of Finance Economics*, 43, 29–77.

Cheung, Y. L. and Mak, S. C. (1992) 'A Study of the International Transmission of Stock Market Fluctuation between the Developed Markets and Asian Pacific Markets', *Applied Financial Economics*, 2, 43–7.

Chowdhury, A. R. (1994) 'Stock Market Interdependencies: Evidence from the Asian NIE's', *Journal of Macroeconomics*, 16, 629–51.

Choudhury, T. (1997) 'Stochastic Trends in Stock Prices: Evidence from Latin American Markets', *Journal of Macroeconomics*, 19, 285–304.

Clements, M. P. and Hendry, D. F. (1995) 'Forecasting in Co-integrated Systems', *Journal of Applied Econometrics*, 10, 127–46.

Corhay, A., Rad, A. T. and Urbain, J. P. (1993) 'Common Stochastic Trends in European Stock Markets', *Economic Letters*, 42, 385–90.

Divecha, A. B., Drach, J. and Stefek, D. (1992) 'Emerging Markets: A Quantitative Perspective', *Journal of Portfolio Management*, 19, 41–50.

Dunis, C. and Karalis, V. (2003) 'Filling Analysis for Missing Data: An Application to Weather Risk Management' in Dunis, C., Laws, J. and Naïm, P. (eds) *Applied Quantitative Methods for Trading and Investment*, John Wiley, Chichester, 381–99.

Engle, R. F. and Granger, C. W. J. (1987) 'Co-integration and Error Correction: Representation, Estimation and Testing', *Econometrica*, 55(2), 251–76.

Engle, R. F. and Yoo B. S. (1987) 'Forecasting and Testing in Co-integrated Systems', *Journal of Econometrics*, 35, 143–59.

Fama, E. F. (1965) 'The Behaviour of Stock Market Prices', *Journal of Business,* 38, 34–105.

Garrett, I. and Spyrou, S. (1994) 'Common Stochastic Trends In Emerging Equity Markets'. http://les1.man.ac.uklaf/Staff//Academic/l_Garrett/Research/comtrend.pdf.

Granger, C. W. J. and Newbold, P. (1974) 'Spurious Regressions in Econometrics', *Journal of Econometrics,* 111–20.

Grubel, H. G. (1968) 'Internationally Diversified Portfolio: Welfare Gains and Capital Flows', *American Economic Review,* 59, 1299–314.

Gruber, M., Elton, E., Brown, S. and Goetzamann, W. (2002) *Modern Portfolio Theory and Investment Analysis,* 6th edn, John Wiley, New York, 265–70.

Haldane, A. G. and Hall, S. G. (1991) 'Sterling's Relationship with the Dollar and Deutschmark: 1976–89', *Economic Journal,* 101, 435–43.

Hamilton, J. (1994) *Time Series Analysis,* Princeton University Press, Princeton, NJ.

Harvey, A. C. (1981) *Time Series Models,* Philip Allan, Oxford.

Hoffman, D. L. and Rasche, R. H. (1996) 'Assessing Forecast Performance in a Co-integrated System', *Journal of Applied Econometrics,* 11, 495–517.

Holden, K. and Thompson, J. (1992) 'Co-integration: An Introductory Survey', *British Review of Economic Issues,* 14, 1–55.

International Finance Corporation (1998) *Emerging Stock Markets Factbook,* IFC, Washington, DC.

Johansen, S. (1988) 'Statistical Analysis of Co-integration Vectors', *Journal of Economic Dynamics and Control,* 12, 231–54.

Johansen, S. and Juselius, K. (1990) 'Maximum Likelihood Estimation and Inference on Cointegration — with Applications to the Demand for Money', *Oxford Bulletin of Economics and Statistics,* 52, 160–210.

Jorion, P. (1989) 'Asset Allocation with Hedged and Unhedged Foreign Stocks and Bonds', *Journal of Portfolio Management,* 12, 251–64.

JP Morgan (1994) *RiskMetrics Technical Document,* Morgan Guaranty Trust Company, New York.

Kasa, K. (1992) 'Common Stochastic Trends in International Stock Markets', *Journal of Monetary Economics,* 29, 95–124.

Kaplanis, E. C. (1988) 'Stability and Forecasting of the Co-movement Measures of International Stock Market Returns', *Journal of International Money and Finance,* 7, 63–75.

Koch, P. D. and Koch, T. W. (1991) 'Evolution in Dynamic Linkage across Daily National Stock Indexes', *American Economic Review,* 81, 819–40.

Lessard, D. (1973) 'International Portfolio Diversification: A Multivariate Analysis for a Group of Latin American Countries', *Journal of Finance,* 28, 619–33.

Levy, H. and Sarnat, M. (1970) International Diversification of Investment Portfolios', *American Economic Review,* 60, 668–75.

Longin, F. and Solnik, B. (1995) 'Is the International Correlation of Equity Returns Constant: 1960–1990?', *Journal of International Money and Finance,* 14, 3–26.

Lütkepohl, H., Saikkonen, P. and Trenkler, C. (2001) 'Maximum Eigenvalue versus Trace Tests for the Co-integrating Rank of a VAR Process', *Econometrics Journal,* 4, 287–310.

Markowitz, H. M. (1952) 'Portfolio Selection', *Journal of Finance,* 7, 77–91.

Markowitz, H. M. (1959) *Portfolio Selection, Efficient Diversification of Investments,* John Wiley, New York.

Naka, A. and Tufte, D. (1997) 'Examining Impulse Response Functions in Co-integrated Systems', *Applied Economics,* 29, 1593–603.
Ng, H. T. (2002) 'Stock Market Linkages in South-East Asia', *Asian Economic Journal,* 16, 353–77.
Phillips, P. C. B. (1986) 'Understanding Spurious Regressions in Econometrics', *Journal of Econometrics,* 33, 311–30.
Phillips, P. C. B. and Perron, P. (1998) 'Testing for a Unit Root in Time Series Regression', *Biometrika,* 75, 335–46.
Serletis, A. and King, M. (1997) 'Common Stochastic Trends and Convergence of European Union Stock Markets', *Manchester School of Economic Social Studies,* 65, 44–57.
Solnik, B. (1974) 'Why not Diversify Internationally Rather than Domestically?', *Financial Analysts Journal,* 30, 48–54.
Solnik, B. (1996), *International Investments.* 3rd edn, Addison-Wesley, Reading, MA.
Solnik, B. and Noetzlin, B. (1982) 'Optimal International Asset Allocation', *Journal of Portfolio Management,* 7, 1–32.
Tobin, J. (1958) 'Liquidity Preference as Behavior Towards Risk', *Review of Economic Studies,* 25, 68–5.
Toda, H. Y. and Yamamoto, T. (1995) 'Statistical Inference in Vector Auto-Regressions with Possibly Integrated Processes', *Journal of Econometrics,* 66, 225–50.

Appendix 1: Johansen test for multiple cointegration

Table 8A1 UK, Indonesia, Philippines and Malaysia

Hypothesis		Trace 5% critical value	Eigenvalue 5%	Trace test statistic	Eigenvalue statistic
H0	H1				
$r = 0$	$r > 0$	47.21	27.07	51.48	32.2
$r \leq 1$	$r > 1$	29.68	20.97	19.28	12.4
$r \leq 2$	$r > 2$	15.41	14.07	6.88	6.15
$r \leq 3$	$r > 3$	3.76	3.76	0.74	0.74

Conclusion: Both tests indicate one cointegrating vector.

Table 8A2 US, Indonesia, Philippines and Malaysia

Hypothesis		Trace 5% critical value	Eigenvalue 5%	Trace test statistic	Eigenvalue statistic
H0	H1				
$r = 0$	$r > 0$	47.21	27.07	48.64	32.33
$r \leq 1$	$r > 1$	29.68	20.97	16.31	10.25
$r \leq 2$	$r > 2$	15.41	14.07	6.06	5.5
$r \leq 3$	$r > 3$	3.76	3.76	0.56	0.56

Conclusion: Both tests indicate one cointegrating vector.

Table 8A3 Japan, Indonesia, Philippines and Malaysia

Hypothesis H0	H1	Trace 5% critical value	Eigenvalue 5%	Trace test statistic	Eigenvalue statistic
$r = 0$	$r > 0$	47.21	27.07	48.64	32.33
$r \leq 1$	$r > 1$	29.68	20.97	16.31	10.25
$r \leq 2$	$r > 2$	15.41	14.07	6.06	5.5
$r \leq 3$	$r > 3$	3.76	3.76	0.56	0.56

Conclusion: Both tests indicate one cointegrating vector.

Table 8A4 UK, Korea, China, India and Taiwan

Hypothesis H0	H1	Trace 5% critical value	Eigenvalue 5%	Trace test statistic	Eigenvalue statistic
$r = 0$	$r > 0$	68.52	33.46	75.68	38.32
$r \leq 1$	$r > 1$	47.21	27.07	37.36	16.39
$r \leq 2$	$r > 2$	29.68	20.97	20.96	13.36
$r \leq 3$	$r > 3$	15.41	14.07	7.61	5.41
$r \leq 4$	$r > 4$	3.76	3.76	2.19	2.19

Conclusion: Both tests indicate one cointegrating vector.

Table 8A5 US, Korea, China, India and Taiwan

Hypothesis H0	H1	Trace 5% critical value	Eigenvalue 5%	Trace test statistic	Eigenvalue statistic
$r = 0$	$r > 0$	68.52	33.46	74.22	37.74
$r \leq 1$	$r > 1$	47.21	27.07	36.48	17.05
$r \leq 2$	$r > 2$	29.68	20.97	19.42	12.62
$r \leq 3$	$r > 3$	15.41	14.07	6.81	4.67
$r \leq 4$	$r > 4$	3.76	3.76	2.14	2.14

Conclusion: Both tests indicate one cointegrating vector.

Table 8A6 UK, Korea, China, India and Taiwan

Hypothesis H0	H1	Trace 5% critical value	Eigenvalue 5%	Trace test statistic	Eigenvalue statistic
$r = 0$	$r > 0$	68.52	33.46	69.62	27.64
$r \leq 1$	$r > 1$	47.21	27.07	41.98	23.34
$r \leq 2$	$r > 2$	29.68	20.97	18.64	9.81
$r \leq 3$	$r > 3$	15.41	14.07	8.82	4.82
$r \leq 4$	$r > 4$	3.76	3.76	4.00	4.00

Conclusion: Trace test indicates one cointegrating vector.

Appendix 2: Variance decomposition model with the US as the 'established' market

Table 8A7

Variance decomposition of DLUS					
Day	DUS	DMAL	DINDO	DPHIL	VE
1	100.00	0.00	0.00	0.00	0.00
2	99.77	0.11	0.12	0.00	0.23
5	99.35	0.24	0.13	0.28	0.65
9	99.35	0.24	0.13	0.28	0.65
10	99.35	0.24	0.13	0.28	0.65
Variance decomposition of DLMAL					
Day	DUS	DMAL	DINDO	DPHIL	VE
1	0.00	100.00	0.00	0.00	0.00
2	6.63	93.32	0.04	0.01	6.68
5	6.66	92.71	0.16	0.47	7.29
9	6.66	92.71	0.16	0.47	7.29
10	6.66	92.71	0.16	0.47	7.29
Variance decomposition of DLINDO					
Day	DUS	DMAL	DINDO	DPHIL	VE
1	0.03	1.61	98.36	0.00	1.64
2	1.71	1.57	96.71	0.00	3.29
5	1.73	1.88	96.29	0.10	3.71
9	1.73	1.88	96.29	0.10	3.71
10	1.73	1.88	96.29	0.10	3.71

Variance decomposition of DLUS						
Day	DUS	DTAI	DCHIN	DKOREA	DINDIA	VE
1	100.00	0.00	0.00	0.00	0.00	0.00
2	99.82	0.03	0.08	0.07	0.00	0.18
5	99.07	0.05	0.09	0.79	0.01	0.93
9	99.07	0.05	0.09	0.79	0.01	0.93
10	99.07	0.05	0.09	0.79	0.01	0.93
Variance decomposition of DLTAI						
Day	DUS	DTAI	DCHIN	DKOREA	DINDIA	VE
1	0.72	99.28	0.00	0.00	0.00	0.72
2	9.89	88.90	0.13	0.71	0.38	11.10
5	10.24	87.71	0.51	0.76	0.78	12.29
9	10.24	87.71	0.51	0.76	0.78	12.29
10	10.24	87.71	0.51	0.76	0.78	12.29
Variance decomposition of DLCHIN						
Day	DUS	DTAI	DCHIN	DKOREA	DINDIA	VE
1	0.65	3.00	96.35	0.00	0.00	3.65
2	9.70	2.91	87.13	0.18	0.07	12.87
5	9.80	2.92	86.63	0.58	0.07	13.37
9	9.80	2.92	86.63	0.58	0.07	13.37
10	9.80	2.92	86.63	0.58	0.07	13.37

(Continued)

Table 8A7 Continued

Variance decomposition of DLPHIL					
Day	DUS	DMAL	DINDO	DPHIL	VE
1	0.01	2.01	0.94	97.04	2.96
2	3.82	2.14	1.08	92.96	7.04
5	3.97	2.14	1.09	92.80	7.20
9	3.97	2.14	1.09	92.80	7.20
10	3.97	2.14	1.09	92.80	7.20

Variance decomposition of DKOREA						
Day	DUS	DTAI	DCHIN	DKOREA	DINDIA	VE
1	1.24	11.55	6.20	81.01	0.00	18.99
2	15.38	9.85	5.47	69.02	0.28	30.98
5	15.33	9.85	5.45	68.82	0.55	31.18
9	15.33	9.85	5.45	68.82	0.55	31.18
10	15.33	9.85	5.45	68.82	0.55	31.18

Variance decomposition of DLINDIA						
Day	DUS	DTAI	DCHIN	DKOREA	DINDIA	VE
1	0.40	2.38	1.53	2.63	93.05	6.95
2	2.75	2.30	1.59	2.53	90.83	9.17
5	3.07	2.46	1.68	2.52	90.27	9.73
9	3.07	2.46	1.68	2.52	90.27	9.73
10	3.07	2.46	1.68	2.52	90.27	9.73

Note: VE denotes the percentage of variance explained by other markets.

Appendix 3: Variance decomposition model with the UK as the 'established' market

Table 8A8

Variance decomposition of DLUK						Variance decomposition of DLUK						
Day	DUS	DMAL	DINDO	DPHIL	VE	Day	DUS	DTAI	DCHIN	DKOREA	DINDIA	VE
1	100.00	0.00	0.00	0.00	0.00	1	100.00	0.00	0.00	0.00	0.00	0.00
2	99.16	0.57	0.25	0.01	0.84	2	99.60	0.02	0.08	0.01	0.16	0.40
5	98.75	0.92	0.25	0.08	1.25	5	99.59	0.02	0.09	0.02	0.16	0.41
9	98.74	0.92	0.25	0.08	1.26	9	99.59	0.02	0.09	0.02	0.16	0.41
10	98.74	0.92	0.25	0.08	1.26	10	99.59	0.02	0.09	0.02	0.16	0.41
Variance decomposition of DLMAL						Variance decomposition of DLTAI						
Day	DUS	DMAL	DINDO	DPHIL	VE	Day	DUS	DTAI	DCHIN	DKOREA	DINDIA	VE
1	0.23	99.77	0.00	0.00	0.23	1	1.23	98.77	0.00	0.00	0.00	1.23
2	2.04	97.91	0.03	0.02	2.09	2	2.88	95.64	0.25	0.86	0.37	4.36
5	2.03	97.37	0.15	0.11	2.63	5	3.33	94.49	0.59	0.86	0.74	5.51
9	2.03	97.37	0.15	0.11	2.63	9	3.33	94.49	0.59	0.86	0.74	5.51
10	2.03	97.37	0.15	0.11	2.69	10	3.33	94.49	0.59	0.86	0.74	5.52
Variance decomposition of DLINDO						Variance decomposition of DLCHIN						
Day	DUS	DMAL	DINDO	DPHIL	VE	Day	DUS	DTAI	DCHIN	DKOREA	DINDIA	VE
1	0.36	2.12	97.52	0.00	2.48	1	1.72	5.24	93.04	0.00	0.00	6.96
2	0.82	2.09	97.08	0.01	2.92	2	3.50	5.26	90.98	0.16	0.10	9.02
5	0.90	2.42	96.58	0.11	3.42	5	3.83	5.21	90.26	0.59	0.11	9.74
9	0.90	2.42	96.58	0.11	3.42	9	3.83	5.21	90.26	0.59	0.11	9.74
10	0.90	2.42	96.58	0.11	3.42	10	3.83	5.21	90.26	0.59	0.11	9.74

(Continued)

Table 8A8 Continued

Variance decomposition of DLPHIL

Day	DUS	DMAL	DINDO	DPHIL	VE
1	0.16	2.79	1.04	96.02	3.98
2	2.73	2.94	1.16	93.17	6.83
5	2.83	2.93	1.17	93.06	6.94
9	2.83	2.94	1.17	93.06	6.94
10	2.83	2.94	1.17	93.06	6.94

Variance decomposition of DLKOREA

Day	DUS	DTAI	DCHIN	DKOREA	DINDIA	VE
1	3.24	15.33	7.29	74.14	0.00	25.86
2	8.04	14.54	7.06	70.14	0.22	29.86
5	8.04	14.48	7.02	69.96	0.50	30.04
9	8.04	14.48	7.02	69.96	0.50	30.04
10	8.04	14.48	7.02	69.96	0.50	30.04

Variance decomposition of DLINDIA

Day	DUS	DTAI	DCHIN	DKOREA	DINDIA	VE
1	1.39	2.93	1.55	2.25	91.87	8.13
2	3.60	2.86	1.59	2.17	89.77	10.23
5	3.68	3.06	1.69	2.17	89.40	10.60
9	3.68	3.06	1.69	2.17	89.40	10.60
10	3.68	3.06	1.69	2.17	89.40	10.60

Note: VE denotes the percentage of variance explained by other markets.

Appendix 4: Variance decomposition model with Japan as the 'established' market

Table 8A9

Variance decomposition of DLJAPAN						Variance decomposition of DLJAPAN						
Day	DUS	DMAL	DINDO	DPHIL	VE	Day	DUS	DTAI	DCHIN	DKOREA	DINDIA	VE
1	100.00	0.00	0.00	0.00	0.00	1	100.00	0.00	0.00	0.00	0.00	0.00
2	99.70	0.00	0.28	0.02	0.30	2	99.67	0.25	0.01	0.38	0.38	1.33
5	98.64	0.05	0.29	0.02	0.36	5	98.15	0.32	0.01	1.05	0.46	1.85
9	98.64	0.05	0.29	0.02	0.36	9	98.15	0.32	0.01	1.05	0.46	1.85
10	98.64	0.05	0.29	0.02	0.36	10	98.15	0.32	0.01	1.05	0.46	1.85
Variance decomposition of DLMAL						Variance decomposition of DLTAI						
Day	DUS	DMAL	DINDO	DPHIL	VE	Day	DUS	DTAI	DCHIN	DKOREA	DINDIA	VE
1	4.75	95.25	0.00	0.00	4.75	1	5.90	94.10	0.00	0.00	0.00	5.90
2	4.55	95.37	0.07	0.01	4.63	2	6.63	91.77	0.21	0.93	0.46	8.23
5	4.52	94.85	0.20	0.43	5.15	5	6.76	90.90	0.54	0.92	0.87	9.10
9	4.52	94.85	0.20	0.43	5.15	9	6.76	90.90	0.54	0.92	0.87	9.10
10	4.52	94.85	0.20	0.43	5.15	10	6.76	90.90	0.54	0.92	0.87	9.10
Variance decomposition of DLINDO						Variance decomposition of DLCHIN						
Day	DUS	DMAL	DINDO	DPHIL	VE	Day	DUS	DTAI	DCHIN	DKOREA	DINDIA	VE
1	2.34	1.51	96.15	0.00	3.85	1	10.91	3.38	85.71	0.00	0.00	14.29
2	2.49	1.52	95.99	0.00	4.01	2	11.08	3.34	84.82	0.73	0.02	15.18
5	2.49	1.87	95.53	0.11	4.47	5	11.27	3.34	84.36	1.00	0.03	15.64
9	2.49	1.87	95.52	0.11	4.48	9	11.27	3.34	84.36	1.00	0.03	15.64
10	2.49	1.87	95.52	0.11	4.48	10	11.27	3.34	84.36	1.00	0.03	15.64

(Continued)

Table 8A9 Continued

Variance decomposition of DLPHIL						Variance decomposition of DLKOREA						
Day	DUS	DMAL	DINDO	DPHIL	VE	Day	DUS	DTAI	DCHIN	DKOREA	DINDIA	VE
1	2.54	2.41	0.90	94.6	5.84	1	15.67	11.24	4.61	68.48	0.00	31.52
2	2.57	2.64	1.09	93.71	6.29	2	15.56	11.42	4.61	68.02	0.39	31.98
5	2.61	2.63	1.11	93.65	6.35	5	15.49	11.38	4.59	67.87	0.67	32.13
9	2.61	2.63	1.11	93.65	6.35	9	15.49	11.38	4.59	67.87	0.67	32.13
10	2.61	2.63	1.11	93.65	6.35	10	15.49	11.38	4.59	67.87	0.67	32.13
						Variance decomposition of DLINDIA						
						Day	DUS	DTAI	DCHIN	DKOREA	DINDIA	VE
						1	3.04	2.53	1.23	2.38	90.81	9.19
						2	2.99	2.64	1.22	2.39	90.76	9.24
						5	3.16	2.78	1.29	2.38	90.38	9.62
						9	3.16	2.78	1.29	2.38	90.38	9.62
						10	3.16	2.78	1.29	2.38	90.38	9.62

Note: VE denotes the percentage of variance explained by other markets.

9

Measuring Investor Sentiment in Equity Markets

Arindam Bandopadhyaya
is Chairman and Associate Professor of Finance in the Accounting and Finance Department at UMASS-Boston. He is also Director of the College of Management's Finance Services Forum. He has published in leading journals in economics and finance and has presented his work at various conferences. He is the recipient of the Dean's Award for Distinguished Research and several awards for teaching excellence in the College of Management.

*Anne Leah Jones**
is an assistant professor of accounting in the Accounting and Finance Department at UMASS-Boston. She is a research associate with the College of Management's Financial Services Forum and has received a conference award for Best Paper by a New Faculty Member. She is also a certified public accountant and worked for several years as an auditor and tax specialist at Ernst and Young.

**Accounting and Finance Department, College of Management, University of Massachusetts, Boston, MA, USA. E-mail: anne.jones@umb.edu*

Introduction

Traditional research on asset pricing has focused on fundamental, firm-specific and economy-wide factors that affect asset prices. Recently, however, some researchers have turned to investor psychology to explain asset-price behaviour. It was previously assumed that there is little correlation among the sentiments of investors. The differing sentiments thus offset each other, and there is no resulting effect on market prices. If, however, there is enough of a consensus among investors, their viewpoints will not offset and will instead become an integral part of the price-setting process. In fact, some researchers (eg Eichengreen and Mody, 1998) suggest that a change in one set of asset prices may, especially in the short run, trigger changes elsewhere, because such a change engenders shifts in

---

Reprinted from 'Measuring investor sentiment in equity markets' by Arindam Bandopadhyaya and Anne Leah Jones in *Journal of Asset Management*, 7, 2006, pp. 208–215, DOI:10.1057/palgrave.jam.2240214. With kind permission from Palgrave Macmillan Ltd.

the market's attitude towards risk (ie because there is a change in investor sentiment). Such shifts in risk attitudes may explain short-term movements in asset prices better than any other set of fundamental factors (eg see Baek *et al.* (2005). Other studies have also recognised that investor sentiment may be an important component of the market pricing process (see Fisher and Statman, 2000; Baker and Wurgler, 2006).

Many investor sentiment measures have been identified in the academic literature and in the popular press. Dennis and Mayhew (2002) have used the Put–Call Ratio, Randall *et al.* (2003) use Net Cash Flow into Mutual Funds, Lashgari (2000) uses the Barron's Confidence Index, Baker and Wurgler (2006) use the Issuance Percentage, Whaley (2000) uses the VIX-Investor Fear Gauge, and Kumar and Persaud (2002) employ the Risk Appetite Index (RAI). A more detailed list of studies that use these and other investor sentiment measures appears in Table 9.1.

This paper shows that the risk appetite measure developed by Persaud (1996) for currency markets can be successfully adapted to measure investor sentiment in an equity market using publicly available data. Using Persaud's 1996 methodology, this study develops and quantifies an Equity Market Sentiment Index (EMSI) for a group of firms in an equity market index. In prior studies, the Put–Call Ratio and the VIX-Investor Fear Gauge were used as measures of investor sentiment in equity markets. As argued in Kumar and Persaud (2002), however, these measures could be measuring changes in the underlying risk of the market itself just as easily as they could be measuring changes in investor attitude towards that risk; it is not possible to isolate the two phenomena. The advantage of the RAI developed in Persaud (1996) and the EMSI constructed in this paper is that changes to the underlying riskiness of the market do not directly affect the proposed measures, and thus these measures more accurately reflect the changes in the market's attitude towards risk. The RAI and the EMSI speak specifically to the risk/return trade-off embedded in prices and therefore focus solely on the market's willingness to accept whatever risks are inherent in the market at a given time.

The EMSI is constructed using stock market price data for firms listed in the Massachusetts Bloomberg Index (MBI).[1] It is found that changes in the EMSI are closely related to news items regarding key firms in Massachusetts as well as to news reports on the condition of the Massachusetts economy as a whole. It is also found that changes in the MBI are related to the EMSI. In fact, the results indicate that lagged values of the EMSI better explain changes in the MBI than do past changes in the MBI itself (ie MBI's own price momentum).

Table 9.1 Measures of market sentiment used in prior research

Name	How measured	Studies
1. Optimism/Pessimism about the Economy		
Index of Consumer Confidence	Survey by Conference Board www.conferenceboard.org	Fisher and Statman (2003)
Consumer Confidence Index	Survey by U Mich.- monthly	Charoenrook (2003)
		Fisher and Statman (2003)
2. Optimism/Pessimism about the Stock Market		
Put/call ratio	Puts outstanding/Calls outstanding	Dennis and Mayhew (2002)
Trin. statistic	Vol Decl issues/# Del/Vol Adv issues/# Adv	NO ACADEMIC REF
Mutual Fund Cash positions	% cash held in MFs	Gup (1973)
		Branch (1976)
	Net cash flow into MF's	Randall *et al.* (2003)
Mutual Fund redemptions	Net redemptions/Total assets	Neal and Wheatley (1998)
AAII Survey	Survey of individual investors	Fisher and Statman (2000, 2003)
Investors Intelligence Survey	Survey of newsletter writers	Fisher and Statman (2000)
Barron's confidence index	Aaa yield-Bbb yield	Lashgari (2000)
TED Spread	Tbill futures yield – Eurodollar futures yield	Lashgari (2000)
Merrill Lynch Survey	Wall St. sell-side analysts	Fisher and Statman (2000, 2003)
3. Riskiness of the Stock Market		
Issuance %	Gross annual equities issued/Gross ann. debt & equ. issued	Baker and Wurgler (2006)
RIPO	Avg. ann. first-day returns on IPOs	Baker and Wurgler (2006)
Turnover	Reported sh.vol./avg shs listed NYSE (logged & detrended)	Baker and Wurgler (2006)
Closed-end fund discount	Y/E, value wtd. avg. disc. on closed-end mutual funds	Baker and Wurgler (2006)
		Neal and Wheatley (1998)
		Lee *et al.* (1991)
		Chopra *et al.* (1993)
Market liquidity	Reported share volume/Avg # of shares	Baker and Stein (2002 WP)
NYSE seat prices	Trading volume or quoted bid-ask spread	Keim and Madhavan (2000)
4. Riskiness of an individual stock		
Beta	CAPM	Various
5. Risk aversion		
Risk Appetite Index	Spearman Rank correlation volatility vs excess returns	Kumar and Persaud (2002)
VIX – Investor Fear Gauge	Implied option volatility	Whaley (2000)

The rest of the paper is organised as follows. The second section outlines the construction of the EMSI. Empirical results and discussion appear in the third section. The fourth section concludes.

The construction of the equity market sentiment index

Persaud (1996) developed a measure of the market's attitude towards risk – a measure that he describes as the market's *appetite* for risk – in the context of currency markets.[2] He argues that, over the short run in the foreign exchange market, the market's changing appetite for risk is a dominant force and at times is the most influential factor affecting currency returns. He goes on to suggest that, if the market's appetite for risk were fixed, exchange rate changes would be driven only by unanticipated shifts in economic risk. If the appetite for risk grows and economic risks are unchanged, investors will feel overcompensated for these risk levels and the sense of overcompensation will grow as the level of risk grows.[3] As investors take advantage of what they see as an improving risk-return trade-off, currency values will change in line with their risk. High-risk currencies should appreciate more than low-risk ones, and the riskiest currency should rally the most.[4] Thus, a RAI could be constructed based upon the strength of the correlation between the *order* of currency performance and the *order* of currency risk.

This paper demonstrates that the technique developed in Persaud (1996) can be applied to an equity market setting by constructing the EMSI for a group of firms in the MBI. The MBI follows 242 firms which span more than 50 industries and range in size from \$2 million to \$42 billion in market capitalisation. From data over the period from 2nd July, 2003, to 1st July, 2004, daily returns are computed for each of the securities in the MBI. For each of the securities, the average standard deviation of the daily returns over the previous five days (the 'historic volatility') is also computed for each day of the sample period.[5] Then the daily rate of return and the historic volatility are ranked, and the Spearman rank correlation coefficient between the *rank* of the daily returns for each firm and the *rank* of the historic volatility of the returns for each firm is computed, and the result is multipled by 100. The EMSI is therefore computed as follows

$$\text{EMSI} = \frac{\sum\left(R_{ir}-\bar{R}_r\right)\left(R_{iv}-\bar{R}_v\right)}{\left[\sum\left(R_{ir}-\bar{R}_r\right)^2\sum\left(R_{iv}-\bar{R}_v\right)^2\right]^{1/2}} \star 100; -100 \leq \mathbf{EM\Sigma I} \leq +100$$

where R_{ir} and R_{iv} are the rank of the daily return and the historical volatility for security *i*, respectively, and $\bar{R}_r$ and $\bar{R}_v$ are the population mean return and historical volatility rankings, respectively.

Empirical results and discussion

Figure 9.1 presents the EMSI for the one-year sample time period. EMSI ranges from a high of 48.09 to a low of −35.44. It averages 4.20 for the year with a standard deviation of 16.62. These EMSI values are placed into five categories. For values between −10 and +10, the market is classified as risk-neutral; for values between −10 and −30, the market is labelled moderately risk-averse and, for values <−30, the market is considered highly risk-averse. Similarly, if EMSI falls between +10 and +30, the market is labelled moderately risk-seeking and, if the index exceeds +30, the market is considered highly risk-seeking. During the sample period, there were 17 days on which the market was highly risk-seeking and 78 days on which the market was moderately risk-seeking. The market was risk-neutral for 109 days, and exhibited moderately and highly risk- averse behaviour for 42 and 6 days, respectively. For a summary of these categories, refer to Table 9.2.

Movements in the EMSI capture both positive and negative news as reported in the *Boston Globe,* New England's leading newspaper, concerning Massachusetts firms and the region's economy. A sample of news events and their impact on the EMSI appear in Table 9.3. For example, on 8th August, 2003 when the *Globe* reported that the local economy was building steam, the EMSI increased by 31 points in a four-day period. On 11th September of that year, when the *Globe* reported that the high-tech sector may be poised for new hiring, the EMSI gained 36 points in one day. When news hit that Putnam Investment's asset values fell by $14 billion, the EMSI dropped by 51 points in two days and, when the Commonwealth later charged Prudential with illegal trading, the EMSI again declined 38 points in three days. In reaction to a 6th April, 2004, *Globe* story which indicated that Bank of America planned to cut 12,500 jobs, the EMSI plummeted 42 points and, later in May, when it appeared that the Bank of America/Fleet Bank merger might cost Massachusetts 500 jobs, the EMSI declined another 26 points. Lastly, the EMSI rose 25 points after a June 2004 story regarding a boost in hiring by Boston employers.

Not only do the movements in EMSI correspond to positive and negative news events affecting firms in Massachusetts and the economy of Massachusetts, but changes in the EMSI also closely replicate changes

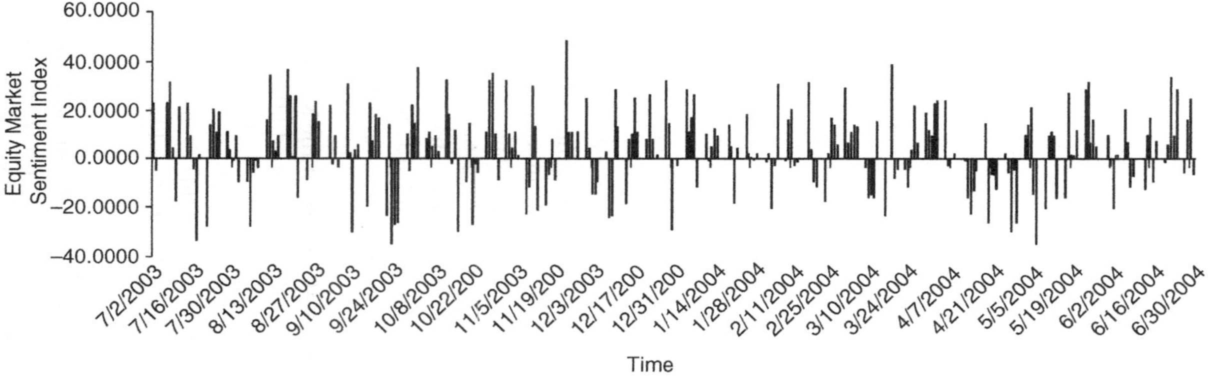

Figure 9.1 Equity Market Sentiment Index: 2nd July, 2003–1st July, 2004

Table 9.2 Risk categorisation of daily EMSI figures

Range of EMSI	Category	Number of days
–30 and below	Highly risk averse	6
–10 to –30	Moderately risk averse	42
10 to +10	Risk neutral	109
+10 to +30	Moderately risk seeking	78
+30 and above	Highly risk seeking	17

in the MBI. The EMSI and the MBI return for the same trading day have a significant correlation coefficient of 74.84 per cent. To investigate the explanatory power of the EMSI in greater detail, the following equation is first posited

$$\mathrm{MBI}_t = \beta_0 + \beta_1\,\mathrm{MBI}_{t-1} + \beta_2\,\mathrm{EMSI}_t + \varepsilon_t \tag{2}$$

where MBI_t is the return on the Massachusetts Bloomberg Index from day $t-1$ to day t, and EMSI_t is the Equity Market Sentiment Index (see Equation 1) on day t.

While it was not possible to confirm whether EMSI Granger causes MBI return or not, results indicate that the EMSI is able to explain changes in the MBI returns. The results from an estimation of Equation (1), which appear in Table 9.4, indicate that a majority of the variation in MBI_t is explained by the two independent variables MBI_{t-1} and EMSI_t ($R^2 = 0.56$). Interestingly, while MBI_{t-1} (the lagged value of the return in MBI) has an insignificant impact on the dependent variable MBI_t, the coefficient on EMSI_t is highly significant. This implies that returns in the MBI for any given day were primarily driven not by returns on the previous day, but by the risk-seeking behaviour of market participants for that particular day.

To investigate the impact of the EMSI on the MBI further, the following equation is estimated, which includes additional lagged values of the EMSI and the MBI[6]

$$\begin{aligned}\mathrm{MBI}_t = {} & \beta_0 + \beta_1\,\mathrm{MBI}_{t-1} + \beta_2\,\mathrm{MBI}_{t-2} + \beta_3\,\mathrm{MBI}_{t-3} + \beta_4\,\mathrm{MBI}_{t-4} + \beta_5\,\mathrm{MBI}_{t-5} \\ & + \beta_6\,\mathrm{MBI}_{t-6} + \delta_0\mathrm{EMSI}_t + \delta_1\mathrm{EMSI}_{t-1} + \delta_2\mathrm{EMSI}_{t-2} + \delta_3\mathrm{EMSI}_{t-3} \\ & + \delta_4\mathrm{EMSI}_{t-4} + \delta_5\mathrm{EMSI}_{t-5} + \varepsilon_t\end{aligned} \tag{3}$$

(MBI_t and EMSI_t are defined earlier). To avoid autocorrelation problems associated with estimating Equation (3) using ordinary least squares, the polynomial distributed lagged model was used (see Harvey, 1990). The results from the estimation of Equation (3) appear in Table 9.5.

Table 9.3 News and EMSI

News	Fact date	Index change (up/down)	From (date)	To (date)
Confidence among mass. Firms leaps	2-Jul-03	▲ 36 (–5 to 31)	3-Jul-03	8-Jul-03
An ailing image: drug industry's tenacious price protection stirs anger	11-Jul-03	▼ 56 (23 to –33)	14-Jul-03	17-Jul-03
Data suggest economy building steam	8-Aug-03	▲ 31 (–3 to 34)	8-Aug-03	12-Aug-03
Bay state jobless rate declines	16-Aug-03	▼ 52 (36 to –16)	18-Aug-03	22-Aug-03
Investors' loyalty facing test	10-Sep-03	▲ 60 (30 to –30)	10-Sep-03	11-Sep-03
'Now hiring' returning to high tech's vocabulary	11-Sep-03	▼ 36 (–30 to 6)	11-Sep-03	12-Sep-03
A wary eye on the bulls: the dollar could lose value	23-Sep-03	▲ 49 (14 to –35)	23-Sep-03	24-Sep-03
State revenue up, but disappointing	2-Oct-03	▼ 34 (37 to 3)	3-Oct-03	10-Oct-03
Investor habits likely to change: top executive at putnam investments resigned	4-Nov-03	▲ 47 (25 to –23)	4-Nov-03	10-Nov-03
Putnam assets fall by $14b	11-Nov-03	▼ 51 (30 to –21)	12-Nov-03	14-Nov-03
In dividends we trust: biggest increase in payouts	20-Nov-03	▲ 57 (–9 to 48)	20-Nov-03	25-Nov-03
Fund investors rethinking their strategy	28-Nov-03	▼ 50 (25 to –25)	1-Dec-03	9-Dec-03
Survey: mass. Losing anchor companies	9-Dec-03	▲ 25 (0 to –25)	9-Dec-03	10-Dec-03
State charges prudential allowed illegal trading	12-Dec-03	▼ 38 (20 to –18)	12-Dec-03	15-Dec-03
$750b vow for lending draws fire	8-Jan-04	▲ 37 (25 to –12)	8-Jan-04	9-Jan-04
Mfs appeared aware of market timing	16-Jan-04	▼ 29 (10 to –19)	16-Jan-04	22-Jan-04
Rebuilding a high-tech giant	22-Jan-04	▲ 37 (–19 to 18)	22-Jan-04	26-Jan-04
No bubble billionaires: boston scientific shares to an all-time high	5-Feb-04	▼ 46 (–15 to 31)	5-Feb-04	6-Feb-04
Great numbers, but show us your worst: the mutual fund industry has declared open season	22-Feb-04	▲ 34 (–17 to 17)	23-Feb-04	25-Feb-04
The good and the bad of a fund closing	7-Mar-04	▼ 29 (10 to –19)	7-Mar-04	9-Mar-04
Trustees on the hot seat	16-Mar-04	▲ 51 (39 to –12)	17-Mar-04	23-Mar-04
Mutual fund firms adding disclaimers	22-Mar-04	▼ 34 (–12 to 22)	23-Mar-04	25-Mar-04
Bank of america to cut 12,500 jobs	6-Apr-04	▲ 42 (20 to –22)	6-Apr-04	14-Apr-04
Emc quarterly earnings and revenues post gains	16-Apr-04	▼ 24 (–10 to 14)	16-Apr-04	19-Apr-04
Growth solid in quarter: 4.2% rise in gdp	30-Apr-04	▲ 47 (–26 to 21)	30-Apr-04	5-May-04
Sign of rebound: small firms thinking bigger	9-May-04	▼ 46 (–35 to 11)	9-May-04	12-May-04
Merger to claim 500 jobs: BOA says losses will hit mass. over 2 years	14-May-04	▲ 26 (10 to –16)	14-May-04	18-May-04
Numbers down, chins up at merged biotechs	18-May-04	▼ 48 (–16 to 32)	18-May-04	25-May-04
Strategic fit: boston scientific pays $740m for microelectronic	2-Jun-04	▲ 35 (–15 to 20)	2-Jun-04	7-Feb-04
Boston employers are planning to boost hiring	15-Jun-04	▼ 25 (9 to 34)	15-Jun-04	23-Jun-04

Table 9.4 Explanation of Massachusetts Bloomberg Index returns using ordinary least squares estimates[a]

Variable	Coefficient	*t*-statistic	*p*-value
Constant	−0.001321	−2.96277	0.0033
MBI_{t-1}	0.040734	0.977536	0.3342
$EMSI_t$	0.046143	17.78022	0.0000
R-squared	0.561510		
Adjusted *R*-squared		0.557973	
Durbin Watson statistic		2.231518	
F statistic		158.7884	
Value (*F* statistic)		0.0000	

[a]$MBI_t = \beta_0 + \beta_1 MBI_{t-1} + \beta_2 EMSI_t + \varepsilon_t$
MBI_t = Massachusetts Bloomberg Index return from day $t-1$ to t
MBI_{t-1} = one period lagged value of MBI_t
$EMSI_t$ = Equity Market Sentiment Index on day t

Table 9.5 Explanation of Massachusetts Bloomberg Index returns using polynomial distributed lagged model estimates[a]

Variable	Coefficient	*t*-statistic
MBI_{t-1}	−0.24937	−4.63278**
MBI_{t-2}	−0.08360	−1.99927*
MBI_{t-3}	0.02330	0.51883
MBI_{t-4}	0.07134	1.68805
MBI_{t-5}	0.06051	1.88195
MBI_{t-6}	−0.00919	−0.22753
Sum of lags	−0.18702	−1.09072
$EMSI_t$	0.03873	16.3857**
$EMSI_{t-1}$	0.02262	13.0613**
$EMSI_{t-2}$	0.01043	4.48360**
$EMSI_{t-3}$	0.00215	0.86171
$EMSI_{t-4}$	−0.00221	−0.93336
$EMSI_{t-5}$	−0.00265	−0.82559
Sum of lags	0.06908	7.47905**
R-squared	0.570109	
Adjusted *R*-squared	0.559317	
Durbin Watson statistic	1.846193	
F statistic	52.82586	
Value (*F* statistic)	0.0000	

* Denotes significance at 5 per cent level.
** Denotes significance at 1 per cent level.
[a]$MBI_t = \beta_0 + \beta_1 MBI_{t-1} + \beta_2 MBI_{t-2} + \beta_3 MBI_{t-3} + \beta_4 MBI_{t-4} + \beta_5 MBI_{t-5} + \beta_6 MBI_{t-6} + \delta_0 EMSI_t + \delta_1 EMSI_{t-1} + \delta_2 EMSI_{t-2} + \delta_3 EMSI_{t-3} + \delta_4 EMSI_{t-4} + \delta_5 EMSI_{t-5} + \varepsilon_t$
MBI_t = Massachusetts Bloomberg Index return from day $t-1$ to t
MBI_{t-i} = i period lagged value of MBI_t
$EMSI_t$ = Equity Market Sentiment Index for Massachusetts on day t
$EMSI_{t-i}$ = i period lagged value of EMSI t

A number of important observations emerge from an examination of Table 9.5. A comparison of the *t*-ratios across the different lagged variables indicates that the most significant variables explaining MBI_t are the contemporaneous and one-day lagged values of the EMSI. The second lagged value of the EMSI is significant as well. Although they are relatively less significant, the lagged values of MBI_t do play a significant role in the equation; however, they lose their significance after two lags. Most importantly, while the sum of all the lagged values of MBI_t jointly does not significantly affect MBI_t, the lagged values of $EMSI_t$ combined do play a significant role. These results suggest that the EMSI better explains MBI returns than do past returns of the MBI itself.

Conclusion

There has been growing interest in investor psychology as a potential explanation for stock price movements. This study, using a technique developed in Persaud (1996), constructs a measure called the Equity Market Sentiment Index (EMSI), which uses publicly available data to measure the market's willingness to accept the risks inherent in an equity market at a given point in time. This measure relates the rank of a stock's riskiness to the rank of its return and therefore directly measures the market's pricing of the risk-return trade-off.

From data for the portfolio of firms included in the MBI, it is found that the EMSI captures Massachusetts-related news events as reported in the *Boston Globe* and is highly correlated with the MBI. Moreover, daily price movements in the MBI are significantly related to investor sentiment. In fact, the results indicate that lagged values of the EMSI explain changes in the market index value better than lagged values of the market index itself. This has important implications, as it appears that short-run changes in the market index value are driven primarily by investor sentiment rather than by the index's own price momentum. Researchers and practitioners should pay close attention to investor sentiment as a determinant of changes in financial markets.

Acknowledgments

The authors wish to thank Atreya Chakraborty and Bill Koehler for valuable comments and suggestions, and Jorge Barrero for excellent research assistance.

Notes

1. The Massachusetts Bloomberg Index follows the performance of public companies which are either based in or do considerable business in Massachusetts. This Massachusetts Bloomberg Index closely approximates other indices that contain a larger collection of firms.
2. Persaud discusses the risk appetite in a research report published by JP Morgan Securities Ltd. This idea has received attention in the 'Economics Focus' series in the *Economist* (1996), and in a 1998 conference on business cycles organised by the Federal Reserve Bank of Boston. Other studies (eg Baek *et al.* (2005) have used Persaud's notion of risk appetite to construct risk appetite indices applicable to different contexts.
3. In Persaud, the risk of a currency is proxied by the yield on the bonds denominated in that currency.
4. The reverse argument applies when the risk appetite falls. High- risk (or high-yielding) currencies would be devalued more than those perceived to be safe.
5. Results do not change if standard deviations of returns over a different number of days are used.
6. Standard specification tests were used to determine the appropriate number of lags included for both variables.

References

Baek, I.-M., Bandopadhyaya, A. and Du, C. (2005), 'Determinants of Market Assessed Sovereign Risk: Economic Fundamentals or Market Risk Appetite?' *Journal of International Money and Finance,* 24(4), 533–48.

Baker, M. and Stein, J. (2002) 'Market Liquidity as a Sentiment Indicator', Harvard Institute Research Working Paper, No. 1977.

Baker, M. and Wurgler, J. (2006) 'Investor Sentiment and the Cross- section of Stock Returns', *Journal of Finance,* 61(4), forthcoming.

Branch, B. (1976) 'The Predictive Power of Stock Market Indicators', *Journal of Financial and Quantitative Analysis,* 11(2), 269–86.

Charoenrook, A. (2003) 'Change in Consumer Sentiment and Aggregate Stock Market Returns', Working Paper, The Owen Graduate School of Management, Vanderbilt University.

Chopra, N., Lee, C. M. C., Schleifer, A. and Thaler, R. H. (1993) 'Yes, Discounts on Closed-End Funds Are a Sentiment Index', *Journal of Finance,* 48, 801–8.

Dennis, P. and Mayhew, S. (2002) 'Risk-Neutral Skewness: Evidence from Stock Options', *Journal of Financial & Quantitative Analysis,* 37(3), 471–93.

Eichengreen, B. and Mody, A. (1998) 'Interest Rates in the North and Capital Flows to the South: Is There a Missing Link?', *International Finance,* 1(1), 35–58.

Fisher, K. L. and Statman, M. (2000) 'Investor Sentiment and Stock Returns', *Financial Analysts Journal,* 56(2), 16–23.

Fisher, K. L. and Statman, M. (2003) 'Consumer Confidence and Stock Returns', *Journal of Portfolio Management,* 30(1), 115–28.

Gup, B. E. (1973) 'A Note on Stock Market Indicators and Stock Prices', *Journal of Financial & Quantitative Analysis,* 8(4), 673–85.

Harvey, A. C. (1990) The Econometric Analysis of Time Series, The MIT Press, Cambridge, MA.

Keim, D. B. and Madhavan, A. (2000) 'The Relation between Stock Market Movements and NYSE Seat Prices', *Journal of Finance,* 55(6), 2817–41.

Kumar, M. S. and Persaud, A. (2002) 'Pure Contagion and Investors' Shifting Risk Appetite: Analytical Issues and Empirical Evidence', *International Finance,* 5(3), 401–36.

Lashgari, M. (2000) 'The Role of TED Spread and Confidence Index in Explaining the Behavior of Stock Prices', *American Business Review,* 18(2), 9–11.

Lee, C., Schleifer, A. and Thaler, R. H. (1991) 'Investor Sentiment and the Closed-End Fund Puzzle', *Journal of Finance,* 46, 75–109.

Neal, R. and Wheatley, S. M. (1998) 'Do Measures of Investor Sentiment Predict Returns?', *Journal of Financial & Quantitative Analysis,* 33(4), 523–48.

Persaud, A. (1996) *Investors' Changing Appetite for Risk,* J.P. Morgan Securities Ltd., Global FX Research.

Randall, M. R., Suk, D. Y. and Tully, S. W. (2003) 'Mutual Fund Cash Flows and Stock Market Performance', *Journal of Investing,* 12(1), 78–81.

Whaley, R. E. (2000) 'The Investor Fear Gauge', *Journal of Portfolio Management,* 26(3).

10
Incorporating Estimation Errors into Portfolio Selection: Robust Portfolio Construction

*Sebastián Ceria**
is President and CEO of Axioma, Inc., a New York-based company that produces portfolio construction analytics. Before founding Axioma, he was an associate professor of decision, risk and operations at Columbia Business School from 1993 to 1998. He completed his PhD in Operations Research at Carnegie Mellon University's Graduate School of Industrial Administation.

Robert A. Stubbs
is Director of Research and Development, for Axioma, Inc., where he develops specialised optimisation solution techniques for financial problems and improved portfolio management methodologies and software. He earned a PhD in Industrial Engineering and Management Science and a Master of Science degree in Industrial Engineering and Management Science from Northwestern University, and a Bachelor of Science degree in Applied Mathmetics from Auburn University.

**Axioma. Inc., 100 5th Avenue, Suite 901, New York, NY 10011, USA*
Tel: +1 (212) 901 1000, Fax: +1 (212) 901 1911; e-mail: sceria@axiomainc.com

Introduction

More than 50 years have elapsed since Markowitz (1952) first introduced his Nobel Prize-winning work on mean-variance portfolio optimisation. His work led to the creation of the field now known as Modern Portfolio Theory (MPT). Throughout this time, MPT has had many followers but has also been challenged by sceptics at academic and financial institutions alike. Today, even though MPT is still widely accepted as the primary theoretical framework for portfolio construction, its employment by investment professionals is not as ubiquitous as one might expect. There are several reasons for the lack of acceptance

Reprinted from 'Incorporating estimation errors into portfolio selection: Robust portfolio construction' by Sebastián Ceria and Robert A. Stubbs in *Journal of Asset Management*, 7, 2006, pp. 109–127, DOI:10.1057/palgrave.jam.2240207. With kind permission from Palgrave Macmillan Ltd.

of MPT among practitioners, but perhaps the most significant is the argument that 'optimal' portfolios obtained through the mean-variance approach are often 'counterintuitive', 'inexplicable' and 'overly sensitive to the input parameters'.

The fact that mean variance 'optimal' portfolios are sensitive to small changes in input data is well documented in the literature. Chopra (1993) shows that even slight changes to the estimates of expected returns or risk can produce vastly different mean-variance optimised portfolios. Best and Grauer (1991) analyse the sensitivity of optimal portfolios to changes in expected return estimates. Instead of focusing on the weights of the assets in optimal portfolios, others have focused on the financial impact of mean-variance efficient portfolios computed from estimates. Jobson and Korkie (1981) show that even an equal-weighted portfolio can have a greater Sharpe ratio than an optimal mean-variance portfolio computed using estimated inputs. Broadie (1993) shows how the estimated efficient frontier overestimates the expected returns of portfolios for varying levels of estimation errors. Because of the ill-effects of estimation errors on optimal portfolios, portfolio optimisation has been called 'error maximisation' (See Michaud, 1989). Michaud argues that mean-variance optimisation overweights those assets with a large estimated return to estimated variance ratio (under weights those with a low ratio) and that these are precisely the assets likely to have large estimation errors.

It is widely believed that most of the estimation risk in optimal portfolios is due to errors in estimates of expected returns, and not in the estimates of risk. Chopra and Ziemba (1993) argue that cash-equivalent losses due to errors in estimates of expected returns are an order of magnitude greater than those for errors in estimates of variances or covariances. Many portfolio managers concur, saying that their confidence in risk estimates is much greater than their confidence in expected return estimates.

In order to cope with the effect of estimation errors in the estimates of expected returns, attempts have been made to create better and more stable mean-variance optimal portfolios by using expected return estimators that have a better behaviour when used in the context of the mean-variance framework. One of the more common techniques is the use of James–Stein estimators (see Jobson and Korkie, 1981). These estimators shrink the expected returns towards the average expected return based on the volatility of the asset and the distance of its expected return from the average. Jorion (1985) developed a similar technique that shrinks the expected return estimate towards the minimum variance portfolio. More recently, Black and Litterman (1990) have developed a new Bayesian approach for producing stable expected return estimates that combines equilibrium expected returns and investors' views on specific assets or weighted groups of assets. The area of robust statistics (see Cavadini *et al.*, 2002) has recently been employed to create stable expected return estimates as well.

While strides have been made to improve estimates of expected returns, there will always be errors in these estimates because of the inherent stochastic nature of the asset return process. Even a portfolio manager employing Bayesian estimators such as James–Stein or Black–Litterman will admit that estimation error remains a factor in the 'corrected' estimates of expected returns, even if it is significantly less than that obtained without the use of these methods. In fact, the main premise of Bayesian statistics is that estimates do have distributions. This has led some authors to consider ways in which to account for estimation errors directly in the portfolio construction process.

One possible strategy for considering estimation error is to increase the risk-aversion parameter or modify the risk estimates by increasing the overall volatility. Since the estimated efficient frontier is an overestimate of the true efficient frontier because of the error-maximisation property, it can be argued that by increasing the risk-aversion parameter, the resulting portfolio on the actual frontier will be closer to the true frontier. Horst *et al.* (2001) show how to create an optimal pseudo risk-aversion parameter to use in a mean-variance optimisation problem rather than using the actual risk-aversion parameter. One problem with this approach is that it assumes that the covariance matrix of the estimation error is a constant multiple of the covariance matrix of returns, which is rarely the case in practice. Since expected return estimates are typically generated independent of the factor risk model, the distribution of the estimation error is likely to be quite different from that of the risk model.

Another development that has recently received much attention is the portfolio resampling methodology of Michaud (1999). Michaud introduces a statistical resampling technique that indirectly considers estimation error by averaging the individual optimal portfolios that result from optimising with respect to many randomly generated expected-return and risk estimates. Portfolio resampling, however, is a somewhat *ad hoc* methodology that has many pitfalls (see Scherer, 2002). Because portfolio resampling is a simulation procedure in which each iteration involves a resampling of a time-series, creating mean-variance input estimators and determining the optimal portfolio, it is overly time-consuming to compute. Like the modified risk-aversion parameter approach, portfolio resampling does not actually consider the portfolio manager's estimation error. It only considers the error of estimating a mean and covariance matrix from a simulated time-series from a stationary return process using the expected returns and covariance matrix to generate the time-series. Additionally, the resulting optimal portfolio does not necessarily satisfy all constraints. If a non-convex constraint, eg a limit on the number of assets in the portfolio, is present, the average of portfolios that satisfy the constraints individually will not necessarily satisfy the constraints.

Others have proposed adding constraints to control the ill-effects of estimation error on optimisation generated portfolios. While some constraints can reduce the sensitivity of optimal portfolios to changes in inputs, this paper shows that constraints can actually exacerbate the problem. Furthermore, it shows that that the overestimate of expected return of an optimal portfolio can also be exacerbated by the presence of constraints.

This paper discusses an optimisation methodology known as robust optimisation, which considers uncertainty in unknown parameters directly and explicitly in the optimisation problem. It is generally concerned with ensuring that decisions are 'adequate' even if estimates of the input parameters are incorrect. Robust optimisation was introduced by Ben-Tal and Nemirovski (1997) for robust truss topology design. In a paper that describes several applications of robust optimisation, Lobo *et al.* (1998) introduced the concept of considering the distribution of estimation errors of expected returns explicitly in a portfolio optimization problem. Since then, Goldfarb and Iyengar (2003) consider uncertainties in the factor exposure matrix of a factor risk model directly in the portfolio optimisation problem.

Robust portfolio optimisation is a fundamentally different way of handling estimation error in the portfolio construction process. Unlike the previously mentioned approaches, robust optimisation considers the estimation error directly in the optimisation problem itself. Here, a financial motivation is given for using robust portfolio optimisation as a means of considering errors in the expected return estimates directly in the portfolio construction process. This motivation allows one to see that the 'standard' formulation is only applicable in certain cases. The fourth section introduces modified forms of robust mean-variance optimisation that are applicable in other commonly used portfolio management strategies. Many of the results in this paper were first presented at a practitioners conference in April of 2003 by Ceria (see Ceria and Stubbs, 2003). Since then, a number of other authors have independently proposed an approach similar to the present authors'. Of particular relevance is the paper of Garlappi *et al.* (2004).

This paper introduces an optimisation methodology that significantly reduces some of the ill-effects of portfolio optimisation that are caused by estimation error in expected return estimates. It is shows that errors in expected return estimates can lead to optimal portfolios whose weights are significantly different from those in the true optimal portfolio and whose expected return is significantly overestimated. It is shows that this can be particularly true in the presence of commonly found types of constraints. We discuss a 'standard' robust optimisation methodology that alleviates some of these ill-effects and introduces new variants that more effectively handle the difficulties caused by estimation error in commonly used portfolio management strategies. Finally, some computational results are discussed that demonstrate the potentially significant economic benefits of investing in portfolios computed using standard robust optimisation and the variants introduced here.

Estimation errors and classical mean-variance optimisation

It is a well-documented fact in the investment management literature that mean-variance optimisers are very sensitive to small variations in expected returns. Slightly different expected return vectors can lead to drastically different portfolios. The seemingly unexplainable changes in asset weights due to small perturbations in expected returns are not the only pitfall of classical mean-variance optimisation. Because of the error-maximisation effect, it is typically the case that the expected return is significantly overestimated.

In order to understand better the effect of estimation error in expected returns on optimal portfolios, consider the following example. Suppose there are two assets where the objective is to maximise expected return subject to a budget constraint that forces full investment between the two assets, and a constraint that limits the total active risk to be no more than 10 per cent with respect to the benchmark portfolio (shown as point 'M' in Figure 10.1). The estimates of expected returns and standard deviations of the two assets are given in Table 10.1. It is assumed that the correlation between the two assets is 0.7. The feasible region of this example is illustrated in Figure 10.1 as the intersection of the shaded ellipsoidal region and the budget constraint, ie the feasible region of this example is simply the line segment between points A and B.

Using column 'Alpha 1' from Table 10.1 as the estimates of expected returns, the optimal portfolio is at point A in Figure 10.1. Using the slightly different expected returns given in column 'Alpha 2', the

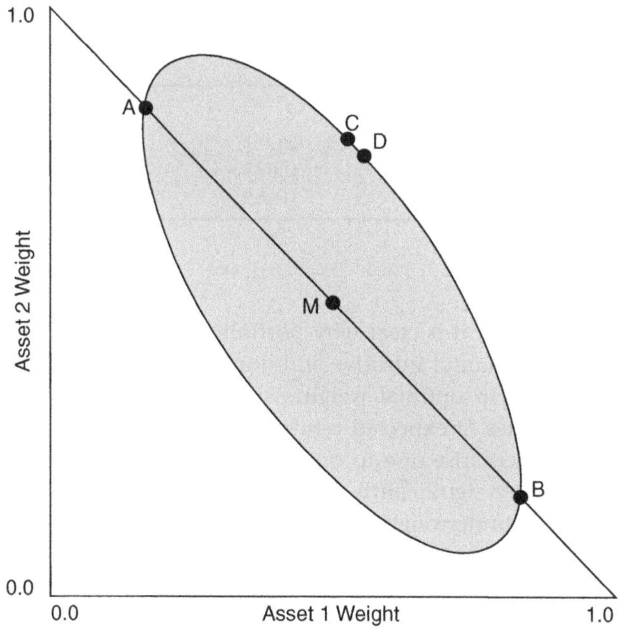

Figure 10.1 Feasible region for example 1

Table 10.1 Expected returns and standard deviations for example 1

Asset	Benchmark weights	Alpha 1 (%)	Alpha 2 (%)	True Alpha (%)	Return Std. Dev. (%)	Alpha Std. Dev. (%)
Asset 1	0.5	2.4	2.5	2.48	0.42	0.5
Asset 2	0.5	2.5	2.4	2.42	0.33	0.5

optimal portfolio is at point B. (The values of the portfolio weights are given in Table 10.2.) This example shows that with only a very small change in the estimates of expected returns of the assets, the weights of the assets in the optimal portfolios changed dramatically. The true optimal solution is at point B with an expected return of 2.46986 per cent. The estimated expected return of points A and B using 'Alpha 1' and 'Alpha 2', respectively, are both 2.4831 per cent. In this example, the expected returns of both optimal portfolios evaluated with respect to their expected return estimates overestimate the true expected return.

Table 10.2 Optimal portfolios for example 1

Attribute	Folio A	Folio B	Folio C	Folio D
Alpha	1	2	1	2
Budget	✓	✓		
Asset 1 weight	0.169	0.831	0.5253	0.5546
Asset 2 weight	0.831	0.169	0.7796	0.7503

From this example, it is clear why portfolio managers find 'optimised' portfolios to be counter intuitive and impractical.

Some changes in optimal weights should be expected when using different estimates of expected returns. Most of the variations in asset weights, however, arise due to optimisers exacerbating the estimation error problem by significantly overweighting assets with an error to the upside and underweighting assets with an error to the downside. Though this behaviour has been described before, the authors are not aware of any studies that have given a precise and intuitive explanation of the error exacerbating effect. The present authors claim that the cause of the 'error maximisation' property of mean-variance optimisers is not only the presence of estimation error, but also the interaction of the estimation error in expected returns with the constraints present in the portfolio optimisation problem.

If we reconsider our example, but drop the budget constraint, then the optimal portfolios with respect to 'Alpha 1' and 'Alpha 2' are points C and D, respectively. Figure 10.1 and Table 10.2 show that the change in optimal portfolio weights with respect to their expected return estimates is much smaller when the budget constraint is dropped. The true optimal solution is at a point on the boundary of the ellipsoid between points C and D with an expected return of 3.191258 per cent. The estimated expected return of points C and D using 'Alpha 1' and 'Alpha 2', respectively, are 3.20972 per cent and 3.18722 per cent. In this example, the expected return of portfolio C evaluated with respect to its expected return estimate overestimates the true expected return, but portfolio D evaluated with respect to its expected return estimate actually underestimates the true expected return. This situation is extremely rare when constraints are present, particularly in higher dimensions.

This simple example was created to illustrate geometrically how slightly different expected return estimates can lead to very different portfolios and how this phenomenon can be exacerbated by the introduction of constraints. It also shows how the error in expected returns is optimised so that the estimated expected return of a portfolio typically overestimates the true expected return. In this small example, the change in expected returns of the portfolios was small, but this was only a two-asset example. To illustrate the error-maximisation effect better, efficient frontiers are considered in a more realistic investment scenario.

As defined by Broadie (1993), the terms 'true frontier', 'estimated frontier', and 'actual frontier' are used to refer to the efficient frontiers computed using the true expected returns (unobservable), estimated expected returns and true expected returns of the portfolios on the estimated frontier, respectively. Specifically, the frontier computed using the true, but unknown, expected returns is referred to as the true frontier. Similarly, the frontier computed using estimates of the expected returns and the true covariance matrix is referred to as the estimated frontier. Finally, the actual frontier is defined as follows. We take the portfolios on the estimated frontier and then calculate their expected returns using the true expected returns. Since we are using the true covariance matrix, the variance of a portfolio on the estimated frontier is the same as the variance on the actual frontier. By definition, the actual frontier will always lie below the true frontier. The estimated frontier can lie anywhere with respect to the other frontiers. If the errors in the expected return estimates have a mean of zero, however, the estimated frontier will lie above the true frontier with extremely high probability, particularly when the investment universe is large.

Using the covariance matrix and expected return vector from Idzorek (2002), we randomly generated a time-series of normally distributed returns and computed the average to use as estimates of expected returns. Using this computed expected-return estimate and the true covariance matrix, we generated an estimated efficient frontier of active risk versus active return where the portfolios were subject to no-shorting constraints and a budget constraint that forces the sum of the weights to be one. Similarly, the true efficient frontier was generated using the original covariance matrix and expected return vector. Finally, the actual 'frontier' was generated by computing the expected return and risk of the portfolios on the estimated frontier with the true covariance and expected return values. The actual 'frontier' is not necessarily concave, as it is not computed as the result of any optimisation, but rather by applying the true expected returns and true covariance to the efficient portfolios in the estimated efficiency frontier. These three frontiers are illustrated in Figure 10.2. Using the same estimate of expected

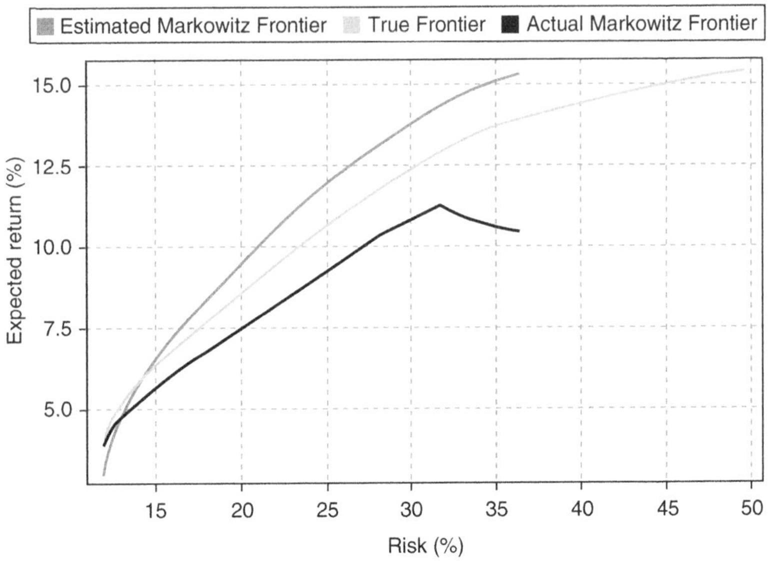

Figure 10.2 Markowitz Efficient Frontiers

returns, we also generated active risk versus active return where we also constrained the active holdings of the assets to be ±3 per cent of the benchmark holding of each asset. These frontiers are illustrated in Figure 10.3. Note how the estimated frontiers significantly over estimate the expected return for most risk levels in both types of frontiers. More importantly, note that the actual frontier lies far below the true frontier in both cases.

This shows that the 'optimal' mean-variance portfolio is not necessarily a good portfolio, ie it is not 'mean-variance efficient'.

In general, it is not known how far the actual expected return may be from the expected return of the mean-variance optimal portfolio. Returning to the example, suppose that the true expected return estimate is some convex combination[1] of the expected return estimates, $(\alpha_1, \alpha_2) = (2.5, 2.4)$ and $(\alpha_1, \alpha_2) = (2.2, 2.7)$ and that one value is no more likely to occur than another. Depending on the point estimate of expected returns used in the mean-variance optimisation problem, the optimal portfolio will be either portfolio A or portfolio B. The actual expected returns of these portfolios for the two extreme expected return estimates are given in Table 10.3. Suppose that the estimate of

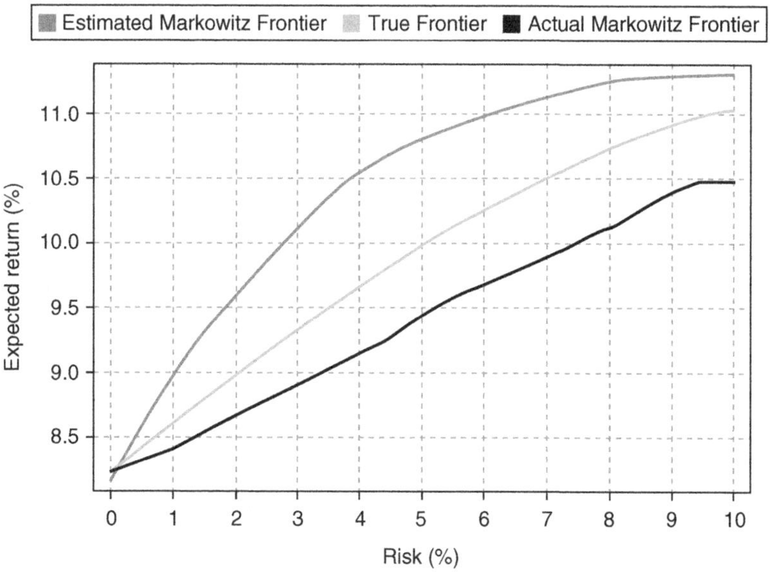

Figure 10.3 Markowitz benchmark-relative efficient frontiers

Table 10.3 Extreme expected return for optimal portfolios

Portfolio	Expected return (2.5, 2.4) (%)	Expected return (2.2, 2.7) (%)
A	2.4169	2.6155
B	2.4831	2.2845

the expected returns leads to optimal portfolio B. In the best scenario, portfolio B will have an expected return that is 0.0662 percentage points greater than that of portfolio A. In the worst-case, however, portfolio B will have an expected return that is 0.331 percentage points less than that of portfolio A. So, by investing in a portfolio that may have an expected return that is 0.0662 percentages points greater than an alternative, there is the risk that the expected return may be as much as 0.331 percentage points less. Since a uniform distribution of expected returns between the two extreme values is assumed, it could be argued that portfolio A is a better, more robust portfolio. That is, the portfolio performs better under more situations within the range of uncertainty of expected returns.

Robust portfolio optimisation

The actual frontier resulting from classical mean-variance optimisation can be far away from both the true and estimated frontiers because of estimation error. The estimated frontier generally lies well above the actual frontier. This study will now analyse just how far apart the estimated and actual frontiers can be over a specified confidence region of the true expected return. It is assumed that the n-dimensional vector of true expected returns α, is normally distributed. Given an estimate of expected return $\bar{\alpha}$ and a covariance matrix Σ of the estimates of expected returns,[2] it is assumed the true expected returns lies inside the confidence region

$$(\alpha - \bar{\alpha})^T \Sigma^{-1} (\alpha - \bar{\alpha}) \leq \kappa^2 \tag{1}$$

with probability 100η per cent where $\kappa^2 = \chi_n^2(1-\eta)$ and χ_n^2 is the inverse cumulative distribution function of the chi-squared distribution with n degrees of freedom.[3]

If the covariance matrix of returns Q is full rank, then one can compute points on the efficient frontier by solving the maximum expected return problem,

$$\begin{array}{ll} \text{maximise} & \bar{\alpha}^T w \\ \text{subject to} & w^T Q w \leq v \end{array} \tag{2}$$

for varying values of v, where α is the expected return estimate, Q is the covariance matrix of returns, and v is the target portfolio variance. It is easy to show that the optimal holdings to this maximum expected return problem are given by

$$w = \sqrt{\frac{v}{\alpha^T Q^{-1} \alpha}} Q^{-1} \alpha$$

Let α^* be the true, but unknown, expected return vector and $\bar{\alpha}$ be an expected return estimate. Recall that the actual frontier is constructed using the true expected return α^*. That is, the true expected return of a portfolio on the estimated from tier is computed as

$$\sqrt{\frac{v}{\bar{\alpha}^T Q^{-1} \bar{\alpha}}} \alpha^{*T} Q^{-1} \bar{\alpha}$$

Let $\tilde{w}$ be the optimal portfolio on the estimated frontier for a given target risk level. Generally, the estimated expected return is greater than the actual expected return because of the 'error maximisation' effect of the optimiser. The question addressed is 'How great can the difference be?' To answer this, consider the maximum difference between the estimated expected return and the actual expected return of $\tilde{w}$. This difference can be written as

$$\bar{\alpha}^T \tilde{w} - \alpha^{\star T} \tilde{w}$$

For a 100η per cent-confidence region of α, the maximum difference between the expected returns on the estimated efficient frontier and the actual efficient frontier is computed by solving

$$\begin{array}{ll} \text{maximise} & \bar{\alpha}^T \tilde{w} - \alpha^T \tilde{w} \\ \text{subject to} & (\alpha - \bar{\alpha})^T \Sigma^{-1} (\alpha - \bar{\alpha}) \leq \kappa^2. \end{array} \tag{3}$$

Note that $\tilde{w}$ is fixed in problem (3). We are optimising over the variable α. The optimal solution to (3) can be shown to be

$$\alpha = \bar{\alpha} - \sqrt{\frac{\kappa^2}{\tilde{w}^T \Sigma \tilde{w}}} \Sigma \tilde{w} \tag{4}$$

Therefore, the lowest possible value of the actual expected return of the portfolio over the given confidence region of true expected returns is computed as

$$\alpha^T \tilde{w} = \bar{\alpha}^T \tilde{w} - \kappa \left\| \Sigma^{1/2} \tilde{w} \right\| \tag{5}$$

and the maximum difference between the estimated frontier and the actual frontier is

$$\bar{\alpha}^T \tilde{w} - (\bar{\alpha}^T \tilde{w} - \kappa \left\| \Sigma^{1/2} \tilde{w} \right\|) = \kappa \left\| \Sigma^{1/2} \tilde{w} \right\| \tag{6}$$

(Throughout this paper, $||\cdot||$ refers to the 2-norm.)

Naturally, one would like this difference to be as small as possible. This would reduce the error-maximisation effect, bring the estimated and actual frontiers closer together, and thus create portfolios that are closer to the true efficient frontier. Simply minimising the distance between the two frontiers, however, will drive the optimal portfolio towards a portfolio that minimises the estimation risk. Clearly, this is not what we want to do. There is no point in considering estimation error if one does not consider the estimates. Instead, we simultaneously want to continue to maximise the expected return of the portfolio so that we are minimising the estimation risk for a given level of estimated expected return. In order to do this, we solve an optimisation problem where we maximise an objective of the form of (5). With this optimisation problem, we will bring the actual and estimated frontiers closer together. We will not be able to guarantee, however, that these frontiers are actually closer to the true frontier.

In this problem, w, the vector of optimal holdings, is not fixed. We optimise over w to find the optimal asset weights. Additionally, any set of portfolio constraints can be added. For instance, a long-only robust portfolio satisfying a budget constraint and a variance constraint can be written as

$$\begin{aligned} \text{maximise} \quad & \bar{\alpha}^T w - \kappa \left\| \Sigma^{1/2} w \right\| \\ \text{subject to} \quad & e^T w = 1 \\ & w^T Q w \leq v \\ & w \geq 0 \end{aligned} \tag{7}$$

where v is a variance target. Note that this problem is exactly the same as a classical mean-variance optimisation problem except for the $\kappa \left\| \Sigma^{1/2} w \right\|$ term in the objective. This term is related to the estimation error and its inclusion in the objective function reduces the effect of estimation error on the optimal portfolio.

There is an important distinction between Q and Σ. Q is the covariance matrix of returns, while Σ is the covariance matrix of estimated expected returns, which is related to the estimation error arising from the process of estimating α, the vector of expected returns. This distinction is even more relevant in practice, where typically Q is obtained from a risk model provider, and is completely independent from Σ which is the result of a proprietary estimation process for α of which the risk model provider is not even aware.

Let us consider just how this additional objective term affects an optimal solution. If one considers equation (4), it can be seen that the expected returns of those assets with positive weights will be effectively[4] adjusted downwards.[5] Similarly, the expected returns of those assets with negative weights, ie short holdings, will be adjusted upwards. The size of the adjustment is controlled by the size of κ, ie the size of the confidence region. Note that the alpha correction term in Equation (4) is constant κ multiplied by the marginal contribution to estimation risk of the assets. Therefore, for a portfolio with a lot of estimation risk in a single asset, the expected return for that asset is effectively adjusted so as to reduce the marginal contribution to the estimation risk of that asset. The purpose of adjusting the expected returns estimates in this way is to counter the error-maximisation effects of portfolio optimisation.

We have just described what we refer to as a robust objective problem. The other forms of classical mean-variance optimisation can also be modelled using robust optimisation. For instance, the maximum utility form of the problem can be written as

$$\begin{aligned} \text{maximise} \quad & \bar{\alpha}^T w - \kappa \left\| \Sigma^{1/2} w \right\| \\ & - p/2 w^T Q w \end{aligned} \tag{8}$$

Similarly, the minimum volatility form of the problem can be written as

$$\begin{aligned} \text{maximise} \quad & w^T Q w \\ \text{subject to} \quad & \bar{\alpha}^T w - \kappa \left\| \Sigma^{1/2} w \right\| \geq r \end{aligned} \tag{9}$$

Problem (7) and its variants cannot be solved by a standard mean-variance optimiser or even a general-purpose quadratic optimiser because the estimation-error term is a 2-norm which contains a square root and cannot be reformulated as a pure quadratic problem. This robust optimisation problem must be solved by either an optimiser capable of handling general convex expressions or a symmetric second-order cone optimiser. Second-order cone optimisation is a relatively new branch of optimisation and special purpose optimisers have been created to solve problems of this type. These specialised solvers can optimize robust optimisation problems in roughly the same amount of time that a mean-variance optimiser can solve the classical problem.

Alternative forms of robust portfolio optimisation

The robust optimisation problem introduced in the previous section three will only adjust the estimates of expected returns downwards if long-only constraints are present. Assuming that each expected return estimate overestimates the true expected return and adjusting all estimates downwards is too pessimistic. Even though there are errors in an expected return estimate, it is not likely that the expected return estimate of each asset is an overestimate of the actual expected return. Similarly, in management of an active fund, the expected returns will be adjusted downwards for any asset with a positive weight. This really does not make sense because this study is interested in active returns. One would not expect our alpha to be adjusted downwards for an asset that already has a negative active weight.

This section introduces new variants of robust optimisation that deal with these issues. It should be noted that the two variants introduced here do not necessarily cover all real-world situations. These variants, along with the standard formulation, do provide ways of handling most commonly found portfolio management strategies. At the end of this section, a more general framework is described under which to view these alternative forms of robust optimisation. This framework can be used to develop other extensions for applicable circumstances.

Zero net alpha-adjustment frontiers

The standard robust optimisation problem discussed in the previous section considered the maximum possible difference between the estimated frontier and the actual frontier. This maximum difference was then minimised. Depending on the goals of the portfolio manager, this approach can potentially be too conservative as the net adjustment to the estimated expected return of a portfolio will always be downwards. If the manager's expected returns are symmetrically distributed around the point estimate, however, one would expect that there are approximately as many expected returns above their estimated values as there are below the true values. It may be more natural and less conservative to build this expectation into the model.

In order to incorporate a zero net alpha-adjustment into the robust problem, (6) is modified by the addition of the linear constraint

$$e^T D(\alpha - \bar{\alpha}) = 0 \tag{10}$$

for some symmetric invertible matrix D to obtain the following

$$\begin{aligned} \text{maximise} \quad & \bar{\alpha}^T \tilde{w} - \alpha^T \tilde{w} \\ \text{subject to} \quad & (\alpha - \bar{\alpha})^T \Sigma^{-1} (\alpha - \bar{\alpha}) \le \kappa^2 \\ & e^T D(\alpha - \bar{\alpha}) = 0 \end{aligned} \tag{11}$$

For now, assume that $D = I$, in which case (10) forces the total net adjustment to the expected returns to be zero. That is, for every basis point decrease in an expected return of an asset, there must be a corresponding gross basis point increase in the expected return of other assets.

$$\alpha = \bar{\alpha} - \sqrt{\frac{\kappa^2}{\left(\Sigma\tilde{w} - \frac{e^T D\Sigma\tilde{w}}{e^T D\Sigma D^T e}\Sigma D^T e\right)^T \Sigma^{-1}\left(\Sigma\tilde{w} - \frac{e^T D\Sigma\tilde{w}}{e^T D\Sigma D^T e}\Sigma D^T e\right)}}\left(\Sigma\tilde{w} - \frac{e^T D\Sigma\tilde{w}}{e^T D\Sigma D^T e}\Sigma D^T e\right) \quad (12)$$

It can be shown that the optimal solution to problem (11) is, (see Equation 12 above).

Therefore,

$$\alpha^T \tilde{w} = \bar{\alpha}^T \tilde{w} - \kappa \left\| \left(\Sigma - \frac{1}{e^T D\Sigma D^T e} \Sigma D^T e e^T D\Sigma\right)^{1/2} \tilde{w} \right\| \quad (13)$$

Instead of having a zero net adjustment of the alphas, one could restrict the alpha region to have a zero net adjustment in standard deviations of the alphas. To do this, one sets $D = L^{-1}$, where $\Sigma = LL^T$ is the Cholesky decomposition of Σ. This forces every standard deviation of upward adjustment in the alphas to be offset by an equal downward adjustment of one standard deviation. Similarly, we could restrict the alpha region to have a zero net adjustment in the variance of alphas in which case one sets $D = \Sigma^{-1}$.

Now, let us consider how this objective is effectively adjusting alphas when $D = \Sigma^{-1}$. In this case, the adjustment term becomes, (see Equation 14 below).

For a problem with a dollar-neutral constraint, ie $e^T \tilde{w} = 0$, the zero-net alpha adjustment form of robust optimisation is equivalent to the standard form. In a fully invested problem, however, there

$$\alpha = \bar{\alpha} - \sqrt{\frac{\kappa^2}{\left(\tilde{w} - \frac{e^T \tilde{w}}{e^T\Sigma^{-1}e}\Sigma^{-1}e\right)^T \Sigma\left(\tilde{w} - \frac{e^T \tilde{w}}{e^T\Sigma^{-1}e}\Sigma^{-1}e\right)}}\,\Sigma\left(\tilde{w} - \frac{e^T \tilde{w}}{e^T\Sigma^{-1}e}\Sigma^{-1}e\right) \quad (14)$$

will be a budget constraint of the form $e^T \tilde{w} = 1$. In this case, the term

$$\frac{e^T \tilde{w}}{e^T\Sigma^{-1}e}\Sigma^{-1}e$$

is exactly the portfolio that minimises estimation error subject to being fully invested. In this case, if a portfolio weight is above that which minimises estimation error, the effective alpha is adjusted downwards. Similarly, if the weight of an asset is below that which minimises estimation error, the effective alpha is adjusted upwards.

Robust active return/active risk frontiers

Thus far, this paper has discussed the classical efficient frontier that demonstrates the trade off between the expected values of total return and total risk. Active managers are more interested in an efficient frontier comparing the expected values of active return and active risk. For a 100η per cent-confidence region of α, the most that the difference between the expected active returns on the estimated efficient frontier and the actual frontier can be is computed by

$$\begin{array}{ll} \text{maximise} & \bar{\alpha}^T(\tilde{w}-b)-\alpha^T(\tilde{w}-b) \\ \text{subject to} & (\alpha-\bar{\alpha})^T\Sigma^{-1}(\alpha-\bar{\alpha})\leq\kappa^2 \end{array} \tag{15}$$

where b is the benchmark holdings. The optimal solution to this problem is

$$\alpha-\bar{\alpha}-\sqrt{\frac{\kappa^2}{(\tilde{w}-b)^T\Sigma(\tilde{w}-b)}}\Sigma(\tilde{w}-b) \tag{16}$$

which implies that

$$\begin{aligned} \alpha^T(\tilde{w}-b) &= \bar{\alpha}^T(\tilde{w}-b) \\ &\quad -\kappa\left\|\Sigma^{1/2}(\tilde{w}-b)\right\| \end{aligned} \tag{17}$$

This gives the following robust optimisation problem for long-only active funds

$$\begin{array}{ll} \text{maximise} & \bar{\alpha}^T w-\kappa\left\|\Sigma^{1/2}(\tilde{w}-b)\right\| \\ \text{subject to} & e^T w=1 \\ & (w-b)^T Q(w-b)\leq v \\ & w\geq 0 \end{array} \tag{18}$$

Now, let us see how this variant of robust objective function effectively adjusts expected return estimates. If the holding in an asset is below the benchmark weight, the α is adjusted upwards. Similarly, if the holding in an asset is above the benchmark weight, the α for that particular asset is adjusted downwards. This behaviour is much more intuitive and performs much better in practice for active strategies.

General robust optimisation framework

All three forms of robust portfolio optimisation discussed thus far can all be cast in a single generalised form. Note that the only difference between Equations (4), (12) and (16) is the model portfolio that is compared with the vector of portfolio holdings $\tilde{w}$, in constructing the expected return adjustments. Let z be the generic 'model' portfolio. Then the generic expected return adjustment can be written as

$$\alpha - \bar{\alpha} - \sqrt{\frac{\kappa^2}{(\tilde{w}-z)^T\Sigma(\tilde{w}-z)}}\Sigma(\tilde{w}-z) \tag{19}$$

In Equations (4), (12) and (16), z is

$0, \dfrac{e^T D\Sigma\tilde{w}}{e^T D\Sigma D^T e} D^T e$ and b, respectively.

Note that z can be dependent on $\tilde{w}$ as it is for the zero-net alpha case.

This generic framework allows for the construction of other alternative forms of robust portfolio optimisation. Both of the alternatives introduced were created to prevent robust optimisation from adjusting alphas based on anything other than estimation error. For example, in the case of the active manager that measures performance relative to a benchmark, the portfolio weights are compared with the benchmark to expected returns from being adjusted because of the active manager's constraints. Similarly, in the case of a fully invested fund, the zero-net alpha adjustment that compares the portfolio weights with the fully invested minimum estimation error portfolio was introduced. The adjustment prevents the expected returns from always being adjusted downwards because of the fully invested constraint.

For different investment strategies, other constraints may force the expected returns to be adjusted in a particular way, even if it is not suggested by estimation error. In these cases, the general form can be used to create an effective robust portfolio construction strategy.

Numerical experiments

In order to measure the effect of the proposed methodology on the efficient frontiers, the experiments used to produce Figure 10.2 were

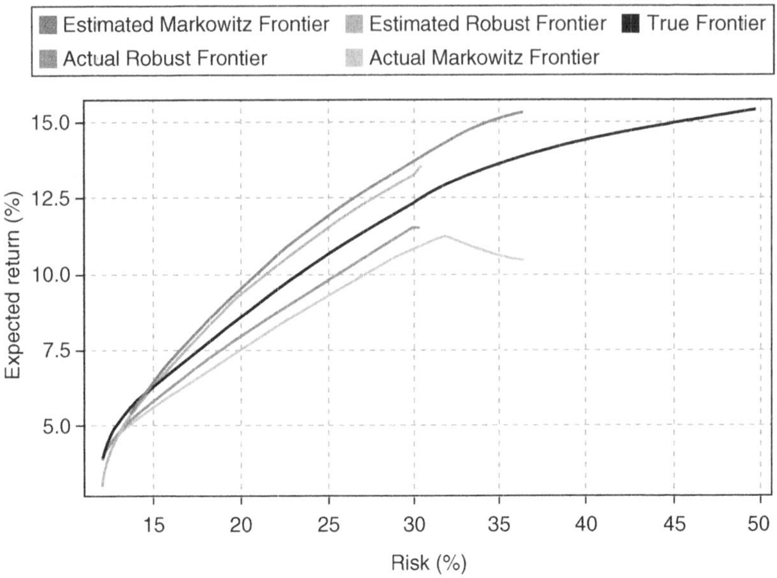

Figure 10.4 Robust efficient frontiers

re-run using robust optimisation. With $D = I$, efficient frontiers were generated using both the standard mean-variance problem and the equivalent robust optimisation problem and compared them with the true frontier as in Figure 10.2. These frontiers are illustrated in Figure 10.4. Similarly, the efficient frontier of active risk versus active return was generated using both classical mean-variance optimisation and the equivalent robust counterpart. These frontiers are illustrated in Figure 10.5. Incorporating the estimation error into the portfolio construction process significantly reduced its effect on the optimal portfolio. In both cases, the predicted return for any given risk level was not exaggerated nearly as much. More importantly, the actual robust frontiers are much closer to the true frontiers than are the actual mean-variance frontiers.

As expected, the computational experiments show that when using robust optimisation, the actual and estimated frontiers lie closer to each other. This is due to the objective function in the robust optimisation problem being based on reducing the distance between the predicted and actual frontiers. The real goal, however, is to get these frontiers not only closer together, but also closer to the true efficient frontier. It is believed that this result will be very difficult to establish theoretically,

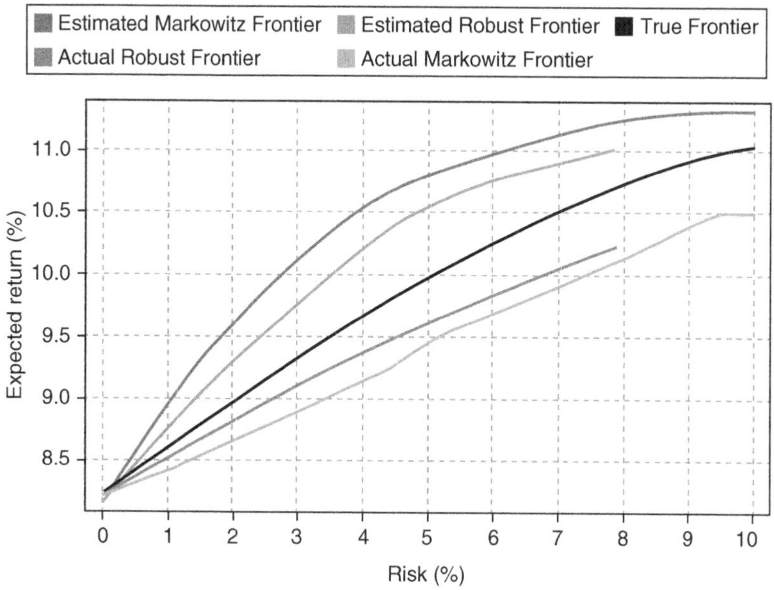

Figure 10.5 Robust Active Return Efficient Frontiers

and for this reason we demonstrated it empirically by running a very large number of computational experiments, which are outlined below.

While frontiers help illustrate the effect of robust optimisation, they only represent one rebalancing period. One cannot say that portfolios constructed using robust optimisation will outperform those constructed using classical mean-variance optimisation each month with certainty. It is argued, however, that portfolios constructed using robust optimisation do outperform those constructed using classical mean-variance optimisation the majority of the time. To demonstrate this, simulated backtests were run using the various forms of robust optimisation described in this paper.

For each simulated backtest, a time-series of monthly returns was generated using the excess expected returns and covariance matrix from Idzorek (2002) for 30 US equities. For each month, a mean vector of returns μ is computed using the previous number of historical periods, T, specified in the backtest. The sample covariance matrix of returns, S, is computed over the same time horizon. For each month, an expected return estimate $\alpha = (1 - \lambda)\mu + \lambda r$ is computed, where r is that month's realised returns, and $0 \leq \lambda \leq 1$ is a parameter specified in the backtest.

Table 10.4 Backtest results for long-short dollar-neutral strategy

Lambda	Kappa	Markowitz Ann. Ret. (%)	Robust Ann. Ret. (%)	Robust Win (%)
0.025	1	2.06	2.90	82
0.025	2	2.06	3.62	80
0.025	3	2.06	4.22	83
0.025	4	2.06	4.71	83
0.050	1	10.53	11.3	79
0.050	2	10.53	11.92	78
0.050	3	10.53	12.38	76
0.050	4	10.53	12.66	76

The value of α used in the backtests intentionally contains some look-ahead bias that is designed to simulate portfolio managers' information.

The estimation error matrix $\Sigma = (1 - \lambda)\ S$, is used in the robust objective term for each backtest. The value of κ used in each backtest is specified in the results tables. All results are based on 100 different runs of the backtests using different seeds for the random number generation. All backtests cover 120 periods, or 10 years of monthly rebalancings.

The first set of backtests simulate a long-short dollar-neutral strategy with a limit on the total risk of 10 per cent. Asset weights were constrained to be within ± 25 per cent of the amount invested. The portfolio is also restricted so that the maximum total value of the long positions is equal to the amount invested in order to restrict leverage. The value of T in each of the backtests was 120. The results are shown in Table 10.4. The columns labeled 'Ann. Ret.' give the average annualised return over all 100 simulations. The column 'Robust win (%)' gives the percentage of the simulations in which the total return using robust optimisation was greater than the total return using classical mean-variance optimisation. In these tests, the total excess returns for the robust backtests were greater than the total excess returns for the classical tests between 76 and 83 per cent of the time. Also note that the average annualised return of the robust portfolios is between 84 and 265 basis points greater than the average annualised return of the classical portfolios.

The second set of backtests simulate a long-only maximum return strategy. Here, expected returns in a fully invested long-only portfolio are maximised with a limit of 20 per cent expected total risk. In these backtests, the monthly round-trip turnover as also limited to be at most 15 per cent by imposing a linear constraint in the portfolio construction

Table 10.5 Backtest results for long-only maximum total return strategy

Lambda	Kappa	Markowitz Ann. Ret. (%)	Robust Ann. Ret. (%)	Robust Win (%)
0.075	1	11.93	12.30	87
0.075	3	11.93	12.59	81
0.075	5	11.93	12.78	75
0.075	7	11.93	12.77	68
0.100	1	14.04	14.46	84
0.100	3	14.04	14.82	81
0.100	5	14.04	14.97	74
0.100	7	14.04	14.97	68

Table 10.6 Backtest results for long-only active strategy

Lambda	Kappa	Markowitz Ann. Ret. (%)	Robust Ann. Ret. (%)	Robust Win (%)
0.025	1	1.59	1.69	69
0.025	3	1.59	1.85	68
0.025	5	1.59	1.98	70
0.025	7	1.59	2.02	65
0.050	1	3.35	3.48	76
0.050	3	3.35	3.68	78
0.050	5	3.35	3.80	75
0.050	7	3.35	3.80	65

problem. The zero-net alpha adjustment version of robust optimisation introduced earlier was used to construct the robust portfolios. The value of T in each of the backtests was 120. The results are shown in Table 10.5. In these tests, the total excess returns for the robust backtests were greater than the total excess returns for the classical tests between 68 and 87 per cent of the time. Also note that the average annualised excess return of the robust portfolios is between 37 and 93 basis points greater than the average annualised excess return of the classical portfolios.

The last set of backtests simulate a long-only active strategy. The portfolios are constrained to be fully invested, have at most a 3 per cent active risk, and the asset weights must be within ± 10 per cent of the investment size of the benchmark weights. In these backtests, we also limited the monthly roundtrip turn over to be atmost 15 per cent. The active return/active risk version of robust optimisation introduced in Section 4.2 was used to construct the robust portfolios. Again, the value of T in each of the backtests was 120. The results of these backtests are given in Table 10.6. The results are based on active returns rather than excess returns, but otherwise show the same type of information as did the previous tables. Again, the total returns for the robust backtests were greater than the total returns for the classical tests. This time, the robust portfolios were superior between 65 and 78 per cent of the time. The average annualised active return of the robust portfolios is between 10 and 45 basis points greater than the average annualised active return of the classical portfolios.

Conclusions

The authors believe that one of the main reasons why modern portfolio theory is not being fully used in practical portfolio management is the fact that the result from a classical mean-variance framework are unstable and too sensitive to expected return estimates. It is argued that these ill-effects of classical portfolio optimisation are caused by the error-maximisation property. The robust optimisation technology described in this paper directly addresses these issues.

The frontier illustrations show that portfolios generated using robust optimisation may be closer to the true efficient frontier. The backtesting results indicate that portfolios constructed using robust optimisation outperformed those created using traditional mean-variance optimisation in the majority of cases. The realised returns were greater when using robust optimisation. The authors believe that the reason for this is that more information is transfered to the portfolios when constructing them using robust optimisation. Classical optimisation will tend to overweight assets with positive estimation error in the expected returns. Because of this, portfolios constructed using mean-variance optimisation typically represent less information from the true expected returns. That is, the portfolios constructed using robust optimisation usually have a higher correlation between the true expected returns and the alphas implied from the portfolio than do those portfolios constructed using robust optimisation.

Robust optimisation is a fairly new optimisation methodology that has not yet found widespread use in the financial community. Robust portfolio optimisation problem is indeed a more complex optimisation problem, but one that can be efficiently handled by a class of interior-point optimisers that are capable of handling second-order cone constraints. Therefore, based on the computational results in this paper, the authors believe that robust portfolio optimisation is a practical and effective portfolio construction methodology.

Notes

1. A convex combination of two vectors *a* and *b* is defined to be $\lambda a + (1 - \lambda)b$ where $0 \leq l \leq 1$.
2. Σ is a symmetric positive definite matrix.
3. We do not need to assume normality. It is only required that the distribution is elliptical. An elliptic distribution is a symmetric distribution such that any minimum volume confidence region of the distribution is defined by an n-dimensional ellipsoid of the form of Equation (1).
4. The effective alpha, or effectively adjusted expected return, is defined as the value of a determined by Equation (4) or the related equation for a variant of (6) for the optimal solution to the robust optimisation problem.
5. When considering adjustments of expected returns, we assume that Σ is a diagonal matrix so that we can easily conceptualise the effective expected-return adjustments without worrying about any interactions between the adjustments. That is, assuming a diagonal matrix, Σ, means that the adjustment to the expected return for asset i is dependent upon the weight of asset *i*, but no others. This is not to say that the adjustments are truly independent, though. Constraints may force one weight to go up if another goes down, which implicitly creates an interrelationship between the alpha adjustments. Because Σ is positive definite, a diagonal Σ will have all positive elements.

References

Ben-Tal, A. and Nemirovski, A. S. (1997) 'Robust Truss Topology Design via Semidefinite Programming', *SIAM Journal on Optimization,* 7(4): 991–1016.

Best, M.J. and Grauer, R. R. (1991) 'On the Sensitivity of Mean-variance Efficient Portfolios to Changes in Asset Means: Some Analytical and Computational Results', *Review of Financial Studies,* 4(2); 315–342.

Black, F. and Litterman, R. (1990) 'Asset Allocation: Combining Investors' Views with Market Equilibrium', Technical report, Goldman, Sachs, *Fixed Income Research,* September.

Broadie, M. (1993) 'Computing Efficient Frontiers using Estimated Parameters', Annals of Operations Research: *Special Issue on Financial Engineering,* 45; 21–58.

Cavadini, H., Sbuelz, A. and Trojani, F. (2002) 'A Simplified Way of Incorporating Model Risk, Estimation Risk, and Robustness in Mean Variance Portfolio Management', Technical Report,University of Southern Switzerland.

Ceria, S. and Stubbs, R. A. (2003) 'Overcoming Estimation Error in Portfolio Construction: Update in the Latest Developments in Optimisation', paper presented at CQA Conference in Las Vegas, NV, April.

Chopra, V. and Ziemba, W. T. (1993) 'The Effects of Errors in Means, Variances, and Covariances on Optimal Portfolio Choice', *Journal of Portfolio Management,*Winter, 6–11.

Chopra, V. K. (1993) 'Mean-variance revisited: Near-optimal Portfolios and Sensitivity to Input Variations', *Russell Research Commentaries,* December.

Garlappi, L., Uppal, R. and Wang, T. (2004) 'Portfolio Selection with Parameter and Model Uncertainty: A Multi-prior Approach', Technical Report, McCombs School of Business, The University of Texas at Austin, Austin, TX 78712, April.

Goldfarb, D. and Iyengar, G. (2003) 'Robust Portfolio Selection Problems', *Mathematics of Operations Research*, 28(1), 1–38.

Horst, J. R. ter, de Roon, F. A. and Werker, B. J. M. (2001) 'Incorporating Estimation Risk in Portfolio Choice', Technical Report, Department of Finance and Center, Tilburg University, Netherlands, January.

Idzorek, T. (2002) 'A Step-by-step Guide to the Black–Litterman Model', Technical Report, Duke University.

Jobson, J. D. and Korki, R. (1981) 'Putting Markowitz Theory to Work', *Journal of Portfolio Management, 7,* 70–74.

Jorion, P. (1985) 'International Portfolio Diversification with Estimation Risk', *The Journal of Business,* 58(3), 259–278.

Lobo, M., Vandenberghe, L., Boyd, S. and Lebret, H. (1985) 'Applications of Second-order Cone Programming', *Linear Algebra and its Application,* 284, 193–228.

Markowitz, H. (1952) Portfolio selection', *Journal of Finance,* VII(1),77–91.

Michaud, R. (1989) 'The Markowitz Optimisation Enigma: Is "Optimised" Optimal?' *Financial Analysts Journal,* 45(1), 31–42.

Michaud, R. *'Efficient Asset Management: A Practical Guide to Stock Portfolio Optimization and Asset Allocation',* Harvard Business School Press, Boston, MA.

Scherer, B. (2002) 'Portfolio Resampling: Review and Critique', *Financial Analysts Journal,* 58(6), 98–109.

11

Best-Practice Pension Fund Governance

*Gordon L. Clark**

is the Halford Mackinder Professor of Geography, holds a Professorial Fellowship at St Peter's College, is cross-affiliated with the Institute of Ageing at Oxford University and is currently a Senior Research Associate of the Labor and Worklife Program at Harvard Law School (Cambridge MA). His current research is on pension fund governance, focusing upon trustee decision-making competence and consistency and the design of rules and regulations to enhance the investment performance of these crucial institutions. With Professor John Marshall and Ms Emiko Caerlewy-Smith, he has concluded a two-year project on trustee competence drawing upon the attitudes and decision-making skills of a select group of UK trustees. This work has been published by the National Association of Pension Funds and through the Journal of Pension Economics and Finance (published by Cambridge University Press). Recent books include The Geography of Finance (Oxford University Press, 2007), Pension Fund Capitalism (Oxford University Press, 2000), European Pensions & Global Finance (Oxford University Press, 2003) and Pension Security in the 21st Century (Oxford University Press, 2003). He is also a co-editor of the Oxford Handbook of Pensions and Retirement Income (Oxford University Press, 2006).

Roger Urwin

graduated from Oxford University (Merton College) with an MA in Mathematics and an MSc in Applied Statistics. He qualified as a Fellow of the Institute of Actuaries in 1983. He worked as an investment consultant for Bacon and Woodrow and headed William Mercer's investment practice before joining Gartmore Investment Management in 1987, where he was the Director responsible for two fields: business development and quantitative investment. He joined Watson Wyatt as a partner in 1989 to head up the firm's UK investment consulting practice, taking on the role of the first global head of practice when this was formed in 1995 and he remains in this role with a worldwide team of over 300 in his charge. He has responsibility for a number of the firm's major investment clients, both in the UK and internationally, advising them on all investment issues. He has increasingly concentrated on policy issues, particularly those relating to asset allocation. His clients include a number of big UK pension funds, but he has also done project work for several institutional funds outside the UK that are working to globalise best practice principles. In particular, he has had client consulting involvement in the US, Canada, Netherlands, Switzerland,

---

Reprinted from 'Best practice pension fund governance' by Gordon L. Clark and Roger Urwin in *Journal of Asset Management*, 9, 2008, pp. 2–21, DOI:10.1057/jam.2008.1. With kind permission from Palgrave Macmillan Ltd.

France, Ireland, Hong Kong, Malaysia, Singapore, Korea and Japan. More recently, he has had greater involvement advising the headquarters of multinational companies.

**Oxford University Centre for the Environment, South Parks Rd., Oxford OX1 3QY, UK. Tel: +44 (0) 1865 285072; Fax: +44 (0) 1865 285073;*
E-mail: gordon.clark@ouce.ox.ac.uk

Introduction

Increasing attention is being paid to the performance of institutional funds; whether public or private, large or small, well-governed or not, these institutions have come to play crucial roles in under-writing the welfare of many citizens of developed and developing countries. In terms of the volume of assets managed by these institutions, it is estimated that, as of 2006, across the world pension funds accounted for $US25,000bn, endowments and foundations $4bn, and the emerging sovereign funds $4bn.[1] The price of poor performance is very high (as is noted by many commentators and academics; see Ambachtsheer (2007a) and Lerner *et al.* (2007)). Inevitably, institutional performance is conditioned by the inherited practices of various bodies that are responsible for these funds. At the same time, we should not be content with simply relying upon the past for the future.

In this paper, we begin by distinguishing between the inherited structure of investment institutions – normally framed by statute, property rights, and covenants – and the governance of those institutions – often framed by the rules and procedures that sustain their performance. This distinction is owed, in part, to Williamson (1996, pp. 4–5) who noted institutional structure is often difficult to change; by his account, it 'evolves' rather than changes in any substantial sense from one time to the next. Like a number of other theorists of institutional design and performance (eg North, 1990), he suggests that 'governance' is an essential ingredient of any institution's functional performance, being the capacity of an organisation to function in ways consistent with desired goals. Institutional structure is, however, not the only determinant of performance: even 'ideal' institutions fail if poorly governed.

Typically, large institutions are organised by formal arrangements of authority and responsibility. Many organisations can provide the interested researcher with figures and maps demonstrating in theory, at least, the proper relationships between line-officers against hierarchically ordered tasks and functions. But the accumulated evidence suggests that formalism is not sufficient as a description of the life of such organisations whether they be general-purpose corporations, financial institutions or pension funds (witness controversy surrounding the agency problems of funds; see Cocco and Volpin, 2007). For many organisations the governance problem is one of orchestrating collective action in a timely and effective fashion given inherited relationships and systems of control; this is especially important in financial institutions that must be adaptive and responsive to market environments that seem to move at the speed of light.

Social scientists often argue that the functional performance of any institution is dependent upon the clarity of *a priori* defined tasks and functions – Merton and Bodie (2005) provide a template for institutional design relevant to the financial industry, arguing that well-governed organisations have functional (means-ends) clarity. We share this opinion, but recognise that the global finance industry is replete with all kinds of institutions that share similar if not the same functions, differentiated by history and geography. Institutional investors are not the same the world over because they come from distinctive national political traditions (Roe, 2006) and particular iterations of social organisation (O'Barr and Conley, 1992). The challenge of institutional governance can be thought to be comprised of two related parts: to facilitate adaptation to the functional imperatives driving performance without institutional (re)design in the short term and to build long-term performance through reform and re-design of institutional structure.

Ambachtsheer (2007a, b) is of the opinion that many pension and retirement income institutions are not 'fit-for-purpose' whatever their jurisdiction and inherited institutional form. On the other hand, it is not self-evident what works nor is it self-evident what does not work – for example, do some US endowment funds 'out-perform' because they are endowment funds or because they are better governed or both (see Lerner *et al.*, 2007)? If nation states are to redesign pension and retirement income institutions to cope with 21st century imperatives like demographic ageing, the sustainability of plan sponsors, and the increasing premium on (and visibility of) financial performance, issues of structural design must be considered in relation to institutional governance. In fact, knowledge of governance best-practice may be essential for the institutional design process – an issue we return to in the closing sections of the paper.

The paper proceeds in the following manner. In the next section we consider the status and significance of best-practice noting that our use of exemplars is designed to help to understand the underlying principles of institutional governance rather than the particular details of each and every case. This is followed in the subsequent section with a statement about the challenges facing asset owners, especially in relation to investment practice and the flux and flows of global financial markets.

We take seriously the insights of Kahneman and Tversky (1979) regarding the cognitive problems of operating in risk environments; we are more optimistic than some about the role that well-governed institutions can play in promoting best-practice (Engel and Weber, 2006).[2] In the following section, we spell out 12 principles of best-practice, recognising that no institution is perfect. This is followed in the fifth section with a series of arguments about what works in resource-constrained situations before closing in the Conclusion with comments about the design of investment institutions like sovereign funds.

Scoping best-practice

Management consulting firms, business schools, and sections of the business press are pre-occupied with best-practice; the subject is increasingly important to organisations worldwide with many now including a formal statement in their charters to the effect that they will strive for best-practice. In many situations, best-practice is derived from global experience not simply their national or regional context. Client advice, teaching, and communication rely upon the synthesis of experience, the identification of core principles and practices, and their transfer to relevant situations. It is also apparent that the market-share of organisations striving for global best-practice is large and growing, as global economic and financial integration challenge the robustness and legitimacy of inherited institutions.

Our analysis of best-practice matches a concern in the funds management industry to identify the principles and practices of good governance. Research suggests the impact of good governance may be as much as 100–300 basis points per year (Ambachtsheer, 2007a; Watson Wyatt, 2006). In a number of instances, our exemplar institutions had instituted their own policies on governance designed to foster learning from peers. For some institutions, governance has become part of their subcommittee system being often located with the audit function.

One development has been the adoption of a 'governance budget' framework to promote the management of governance innovation (Urwin and others, 2001). In part, a fund's governance budget is related to size. But, as we show below, even smaller funds can adopt best-practice standards appropriate to their size and capacity. Our conception of governance is based on three principles:

- Governance is a finite and conceptually measurable resource, and the size of this resource – the governance budget – is associated with expected performances.

- A certain size governance budget is best matched with a certain investment style and strategy, consistent with other budgets that recognise limited resources and the need for skill.
- There are ways to adapt the governance budget over time with implications for long-term investment performance and pay-offs.

As consultants have become involved in evaluating the effectiveness of fund governance, the definition of governance has evolved. For this paper, the 'governance budget' refers to the capacity to create value from effective actions in the chain of institution-defined tasks and functions (Watson Wyatt, 2004).

There are two rather different approaches to the identification of best-practice. Some analysts rely upon large databases of institutional performance using accepted metrics such as the risk-adjusted rate of return over time to benchmark relative virtue. This approach allows for comparative performance measures across different types of institutions performing similar functions; it also allows for the identification of those types of institutions that are, on average, better performing than others (Lerner *et al.,* 2007). The lessons of this approach are twofold: first, those types of institutions that do better than others ought to be emulated and secondly, those institutions that do better than others can be emulated not withstanding their distinctive attributes and inherited traditions (Gertler, 2001).

At the same time, however, there are acknowledged shortcomings with this approach. Using the risk-adjusted rate of return as the performance measure to discriminate best-practice runs the danger of confusing a common measure of performance with rather different objectives – it is widely appreciated that defined benefit schemes seek to maximise returns subject to their long-term liabilities and government regulations regarding sponsor solvency and mandated funding levels. Defined contribution plans, hybrid schemes, and endowment funds may also seek to maximise returns but do so over very different time horizons and for different purposes. In addition, most performance evaluations have difficulty in using past performance to isolate the relevant determinants of future performance. This issue is exacerbated by the high noise to signal ratio of most measures of investment performance, which weaken the significance of statistical inference studies (Urwin, 1998).

The approach followed in this paper is to rely upon exemplars of best-practice by class of institution, thereby being sensitive to their distinctive attributes while drawing lessons between best-in-class exemplars for industry best-practice. Our selection relied on the authors' extensive knowledge of organisations over a sustained period of time with clear evidence of strong decision-making accompanying success in performance. While performance was not our principle selection criteria, almost all of our best-practice funds had a performance margin of 2 per cent per annum or more over their benchmarks. Our selection of exemplars targeted different types of institutions including corporate pension plans, public pension plans, sovereign funds, and endowment funds. They were also taken from six different countries dispersed across North America, Europe, and Asia-Pacific. As expected, no single country has a dominant position in global best-practice.[3]

Identifying exemplars of best-practice may be problematic if industry reputation for high-quality governance is the sole criterion for selection. We run the risk of playing favourites with well-known cases rather than challenging the status quo with heretofore unrecognised innovative instances of best-practice. In this project, we went beyond industry reputation, relying upon our shared knowledge of different cases to scope the field for interesting cases. Of course, case study research is challenging for other reasons including the problems sometimes encountered when seeking access to the exemplars deemed most worthy of study. Likewise, care must be taken when reporting results and synthesising experience such that information shared in confidence is not disclosed to the detriment of respondents. Here, we follow social science guidelines regarding respect for confidentiality and anonymity (Clark, 2003). Throughout, no fund or institution is identified by name because we seek to emphasise the principles of best-practice rather than the details of any one institution (see the Appendix for more details).

The challenge of pension fund governance

Notwithstanding the common acceptance of golden rules such as maximising beneficiary (or other stakeholder) interests, pension institutions are subject to many of the same governance problems of the modern corporation (compare Clark (2006) with Jensen (2000)). Such institutions suffer from substantial agency issues, often of a greater order than most corporations. The list of relevant issues includes the following: pension beneficiaries (principals) are unable to monitor the actions of plan administrators and trustees (agents); there may be more than one principal (if we include DB plan sponsors); and there may be an extensive network of agents (such as investment managers) whose motivations and rewards may be difficult to align and difficult to observe (Black, 1992). For most funds, internal investment costs (the direct costs of trustees and their staff) are substantially smaller than external costs (principally of investment managers and other investment agents). The ratio of external to internal costs is generally of the order 10:1 or greater. This external agent expenditure is rarely observed in other corporations (Watson Wyatt, 2006).

Corporate boards of directors do have significant responsibilities, are subject to legal principles such as fiduciary duty (depending upon the jurisdiction), and face formidable rules and regulations as regards their conduct. Even so, in law due deference is paid to the separate operational responsibilities of managers as well as to the myriad of contractual relationships between stakeholders including employees, service providers, and customers. Managers and key associates often receive performance-related pay, especially where their performance is integral to the generation of income distributed to otherwise passive shareholders in the form of stock-price appreciation and dividends (Roberts, 2004). By contrast, the responsibilities of trustee boards are not normally circumscribed by managers' operational responsibilities, and performance-related pay arrangements are very uncommon. Nor are pension beneficiaries normally able to participate in a market for (pension) control. Their reliance on trustee boards for delivery of promised pensions is exceptionally high (Clark and Monk, 2008).

Not surprisingly, trustees are very much aware of their responsibilities. Given that many trustees are only nominally compensated for their roles and responsibilities, an important motive for serving on such boards is the proffered scope of responsibilities in relation to the welfare of others. Well-governed trustee boards segment and prioritise responsibilities, distinguishing (for example) between beneficiaries' claims for special consideration as regards the nature and value of benefits and the investment of plan assets against a target rate of return (see below).

Well-governed trustee boards tend to allocate the routine issues to plan administrators and rely upon reporting systems to oversee the determination and resolution of claims while allocating the available time and resources to issues like investment strategy and management that may affect the long-term integrity of the institution and payment of pension benefits. Well-governed trustee boards also tend to delegate to internal staff and external service providers the execution of tasks and functions governing those relationships by contract and measures of performance (Clark, 2007a). The asset owners in our study showed awareness of these special characteristics, and all made reference to a number of particular challenges of governance that best-practice must surmount.

The challenge of governance is more than the generic issues that afflict all modern organisations – pension funds operate in global financial markets where the management of risk and uncertainty is

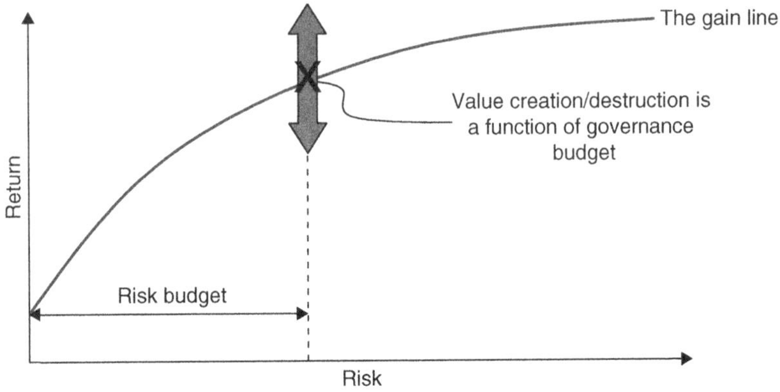

Figure 11.1 Schematic of governance budget and risk budget

crucial to the creation of long-term value. Figure 11.1 demonstrates that governance can create and destroy value shifting the risk-adjusted rate of return above or below the 'gain line' (depending on the risk budget and the governance budget). The implications of this proposition are twofold: first, risk taking against well-defined objectives is an essential ingredient in any well-governed financial institution and secondly, the extent to which risk taking is a deliberate and managed activity depends upon the governance budget allocated to this function within the institution. Poorly governed entities rarely take risk planning seriously and wrongly economise on the governance budget treating it as a cost that limits net financial performance.

(a) Risk management focus

More generally, in our experience we would contend that pension and retirement institutions must be sensitive to the distinctive attributes of financial markets and behaviour. While theories of financial market structure and performance abound, from our research on pension fund investment it is important that fund decision-makers be able to distinguish between moments of 'normal' risk and moments of uncertainty. In addition, this determination must encompass regime shifts in pricing and risk, and their consequences for non-normal return distributions and investing in extreme conditions. The challenge in risk management could be summarised as employing both quantitative and qualitative disciplines in analysing many fast-moving parts of markets – economic, behavioural, and organisational (Shiller, 2002). *The governance challenge here is to function efficiently in the fast changing risk domain, adapting effectively to market signals while recognising that market signals may be subject to unanticipated disruption.*

(b) Time horizon focus

Just as importantly, reaping long-term higher than average rates of return requires integrating short-term positions with long-term goals thereby being sensitive to the sequential nature of investment decision-making. Characteristic of poor performing institutional funds, advisors, decision-makers, and stakeholders tend to come to premature conclusions (Wagner, 2002). Long-term optimising must accommodate short-term opportunism while recognising that the short-time horizons of many stakeholders conditions behaviour such that these actions may not be aligned with long-term goals. Therefore, decision-makers have to make a very big adjustment to take a longer-term view, which risks being 'wrong' in the short term. *The governance challenge here is to act in the short term with respect to long-term goals, utilising decision-procedures to exploit immediate opportunities but penalise impulsiveness.*

(c) Innovative capability

It is widely recognised that financial markets are 'innovation machines' that test investors' fitness to succeed – there are significant rewards for those who are able to identify and exploit unacknowledged market opportunities just as there are enormous rewards for those who create markets and financial products to price and distribute risk (as in alternative investments, infrastructure, and derivates, etc). Recognising the increasing clock speed of markets and strategies places real-time processes at an advantage. Many funds use calendar-time processes, often through a quarterly meeting cycle, making their decisions insufficiently responsive to opportunities and threats. *The governance challenge here is to exploit the premium from innovation through the application of judgment and experience to new opportunities, recognising that conventional risk-related procedures may be poorly tuned to the frontiers of finance.*

(d) Alignment with a clear mission

Perhaps the greatest governance challenge is to be effective in responding to these governance issues in organisations whose original design, mission, and current size and composition of skills and experience are less than perfect (Clark *et al.*, 2006). For many reasons, pension and retirement income institutions often have a variety of constituents, stakeholders and even competing objectives in the real world of inherited institutions, procedures, and expectations. *The governance challenge here is to build alignment behind clear statements of mission-critical goals, particularly in dealing with multiple stakeholders and complex dependencies, recognising that 'reform' is normally an ongoing process of accommodation and only rarely once-and-for-all instances of idealism.*

(e) Effective management of external agents
Achievement of goals is unrealistic for the vast majority of funds without external delegation. The characteristic approach of the best-practice fund is to employ external managers in a line-up emphasising diversity to limit risk. In assessing the wide field of choices of investment firms, funds need particular skills and processes for dealing with agency issues, given the informational asymmetries about each manager's value proposition. The processes that have evolved to deal with these decisions have been unsystematic. *The governance challenge here is managing the considerable agency issues in using a line-up of managers and other agents that collectively can support the organisation's overall goals.*

Governance best-practice

Our project concentrates on three aspects of asset owner best-practice: the ways in which our exemplars organise their governance practices with respect to institutional coherence, their people, and their processes. In summary terms, *coherence* included consideration of the clarity and focus of investment objectives; *people* included consideration of those involved in investment decision-making including reference to their skills and expertise; and *process* included reference to how investment decision-making is organised and implemented. These three aspects of good governance are distinctive but closely related. When screening the available set of case studies to settle on those that represent best-practice, strengths varied; it was found that some institutions are better on institutional coherence than people and process, in other cases, institutions hoped that a strong decision-making process could overcome shortfalls in coherence and people. We contend that the best-governed institutions are those that follow best-practice across all three dimensions.

In this section we concentrate on the lessons learnt about best-practice according to these headings and selectively illustrate those lessons with reference to some of our exemplars. Consideration is also given to the diversity of institutions represented in our study, noting the experience, for example, of public and private pension funds, endowment funds, and sovereign funds. In the Appendix, we list the case study institutions and their attributes and identify them in this manner so as to maintain anonymity. In the following section, we bring together the findings on best-practice by institutional coherence, people, and process to show how these aspects of good governance interact with one another such that best-practice is reinforced and becomes an endogenous element in value-added investment management.

Best-practice – Institutional Coherence

Many investment institutions have a form and structure that is essentially given: in some cases provided by statute and in other cases nonetheless subject to the interests of political and stakeholder constituencies. One way or another, institutional structure is inherited and, if reform is on the agenda, is subject to negotiation and compromise (Roe, 2006). The trick in so many of our institutions, public and private, is to ensure a match between what is inherited with respect to the long-term interests of beneficiaries and other stakeholders. Here, our findings can be summarised as follows.

1. *Clarity of the mission and the commitment of stakeholders to the mission statement.* In our exemplary cases, abstract golden-rules such as maximising beneficiary welfare were augmented with second-order mission statements such that board members, the senior staff, and stakeholders inside and outside of the institution were able to match the golden rule with an accepted operational goal such as a target yearly real rate of return allowing for liabilities subject to agreed risk parameters. Such funds also developed a set of other supporting goals to support success with their primary goals. The clarity apparent in the funds in our best-practice group is very uncommon in the authors' experience.
2. *A highly competent investment function tasked with clearly specified responsibilities and with clear accountability to the institution was characteristic of our exemplars.* This arrangement often included an explicit 'map' of institutional authority, distinguishing the responsibilities of trust boards, executives, and service providers. In some cases, there were formal 'charters' providing each element in the governance chain with a mandate for their tasks and functions. In other cases, where charters were not incorporated into standing orders, trust boards sought to provide a clear demarcation of responsibilities, typically distinguishing between strategy and its implementation and execution. The key element for most funds is the executive group,

including a Chief Investment Officer with significant delegated responsibility. Our exemplars sought to 'govern' their management by reference to delegated tasks and responsibilities, specified by contract and set in relation to the mission statement and operational goals of the institutions. We have noted elsewhere that many investment institutions blur delegation and deference, often relying upon their senior staff for support in decision-making without clarifying performance objectives, incentives, and sanctions (Clark, 2007a).

3. *Most importantly, we observed that institutional coherence was sustained in most cases by resourcing each element in the investment process and governance chain with an appropriate time and resources budget.* Unfortunately, resourcing is often seen as a cost to the institution rather than a long-term investment in the coherence of the institution as a functional entity. Our exemplars demonstrated a keen awareness of the value that could be created by internal resources if appropriately targeted.

Best-practice – People

It is, perhaps, a truism that the human capital or talent of any organisation is its most important asset. This is certainly an important theme in contemporary research on industry and firm-related differences in productivity and market performance and is especially important in the financial and service-related industries that overlap with pension and retirement income institutions. Nonetheless, institutions vary a great deal in terms of their ability to select trustees, employ senior staff, and generally govern themselves as human capital-enhancing organisations (Ambachtsheer *et al.*, 2007). Here, our findings were as follows.

4. *Leadership has a strong and demonstrable effect on institutional performance, being evident at the board level (particularly in the activities of the chairperson) through to the execution of delegated tasks and functions.* Our exemplars sought out highly qualified and respected board chairpersons and charged them with encouraging a culture of accountability and responsibility among board members. This commitment also appears to pay dividends in the selection of senior staff of pension and retirement income institutions, especially when that is matched by a commitment to management by goals and objectives.
5. *To the extent trust chairpersons and their boards are able to select their colleagues, three desired qualities guide selection: demonstrable numeric skills, a capacity for logical thinking, and an ability to think about risk*

in the probability domain. Collegiality is important, but it was often noted that shared competencies combined with peer recognition for experience and ability tended to enhance collective decision-making, whereas disparate and unmatched abilities tend to be a drag on board decision-making (Clark *et al.,* 2006). This issue is under-recognised, with many institutions assuming that commitment, training, and experience can overcome deficiencies. Our exemplars recognised that these competencies are not easy to instil, and so selection of board and staff becomes a critical function. In some cases, our exemplars were able to fashion human resource policies that took advantage of the unique characteristics of their institutions while fashioning tasks and functions that were different than financial institutions.

6. *Effective compensation practices are used to build bench-strength and align actions to the mission, with different strategies working according to fund context.* Compensation is an important issue. In many cases, our respondents acknowledged that corporate staffing policies and remuneration schemes, public sector scrutiny of salaries and benefits, and the remarkable bonus schemes of bulge-bracket financial firms make head-to-head competition on compensation difficult. This issue has been particularly challenging with respect to key staff members. Different issues arise for board or investment committee members, where in some of our exemplars, payments are set to match the standards set in the mutual fund industry. Whatever the strategy is used, systems of 'reward' are explicitly linked to the mission and performance of the institution and the sense of common responsibility for its performance against objectives. We observed that many funds have acquiesced to a double-standard in compensation – paying limited packages in-house and paying fees that support much more substantial packages externally. Our exemplars have recognised the contradiction implied in this distinction.

Best-practice – Process

By our analysis, institutional coherence and the people involved in decision-making are essential pre-conditions for a high-performance pension and financial institution. Without a clear mission statement and operational goals and the people to frame and implement an appropriate investment strategy, a disciplined investment process will not deliver desired results. On the other hand, with both preconditions in place the evidence suggests that the process of investment decision-making was the most important means of reaping the potential value of an institution. It was also noted that this element in the governance chain was that which the institution could most control. Our findings were as follows.

7. *Our exemplars rely upon a process centred on strong beliefs and an investment philosophy claiming fund-wide support that aligns with operational goals and informs investment decision-making.* Only with a clear and accepted belief structure can an institution sustain its competitive edge in financial markets. In our research, we observed exemplars focus upon four main areas of this issue: (1) asset class and security pricing including the 'fair' prices of investment opportunities, the reasons why mis-pricing can occur, and the degree to which mis-pricing is a systematic fact of life; (2) the fund's ability (or its comparative advantage) in exploiting such identified opportunities; (3) how the fund might develop and integrate these beliefs into its investment strategy; and (4) what these strategies can produce, in value-added and risk terms, across the whole portfolio. Many institutions distinguish between different types of strategic issues and the appropriate location of decision-making relevant to those issues particularly between investment committees and the executive. For example, in many cases the most developed investment beliefs are located at the executive level. But it is still critical for an informed board to build their own beliefs and deal effectively with those of the executive.
8. *Our exemplars frame the decision-making process by reference to the institution's comparative advantages and disadvantages.* Few investment institutions are able to operate effectively in all investment domains (some are better suited to public markets, whereas others may have the capacity to operate most effectively in private markets or exotic products). The best-practice process of decision-making takes into account an institution's own capacities and its acknowledged limits and acts accordingly. This includes deciding on the degree of delegation, choosing to act in a primary investment role, selecting individual investments in some areas, or acting as a manager of managers in other areas where investments would be selected by outside managers. Funds varied in their degree of use of external managers, but it is interesting that none managed all assets in-house.
9. *Our exemplars frame the investment process by reference to a risk budget aligned to fund goals incorporating an accurate and integrated view of alpha and beta.* Many of our institutions utilise an absolute return ethos, constrained by a risk budget, which is explicit about the desired relative contributions of alpha and beta to overall fund

performance. This is a quantitative decision-making framework reinforcing the significance of trustee skills and qualities that sustain consistent method-based decision-making (Clark *et al.*, 2007). While the increased opportunity to separate alpha and beta has attracted many funds' attention, most of the exemplars in our group concentrated on improved alpha and beta transparency in their line-up, but most did not go as far as more formal alpha-beta transport. They all sought clarity over how to manage a judicious mix of alpha and beta consistent with their goals.

10. *Recognising the time-dependent nature of investment performance, best-practice institutions utilise decision-making systems that function in real time not calendar time.* There are various ways of doing this, including devolving decision-making to expert sub-committees, most of which involve greater delegation of time-dependent decision-making to executives or external firms subject to board over-sight. The authors' contend that calendar-time governance is typical of most funds; the crucial issue here is how that is reconciled with real-time markets.
11. *Best-practice masters the effective use of external managers through clearly defined mandates, aligned to goals, and selected with rigorous application of fit-for-purpose criteria.* In other words, best-practice institutions distinguish between the nature and types of decision-making by operational entities taking care not to compromise decision-making at one level by poor decision-making at other levels. Characteristically, best-practice asset owners employ external managers in a line-up emphasising diversity so as to limit risk. Mandate specification is one area of importance. Also fit-for-purpose assessment of firms and products is important. Typically, we found three aspects of suitability: (1) investment efficiency, allowing fully for costs, (2) alignment to the fund's needs to achieve sustainability of performance goals, and (3) an appropriate transparency of process, allowing for an assessment of the product according to its manager skills (alpha) and market return (beta) drivers. While acknowledging that the selection of managers is always problematic, our exemplars showed considerable rigour with applying fit-for-purpose assessment of outside firms and their investment products. They also made frequent reference to the importance of the de-selection process as well as the selection process.
12. *In terms of investment decision-making, best-practice institutions work within a learning culture that deliberately encourages change and challenges the commonplace assumptions of the industry.* In part, this

means that past decisions are evaluated against actual outcomes so as to calibrate the decision-making process while allowing appropriately for noise and signal issues (Clark, 2004). In part, this also means that institutions are routinely turned inside-out by challenging trustee boards and senior executive staff to be innovative within the bounds of institutional capacity. Accelerating change is a given of the funds industry; technology is always moving forward and its effect on the growth of knowledge is positive at an accelerating pace. Knowledge of what works and what does not work in investment is at a premium and is time-sensitive; there is added value in changing with new knowledge and opportunities.

The full list of the 12-factor model of best-practice is summarised in Table 11.1.

Constrained best-practice governance

We are conscious that these findings, when taken together, are idealistic on two fronts. First, none of our exemplars could be said to be at the leading edge of each and every component of best-practice. Secondly, this list is premised on significant internal resources, which many funds do not have available or are unable to mobilise.

We noted that best-practice institutions were generally aware of their own shortcomings on some or all of these issues. In fact, it could be argued that best-practice funds are those that continuously seek to improve their functional performance whatever their inherited structures and practices (comparing Merton and Bodie (2005) with Roe (2006)). That is, there is a self-critical ethos of institutional learning and best-practice; complacency is the enemy of long-term value creation. One key institutional quality we observe in our exemplars is their use of expertise in investment decision-making and, in particular, whether they utilise in-house investment experts. Based on our experience, we can identify three types of fund structure and organisational design (Figure 11.2). The simplest type is widely known, being a system of collective deliberation wherein the board makes decisions on a routine basis with the support of a consultant and external service providers. A more sophisticated version utilises an investment sub-committee subject to the final approval at the board relying, again, on collective decision-making according to the regular meeting schedule (Type 2). In Finding 2, we identified in-house investment expertise as a key factor in best-practice our exemplars utilise to drive real-time decision-making (Type 3).

Table 11.1 Best-practice factors

1. Mission clarity	Clarity of the mission and the commitment of stakeholders to the mission
2. Investment executive	The use of a highly investment-competent investment function tasked with clearly specified responsibilities, with clear accountabilities to the investment committee
3. Effective time budget	Resourcing each element in the investment process with an appropriate budget considering impact and required capabilities
4. Required competencies	Selection to the board and senior staff guided by: numeric skills, capacity for logical thinking, ability to think about risk in the probability domain
5. Leadership	Leadership, being evident at the board, investment committee and executive level, with the key role being the investment committee Chairman
6. Effective compensation	Effective compensation practices used to build bench strength and align actions to the mission, different strategies working according to fund context
7. Strong beliefs	Strong investment philosophy and beliefs commanding fund-wide support that aligns with operational goals and informs all investment decision-making
8. Competitive positioning	Frames the investment philosophy and process by reference to the institution's comparative advantages and disadvantages
9. Risk budget	Frames the investment process by reference to a risk budget aligned to goals and incorporates an accurate view of alpha and beta
10. Real-time decisions	Utilises decision-making systems that function in real time not calendar time
11. Manager line-up process	The effective use of external managers, governed by clear mandates, aligned to goals, selected with rigorous application of fit for purpose criteria
12. Learning organisation	Work to a learning culture which deliberately encourages change and challenges the commonplace assumptions of the industry

As is widely appreciated, the most prevalent organisational forms are those in which there are no significant internal resources deployed supporting multiple-function boards. Rough calculations suggest that if we consider all institutional funds across the world that have assets that are above $2bn (and there are somewhere over 2,000 of these), we would argue that only around 10 per cent of this group are set up as Type 3 with significant delegated investment authority. In part, this is a

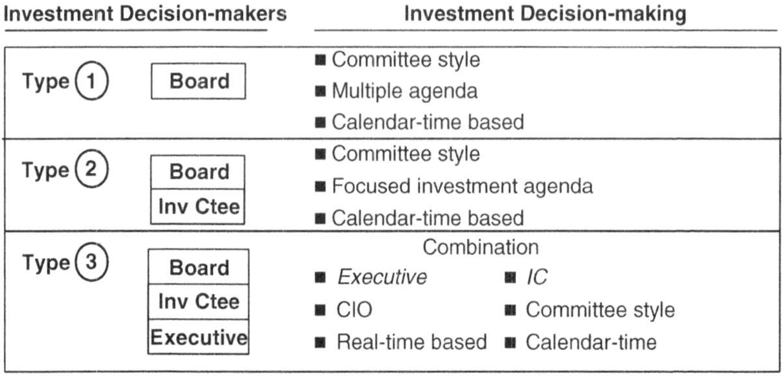

Figure 11.2 Governance types

product of size – the limited resources available from the plan sponsor and the relatively small volume of assets under management – and the limited time available for decision-making by members of the board. Such funds can hardly embrace the full set of best-practice criteria in the short term or even the long term.

With these considerations in mind, Table 11.2 separates the best-practice points between the 'exceptional' group associated with the Type 3 structure with an internal executive, and a 'core' group, which are within the range of all funds that seek to strengthen the formal structure of decision-making. In effect, we believe that formal procedures and requirements can compensate to a degree for a lack of institutional capacity and ability. This is the subject of further research, especially in relation to the consequences of such an organisational strategy for investment performance (see below).

Type 1 and Type 2 fund structures face two significant challenges. First, Finding 5 indicates that there is a strong case for selecting members of the board and investment committees based on the task-related competencies needed to be effective asset owners. This finding comes from our exemplars as well as academic research (see Ambachtsheer *et al.*, 2007; Clark *et al.*, 2006, 2007). However, most boards and investment committees are shaped by a variety of agendas including stakeholder representation sometimes leaving funds with competency deficits relative to the specialised skills required to be effective. We do not dispute the value of a representative board (especially in terms of fund sponsorship and motivation). But we do suggest that the criteria for board selection should be balanced against best-practice such that representation reinforces at least the six-point guidelines as summarised in Table 11.2.

Table 11.2 Best-practice factors by type of fund

Core best-practice factors	
Relevant to all funds, especially Type 1 and 2 funds	
Mission clarity	Clarity of the mission and the commitment of stakeholders to the mission statement
Effective focusing of time	Resourcing each element in the investment process with an appropriate budget considering impact and required capabilities
Leadership	Leadership, being evident at the board/investment committee level, with the key role being the investment committee Chairman
Strong beliefs	Strong investment beliefs commanding fund-wide support that align with goals and informs all investment decision-making
Risk budget framework	Frame the investment process by reference to a risk budget aligned to goals and incorporates an accurate view of alpha and beta
Fit-for-purpose manager line-up	The effective use of external managers, governed by clear mandates, aligned to goals, selected on fit for purpose criteria
Exceptional best-practice factors	
Relevant only to Type 3 funds	
Investment executive	The use of a highly investment-competent investment function tasked with clearly specified responsibilities, with clear accountabilities to the investment committee
Required competencies	Selection to the board and senior staff guided by: numeric skills, capacity for logical thinking, ability to think about risk in the probability domain
Effective compensation	Effective compensation practices used to build bench strength and align actions to the mission, different strategies working according to fund context
Competitive positioning	Frame the investment philosophy and process by reference to the institution's comparative advantages and disadvantages
Real-time decisions	Utilise decision-making systems that function in real time not calendar time
Learning organisation	Work to a learning culture which deliberately encourages change and challenges the commonplace assumptions of the industry

Secondly, Finding 10 sets out the normative role of 'real-time' investing. Type 1 and Type 2 funds cannot employ a real-time approach given their reliance on the periodic meetings of their boards and/or investment committees. This limitation is likely to have its costs, not least involving opportunities that such funds are forced to forego (see below). On the other hand, in these cases, best-practice should recognise the institutional limits of such entities against competing market players eschewing active management for passive management such that the elements listed in Table 11.2 are focused on beta not alpha activities. Elsewhere, Clark (2004) has argued that size is a real constraint on governance capacity and performance; over the long term, it is arguable that such resource-constrained institutions should seek ways of sharing resources or merging into larger entities.

Best-practice investment strategy

This study concentrates on governance best-practice. In our interviews, it also became apparent that funds' governance budgets are associated with particular institutional capacities and features. At its simplest, an appropriate governance budget is a precondition for an effective investment strategy, recognising the limits imposed by fund size and committed resources including time and expertise (noted above). More generally, the governance budget is also a strategic instrument framed according to funds' ambitions in relation to long-term investment objectives. Our exemplars were, more often than not, deliberate about their chosen governance procedures and practices, treating governance as an investment in realising their objectives. Here, a balance is normally struck between short-term cost efficiency and long-term fund performance (even if it is sometimes difficult calibrating the value created by effective governance).

Matching the significance we attribute to formal governance procedures, especially in Type 1 and Type 2 institutions, we suggest that those procedures are matched on the investment side of the equation by certain characteristics. Basically, lower governance budget arrangements are consistent with less complicated or sophisticated arrangements. If this is not the case, we expect some difficulties with such funds' implementation of complex arrangements. The 'value drivers' that funds can use are summarised in Table 11.3 where, on the left-hand side of the table, the first four drivers of value are deemed appropriate to all types of funds. The second set of four value drivers imply a level of discretion and flexibility with respect to investment policy that Type 1 and Type 2

Table 11.3 Investment value drivers

Strategic allocation to equities and bonds	The strategic mix of equities and bonds over time allows some opportunity for added value	Within the range of all types of governance
Liability-driven investment	Hedging unrewarded risks, in particular interest rate and inflation risks, is a simple way to create value (essentially by avoiding destroying value)	
Use of alternative benchmarks/ enhanced indices	This refers to the use of alternative benchmarks ('beta primes') which may have higher returns per unit risk than traditional capitalisation weighted benchmarks	
Strategic allocation to alternatives/ absolute return mandates	Allocations to alternative assets should improve portfolio efficiency (contributing return and/or diversification) but carry heavy implementation and monitoring burdens	
Diversity in alpha selections/multiple active managers	This is a difficult area within which to add value, and value creation ideally requires large line-ups of managers with the attendant governance requirements	Within range of Type 3 governance funds
Diversity in beta selections/wider risk budget flexibility	Diversity in beta sources is deliberately targeting a more even exposure to a wide array of market return drivers which may be helped by using leverage and risk weighting	
Long-term mandates to capture skill term premium	This is about avoiding the efficiency costs of benchmark constraints and unnecessary costs of excessive short-term turnover, exploiting a 'discomfort premium' and sometimes using activism approaches	
Dynamic strategic allocations	Belief that asset classes can be temporarily expensive, or cheap, suggests a dynamic medium-term approach to asset allocation based on relatively frequent assessment of relative value	

funds would have difficulty in sustaining given their resources. This is the domain of Type 3 institutions, those characterised by a large volume of assets under management and organisational resources including time, commitment, and real-time investing.

Of course, operating in this domain is very challenging. For instance, hiring, monitoring, and replacing active managers is a time-consuming process that demands a level of internal expertise among senior staff that is difficult if not impossible to provide in Type 1 and Type 2 organisations. Furthermore, once we move into time-dependent portfolio optimisation using leverage and risk weighting, senior management must be able to make tactical decisions backed by boards that appreciate the nature and scope of the risks assumed. While we are sometimes told that 'trust' between staff and boards is an essential ingredient in investment management in these circumstances, we also note that best-practice is less about trust and more about contract wherein staff are set responsibilities and performance parameters with appropriate levels of compensation.

In these circumstances, our exemplars tend to treat governance as an instrument of management as well as an instrument of control. As a result, some of the most effective Type 3 institutions are those that have made governance design and oversight a standing sub-committee of the board with responsibility for monitoring board performance and its relationships with senior staff and the myriad of consultants and service providers who populate the industry. That is, our exemplars have sought to identify best-practice forms of governance and mechanisms of accountability. These are summarised in Table 11.4. So, for example, our exemplars are conscious of the costs for decision-making of a large board recognising that many members (normally more than nine) tend to fracture collegiality (Sunstein, 2005) and add a degree of heterogeneity in board member competence that undercuts competent decision-making (Clark *et al.*, 2006). Not surprisingly, our exemplars have become active in the recruitment and nomination of board members even if, in the end, they do not normally control the selection process.

Just as our exemplars have developed mechanisms to govern their relationships with senior staff and external service providers, boards have sought to enhance their own systems of accountability. So, for example, some boards have created subcommittees or have used their audit committees to make governance an ongoing issue of scrutiny and oversight. Some of our exemplars have instituted yearly reviews of board member performance in conjunction with longer-term contracts designed to capture the expertise and specialised learning that comes with commitment. Significantly, some funds have introduced trustee compensation schemes, matching the obligations historically associated with the trust institution (Langbein, 1997) with a realistic assessment of the roles and responsibilities of board members.

Table 11.4 Best-practice board/investment committees

	'Best practice'		'Best practice'
Number	• Ideally 6–8	Governance reporting	• Substantial disclosures • Governance beliefs/ principles
Board member tenure	• Three-year terms • No term limits • Long tenures desirable • Organisational memory	Number of meetings/days per annum	• 6–8 days Board • 3–4 days Sub-Ctees
Control over new board members	• Investment competency • Fit with team	Board core agenda	• Items covered by impact • Limited time on alpha • Traffic light protocols for reporting/escalating
Board member evaluation	• Annual process • Performance management		
Board compensation	• Full market rates • Time element	Board variable agenda	• Joint Ch/CIO agreement • Commitment to education/development
Board committees	• Audit • Governance and HR		

Conclusions

Governance is on the agenda of many of the world's leading pension and investment institutions. Prompted by the challenges posed by global financial markets and closer scrutiny of performance by sponsors and stakeholders, investment by goals and objectives has demanded innovation in how funds are governed. We note that setting targets and constraints such as rates of return and stable contribution rates has had a salutary effect in many institutions, challenging past practices and encouraging focus upon organisational coherence, the people involved, and decision-making processes. We also note that these initiatives can be found in many different national settings and across a broad array of institutional forms (including sovereign funds, endowment funds, public and private sector funds, etc).

In this paper we have used exemplars to illustrate these developments, drawing inspiration from a select group of institutions that have shared with us their governance strategies and practices. In each and every case study, respondents have emphasised that governance is best treated as an investment in long-term performance rather than a short-term cost to be carved out of sponsor contributions or investment returns. In part, the governance budget is part of the management of risk and return. More importantly, the governance budget is part of any institution's commitment to strategic investment management recognising the frontiers of financial engineering and the challenges that face any institution when operating in the real-time world of financial markets.

As suggested, our exemplars provide insights about best-practice governance. These are summarised in Figures 11.1 and 11.2 and Tables 11.1–11.4. Nonetheless, we recognise that these insights represent a high hurdle for any institution and its board members and senior staff; it is arguable that our exemplars have certain advantages such as size and structure that have allowed them to develop their distinctive approaches to governance. In many cases, a large pool of assets or the prestige of the fund concerned has provided an effective platform for developing best-practice governance. In other cases, leadership has been an essential ingredient in institutional innovation. Nonetheless, we could identify, as readers could identify, similarly sized institutions that seem to lack a commitment to best-practice (as implied by Lerner *et al.*, 2007).

We would also suggest that these findings could be used to inform debate over the design of the new sovereign funds that have come to occupy an important place in national savings programmes. In some countries, these institutions have become a means of realising the apparent advantages of scale and scope in the context of declining coverage rates by occupational and industry pension plans. In other countries, sovereign funds have been a mechanism for mobilising social security assets for placement in global financial markets in the hope of reaping higher rates of return. In yet other countries, sovereign funds are strategic investment vehicles for foreign reserves and earnings. Whatever their origins, sovereign funds are likely to be as important for 21st century markets as Anglo-American pension funds were for the second half of the 20th century (Clowes, 2000).

Sovereign funds face significant challenges in implementing best-practice governance. In some cases, the objectives of such institutions are unclear and subject to unresolved debate. In other cases, governing boards are quite large and heterogeneous in terms of the skills and aptitudes of those appointed. When combined with poorly specified responsibilities, the process of investment decision-making can become a competition for power and influence rather than a process responsive to the five challenges of governance that underpin this paper. In these cases, inadequate governance may translate into unrealised promises of national wealth. Just because an institution controls a large volume of assets does not mean that it is a well-governed entity.

Our evaluative framework and 12 findings have significant implications for the design of these types of institutions. For example, we have suggested that return targets and contribution constraints have played a vital role in focusing boards on the nature and scope of their governance processes (Finding 1). Likewise, we have suggested that investment institutions deserve to be governed in a deliberate manner with formal charters or mandates used to set roles, responsibilities, and accountabilities (Finding 2). And we have emphasised that governance is an investment not just a cost (Finding 3). Most importantly, we focused on people and process emphasising that those involved ought to have certain types of skills and aptitudes (Findings 4–6) as well as carry out well-defined responsibilities in a disciplined investment process (Findings 7–12).

Acknowledgments

The authors wish to thank the funds and institutions that participated in the study recognising that most requested anonymity and, as such, cannot be formally identified. The authors also wish to thank their colleagues at both institutions including Emiko Caerlewy-Smith, Tessa Hebb, Lisa Hagerman, John Marshall, and Dorothee Franzen (at Oxford) and Michael Orszag, Carole Judd and Lloyd Raynor (at Watson Wyatt). Keith Ambachtsheer, Charles Ellis, Adam Dixon, and Ashby Monk made useful comments on a previous draft. Research on pension fund governance at Oxford has been supported by the National Association of Pension Funds (United Kingdom), the Lupina Foundation (Toronto), and the Rockefeller and Ford foundations. None of the above should be held responsible for any comments or opinions expressed herein, especially any misapprehension of the lessons to be drawn from particular instances of best-practice value-creating investing.

Notes

1. Here, we refer to data collected by Watson Wyatt through the Global Pension Asset Study of 2007; further details are available at www.watsonwyatt.com.
2. See also the recent commitment shown by the CFA Institute in promoting a code of conduct for pension scheme governing bodies wherein the code will require members to 'take actions that are consistent with the established mission of the scheme' and 'regularly review the efficiency and effectiveness of the scheme's success in meeting its goals'. See www.cfainstitute.org.
3. Note that we focus upon governance principles and policies in this paper and ignore, for the moment, the distinctive regulatory and legislative

environments within which our chosen funds operate. This is not because we think this is irrelevant, quite the contrary. Rather, our emphasis on principles and policies is such that we believe that over the long term the regulatory environment ought to enable best-practice rather than constrain best-practice. See Clark (2007a, b).

References

Ambachtsheer, K. (2007a) *Pension Revolution: A Solution to the Pensions Crisis,* John Wiley, New York.

Ambachtsheer, K. (2007b) 'The Three Grades of Pension Fund Governance Quality: Bad, Better, and Best', mimeo, Rotman International Center for Pension Management, University of Toronto, Toronto.

Ambachtsheer, K., Capelle, R. and Lum, H. (2007) 'The State of Global Pension Fund Governance Today: Board Competency still a Problem', mimeo, Rotman International Center for Pension Management, University of Toronto, Toronto.

Black, B. (1992) 'Agents Watching Agents: The Promise of Institutional Voice', *UCLA Law Review,* 39, 811–893.

Clark, G. L. (2003) *European Pensions & Global Finance,* Oxford University Press, Oxford.

Clark, G. L. (2004) 'Pension Fund Governance: Expertise and Organisational Form', *Journal of Pension Economics and Finance,* 3, 233–253.

Clark, G. L. (2006) 'Regulation of Pension Fund Governance', in G. L. Clark, A. Munnell and M. Orszag (eds.) *The Oxford Handbook of Pensions and Retirement Income,* Oxford University Press, Oxford, 483–500.

Clark, G. L. (2007a) 'Expertise and Representation in Financial Institutions: UK Legislation on Pension Fund Governance and US Regulation of the Mutual Fund Industry', *21st Century Society: Journal of the Academy of Social Sciences,* 2, 1–23.

Clark, G. L. (2007b) 'Governing Finance: Reconciling Functional Performance with Stakeholder Representation', Working Paper 07-08, Oxford University Centre for the Environment, Oxford.

Clark, G. L., Caerlewy-Smith, E. and Marshall, J. (2006) 'Pension Fund Trustee Competence: Decision Making in Problems Relevant to Investment Practice', *Journal of Pension Economics and Finance,* 5, 91–110.

Clark, G. L., Caerlewy-Smith, E. and Marshall, J. (2007) 'The Consistency of UK Pension Fund Trustee Decision-Making', *Journal of Pension Economics and Finance,* 6, 67–86.

Clark, G. L. and Monk, A. H. B. (2008) 'Conceptualizing the Defined Benefit Pension Promise: Implications from a Survey of Expert Opinion', *Benefits Quarterly,* 24, 7–18.

Clowes, M. J. (2000) *The Money Flood: How Pension Funds Revolutionized Investing,* Wiley, New York.

Cocco, J. F. and Volpin, P. F. (2007) 'Corporate Governance of Pension Plans: The UK Evidence', *Financial Analysts Journal,* 63(1), 70–83.

Engel, C. and Weber, E. U. (2006) 'The Impact of Institutions on the Decision How to Decide', MPI Collective Goods Preprint No. 2006/19. Available at SSRN: http://ssrn.com/abstract=93502.

Gertler, M. S. (2001) 'Best Practice? Geography, Learning and the Institutional Limits to Strong Convergence', *Journal of Economic Geography,* 1, 5–26.
Jensen, M. (2000) *A Theory of the Firm: Governance, Residual Claims, and Organizational Forms,* Harvard University Press, Cambridge, MA.
Kahneman, D. and Tversky, A. (1979) 'Prospect Theory: An Analysis of Decisions Under Risk', *Econometrica,* 47, 263–291.
Langbein, J. (1997) 'The Secret Life of a Trust: The Trust as an Instrument of Commerce', *Yale Law Journal,* 107, 165–189.
Lerner, J., Schoar, A. and Wongsunwai, W. (2007) 'Smart Institutions, Foolish Choices: The Limited Partner Performance Puzzle', *Journal of Finance,* 62, 731–764.
Merton, R. and Bodie, Z. (2005) 'The Design of Financial Systems: Towards a Synthesis of Function and Structure', *Journal of Investment Management,* 3, 1–23.
North, D. C. (1990) *Institutions, Institutional Change and Economic Performance,* Cambridge University Press, Cambridge.
O'Barr, W. and Conley, J. (1992) *Fortune and Folly,* Wiley, New York.
Roberts, J. (2004) *The Modern Firm: Organizational Design for Performance and Growth,* Oxford University Press, Oxford.
Roe, M. J. (2006) 'Legal Origins, Politics, and Stock Markets', *Harvard Law Review,* 120, 460–527.
Shiller, R. J. (2002) 'Bubbles, Human Judgement, and Expert Opinion', *Financial Analysts Journal,* 58(3), 18–26.
Sunstein, C. (2005) 'Group Judgements: Statistical Means, Deliberation, and Information Markets', *New York University Law Review,* 80, 962–1049.
Urwin, R. (1998) *Avoiding Disappointment in Investment Manager Selection,* International Association of Consulting Actuaries, London.
Urwin, R., Breban, S., Hodgson, T. and Hunt, A. (2001) 'Risk Budgeting in Pension Investment', *Annals of the Faculty of Actuaries,* 7, 319–364.
Wagner, R. K. (2002) 'Smart People Doing Dumb Things: The Case of Managerial Incompetence', in R. J. Sternberg (ed.), *Why Smart People Can Be So Stupid,* Yale University Press, New Haven, 42–63.
Watson Wyatt (2004) *Remapping,* Reigate.
Watson Wyatt (2006) *Changing Lanes,* Reigate.
Williamson, O. (1996) *The Mechanisms of Governance,* Oxford University Press, Oxford.

Appendix

Case study exemplars

Shown below are brief sketches of the institutions that were the basis of our case studies. Inevitably, these sketches are shallow and indicative rather than definitive, and properly so given our undertakings regarding confidentiality. Whereever possible, interviews were conducted with the CEO or CIO of the institution, or nominee; certainly, someone with insight regarding its investment performance and knowledge of the nature and scope of the governance issues encountered therein. The procedures governing the interviews including the stages of the process are explained in more detail in Clark (2003) and conform to standard social science practices.

Funds ranged in size from $5bn to $100bn. Five funds were located in North America, three in Europe and two in Asia-Pacific.

Fund A: a large, multi-employer, state-sponsored fund investing on behalf of the participating public sector defined benefit pension plans.

Fund B: a large, multinational company cross-listed between three stock exchanges, with substantial consolidated pension liabilities principally DB in nature.

Fund C: a very large, multi-employer industry fund offering a range of retirement plans including hybrid versions of defined benefit and defined contribution plans.

Fund D: an industry fund operating in a competitive national market for investment management and related services in the defined contribution environment.

Fund E: a corporate defined benefit pension plan with an in-house investment division to manage its pension assets.

Fund F: a global company with significant worldwide pension assets in particular with large US DB plans.

Fund G: a major endowment fund with a long-term commitment to the growth and stability of its university sponsor.

Fund H: a leading global endowment fund with a mandate in perpetuity in the interests of research.

Fund I: a national pension and retirement savings institution operating on behalf of national and the second pillar of government investment provision.

Fund J: a national pension fund operating in a unitary state, with responsibility for the investment of mandatory individual contributions for supplementing the basic pension.

12
Fundamental Indexation in Europe

Julius Hemminki
graduated as MSc (Econ) from Helsinki School of Economics (major in finance). He works as a project controller at ABB.

*Vesa Puttonen**
is Professor of Finance at the Helsinki School of Economics. His areas of expertise include topics such as risk management, derivatives, mutual funds and behavioural finance. He acts as Chairman of the Board of Arvo Asset Management Ltd.

**Helsinki School of Economics, Runeberginkatu 22-24, FI-00100 Helsinki, Finland. Tel: +358 9 43138405; Fax: 358 9 43138678; E-mail: vesa.puttonen@hse.fi*

Introduction

According to the Capital Asset Pricing Model (CAPM), a capitalisation-weighted market portfolio is mean–variance optimal. From this, one could conclude that an average investor could not do better than just hold a market portfolio. Arnott *et al.* (2005) demonstrate that investors can do much better than capitalisation-weighted market indexes. Their paper provides evidence on fundamental equity market indexes that deliver superior mean–variance performance. The study was conducted with US companies and the returns were compared to the S&P 500 index. Arnott *et al.* suggest four reasons for the excess return of the fundamental index portfolios over the S&P 500; superior market portfolio construction, price inefficiency, additional exposure to distress risk, or a combination of the three[1].

Hsu (2006) shows that if stock prices are inefficient in the sense that they do not fully reflect firm fundamentals, market capitalisation-weighted portfolios are sub-optimal. This is because under-prices stocks will have smaller capitalisations than their fair equity value, and similarly, over-prices stocks will have larger capitalisations than their fair value. Treynor (2005) also shows that as prices are noisy and do not

Reprinted from 'Fundamental indexation in Europe' by Julius Hemminki and Vesa Puttonen in *Journal of Asset Management* 8, 2008, pp. 401–405, DOI:10.1057/palgrave.jam.2250090. With kind permission from Palgrave Macmillan Ltd.

fully reflect firm fundamentals, traditional capitalisation-weighting schemes are likely to be sub-optimal.

We examine the benefits of fundamental indexation using European data. The fundamental values are book value of equity, total employment, sales, cash flow, and dividend. The results indicate that these fundamental indexes are more mean–variance efficient than the traditional capitalisation-weighted index. Some of these fundamental portfolios produce consistent and significant benefits compared to the capitalisation-weighted portfolio.

Data

The period under review in this study is from January 1996 to December 2006, an 11-year period covering both bear and bull markets. The Dow Jones Euro Stoxx 50 index data would have been available starting from 1986, but the necessary company data were insufficient prior to 1996. The company-level data include financial statement information as well as market information.

All DJ Stoxx indexes are derived from one original source: the Dow Jones World index. This world index is a global stock universe currently comprising about 6,500 components representing 95 per cent of the worldwide free float market capitalisation. The DJ Euro Stoxx 50 is derived from the DJ Euro Stoxx Total Market index, which covers approximately 95 per cent of the free float market capitalisation of the 12 Eurozone countries, namely, Austria, Belgium, Finland, France, Germany, Greece, Ireland, Italy, Luxembourg, the Netherlands, Portugal, and Spain. The DJ Euro Stoxx 50 index provides a blue-chip representation of supersector leaders in the Eurozone. The index covers 50 stocks from the Eurozone countries and it captures approximately 60 per cent of the free float market capitalisation of the DJ Euro Stoxx Total Market index (www.stoxx.com). This means that the DJ Euro Stoxx 50 represents the total market quite well although it covers only 50 companies.

The DJ Euro Stoxx 50 index includes shares from 50 of the largest companies by capitalisation in the Eurozone. The index is licensed to financial institutions to serve as an underlying asset for a wide range of investment products such as exchange-traded funds (ETF). It is weighted by market capitalisation and each component's weight is capped at 10 per cent of the index's total free float market capitalisation. The composition of the index is reviewed annually in September. The DJ Euro Stoxx 50 index was first introduced in 1998, and there are daily historical data available dating back to 1986. The historical data include component lists, price and return data of the index, and change logs of the components.

In order to construct a corresponding portfolio by using fundamental values as weights, and to calculate the required risk and return figures, financial statements information and market information was needed. This information was retrieved from Worldscope database by using Thomson ONE Banker-Analytics.

The fundamental values were retrieved for each company for every year. The book value of equity, sales, dividend, and total employment figures were available directly from the database. Cash flow information needed to be calculated from the cash flow for each set of share figures. These fundamental values were used to construct and weight different portfolios. In addition, the market cap value was retrieved yearly for each company. This was necessary to reproduce a reference portfolio that corresponds to the DJ Euro Stoxx 50 index.

Construction of portfolios

Eight different portfolios are investigated in this study, including, of course, the DJ Euro Stoxx 50 index portfolio and one that we call the Reference portfolio. The remaining portfolios are weighted according to the fundamental values: book value of equity, cash flow, sales, dividend, and total employment. In addition, a composite portfolio is constructed. Arnott *et al.* (2005) state that adopting fundamental indexation is more than simply changing the basis for weighting the stocks in an index. They argue that if stocks are simply re-weighted in the index, a large number of companies with substantial book value that are trading at a low price-to-book ratio are missed. This would lead to a portfolio that is concentrated primarily in stocks that are large in both capitalisation and book value.

The DJ Euro Stoxx 50 index portfolio and the Reference portfolio are both capitalisation-weighted portfolios. In principle, these two portfolios should be identical in weighting and in performance, but as we show, they are not in fact exactly identical. The reason for this is that the composition of the DJ Euro Stoxx 50 index is reviewed annually in September. All the re-weighted portfolios, including the Reference portfolio, are weighted according to the information at year end and these weights are retained for the following year. Therefore, it is more accurate to compare the fundamental value-weighted portfolios to the Reference portfolio than to the DJ Euro Stoxx 50 index portfolio. The reason why re-weighted portfolios are not weighted simultaneously with the DJ Euro Stoxx 50 index portfolio in September is simply that most of the necessary data are available only on an annual basis.

In the Book Value portfolio, the components are re-weighted on the last trading day of each year according to their book value of equity at year end. The portfolio is kept untouched the following year until at year end a new set of components are chosen according to the DJ Euro Stoxx 50 index portfolio and these components are re-weighted again.

Every component in the employment portfolio is re-weighted on the last trading day of each year according to its average yearly number of employees. This means that if a company had 100 employees for the first six months and 80 employees for the second six months of the year, the average yearly number of employees would be 90.

The Cash Flow portfolio is re-weighted on the last trading day of each year according to the components trailing three-year average cash flow. This means that the re-weighting of the portfolio for example for the year 1996 is done according to an average cash flow of the years 1993, 1994, and 1995. When fewer than three years of data are available, the years of data that are available are averaged. Using the three-year average cash flow instead of year-to-year data reduces rebalancing turnover and it should not affect the performance of the portfolio (Arnott *et al.*, 2005).

The Dividend portfolio is re-weighted the same way as the Cash Flow portfolio. It also uses three-year average figures instead of year-to-year data. The dividend payment amount of each company is taken from the company cash flow statement figures.

The Sales portfolio is also re-weighted using the three-year average figures to reduce rebalancing turnover. Sales figures are retrieved from the database and, with very few exceptions, the data received are complete.

The Composite portfolio is weighted by using all of the five fundamental value portfolios. The weights of each company in the five fundamental portfolios are combined in equal proportions and each company is re-weighted in the Composite portfolio by this combined weight.

Analysis and results

The reference portfolio versus the DJ Euro Stoxx 50 index

The capitalisation-weighted Reference portfolio is first constructed to represent the performance of the DJ Euro Stoxx 50 index. The returns are compared for the observation period from 1996 to 2006.

Table 12.1 The comparison of performance of the Reference Portfolio and the DJ Euro Stoxx 50 index

January 1996–December 2006					
Portfolio	**Ending value of €100**	**Geometric return (%)**	**Volatility (%)**	**Excess return versus reference (%)**	**Tracking error**
Reference Portfolio	348.13	12.01	24.00	0.00	0.00
Euro Stoxx 50 Index	342.82	11.85	24.28	−0.16	2.54

As expected, the returns of the DJ Euro Stoxx 50 index and the Reference portfolio are almost identical. Table 12.1 presents the performance of the two portfolios.

The Reference portfolio has a slightly higher ending value: 348.13 EUR versus 342.82 EUR. This gives a geometric return of 12.01 per cent for the Reference portfolio and 11.85 per cent for the DJ Euro Stoxx 50 index over the sample period. As a contrary to the ending value, the Reference portfolio has a slightly lower standard deviation (24.00 per cent versus 24.28 per cent). The tracking error, which represents the difference between a DJ Euro Stoxx 50 index return and the Reference portfolio return, is naturally very low.

One might expect the returns of the DJ Euro Stoxx 50 index and the Reference Portfolio to be identical. The reason for the differences is that the composition of the DJ Euro Stoxx 50 index is reviewed annually in September, whereas the Reference portfolio is weighted according to the information at year end. During the four-month difference in reviewing the portfolio, capitalisation values of the companies may change so that they lead to differences in weighting the companies. These differences are, however, small and we use the capitalisation-weighted Reference portfolio as the benchmark for the fundamental portfolios.

Relative performance of fundamental portfolios

Table 12.2 shows the return attributes of the fundamental indexes. All fundamental portfolios are able to produce higher returns than the capitalisation-weighted market index. The fundamental portfolios outperform the capitalisation-weighted market index by an average of 1.76 percentage points a year.

Table 12.2 This table shows the comparison of returns for the observation period from 1996 to 2006. The returns show a theoretical growth in value of the portfolio, assuming that dividends are re-invested to purchase additional units of equity at the closing price applicable on the ex-dividend date. The Reference portfolio is a capitalisation-weighted portfolio based on the DJ Euro Stoxx 50 index

	Ending value of €100	**Geometric return**	**Volatility**	**Excess return vs. reference**	**Sharpe ratio**	**Tracking error vs. Ref.**	***t*-statistic for Excess Return**
Portfolio							
Book value	415.92	13.83	24.51	1.83%	0.546	2.57%	2.41
Employee	368.25	12.58	24.30	0.57	0.501	3.53	0.63
Sales	403.76	13.63	23.07	1.52	0.555	4.14	1.04
Cash flow	414.81	13.81	24.47	1.80	0.548	5.72	1.09
Dividend	461.69	14.92	22.67	2.91	0.614	3.39	2.33
Composite	413.45	13.77	23.62	1.76	0.556	2.60	2.06
Reference	348.13	12.01%	24.00%	–	0.477	–	–

The evidence for the excess returns is positive but not statistically significant for all fundamental portfolios. This can be explained by the relatively short observation period compared with the 43-year period of Arnott *et al.* (2005).

Robust evidence shows that the Book Value portfolio, the Dividend portfolio, and the Composite portfolio produce higher returns than the capitalisation-weighted market index. The evidence also indicates that the Sales portfolio and the Cash Flow portfolio produce higher returns, but the findings are not statistically significant. The Employee portfolio is able to produce only slightly higher returns than the capitalisation-weighted index.

The risk level of the portfolios is measured by a standard deviation of returns. Three of the fundamental portfolios have a lower risk level than the capitalisation-weighted market index. These are the Sales portfolio, the Dividend portfolio, and the Composite portfolio. The Book Value portfolio, the Employees portfolio, and the Cash Flow portfolio have slightly higher risk levels than the capitalisation-weighted market index. All fundamental portfolios yield higher risk-adjusted returns (Sharpe ratio) than the Reference portfolio.

Conclusions

We provide further evidence that by practicing fundamental indexation, an investor could realise superior performance than by investing in a capitalisation-weighted market portfolio. Six different fundamental portfolios were constructed by using various fundamental values as weights. The performances of these fundamental portfolios were compared to a capitalisation-weighted market portfolio based on the DJ Euro Stoxx 50 index.

In conclusion, we show that by re-weighting a capitalisation-weighted market index by certain fundamental values, it is possible to produce consistently higher returns and higher risk-adjusted returns. Our findings are very similar to those of Arnott *et al.* (2005), suggesting that if market prices are noisy, traditional capitalisation-weighting leads to sub-optimal portfolios. Arnott *et al.* (2005) report statistically more significant findings that can be explained with a longer observation period (43 years of US data versus 10 years of European data).

Our findings suggest that in fundamental indexation, an investor should use the book value of equity or the dividend amount as fundamental values, or construct a composite portfolio. When managing fees and transaction costs are expected to be the same, whether an index fund is based on a traditional capitalisation-weighted market index or a fundamental-weighted index, the fundamental-weighted index fund should consistently outperform its capitalisation-weighted benchmark in net returns.

Acknowledgments

We thank Robert Arnott and Antti Pirjetä for comments.

Note

1. Arnott *et al.* (2005) provide an extensive list of relevant literature on the topic. There is a vast stream of literature on 'Value' strategies that call for buying stocks with a low price relative to earnings, dividends, book assets, cash flow, or other measures of fundamental value. In addition to the literature in Arnott *et al.* (2005), one may add Chan and Lakonishok (2004), Lakonishok *et al.* (1994), and Fama and French (1998, 2004) as cornerstone articles in the field.

References

Arnott, R. D., Hsu, J. and Moore, P. (2005) 'Fundamental Indexation', *Financial Analysts Journal*, 61(2), 83–99.

Chan, L. K. C. and Lakonishok, J. (2004) 'Value and Growth Investing: Review and Update', *Financial Analysts Journal*, 60(1), 71–86.

Fama, E. F. and French, K. R. (1998) 'Value Versus Growth: The International Evidence', *Journal of Finance*, 53(6), 1975–1999.

Fama, E. F. and French, K. R. (2004) 'The Capital Asset Pricing Model: Theory and Evidence', *Journal of Economic Perspectives*, 18(3), 25–46.

Hsu, J. C. (2006) 'Cap-Weighted Portfolios are Sub-Optimal Portfolios', *Journal of Investment Management*, 4(3), 1–10.

Lakonishok, J., Shleifer, A. and Vishny, R. W. (1994) 'Contrarian Investment, Extrapolation, and Risk', *Journal of Finance*, 49(5), 1541–1578.

Treynor, J. (2005) 'Why Market-Valuation-Indifferent Indexing Works', *Financial Analysts Journal*, 61(5), 65–69.

13

Fundamental Indexation: An Active Value Strategy in Disguise

*David Blitz**
is the Head of Quantitative Equity Research at the Quantitative Strategies Department of Robeco Asset Management.

Laurens Swinkels
is an assistant professor in Finance at the Erasmus School of Economics in Rotterdam and is affiliated with the Erasmus Research Institute of Management. He is also a senior researcher at the Quantitative Strategies Department of Robeco Asset Management.

**Coolsingel 120, NL-3011 AG Rotterdam, The Netherlands.*
Tel: +31 10 224 2079; Fax: +31 10 224 2110; E-mail: d.c.blitz@robeco.nl

Introduction

Arnott *et al.* (2005) propose a novel investment approach, which they call fundamental indexation. The main idea behind fundamental indexation, or fundamental indexing, is to create an index in which stocks are weighted by economic fundamentals, such as book value, sales and/or earnings, instead of by market capitalisation. An important argument put forward by fundamental indexers is that capitalisation-weighted indices are inferior because they necessarily invest more in overvalued stocks and less in undervalued stocks. This is, however, disputed by, among others, Perold (2007), who argues that capitalisation weighting does not, by itself, create a performance drag. At present, the debate between proponents and critics of fundamental indexing continues to rage on.[1]

In this paper, we compare fundamental indices with their traditional cap-weighted counterparts. First, we argue that fundamental indices are, essentially, nothing more than a new breed of value indices. Arguably,

Reprinted from 'Fundamental indexation: An active value strategy in disguise' by David blitz and Laurens Swinkels in *Journal of Asset Management*, 9, 2008, pp. 264–269, DOI:10.1057/jam.2008.23. With kind permission from Palgrave Macmillan Ltd.

fundamental indices are more elegant than traditional value indices, but the key underlying idea remains the same. Next, we argue that a fundamental index bears more resemblance to an active investment strategy than to a traditional passive index. Having concluded that a fundamental index is an active value strategy, we next discuss whether fundamental indexing is the most efficient way to capture the value premium. We conclude that fundamental indexation is very likely to be inferior compared to more sophisticated quantitative investment strategies.

Fundamental indices capture the value premium

The weights of stocks in a traditional index are proportional to their market capitalisations. Fundamental indices, however, weight stocks in proportion to their economic fundamentals. Thus, weights differences are entirely due to differences in valuation levels, that is, ratios of fundamental value-to-market value. For example, if a fundamental index is created based on book values, then the weight differences compared to a market-capitalisation-weighted index are entirely due to differences in the book-to-market ratios of the stocks included in the index. In other words, compared to a market-capitalisation-weighted index, a fundamental index simply overweights value stocks and underweights growth stocks; a fact which is also recognized by, for example, Asness (2006). This implies that fundamental indices are essentially a new breed of value indices. Of course, value (and growth) indices have been around for many years already, but traditionally these tend to be based on a different, arguably less sophisticated approach. The traditional approach consists of first classifying each stock as either a value stock or a growth stock, and then creating a value (or growth) index by market-capitalisation-weighting all value (or growth) stocks.[2] Splitting up the universe into two mutually exclusive parts is a rather crude approach compared to fundamental indices, which elegantly reweight the entire universe of stocks based on fundamental values.

Since the weight differences between a fundamental index and a traditional index are entirely due to differences in valuation levels, any difference in return between a fundamental index and a traditional index must be due to the difference in return between value and growth stocks. Crucially, the proponents of fundamental indexation claim that capitalisation weighting by itself introduces a drag on performance, because in a market-capitalisation-weighted index overvalued stocks tend to be overrepresented and undervalued stocks tend to be underrepresented. See, for example, Arnott *et al.* (2005), Treynor (2005), and Hsu (2006). A fundamentally weighted index is claimed to be superior by avoiding this pitfall. Perold (2007), however, correctly points out that this reasoning hinges critically on the assumption that the mispricing of a stock is, to some extent, predictable by considering the difference between its market price and fundamentals. In other words, the proponents of fundamental indexation assume that stocks with high valuation ratios are more likely to be overvalued than stocks with low valuation ratios. Empirically, there is indeed a large amount of evidence for a so-called value premium, as, historically, value stocks have outperformed growth stocks. This also explains the finding that fundamental indices have outperformed market-capitalisation-weighted indices historically. A historical outperformance, due to being exposed to an already-known return irregularity, is, however, something that is quite different from a superior theoretical performance, as a result of avoiding some structural drag on performance that is supposedly associated with capitalisation-weighted indices.[3] As Perold (2007) and Kaplan (2008) argue, if we assume that pricing errors are random (in particular, unrelated to valuation ratios), the theoretical case for a systematic outperformance of fundamental indexation breaks down.

We can illustrate the strong value tilt of fundamental indices by regressing the returns of the RAFI 1000 index (the Research Affiliates Fundamental Index for the top 1000 US equities) on the returns of traditional market-factor indices. The results of these regressions are displayed in Table 13.1. We observe that when we compare the fundamental indexing strategy to the market index, the alpha amounts to 0.19 per cent per month if we use the Fama–French market factor over the 1962–2005 period, and 0.26 per cent per month if we use the Russell 1000 index over the 1979–2005 period. Both are highly significant from an economical and a statistical point of view. These analyses, however, do not take into account the value tilt that characterises fundamental indexing portfolios. When we add the value and small-capitalisation factor of Fama and French (1992), we see that the fundamental indexation strategy has, on average, a large and highly significant (*t*-statistic over 30) exposure of 0.36 towards the value factor.[4] The loading on the small-capitalisation factor is small and negative with –0.07. The results using Russell index data are very similar, with a beta of 0.38 with regard to the Russell 1000 value/growth return difference, associated with a highly significant *t*-statistic of over 30. Thus, these regression results provide strong empirical support for the theoretical observation that fundamental indices are tilted towards value stocks. Particularly interesting is the finding that, after adjusting for this value tilt, the alpha of the RAFI 1000 index drops sharply to an insignificant –0.02 per cent per month

Table 13.1 Regression results

	CAPM		Fama–French three-factor	
	Coefficient	*t*-statistic	Coefficient	*t*-statistic
Sample period: January 1962–December 2005				
Alpha	0.19%	3.5	−0.02%	−0.5
Market–risk free	0.91	74.6	1.02	131.8
Small minus big (SMB)	–	–	−0.07	−7.0
Value minus growth (HML)	–	–	0.36	30.9
Sample period: January 1979–December 2005				
Alpha	0.26%	3.8	0.10%	2.9
Russell 1000–risk free	0.91	59.7	1.01	120.8
Russell 1000 value–growth	–	–	0.38	30.6

Dependent variable is the historical, simulated RAFI 1000 index minus the risk-free rate of return.
Sources: Kenneth French website, Datastream.

in the Fama–French analysis and 0.10 per cent per month, or 1.2 per cent per annum, in the case of the Russell data. Thus, we conclude that after adjusting for style exposures, fundamental indexation offers zero, or at best a small positive added value. We can interpret a possible small, positive added value positively, namely as evidence that fundamental indexation might constitute a more effective value strategy than traditional value indices. The alpha, however, might also simply reflect some hindsight wisdom or biases in the construction of the historical RAFI 1000 returns, which are after all only based on a back-test. Thus, even the small, positive alpha might turn out to be an illusion going forward.

Fundamental indices resemble active strategies

A fundamental index differs from traditional capitalisation-weighted indices in several important ways. First, the market capitalisation weighted index is unique in the sense that it is the only portfolio that every investor can hold.[5] Fundamental indices, on the other hand, cannot be held in equilibrium by every investor.[6] For every stock that is overweighted by fundamental investors, there must, by definition, be some other investor who actively underweights the same stock, and vice versa. Thus, for fundamental investors to outperform against a capitalisation-weighted index, there must be some other group of investors with opposing views who underperform, and vice versa. It is not immediately clear, however, which investor characteristics determine whether it is optimal to be a fundamental indexer or not. The proponents of fundamental indexation also fail to explain why, in equilibrium, a certain group of investors would want to invest in fundamentally unattractive stocks.

Secondly, contrary to a market-capitalisation-weighted index, a fundamental index does not represent a passive, buy-and-hold strategy. Mirroring a cap-weight index requires no turnover, except in the case of index changes due to new share issuance. A fundamental index, on the other hand, requires some kind of rebalancing strategy, as changes in stock prices continuously push weights away from their fundamental target levels. In the absence of transaction costs, the ideal fundamental index would be rebalanced continuously. Note, however, that a continuously rebalanced fundamental index will exhibit a negative exposure towards momentum compared to a capitalisation-weighted index, as it continuously needs to sell stocks that have done well (for which the weight has increased) and buy stocks that have done poorly (for which the weight has decreased). This may explain why fundamental index providers propose low rebalancing frequencies that make their indices deviate more from the theoretical ideal. In addition to saving on transaction costs, this prevents the fundamental indices from obtaining a large negative exposure to the momentum effect, which historically would have hurt their performance.[7]

Thirdly, several subjective choices need to be made in order to define a fundamental index. Most notably, which particular fundamentals are considered in the construction of the index (eg book value, sales, earnings, cash-flow, dividends, etc) and how exactly should these be defined to construct the index. Also, relating to our previous point, a rebalancing strategy needs to be defined.

In sum, it is not clear who holds the fundamental indexing portfolio in equilibrium, fundamental indexation does not represent a buy-and-hold strategy and fundamental indexation requires subjective choices. These characteristics of fundamental indices actually bear more resemblance to an active investment strategy than to traditional passive indices. Based on these observations, we conclude that fundamental indexation is essentially an active value strategy disguised as an index.

Fundamental indexation is a sub-optimal quantitative strategy

In the previous sections, we concluded that fundamental indexing is simply a way to gain exposure to the well-known value premium. Although this is not something unique, it might still be a useful idea in practice.

For example, there could remain a case for fundamental indexation if it is a highly efficient way of capturing the value premium. Fundamental indexation is in fact more likely to be a sub-optimal way of benefiting from the value premium. This is because fundamental indices are primarily designed for simplicity and appeal, and not for optimal risk/return characteristics, as measured by the Sharpe ratio or information ratio, for example. Arnott *et al.* (2005) report a Sharpe ratio improvement from 0.301 to 0.444, and an associated information ratio of 0.47 for fundamental indexation.[8] Although these figures are not bad, they are also not spectacular. Furthermore, the outperformance is not very consistent over time, as it tends to be concentrated in certain periods (such as the post-2000 period), and is even negative during others (such as the 1990s). Quantitative value strategies that are specifically designed for optimal risk/return characteristics should therefore be able to beat fundamental indexation strategies, not just historically but also in the future.

Furthermore, it is important to realise that fundamental indexation is trying to benefit solely from the value premium, which happens to be just one particular well-known empirical return irregularity. Multi-factor quantitative investment strategies allow investors to benefit from many more anomalies, which have been documented empirically, such as the medium-term price momentum effect (Jegadeesh and Titman, 1993), the short-term reversal effect (Jegadeesh, 1990), the earnings momentum effect (Chan *et al.*, 1996), the accruals effect (Sloan, 1996), and the low volatility effect (Blitz and van Vliet, 2007). Not surprisingly, multi-factor quantitative investment strategies are able to generate significantly better results (typically information ratios well above 1) over the same period as studied by Arnott *et al.* (2005). These anomalies together could, in similar spirit to a fundamental index, be captured in a 'behavioural finance index' that could be tracked by passive managers or serve as a benchmark for (quantitative) active portfolio managers.

We conclude that although fundamental indices may appear to be an appealing alternative to traditional market-capitalisation-weighted indices, their risk–return characteristics are dominated by more sophisticated quantitative strategies, which allow for more flexibility with regard to exploiting the value effect, and which are able to benefit from other return irregularities as well.

Conclusion

In this paper, we have examined the added value of the appealing new concept of fundamental indexation. First, we have argued that because the weight differences between a fundamental index and a market-capitalisation-weighted index are entirely due to differences in valuation ratios, that is, fundamental values compared to market capitalisations, fundamental indices are by definition nothing more than a new breed of value indices. Next, we have argued that fundamental indices more resemble active investment strategies than classic passive indices because (i) they appear to be inconsistent with market equilibrium, (ii) they do not represent a buy-and-hold strategy, and (iii) they require several subjective choices. Because fundamental indices are primarily designed for simplicity and appeal, they are unlikely to be the most efficient way of benefiting from the value premium. The risk/return characteristics of fundamental indices are likely to be even more inferior compared to more sophisticated quantitative strategies, which also try to exploit other anomalies in addition to the value effect.

Acknowledgments

Fundamental Indexation is the patent-pending proprietary property and registered trademark of Research Affiliates LLC. We thank Clifford Asness and Thierry Post for valuable comments on an earlier version of this paper. The views expressed in this paper are not necessarily shared by Robeco or any of its subsidiaries.

Notes

1. See, for example, the papers of Arnott and Markowitz (2008), Perold (2008), Treynor (2008), and Hsu (2008), all of which appeared in the March/April 2008 edition of the *Financial Analysts' Journal.*
2. More recently, refinements have been introduced that allow some stocks to be, for example, 50 per cent value and 50 per cent growth, but the principle has remained the same.
3. Hemminki and Puttonen (2008) document that fundamental indexation has also generated higher returns in Europe. However, as Asness (2006) points out, this does not come as a surprise, given the fact that Fama and French (1998) already observe that the value effect is an international phenomenon. Estrada (2008) prefers an international value strategy above an international fundamental indexation strategy.
4. As the cross-sectional dispersion in fundamental characteristics might change over time, the exposure to the value factor might also be time-varying. We report the long-term average exposure here.
5. For a vivid discussion of this point, see Asness (2006).
6. Except of course for the trivial case in which the two happen to be exactly the same.

7. The RAFI 1000 still has a slightly negative exposure to the momentum strategy from Fama's website.
8. This information ratio was derived by taking the reported outperformance of 2.15 per cent and dividing this by the associated tracking error of 4.57 per cent.

References

Arnott, R. D., Hsu, J. and Moore, P. (2005) 'Fundamental Indexation', *Financial Analysts' Journal,* 61(2), 83–99.

Arnott, R. D. and Markowitz, H. M. (2008) 'Fundamentally Flawed Indexing: Comments', *Financial Analysts' Journal,* 64(2), 12–14.

Asness, C. (2006) 'The Value of Fundamental Indexation', *Institutional Investor,* (October), 94–99.

Blitz, D. C. and van Vliet, P. (2007) 'The Volatility Effect', *Journal of Portfolio Management,* 34(1), 102–113.

Chan, L. K. C., Jegadeesh, N. and Lakonishok, J. (1996) 'Momentum Strategies', *Journal of Finance,* 51(5), 1681–1713.

Estrada, J. (2008) 'Fundamental Indexation and International Diversification', *Journal of Portfolio Management,* 34(3), 93–109.

Fama, E. F. and French, K. R. (1992) 'The Cross-Section of Expected Stock Returns', *Journal of Finance,* 47(2), 427–465.

Fama, E. F. and French, K. R. (1998) 'Values versus Growth: The International Evidence', *Journal of Finance,* 53(6), 1975–1999.

Hemminki, J. and Puttonen, V. (2008) 'Fundamental Indexation in Europe', *Journal of Asset Management,* 8(6), 401–405.

Hsu, J. (2006) 'Cap-Weighted Portfolios are Sub-Optimal Portfolios', *Journal of Investment Management,* 4(3), 44–53.

Hsu, J. (2008) 'Why Fundamental Indexation Might – or Might Not – Work: A Comment', *Financial Analysts' Journal,* 64(2), 17–18.

Jegadeesh, N. (1990) 'Evidence of Predictable Behavior of Security Returns', *Journal of Finance,* 45(3), 881–898.

Jegadeesh, N. and Titman, S. (1993) 'Returns to Buying Winners and Selling Losers: Implications for Stock Market Efficiency', *Journal of Finance,* 48(1), 65–91.

Kaplan, P. D. (2008) 'Why Fundamental Indexation Might – or Might not – Work', *Financial analysts' Journal,* 64(1), 32–39.

Perold, A. F. (2007) 'Fundamentally Flawed Indexing', *Financial Analysts' Journal,* 63(6), 31–37.

Perold, A. F. (2008) 'Fundamentally Flawed Indexing: Author Response', *Financial Analysts' Journal,* 64(2), 14–17.

Sloan, R. G. (1996) 'Do Stock Prices Fully Reflect Information in Accruals and Cash Flows About Future Earnings', *Accounting Review,* 71, 289–315.

Treynor, J. (2005) 'Why Market-Valuation-Indifferent Indexing Works', *Financial Analysts' Journal,* 61(5), 65–69.

Treynor, J. (2008) 'Fundamentally Flawed Indexing: Comments', *Financial Analysts' Journal,* 64(2), 14.

14
A Robust Optimization Approach to Pension Fund Management

Garud Iyengar
is an associate professor in the Industrial Engineering and Operations Research Department at Columbia University. He has a PhD in Electrical Engineering from Stanford University and an undergraduate degree in Electrical Engineering from the Indian Institute of Technology at Kanpur. Iyengar's research interests include convex optimization, robust optimization, combinatorial optimization, mathematical and computational finance, mathematical biology, communication and information theory. His research has appeared in the IEEE Transactions on Information Theory, Mathematical Finance, Computational Finance, Mathematics of Operations Research, *and* Mathematical Programming.

Alfred Ka Chun Ma
is presently an assistant professor in the Department of Finance at The Chinese University of Hong Kong. He obtained his PhD from the Industrial Engineering and Operations Research department at Columbia University and BSc and MPhil in Mathematics from The Chinese University of Hong Kong. He has worked in Goldman Sachs in New York as a summer associate and he is an associate of Society of Actuaries.

Introduction

Pension plans in the United States come in two varieties. Defined contribution pension plans specify the contribution of the corporation. The employees have the right to invest the corporation's contribution and their own contribution in a limited set of funds. The participants in a defined contribution pension plan are responsible for making all the investment decisions and bear all the risks associated with these decisions; thus, the benefit to the participants is uncertain. In contrast,

---

Reprinted from 'A robust optimization approach to pension fund management' by Garud Iyengar and Alfred Ka Chun Ma in *Journal of Asset Management*, 11, 2010, pp. 163–177, DOI:10.1057/jam.2010.9. With kind permission from Palgrave Macmillan Ltd.

defined benefit pension plans specify the benefits due to plan participants. The plan sponsor, that is the corporation, makes all the investment decisions in a defined benefit pension plan and bears all the investment risk. Defined benefit plans have been in the news in the past few years because some firms face the prospect of bankruptcy over severely underfunded pension plans. Consequently, there is a need to develop models that account for uncertainty in future market conditions and plan accordingly.

Pension fund management is an instance of the asset-liability management problem (see, for example, Consigli and Dempster, 1998; Klaassen, 1998; Drijver *et al,* 2000; Sodhi, 2005) in which the goal of the decision maker is to manage the capital invested into a set of assets in order to meet obligations at the minimum possible cost. The typical modeling paradigm adopted in the literature is to model the uncertainty in market conditions as random variables with a known distribution, formulate the asset-liability management problem (and, hence, also the specific case of the pension fund management problem) as a stochastic program, and solve the problem by sampling the market conditions from the given distributions. All sampling-based methods suffer from the curse-of-dimensionality and become intractable as the number of decisions increases, that is either the number of assets in the portfolio or the number of decision epoch increases. In this article, we propose a robust optimization-based approach as an alternative to the stochastic programming based-methods.

Robust optimization is a methodology for explicitly incorporating the effect of parameter uncertainty in optimization problems (Ben-Tal *et al,* 2000; Ben-Tal and Nemirovski, 2001). In this approach, the parameter values are assumed to belong to known and bounded uncertainty sets, and the solution is computed assuming the worst-case behavior of the parameters. Thus, robust solutions are conservative. This is particularly appropriate for pension fund management. Typically, the uncertainty sets correspond to confidence regions around point estimates of the parameters; consequently, one is able to provide probabilistic guarantees on the performance of the robust solution. For a very large class of uncertainty sets, the computational effort required to solve the robust optimization problem is polynomial in the size of the problem (Ben-Tal and Nemirovski, 2001; Goldfarb and Iyengar, 2003) – in contrast, the computational complexity of the stochastic programming-based methods is exponential in the problem size. Consequently, robust methods are likely to become a computationally tractable alternative to stochastic programming-based methods.

A pension fund management problem involves optimizing a given objective, for example minimizing the discounted value of all contributions, while ensuring that the fund is always able to meet its liabilities. In addition, the fund's holdings must also satisfy regulatory requirements. We assume that the parameters of the financial markets of relevance to pension fund management, for example the yield curve, the expected return and volatility on an equity index and so on, are described by factors that evolve according to a stochastic differential equation. In this setting, we show that the pension fund management problem can be formulated as a chance-constrained optimization problem. However, the random variables in the chance constraints are nonlinear functions of the underlying factors. We use the Itô-Taylor expansion to linearize the nonlinear chance constraints and show that the linearized chance constraints can be approximated by second-order cone (SOC) constraints. Thus, the pension fund management problem can be approximated by a second-order cone program (SOCP). This implies that very large-scale problems can be solved efficiently both in theory (Alizadeh and Goldfarb, 2003) and in practice (Andersen and Andersen, 2006). Moreover, as a number of commercial solvers, such as MOSEK, CPLEX and Frontline System (supplier of EXCEL SOLVER), provide the capability for solving SOCPs in a numerically robust manner, we expect the robust approach to become the method of choice for solving large-scale pension fund problems.

The rest of the article is organized as follows. In the section 'Robust pension fund management', we show how to use linearization and robust optimization techniques to formulate general pension fund management problems as a SOCPs. In the section 'Numerical example', we report the results of our numerical experiments with a frozen fund and illustrate the robustness of the robust optimization solution. In the 'Concluding remarks' section, we include some concluding remarks.

Robust pension fund management

In this section, we present a robust optimization-based framework for pension fund management. As pension funds evaluate and re-balance their portfolio holdings at best on a quarterly basis, we work with a discrete time model. In this section, we discuss a general framework for approximating the typical constraints and objectives by second-order constraints; we consider a concrete example in the 'Numerical example' section.

Constraints

At each decision epoch $t \in \{0,1,\ldots, T\}$, the pension manager has to make two decisions: select a new portfolio of traded assets and decide the amount of fresh capital to be injected into the fund. Let $\mathbf{x}_t$ denote the number of shares of the traded assets held by the pension fund from time t to time $t+1$, that is over period t, let w_t denote the fresh capital injected into the fund at time t, and let $\tilde{l}_t$ denote the random liability of the pension fund at time t. Then, assuming that the trading costs are negligible, we must have:

$$\tilde{\mathbf{p}}_t^T(\mathbf{x}_{t-1} - \mathbf{x}_t) + w_t - \tilde{l}_t \geq 0, \tag{1}$$

where $\tilde{\mathbf{p}}_t$ denotes the random prices for the traded assets at time t. As the price $\tilde{\mathbf{p}}_t$ is random, and typically has support on the entire positive orthant, one has to ascribe a proper meaning to the uncertain constraint (1). In this article, we approximate the uncertain liability constraint (1) at time t by the chance constraint

$$\mathrm{P}(\tilde{\mathbf{p}}_t^T(\mathbf{x}_{t-1} - \mathbf{x}_t) + w_t - \tilde{l}_t \geq 0) \geq 1 - \varepsilon, \tag{2}$$

where P denotes the probability measure conditioned on all available information and $\varepsilon > 0$ is the constraint violation probability. Note that we are implicitly assuming that when the event $\tilde{\mathbf{p}}_t^T(\mathbf{x}_{t-1} - \mathbf{x}_t) + w_t < \tilde{l}_t$ occurs, the fund sponsor is able to meet the shortfall using earnings or raising debt. We discuss this in greater detail in the next section on pension fund objectives.

In addition to the budget constraint (1), pension fund holding must also satisfy some regulatory requirements. These requirements typically impose constraints of the form

$$\tilde{\mathbf{p}}_t^T \mathbf{x}_t \geq \beta\left(\sum_{\tau > t} \frac{\tilde{l}_\tau}{(1+\tilde{d})^\tau}\right),$$

where $\tilde{d}$ denotes the (possibly stochastic) nominal interest rate set by the regulatory body and β is a specified funding level. We approximate this uncertain constraint by the chance constraint

$$\mathrm{P}\left(\tilde{\mathbf{p}}_t^T \mathbf{x}_t \geq \beta\left(\sum_{\tau > t} \frac{\tilde{l}_\tau}{(1+\tilde{d})^\tau}\right)\right) \geq 1 - \varepsilon.$$

Thus, the generic chance constraint encountered in the pension fund management problem is of the form

$$\mathrm{P}(\tilde{\mathbf{a}}_t^T \mathbf{y}_t \geq d_t) \geq 1-\varepsilon, \tag{3}$$

where $\tilde{\mathbf{a}}_t$ denotes stochastic parameters such as the prices of assets, liabilities, discount factors and so on, and $\mathbf{y}_t$ and d_t are affine functions of the decision variables $\{(\mathbf{x}_t, w_t)\}_{t=1}^T$.

We assume that the stochastic parameters are described by a factor model:

$$\tilde{\mathbf{a}}_t = f(\mathbf{Z}_t), \tag{4}$$

where f is a sufficiently smooth function mapping the m stochastic factors $\mathbf{Z}_t \in \Re^m$ into the random coefficients $\tilde{\mathbf{a}}_t$, and the m-dimensional vector of factors $\mathbf{Z}_t \in \Re^m$ evolves according to the stochastic differential equation

$$\mathrm{d}\mathbf{Z}_t = \mu(t, \mathbf{Z}_t)\mathrm{d}t + \mathbf{\Sigma}(t, \mathbf{Z}t)\mathrm{d}\mathbf{W}_t, \tag{5}$$

where $\mu(t, \mathbf{Z}_t) \in \Re^{m\times n}$, and $\mathbf{\Sigma}(t, \mathbf{Z}t) \in \Re^{m\times n}$, and n denotes the length of the vector of standard Brownian motions $\mathbf{W}_t$. Most popular financial models in the literature satisfy (4)–(5). For example, it is easy to show that when the universe of assets is a set of treasury bonds and the equity index, the short rates are given by the Hull–White model (Hull and White, 1990), and the equity index evolves according to a geometric Brownian motion, then the price process $\tilde{\mathbf{p}}_t$ for the asset satisfies (4)–(5).

Objective

The most obvious objective for managing a pension fund is to minimize the net present value of all the future contributions:

$$\min \sum_t w_t B_{0,t}, \tag{6}$$

where $B_{0,t}$ denotes the price at time 0 of a zero-coupon bond with face value $F = 1$ maturing at time t. Defined benefit pension funds most often use this objective.

The objective (6) does not account for the impact of the pension contributions on the fund's sponsor. There is evidence that pension contributions w_t have a serious impact on the stock price of the sponsor (Jin *et al*, 2006). We next discuss an objective that explicitly accounts for the impact of the pension fund on the sponsor. The Myers and Majluf pecking order hypothesis (Myers and Majluf, 1984) suggests that the sponsor would first use earnings, and then use debt to finance the pension contributions $\{w_t\}$. We assume that the firm will not be able to issue equity for the purpose of meeting its pension obligations. Suppose w_t^e denotes the portion of the pension fund contribution w_t that is financed directly from the firm's earnings C_t before interest and tax (EBIT). We assume that the earnings C_0 at time $t = 0$ are known and the portion of the earnings invested in the firm grows at a rate r_e. Thus,

$$C_{t+1} = (C_t - w_t^e)(1 + r_e). \tag{7}$$

We also impose the additional constraint that $w_t^e \leq uC_t$, where $u \in [0, 1]$ indicates the maximum fraction of the earnings that can be used for funding pension obligations.

Let w_t^d denote the amount raised in the debt market at time t. We assume that this debt has maturity $D = 1$. Thus, at time $t + 1$, the firm has to repay $(1 + (s_{t,1} + P))w_d$, where $s_{t,1}$ denotes the spot risk-free interest rate at time t for maturity $D = 1$ and P denotes the spread over the risk-free rate that the sponsoring firm needs to pay to raise capital. As interest payments are tax deductible, the effective cost incurred by the firm at time $t + 1$ is $(1 + (1 - \alpha_T)(s_{t,1} + P))w_d$, where α_T denotes the marginal tax rate of the firm. Thus, the discounted cost $c_t^d(P)$ of raising an amount w_t^d in the debt market is given by

$$\begin{aligned} c_t^d(P) &= (1 + (1 - \alpha_T)(s_{t,1} + P))B_{0,t+1}w_t^d \\ &= ((1 - \alpha_T)(1 + s_{t,1})B_{0,t+1} + ((1 - \alpha_T)P + \alpha_T)B_{0,t+1})w_t^d \\ &= ((1 - \alpha_T)B_{0,t} + ((1 - \alpha_T) \times P + \alpha_T)B_{0,t+1})w_t^d, \end{aligned} \tag{8}$$

where we have used the identify $B_{0,t+1}(1 + s_{t,1}) = B_{0,t}$.

The spread P is not a constant – it is a function of the credit rating of the sponsoring firm. Therefore, in order to use $c_t^d(P)$ to model the cost of debt, we have to ensure that the credit rating of the firm remains above a certain level. We assume that the credit rating of the firm is a function of the interest coverage (IC), and a firm has a credit rating Q provided $IC \in [\alpha(Q), \beta(Q)]$ and in this case the spread is given by $P(Q)$

(Damodaran, 2004). We also assume that the function mapping interest coverage IC to the credit rating Q is fixed over time. As we assume that each debt offering has a duration $D = 1$, it follows that the interest coverage IC_t is given by

$$IC_t = \frac{C_t}{(s_{t,1} + P)w_t^d}.$$

Suppose the firm maintains a debt rating $Q \geq \underline{Q}$, then the spread $P \leq P(\underline{Q})$, and we can use $c_t^d(P(\underline{Q}))$ to estimate the cost of debt. The chance constraint

$$\mathrm{P}(\alpha(\underline{Q})(s_{t,1}(\mathbf{Z}_t + (P(\underline{Q}))w_t^d \leq C_t) \geq 1 - \varepsilon, \tag{9}$$

where we write $s_{t,1}(\mathbf{Z}_t)$ to emphasize that $s_{t,1}$ is a function of the factors $\mathbf{Z}_t$, ensures that $Q \geq \underline{Q}$ with high probability and we can use $c_t^d(P(\underline{Q}))$ to approximate the cost of debt. The constraint (9) also belongs to the general class of chance constraints described in (3).

We adopt $c_t^d(P(\underline{Q}))$ defined in (8) as the objective. Thus, the pension fund management optimization problem is given by the chance-constrained problem

$$\min \sum_t c_t^d(P(\underline{Q}))$$

s.t.

$$\mathrm{P}(\tilde{\mathbf{a}}_t^T \mathbf{y}_t \geq d_t,\ t = 1,\ldots, T) \geq 1 - \varepsilon, \tag{10}$$

In general, chance-constrained optimization problems are difficult to solve. In most cases, the problem is non-convex. Except for a few special cases, one has to resort to sampling to solve chance-constrained problems. Consequently, the complexity of solving chance-constrained problems is exponential in the problem dimension. In the next section, we construct a tractable approximation to (10).

Linearization and robust constraints

Let $\mathbf{f} = (f_1,\ldots,f_l)$: $\Re^m \rightarrow \Re^l$ denote the function that defines the stochastic parameters $\mathbf{a}_t$ in terms of the factors $\mathbf{Z}_t$ at time t. By Itô's lemma (see Chang (2004) for example),

$$\mathbf{df}_t(\mathbf{Z}) = \boldsymbol{\mu}^f(t, \mathbf{Z})\mathrm{d}t + \Sigma^f(t, \mathbf{Z})\mathrm{d}\mathbf{W}_t, \tag{11}$$

where

$$\begin{aligned}\mu^f(t, \mathbf{Z}) &= \mathbf{J}_f(\mathbf{Z})\mu(t, \mathbf{Z}) + \frac{1}{2}\eta_f, \Sigma^f(t, \mathbf{Z}) \\ &= \mathbf{J}_f(\mathbf{Z})\Sigma(t, \mathbf{Z})\mathrm{d}\mathbf{W}_t, \\ \eta_f &= [\mathrm{tr}(\Sigma(t, \mathbf{Z})\Sigma(t, \mathbf{Z})^T \mathbf{H}_1(\mathbf{Z})), \ldots, \\ &\quad \mathrm{tr}(\Sigma(t, \mathbf{Z})\Sigma(t, \mathbf{Z})^T \mathbf{H}_l(\mathbf{Z}))]^T,\end{aligned}$$

$\mathbf{J}_f(\mathbf{Z})$ denotes the Jacobian matrix of $\mathbf{f}$, $\mathbf{H}_i(\mathbf{Z})$ denotes the Hessian matrix of f_i with respect to the factors, and $\mathrm{tr}(\cdot)$ denotes the trace of a matrix. We approximate

$$\mathbf{f}_t \approx \mathbf{f}_0 + \mu_0^f t + \Sigma_0^f \mathbf{W}_t, \tag{12}$$

where

$$\begin{aligned}\mu_0^f &= \mathbf{J}_f(\mathbf{Z})\mu(t, \mathbf{Z}) + \frac{1}{2}\eta_f\Big|_{\mathbf{Z}=\mathbf{Z}_0}, \\ \Sigma_0^f &= \mathbf{J}_f(\mathbf{Z})\Sigma(t, \mathbf{Z})\Big|_{\mathbf{Z}=\mathbf{Z}_0},\end{aligned}$$

that is, we evaluate the coefficients at time $t = 0$ and then let $\mathbf{f}_t$ evolve according to a Gaussian process. Thus, $\mathbf{f}_t \sim N(\mathbf{f}_0 + t\mu_0^f, t\Sigma_0^f)$. We discuss the impact of this approximation in the section 'Numerical example'.

We can now approximate the generic chance constraint (3) by

$$\mathrm{P}((\mathbf{f}_0 + \mu_0^f t + \boldsymbol{\Sigma}_0^f \mathbf{W} t)^T \mathbf{y}_t \geq d_t) \geq 1 - \varepsilon. \tag{13}$$

Let $\Phi(\cdot)$ denote the cumulative density function of the standard normal random variable. Then $\mathrm{P}(\|\mathbf{W}_t\| \leq t\Phi^{-1}(1 - \varepsilon)) = 1 - \varepsilon$, and it follows that (13) holds if

$$(\mathbf{f}_0 + \mu_0^f t + \Sigma_0^f \mathbf{w})^T \mathbf{y}_t \geq d_t \text{ for all } \|\mathbf{w}\| \leq \sqrt{t}\Phi^{-1}(1-\varepsilon). \tag{14}$$

A constraint of the form (14) is called a robust constraint (Ben-Tal and Nemirovski, 2002). Note that the robust constraint (14) is a conservative approximation for the chance constraint. Using the Cauchy–Schwarz inequality, (14) can be written as

$$(\mathbf{f}_0 + \mu_0^f t)^T \mathbf{y}_t - d_t \geq \sqrt{t}\Phi^{-1}(1-\varepsilon) \times \|\Sigma_0^f \mathbf{y}_t\|_2, \tag{15}$$

where $||\mathbf{x}||_2 = \sqrt{\mathbf{x}^T\mathbf{x}}$ denote the L_2-norm. The constraint (15) is of the form

$$||\mathbf{Bx} - \mathbf{a}||_2 \leq \mathbf{d}^T\mathbf{x} + c,$$

where **B**, **a**, **d**, and c are constants and **x** is the decision variable. Constraints of this form are called SOC constraints.

SOC programming approximation for pension fund management

In a pension fund management problem, we have at least one constraint of the form (3) at each decision epoch t. Suppose we have K chance constraints in total. We want to guarantee that all the chance constraints hold with probability at least η. We set $\varepsilon = \eta/K$ for each chance constraint of the form $\mathrm{P}(\mathbf{C}_i) \geq 1 - \varepsilon$, $i = 1, \ldots, K$. The Bonferroni inequality (see for example Boros and Prékopa, 1989) implies that

$$\begin{aligned} \mathrm{P}\left(\bigcap_{i=1}^{K} \mathbf{C}_i\right) &\geq 1 - \sum_{i=1}^{K}(1 - P(\mathbf{C}_i)) \\ &\geq 1 - \sum_{i=1}^{K}\frac{\eta}{K} = 1 - \eta, \end{aligned} \tag{16}$$

that is, by setting a more conservative target for each chance constraint, the Bonferroni inequality guarantees that all the chance constraints hold simultaneously. We use $\varepsilon = \eta/K$ in constraints of the form (15) to approximate each chance constraint by an SOC constraint. Thus, the resulting optimization problem is of the form

$$\min \sum_t c_t^d(P(\underline{Q}))$$

s. t.

$$||\mathbf{B}_i\mathbf{y} - \mathbf{a}_i||_2 \leq \mathbf{d}_i^T\mathbf{x} + c_i,\ i = 1, \ldots, K, \tag{17}$$

that is, it has one linear objective and several SOC constraints. Such an optimization problem is called an SOCP.

Very large-scale SOCPs can be solved efficiently both in theory (Alizadeh and Goldfarb, 2003) and in practice (Andersen and Andersen, 2006). Moreover, a number of commercial solvers, such as MOSEK, CPLEX and Frontline System (supplier of EXCEL SOLVER), provide the capability for solving SOCPs in a numerically robust manner. As the approximation (12) implies that the pension fund management problem can be approximated by an SOCP, the approach proposed in this article can be used to solve very large-scale pension fund management problems.

Numerical example

In this section, we consider a specific example and formulate the optimization problem that computes the optimal contribution schedule and portfolio holdings for a frozen pension fund using the general framework described in the section 'Robust pension fund management'. A frozen fund is a fund in which all the liabilities l_t are fixed; therefore, there is no actuarial risk and the only risk in the problem is financial risk.

Assets, liabilities and dynamics

We assume that a pension fund invests in an equity index and zero-coupon bonds with face value 1 and maturities up to M years. Thus, the holdings of the fund at time t can be described by the vector

$$\mathbf{x}_t = \begin{bmatrix} \text{Number of shares of 1} - \text{year bond} \\ \vdots \\ \text{Number of shares of M} - \text{year bond} \\ \text{Number of shares of equity} \end{bmatrix} \in \Re^{M+1}.$$

Note that, if the equity investment is specified as a broad market index, we can use the index to denote price even if it is not possible to invest in the market index directly. As long as the index is used consistently over time, the investment returns can still be correctly calculated in the model. At time $t+1$, all the bonds in the portfolio have a maturity that is 1 year shorter (the bond with 1-year maturity is now available as cash). Thus, the holding $\mathbf{x}_t + 1$ before any trading at time $t+1$ is given by

$$\hat{\mathbf{x}}_{t+1} = \mathbf{D}\mathbf{x}_t,$$

and $\mathbf{d}^T \boldsymbol{x}_t$ is available as cash, where

$$D = \begin{bmatrix} 0 & 1 & 0 & 0 & \cdots & 0 \\ 0 & 0 & 1 & 0 & \cdots & 0 \\ \vdots & \ddots & \ddots & \ddots & \ddots & \vdots \\ 0 & 0 & \cdots & 0 & 1 & 0 \\ 0 & 0 & \cdots & 0 & 0 & 0 \\ 0 & 0 & \cdots & 0 & 0 & 1 \end{bmatrix}, \text{ and } \mathbf{d} = \mathbf{e}_1 = \begin{bmatrix} 1 \\ 0 \\ \vdots \\ 0 \end{bmatrix}.$$

The value of the portfolio $\mathbf{x}_t$ at time $t+1$ is given by $\mathbf{p}_{t+1}^T \mathbf{D}\mathbf{x}_t + \mathbf{d}^T \mathbf{x}_t$.

The liability of the pension fund at time t is denoted by l_t and time $t = 0,1, \ldots, T$, that is, the time horizon for the pension fund problem is T. We assume that at time $t = 0$, all the future payments l_t, $t = 0,1, \ldots, T$, are deterministic as in the case of frozen pension funds, that is, the uncertainty in the model is only from the changing financial conditions.

Bond prices and the yield curve

We follow Nelson and Siegel (1987) and assume that the short rates

$$\begin{aligned} s_{t,j} &= Z_t^1 + Z_t^2\left[\frac{1-\exp(-j/\tau)}{j/\tau}\right] \\ &\quad + Z_t^3\left[\frac{1-\exp(-j/\tau)}{j/\tau} - \exp(-j/\tau)\right], \end{aligned} \tag{18}$$

where the factors Z_t^1, Z_t^2 and Z_t^3 refer, respectively, to level, slope and curvature of the yield curve and τ is a constant. We use the Nelson–Siegel model because this model ensures non-negative spot rates $s_{t,j}$ for large $t \gg 1$. This is necessary in our setting as we need to discount liabilities with very long durations.

In the Nelson–Siegel model, the price $B_{t,j}$ at time t of a zero-coupon bond with face value $F = 1$ and maturing at time $t + j$ is given by

$$\begin{aligned} B_{t,j} &= \frac{1}{(1+s_{t,j})^j} \\ &= \left(1 + Z_t^1 + Z_t^2\left[\frac{1-\exp(-j/\tau)}{j/\tau}\right]\right. \\ &\quad \left. + Z_t^3\left[\frac{1-\exp(-j/\tau)}{j/\tau} - \exp(-j/\tau)\right]\right)^{-j}. \end{aligned} \tag{19}$$

Thus, $B_{t,j}$ is a highly nonlinear function of the factors $\mathbf{Z}$. We chose the Nelson–Siegel model to illustrate our framework because a highly nonlinear yield curve is a good test for the linearization technique introduced in the section 'Robust pension fund management'.

We denote the value of the equity index by q_t. We assume that the equity index q_t and the factors $\{Z_t^i : i = 1,\ldots,3\}$ driving the yield curve (18) evolve according to the stochastic differential equation

$$\begin{bmatrix} dZ_t^1 \\ dZ_t^2 \\ dZ_t^3 \\ \dfrac{dq_t}{q_t} \end{bmatrix} = \begin{bmatrix} (m_1 - Z_t^1) \\ (m_2 - Z_t^2) \\ (m_3 - Z_t^3) \\ \mu \end{bmatrix} dt + \mathbf{A} d\mathbf{W}_t, \tag{20}$$

where $\mathbf{W}_t = (W_t^1, W_t^2, W_t^3, W_t^4)^T$, $\{W_t^i\}_{t \geq 0}$, $i = 1, 2, 3, 4$, are independent standard Brownian motions, and the lower triangular matrix $\mathbf{A} \in \Re^{4 \times 4}$ denotes the Cholesky decomposition of the covariance matrix $\mathbf{V} \in \Re^{4 \times 4}$ of the vector $(Z_t^1, \ldots, Z_t^3, q_t)$. The dynamics in (20) imply that each of the factors Z_t^i is an Ornstein–Uhlenbeck process and the equity index q_t is a geometric Brownian motion. The yield curve dynamics given by (20) is similar to the one considered in Fabozzi *et al* (2005). With the above definitions, the price vector is given by

$$\mathbf{p}_t = (B_{t,1}, \ldots, B_{t,M}, q_t)^T.$$

Note that the price vector and the stochastic differential equations (20) conform to the general framework described in the section 'Robust pension fund management'.

Optimization problem

We assume that at time $t = 0$, we determine the contribution w_t and the portfolio $\mathbf{x}_t$ for $t = 0, \ldots, \bar{T} \leq T$. We expect that the pension fund problem will be solved on a rolling-horizon basis, that is, at time $t = 1$, we will recompute the optimal portfolio for the horizon $t = 1, \ldots, \bar{T} + 1$. The horizon $\bar{T}$ is chosen to be long enough so that the impact of the liabilities l_t, $t > \bar{T}$, is minimal.

Let ψ denote the initial holdings of the fund, that is the holdings before rebalancing at time 0. We require that the portfolio $\mathbf{x}_0$ must satisfy

$$\mathbf{p}_0^T \psi + w_0 - l_0 = \mathbf{p}_0^T \mathbf{x}_0, \tag{21}$$

that is, the total value of the portfolio $\mathbf{x}_0$ must equal the difference between the available capital $(\mathbf{p}_0^T \psi + w_0)$ and the liability l_0. Note that (21) implicitly assumes that rebalancing does not incur any transaction costs. Therefore, we can assume, without loss of generality, that the portfolio ψ is held in cash.

The constraint for time $t \geq 1$ is

$$\begin{aligned} &P(\mathbf{p}_t^T \mathbf{D}\mathbf{x}_{t-1} + \mathbf{d}^T \mathbf{x}_{t-1} + w_t - l_t \geq \mathbf{p}_t^T \mathbf{x}_t) \geq 1 - \varepsilon, \\ &t = 1, \ldots, \bar{T} - 1, \end{aligned} \tag{22}$$

where P denotes the probability measure conditioned on the information available at time t = 0. We also require the following target funding level constraint

$$P(\mathbf{p}_{\bar{T}}^T \mathbf{D}\mathbf{x}_{\bar{T}-1} + \mathbf{d}^T \mathbf{x}_{\bar{T}-1} + w_{\bar{T}} \geq l_{\bar{T}} + \beta L_{\bar{T}}) \geq 1 - \varepsilon, \tag{23}$$

to set the target funding level at time $\bar{T}$ to be a fraction β of the future liabilities, where L_t denote the net present value at time t of the entire set of future liability at a fixed discount rate d, that is

$$L_t = \sum_{\tau=t+1}^{T} \frac{l_\tau}{(1+d)^{\tau-t}},$$

and the discount rate d is chosen by the plan sponsor subject to some regulatory constraints. The funding level of a pension fund at time t is defined to be the ratio of the total spot value $\mathbf{p}_t^T \mathbf{x}_t$ of the assets of fund to L_t.

In addition, one may have to impose other constraints that meet regulatory requirements. For example, in the US, pension funds need to maintain a funding level of $\gamma = 90$ per cent and the sponsor is required to contribute if the funding level drops below γ. Such a regularity requirement can be met by imposing constraints of the form:

$$\mathbf{p}_0^T \mathbf{x}_0 \geq \gamma L_0, \tag{24}$$

and

$$P(\mathbf{p}_t^T \mathbf{x}_t \geq \gamma L_t) \geq 1 - \varepsilon, \quad t = 1, \ldots, \bar{T} - 1 \tag{25}$$

See Fabozzi *et al* (2004) for a summary of regulations on pension funds in different countries.

Collecting together all the constraints and using the objective incorporating the corporate structure of the plan sponsor given as an example in the section 'Linearization and robust constraints', we solve the following optimization problem

$$\min \sum_{t=0}^{\bar{T}} ((1-\alpha_T)B_{0,t} + ((1-\alpha_T)P(\underline{Q}) + \alpha_T)B_{0,t+1})w_t^d$$
$$\text{subject to (21), (22),(23),(24),(25),(7) and (9).} \tag{26}$$

In the Appendix section, we discuss how to use the general results in section 'Robust pension fund management' to reformulate (26) into an SOCP.

Discussion

Typically, the pension fund manager only chooses capital allocation to asset classes. The tactical decisions of the particular assets to purchase within each asset class are left to asset managers who are specialists in a particular asset classes. We consider two asset classes – equity and treasury bonds. The solution of the pension fund problem (26) guides the fraction of capital that should be allocated to an asset manager specializing in equity market for tactical asset allocation, and the fraction that should be given to an asset manager specializing in fixed income market. Therefore, the bond portfolio is only a proxy for total fixed income holdings.

We want our robust optimization-based approach to produce conservative portfolios. In constructing (26), we linearize the nonlinear factor dynamics, but then we use Bonferroni's inequality (see (16)), to impose a very conservative chance constraint. It is not immediately clear that the net outcome is a conservative portfolio. We show in the section 'Stationary portfolio selection' that the robust solution is indeed conservative when the risk is measured by the Value-at-Risk (VaR) and the Conditional Value-at-Risk (cVaR).

Problem parameters

Following Fabozzi *et al* (2005) (see also Barrett *et al*, 1995), we set $\tau = 3$. The other parameters used in the example are:

$$Z_0^1 = 4.5794,\ Z_0^2 = -0.3443,$$
$$Z_0^3 = -0.2767,\ q_0, = 1248.29,$$
$$\mu = 0.0783,\ m_1 = 6.1694,$$
$$m_2 = -2.4183,\ m_3 = 0.4244,$$

the covariance matrix

$$\mathbf{V} = \begin{bmatrix} 2.1775 & -4.5778 & 19.3399 & -0.1201 \\ -4.5778 & 15.6181 & -43.6039 & 0.2679 \\ 19.3399 & -43.6039 & 179.7153 & -1.0094 \\ -0.1201 & 0.2679 & -1.0094 & 0.0078 \end{bmatrix},$$

and the correlation matrix

$$\rho = \begin{bmatrix} 1.0000 & -0.2178 & 0.5685 & -0.4008 \\ -0.2178 & 1.0000 & -0.4452 & 0.0945 \\ 0.5685 & -0.4452 & 1.0000 & -0.1149 \\ -0.4008 & 0.0945 & -0.1149 & 1.0000 \end{bmatrix}.$$

Thus, the Cholesky decomposition **A** of **V** is given by

$$\mathrm{A} = \begin{bmatrix} 1.4756 & 0 & 0 & 0 \\ -3.1023 & 2.4482 & 0 & 0 \\ 13.1063 & -1.2027 & 2.5485 & 0 \\ -0.0814 & 0.0063 & 0.0255 & 0.0212 \end{bmatrix}$$

These parameter estimates result in the current yield curve displayed in Figure 14.1. The number of maturities M is set to $M = 10$ in our numerical experiments.

The liability stream used in our numerical experiments is shown in Figure 14.2. The liability stream ends in year $T = 85$. We obtained these data for a frozen pension fund from Goldman Sachs. We set the value of initial holding

$$\mathbf{p}_0^T \psi = 0.8(\mathrm{L}_0 + l_0),$$

Other parameters for this numerical example are set as follows:

(i) We consider the optimal plan for the first 4 years, that is $\bar{T} = 4$.
(ii) The regulation mandated minimum funding level γ is set to $\gamma = 0.9$. Thus, the fund is *underfunded* at time $t = 0$.
(iii) The target funding level β that controls the influence of liabilities beyond $\bar{T}$ is set to $\beta = 0.9$.
(iv) The liabilities are discounted at a nominal discount rate $d = 6$ per cent.
(v) The violation probability $\eta = 1$ per cent (see (16)), that is, all chance constraints in (26) are satisfied with $1–\eta = 99$ per cent probability.

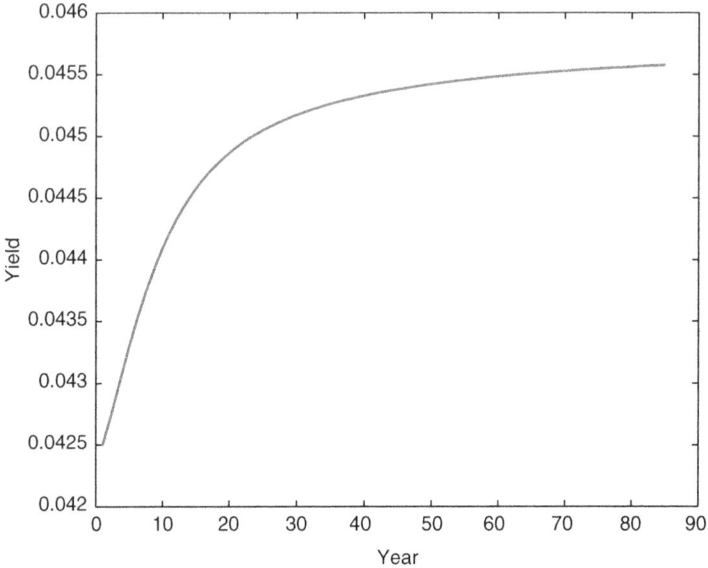

Figure 14.1 Current yield curve

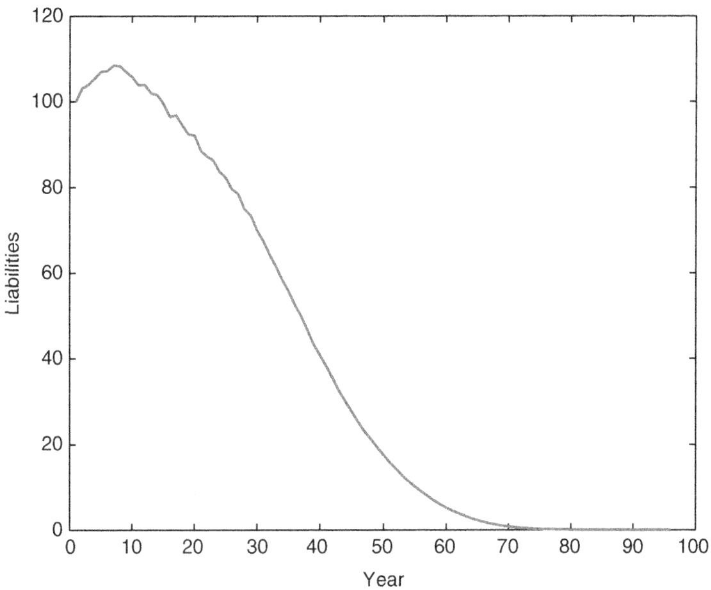

Figure 14.2 Liability as a function of time

(vi) The earnings $C_0 = 500$ and $u = 0.2$, that is, we impose a limit that at most 20 per cent of the earnings can be used to fund the pension plan. We set $r_e = 0.05$.

(vii) The marginal tax rate $\alpha_T = 0.35$ and we assume that the company wants to maintain a credit rating Q = 'A+', that is, $\alpha(\underline{Q}) = 5.5$ and $P(\underline{Q}) = 0.008$ (Damodaran, 2004).

We summarize the values for the parameters as follows.

Parameter	Value
$\bar{T}$	4
γ	0.9
β	0.9
d	6%
η	1%
C_0	500
u	0.2
α_T	0.35
$\alpha(\underline{Q})$	5.5
$\rho(\underline{Q})$	0.008

Stationary portfolio selection

We consider optimal portfolio selection over $\bar{T} = 4$ for a liability stream with time horizon $T = 85$. We consider this setting for simpler presentation and evaluation of the solution. As $\bar{T} \ll T$, we require that portfolio $\mathbf{x}_t$, $t = 1, \ldots, \bar{T}$ be stationary, that is, $\mathbf{x}_0 = \mathbf{x}_1 = \mathbf{x}_2 = \mathbf{x}_3$. In order to investigate the impact of the equity ratio, that is the fraction of the total capital of the fund that is invested in equity, we impose the constraint

$$(B_{1,1},\ldots,B_{1,M})(x_0(1),\ldots,x_0(M))^T = \rho q' x_0(M+1)$$

that sets the equity ratio of the initial portfolio $\mathbf{x}_0$ to $1/(1+\rho)$. We compute $\mathbf{x}_0$ and $\{w_k\}_{k=0}^{\bar{T}}$ by solving

$$\begin{aligned} &\min \sum_{t=0}^{\bar{T}} ((1-\alpha_T)B_{0,t} + ((1-\alpha_T)P(\underline{Q}) + \alpha_T)B_{0,t+1})w_t^d \\ &\text{subject to } \mathbf{x}_0 = \mathbf{x}_1 = \mathbf{x}_2 = \mathbf{x}_3, \\ &(B_{1,1},\ldots,B_{1,M})(x_0(1),\ldots,x_0(M))^T = \rho q' x_0(M+1), \\ &\quad (7), (21), (24), (34), (35), (36), \text{ and } (37). \end{aligned} \tag{27}$$

Table 14.1 and Figure 14.3 shows the worst-case payments as a function of the equity ratio $1/(1+\rho)$ with the probability of constraint satisfaction fixed at $1-\eta = 0.99$. The contribution w_0 increases with increasing equity ratio while the contributions (w_1, w_2, w_3) all decrease with the increase in the equity ratio. The total discounted payment, however, increases with the increase in the equity ratio.

In Table 14.2 we display the worst-case payments as a function of the probability of constraint satisfaction with the equity ratio $1/(1+p)$ fixed at 0.4. As expected, the worst-case contribution decreases with a decrease in constraint satisfaction.

Table 14.1 Worst-case contribution as a function of equity ratio

Equity ratio	w_0	w_1	w_2	w_3	$\sum_{t=0}^{\bar{T}} B_{0,t} w_t$
0.2	239.90	125.00	155.60	180.41	683.69
0.4	283.96	120.04	143.91	163.44	697.36
0.6	348.05	114.88	131.76	145.81	729.92

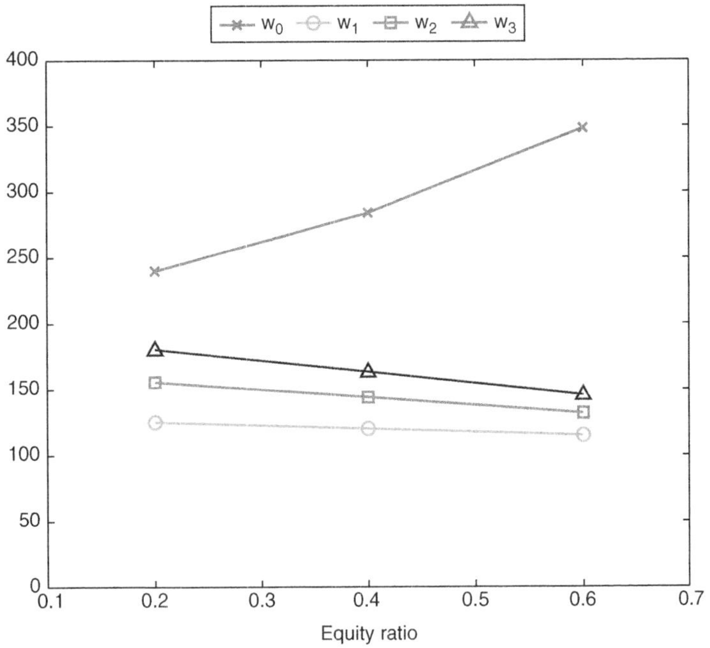

Figure 14.3 Worst-case contribution as a function of equity ratio

Table 14.2 Worst-case contribution as a function of time

Probability	w_0	w_1	w_2	w_3	$\sum_{t=0}^{\bar{T}} B_{0,t} w_t$
0.99	283.96	120.04	143.91	163.44	697.36
0.95	244.27	111.20	130.97	147.34	622.91
0.90	230.03	107.11	125.01	139.95	592.79

Conditional VaR

In this section, we test the effect of linearizing the dynamics by stress–testing the pension fund portfolio using the VaR and CVaR measures.

We simulate the asset prices using the dynamics described by (18)–(20) (that is, we do not linearize the dynamics) and compute the real (as opposed to the worst-case) payments $\bar{w}_t$ required to finance the portfolio strategy. From the constraints (21), (22), (23), (24) and (25), it follows that

$$\bar{w}_t = \begin{cases} \max(l_t + \mathbf{p}_t^T \mathbf{x}_t - \alpha_{t-1}(\mathbf{p}_t^T \mathbf{D} \mathbf{x}_{t-1} \\ \quad + \mathbf{d}^T \mathbf{x}_{t-1}),\ \gamma L_t - \mathbf{p}_t^T \mathbf{x}_t, 0) \\ \quad \text{if } 1 \le t \le \bar{\mathrm{T}}, \\ \max(l_t + \beta L_t - \alpha_{t-1}(\mathbf{p}_t^T \mathbf{D} \mathbf{x}_{t-1} \\ \quad + \mathbf{d}^T \mathbf{x}_{t-1}), 0) \\ \quad \text{if } \mathrm{t} = \bar{\mathrm{T}}, \end{cases} \tag{28}$$

where

$$\alpha_t = \max\left(\frac{\gamma L_t}{\mathbf{p}_t^T \mathbf{x}_t}, 1\right). \tag{29}$$

The variable α_t keeps track of whether the payment $\bar{w}_t$ is needed to maintain the regulation requirement $\gamma L_t / \mathbf{p}_t^T \mathbf{x}_t \le 1$, and the value of the portfolio in the next period will increase or remain unchanged accordingly. Note that, in our numerical experiments, $\mathbf{x}_t$ is fixed over time.

We generated $K = 100000$ independent sample paths and set the shortfall probability

$$\bar{\eta} = \frac{\sum_{k=1}^{K} \max_{0 \le t \le 3} \mathbf{1}(w_t < \bar{w}_t^{(k)})}{K},$$

where $\{\bar{w}_t^{(k)}\}$ denotes the real payments on the k-th simulation run and $\mathbf{1}(\cdot)$ is the indicator function that takes the value 1 when the argument is true and 0 otherwise. Thus, $\bar{\eta}$ is the empirical probability that the real payment $\bar{w}_t$ is larger than the worst case payment w_t. The expected net shortfall $\bar{W}$ was defined as follows.

$$\bar{W} = \frac{\sum_{k=0}^{K}\sum_{t=0}^{\bar{T}} B_{0,t}(\bar{w}_t^{(k)} - w_t)^+}{\sum_{k=0}^{K}\mathbf{1}\left(\sum_{t=0}^{\bar{T}} B_{0,t}(\bar{w}_t^{(k)} - w_t)^+ > 0\right)}, \tag{30}$$

that is $\bar{W}$ is the expected shortfall conditioned on their being a shortfall. We define the Value-at-Risk (VaR_p) at probability p of the discounted total real payment as

$$\mathrm{VaR}_p = \sup_{x\geq 0}\left\{\sum_k \mathbf{1}\left(\sum_{t=0}^{\bar{T}} B_{0,t}\bar{w}_t^{(k)} \geq x\right) \geq (1-p)K\right\}$$

and Conditional Value-at-Risk (CVaR_p) of the discounted total real payment $\sum_{t=0}^{I} B_{0,t}\bar{w}_t$ as

$$\begin{aligned}\mathrm{CvaR}_p = \frac{1}{1-p}\Bigg(&\sum_{k=1}^{K}\left(\sum_{t=0}^{\bar{T}} B_{0,t}\bar{w}_t^{(k)}\right)\\ &\times \mathbf{1}\left(\sum_{t=0}^{\bar{T}} B_{0,t}\bar{w}_t^{(k)} \geq \mathrm{VaR}_p\right)\Bigg).\end{aligned}$$

Table 14.3 plots the shortfall probability $\bar{p}$, the expected shortfall $\bar{W}$, the VaR and CVaR as a function of the probability p. From the numerical results, we can conclude that the linearized robust problem (27) does produce a conservative solution for the true nonlinear problem (note that, this is not guaranteed). In all cases, the empirical shortfall probability is at least an order of magnitude lower than that guaranteed by the robust problem. This result confirms our initial hypothesis that linearizing the dynamics should not result in a significant deterioration in performance.

For a fixed p, let $\tilde{p}$ denote the probability such that the corresponding shortfall probability $\bar{\tilde{p}} \approx 1-p$. For example, for $p = 0.98$, $\tilde{p} = 0.85$ as the corresponding shortfall probability $\bar{\tilde{p}} = 0.0182 \approx 1 - p = 0.02$.

Table 14.3 Simulation results

p	$\bar{p}$	$\overline{w}$	$\sum_{t=0}^{\bar{T}} B_{0,t} w_t$	VaR	CVaR
0.99	0.0014	5.98	697.36	537.40	546.96
0.98	0.0027	5.07	667.48	511.58	521.73
0.97	0.0039	5.41	644.63	496.18	506.83
0.96	0.0050	5.34	632.27	487.12	498.22
0.95	0.0063	5.43	622.91	479.91	491.22
0.90	0.0126	5.64	592.79	456.23	496.00
0.85	0.0182	5.99	574.24	441.90	455.63
0.80	0.0235	6.08	560.48	430.38	445.12

Another such pair is $(p, \tilde{p}) = (0.99, 0.90)$. Then total discounted worst-case payment corresponding to p is approximately equal to the CVaR_p – note that, this is in spite of the fact that the robust problem does *not* minimize the total discounted payment.

Computational efficiency

All numerical computations reported in this work were conducted using Matlab 6.5 and MOSEK 4.0 (Andersen and Andersen, 2006). We used a Windows/32-X86 platform with Intel-PM. A typical portfolio problem had less than 100 constraints and 100 variables and it took no longer than a second for MOSEK to solve the portfolio problem.

Concluding remarks

In this article, we introduce a robust optimization framework for pension fund management that minimizes the worst-case pension contributions of the sponsoring firm. The illustrated model is able to account for some aspects of the corporate structure of the firm, for example cost of debt. The optimal pension plan from the proposed framework is computed by solving an SOCP and is, therefore, very efficient both in theory and in practice. In addition, we show that the framework is very versatile in that it allows us to compute both the optimal plan and also stress test any existing pension plans. The solution to the pension fund management problem is shown to be robust and conservative in the stress testing result.

There are fundamental differences between the robust approach and the stochastic programming approach. In the stochastic programming approach, the evolution of the stochastic parameters is approximated by a tree and one computes an optimal portfolio for each node in the tree taking the evolving information into account. As the tree can be constructed for any stochastic model, the stochastic programming approach is extremely versatile. However, a tree has zero probability and the stochastic programming approach is not able to provide any worst-case guarantees. Moreover, the complexity of the associated optimization problem is exponential in the time horizon and number of assets. In the robust optimization approach, one is able to provide a worst-case probabilistic guarantee; however, the portfolio selection cannot take advantage of evolving information (adjustable robust optimization somewhat mitigates this objection (Ben-Tal *et al*, 2004)). The computational complexity of the robust approach is polynomial in the time horizon and the number of assets. Both of these approaches cannot be implemented in an open-loop manner, and a new optimization problem has to be solved at each decision epoch. In summary, neither of these two approaches are clear winners; however, robust methods are very well suited for solving large-scale pension fund management problems.

Acknowledgements

We thank Mr Armen Avanessians of Goldman Sachs for a gift that helped support this research. We also thank Professor Donald Goldfarb and Dr Erol Hakanoglu for constructive comments. This research was partially supported by NSF grants CCR-00-09972, DMS- 01-04282, DMS 06-06712, ONR grant N000140310514 and DOE grant GE-FG01-92ER-25126.

References

Alizadeh, F. and Goldfarb, D. (2003) Second-order cone programming. *Mathematical Programming* 95: 3–51.

Andersen, E.D. and Andersen, K.D. (2006) The MOSEK optimization toolbox for MATLAB manual Version 4.0, http://www.mosek.com/products/4 0/tools/help/index.html.

Barrett, W.B., Gosnell, T. and Heuson, A. (1995) Yield curve shifts and the selection of immunization strategies. *Journal of Fixed Income* 5(2): 53–64.

Ben-Tal, A. and Nemirovski, A. (2001) *Lectures on Modern Convex Optimization: Analysis, Algorithms, and Engineering Applications*. Philadelphia, USA: Society for Industrial & Applied Math.

Ben-Tal, A. and Nemirovski, A. (2002) Robust optimization – Methodology and applications. *Mathematical Programming* 92(3): 453–480.

Ben-Tal, A., Margalit, T. and Nemirovski, A. (2000) Robust modeling of multi-stage portfolio problems. In: H. Frenk (ed.) *High Performance Optimization*. Dordrecht, The Netherlands: Kluwer Academic Publishers, pp. 303–328.

Ben-Tal, A., Goryashko, A., Guslitzer, E. and Nemirovski, A. (2004) Adjustable robust solutions of uncertain linear programs. *Mathematical Programming* 99(2): 351–376.

$$\begin{aligned}\boldsymbol{\Delta} X_t = \mu + \Gamma_1 \boldsymbol{\Delta} X_{t-1} + \Gamma_2 \boldsymbol{\Delta} X_{t-2} + \ldots + \Gamma_{p-1} \boldsymbol{\Delta} X_{t-p-1} \\ + \boldsymbol{\Pi} X_{t-p-1} + BZ_t = u_t \qquad (1)\end{aligned}$$

Day	DUS	DMAL	DINDO	DPHIL	VE
1	2.54	2.41	0.90	94.6	5.84
2	2.57	2.64	1.09	93.71	6.29
5	2.61	2.63	1.11	93.65	6.35
9	2.61	2.63	1.11	93.65	6.35
10	2.61	2.63	1.11	93.65	6.35

Day	DUS	DTAI	DCHIN	DKOREA	DINDIA	VE
1	15.67	11.24	4.61	68.48	0.00	31.52
2	15.56	11.42	4.61	68.02	0.39	31.98
5	15.49	11.38	4.59	67.87	0.67	32.13
9	15.49	11.38	4.59	67.87	0.67	32.13
10	15.49	11.38	4.59	67.87	0.67	32.13

Boros, E. and Prékopa, A. (1989) Closed form two-sided bounds for probabilities that at least r and exactly r out of n events occur. *Mathematics of Operations Research* 14(2): 317–342.

Chang, F. (2004) *Stochastic Optimization in Continuous Time*. Cambridge, UK: Cambridge University Press.

Consigli, G. and Dempster, M. (1998) Dynamic stochastic programming for asset-liability management. *Annals of Operations Research* 81: 131–161.

Damodaran, A. (2004) *Applied Corporate Finance: A User's Manual*, 2nd edn. Hoboken, NJ: Wiley.

Drijver, S., Haneveld, W. and Vlerk, M. (2000) Asset Liability Management Modeling Using Multistage Mixed-integer Stochastic Programming. University of Groningen. Technical Report.

Fabozzi, F., Focardi, S. and Jonas, C. (2004) *Can Modeling Help Deal with the Pension Funding Crisis*. Houston, TX: The Intertek Group.

Fabozzi, F., Martellini, L. and Priaulet, P. (2005) Predictability in the shape of the term structure of interest rates. *Journal of Fixed Income* 15(1): 40–53.

Goldfarb, D. and Iyengar, G. (2003) Robust convex quadratically constrained programs. *Mathematical Programming Ser B* 97(3): 495–515.

Hull, J. and White, A. (1990) Pricing interest rate derivative securities. *Review of Financial Studies* 3(4): 573–592.

Jin, L., Merton, R. and Bodie, Z. (2006) Do a firm's equity returns reflect the risk of its pension plan? *Journal of Financial Economics* 81(1): 1–26.

Klaassen, P. (1998) Financial asset-pricing theory and stochastic programming models for asset/liability management: A synthesis. *Management Science* 44(1): 31–48.

Myers, S. and Majluf, N. (1984) Corporate financing and investment decisions when firms have information that investors do not have. *Journal of Financial Economics* 13(2): 155–295.

Nelson, C. and Siegel, A. (1987) Parsimonious modeling of yield curves. *Journal of Business* 60(4): 473–489.

Sodhi, M. (2005) LP modeling for asset-liability management: A survey of choices and simplifications. *Operations Research* 53(2): 181–196.

Appendix

Derivation

The Itô-Taylor expansion applied to (19) at time 0 using (18) and (20) implies that

$$B_{t,j} \approx B_{0,j} + \left(\sum_{i=1}^{3} (m_i - Z_0^i) \left. \frac{\partial B_{s,j}}{\partial Z_s^i} \right|_{s=0} + \frac{1}{2} \sum_{i,l=1}^{3} \rho_{il} \left. \frac{\partial^2 B_{s,j}}{\partial (Z_s^i) \partial (Z_s^l)} \right|_{s=0} \right) t + \sum_{i=1}^{3} \left. \frac{\partial B_{s,j}}{\partial Z_s^i} \right|_{s=0} \sum_{k=1}^{4} v_{ik} W_t^k, \tag{A.1}$$

where $\rho_{il} = \sum_{k=1}^{4} v_{ik} v_{kl}$ and $\mathbf{A} = [v_{ij}]$ is the covariance matrix of the factor vector $(W_t^1, \ldots, W_t^4)$. Similarly, for the equity index q_t, we have

$$q_t \approx q_0 + q_0 \mu t + q_0 \sum_{k=1}^{4} v_{4k} W_t^k. \tag{A.2}$$

Thus,

$$\mathbf{p}_t \approx \mathbf{p}_0 + \mu_0^p t + \sum_0^p W_t, \tag{A.3}$$

where

$$\mu_0^p = \begin{bmatrix} \sum_{i=1}^{3} (m_i - Z_0^i) \left.\frac{\partial B_{s,1}}{\partial Z_s^i}\right|_{s=0} + \frac{1}{2} \sum_{i,l=1}^{3} \rho_{il} \left.\frac{\partial^2 B_{s,1}}{\partial (Z_s^i) \partial (Z_s^l)}\right|_{s=0} \\ \vdots \\ \sum_{i=1}^{3} (m_i - Z_0^i) \left.\frac{\partial B_{s,M}}{\partial Z_s^i}\right|_{s=0} + \frac{1}{2} \sum_{i,l=1}^{3} \rho_{il} \left.\frac{\partial^2 B_{s,M}}{\partial (Z_s^i) \partial (Z_s^l)}\right|_{s=0} \\ q_{0\mu} \end{bmatrix} \in \Re^{M+1},$$

and

$$\Sigma_0^p = \begin{bmatrix} \left.\frac{\partial B_{s,1}}{\partial Z_s^1}\right|_{s=0} & \left.\frac{\partial B_{s,1}}{\partial Z_s^2}\right|_{s=0} & \left.\frac{\partial B_{s,1}}{\partial Z_s^3}\right|_{s=0} & \left.\frac{\partial B_{s,1}}{\partial q_s}\right|_{s=0} \\ \vdots & \vdots & \vdots & \vdots \\ \left.\frac{\partial B_{s,M}}{\partial Z_s^1}\right|_{s=0} & \left.\frac{\partial B_{s,M}}{\partial Z_s^2}\right|_{s=0} & \left.\frac{\partial B_{s,M}}{\partial Z_s^3}\right|_{s=0} & \left.\frac{\partial B_{s,M}}{\partial q_s}\right|_{s=0} \\ 0 & 0 & 0 & q_0 \end{bmatrix} \in \Re^{(M+1)\times 4}.$$

It then follows that for all $t = 1, \ldots, \overline{T} - 1$,

$$\begin{aligned} &\mathrm{P}(\mathbf{p}_t^T \mathbf{D}\mathbf{x}_{t-1} + \mathbf{d}^T \mathbf{x}_{t-1} + w_t - l_t \geq \mathbf{p}_t^T \mathbf{x}_t) \\ &= \mathrm{P}(\mathbf{p}_t^T (\mathbf{D}\mathbf{x}_{t-1} - \mathbf{x}_t) + \mathbf{d}^T \mathbf{x}_{t-1} + w_t - l_t \geq 0) \\ &= \mathrm{P}((\mathbf{p}_0 + \mu_0^p t)^T (\mathbf{D}\mathbf{x}_{t-1} - \mathbf{x}_t) + \mathbf{d}^T \mathbf{x}_{t-1} t \\ &\quad + w_t - l_t \geq (\mathbf{D}\mathbf{x}_{t-1} - \mathbf{x}_t)^T \Sigma_0^p W_t) \end{aligned}$$

Since $-(\mathbf{Dx}_{t-1} - \mathbf{x}_t)^T \Sigma_0^p W_t \sim N \times (0, \|(\mathbf{Dx}_{t-1} - \mathbf{x}_t)^T \Sigma_0^p\|_2^2 t)$, if $\varepsilon < 0.5$, we have

$$\begin{aligned}
&(\mathbf{p}_0 + \mu_0^p t)^T(\mathbf{Dx}_{t-1} - \mathbf{x}_t) + \mathbf{d}^T\mathbf{x}_{t-1} + w_t - l_t \\
&\geq \sqrt{t}\Phi^{-1}(1-\varepsilon)\,\|(\mathbf{Dx}_{t-1} - \mathbf{x}_t)^T \Sigma_0^p\|_2 \\
&\Downarrow \\
&\mathrm{P}(\mathbf{p}_t^T\mathbf{Dx}_{t-1} + \mathbf{d}^T\mathbf{x}_{t-1} + w_t - l_t \geq \mathbf{p}_t^T\mathbf{x}_t) \geq 1-\varepsilon,
\end{aligned} \tag{A.4}$$

where $\Phi(\cdot)$ denotes cumulative density function of the standard normal random variable.

Using an analysis similar to the one employed above, the constraint (23) can be reformulated as the SOC constraint

$$\begin{aligned}
&(\mathbf{p}_0 + \mu_0^p \bar{T})^T\mathbf{Dx}_{\bar{T}-1} + \mathbf{d}^T\mathbf{x}_{\bar{T}-1} + w_{\bar{T}} - l_{\bar{T}} - \beta L_{\bar{T}} \\
&\geq \sqrt{\bar{T}}\Phi^{-1}(1-\varepsilon)\,\|(\mathbf{Dx}_{\bar{T}-1})^T \Sigma_0^p\|_2,
\end{aligned} \tag{A.5}$$

and the regulation constraint (25) can be reformulated as the SOC constraint

$$(\mathbf{p}_0 + \mu_0^p t)^T\mathbf{x}_t - \gamma L_t \geq \Phi^{-1}(1-\varepsilon)\sqrt{t}\,\|x_t^T\Sigma_0^p\|_2 \tag{A.6}$$

As the short rates $s_{t,1}$ are described by a Ornstein–Uhlenbeck process whose marginal distribution is normal, it follows that the interest-coverage constraint (9) is equivalent to the linear constraint

$$\begin{aligned}
&\alpha(\underline{Q})\left(E(s_{t,1}) + \sqrt{\mathrm{var}[s_{t,1}]}\Phi^{-1}(1-\varepsilon) + P(\underline{Q})\right)w_t^d \leq C_t, \\
&t = 1,2,\ldots,\bar{T},
\end{aligned} \tag{A.7}$$

where $\mathrm{var}[s_{t,1}]$ denotes the variance of $s_{t,1}$.

Finally, we can solve the following SOCP

$$\begin{aligned}
&\min \sum_{t=0}^{\bar{T}} ((1-\alpha_T)B_{0,t} + ((1-\alpha_T)\times P(\underline{Q}) + \alpha_T)B_{0,t+1})w_t^d \\
&\text{subject to (21), (34), (35), (24), and (36), (7) and (37).}
\end{aligned} \tag{A.8}$$

Index

The manufacturer's authorised representative in the EU is Springer Nature Customer Service Centre GmbH, Europaplatz 3, 69115 Heidelberg, Germany. If you have any concerns regarding our products, please contact ProductSafety@springernature.com

Printed and bound by CPI Group (UK) Ltd, Croydon, CR0 4YY

30/09/2026

02225565-0019